THE JOURNAL OF NEGRO HISTORY, VOL. VII.

BY
CARTER G. WOODSON

BLP PUBLISHING
Eastchester New York

For wholesale please visit:
www.BBWLogistics.com

Available wherever books are sold.
ISBN: 978-1-63652-159-6

THE JOURNAL OF NEGRO HISTORY

VOL. VII,

EDITED BY

CARTER G. WOODSON

CONTENTS

VOL. VII—APRIL, 1922—NO. 2

DOCUMENTS

VOL. VII—JULY, 1922—NO. 3

VOL. VII—OCTOBER, 1922—NO. 4

THE JOURNAL OF NEGRO HISTORY

VOL. VII—JANUARY, 1922—No. 1

CARTER G. WOODSON

SLAVE SOCIETY ON THE SOUTHERN PLANTATION

In the year 1619, memorable in the history of the United States, a Dutch trading vessel carried to the colonists of Virginia twenty Negroes from the West Indies and sold them as slaves, thus laying the foundation of slave society in the American colonies. In the seventeenth century slavery made but little progress in these parts of America, and during that whole period not more than twenty-five thousand slaves were brought to the colonies to work in the tobacco and rice fields of the South or to serve as maids, butlers, and coachmen in the North. The eighteenth century, however, saw a rapid increase in slavery, until the census of 1790, much to the surprise of most observers, showed a slave population of 679,679 living in every State and territory of the country except Massachusetts and Maine.

With the extensive development of various industries in the colonies, slavery soon left the North and was used exclusively in the South. There are several reasons for this shift. In the first place, the colonies of the North were settled by people from the lower and middle classes, who had been accustomed to working for themselves and who thus had no use for slaves, while the South was settled largely by adventurers, who had never worked and who looked upon labor as dishonorable. In the second place, the North had a temperate climate in which any man could safely work, while the heat of the South was so intense that a white man endangered his life by working in it, whereas the Negro was protected by facility of acclimation. Another cause was the difference in soil. The soil of the South was favorable to the growth of cotton, tobacco, rice, and sugar, the cultivation of which crops required large forces of organized and concentrated labor, which the slaves supplied. On the other hand, the soil of the North favored the raising of cereals, which required neither organized nor concentrated labor; for one man working alone was able to produce more than one man working in a group: and thus slave labor was of little or no advantage to the North. Then, too, its soil, lacking the fertility of that of the South, required considerable fertilizing, which slave labor did not have the intelligence to learn. Thus in 1750 the slaves included three per cent of the population of the New England colonies, nine per cent of the middle colonies, and twenty-five per cent of those south of the Potomac River.[1] By the end of the eighteenth century every State north of Maryland, with the exception of New Jersey, had provided for the immediate or gradual abolition of slavery, while the rise of the cotton industry, quickened by the invention of the cotton gin in 1793, had bound the institution on the South.

In order to understand the institutions of the South, it is first necessary to know something about the dominating class of people. The planters, numbering in 1860 about 384,750 and owning 2,308,518 slaves,[2] were first in the social scale and controlled affairs.

"They included an aristocracy or gentry reflecting distinctions of colonial government, and expanding under influences that prevented an amalgamation of widely separated elements."[3]

The home of the planter was usually a large country house of ten or twelve rooms, situated on an elevation, or river bluff. The house was surrounded by a large porch, almost as tall as the house itself, the roofs of which were supported by rows of large white columns. Inside the house there was a large hall, with a wide stairway leading to another hall on the second floor. Opening from the hall on the first floor were the parlors, library and dining room, and, on the second floor, the living rooms of the family. The ceilings were high, and the windows tall and wide. The carpets were very plain, but very heavy, while on the walls were portraits of ancestors, of Washington, or of Calhoun. The house was surrounded by beautiful lawns with tall spreading trees and sometimes marble statues.[4] The home of the planter was indeed picturesque.

The typical planter's family was composed of about twelve sons and daughters, a "tall, lank, and rather weatherworn gentleman, and a slender, soft-voiced, weary-looking mother, unless one counts the inevitable guest or the old-maiden cousin, who, like the furniture or the servants, always formed part of a planter's household."[5] The planter, the master of the plantation, was usually well educated, honorable, and generous. His chief work was managing the plantation. He planned, ordered, and saw to the performance of the work. He also spent much time engaging in politics, caring more for the honor of the public station than for the remuneration, and often went on sporting trips, being used to out-of-door life from boyhood. "The high sense of personal worth, the habit of command, the tyranny engendered by the submission of the prostrate race, made the Southern gentleman jealous in honor, sudden and quick in quarrel,"[6] and, as a result, the duel was very common. Men went about fully armed and used their pistols with slight provocation. They were used to exercising absolute power over their dependents and became furious at opposition; thus a quarrel between one lord and another was, during the earlier period, usually settled by the pistol.

The mistress, usually mother of a large family of her own and over-mother of the pickaninnies, was the "chatelaine of the whole establishment." She supervised the domestic duties, superintended the household industries, was head nurse for the sick, and instructor in religion and morals for the family and for the slaves. She was highly honored and respected by the men, who showed her much consideration. "No patience was had with plans to bring women into competition with the men in the public life; but a generalization of the Pauline advice to the Corinthian church did not hinder the mother from exercising a gentle but firm sway over her husband and sons, while she set the example of virtue and modesty for her daughters."[7]

One of the chief characteristics of the Southern people was their hospitality, which was increased by the fact that they had few opportunities to extend it. Any traveler was welcome to eat at their tables, which were always loaded with meats, breads, seasonal vegetables, relishes, pickles, preserves, jellies, and cakes. He was willingly entertained until he again took up his journey. The general effect of the hospitality upon the status of the Southern society was similar to that of "some rosy afterglow upon a landscape, enhancing the charm of many features, and making attractive others that under a cold white light might mar the whole."[8]

Another prominent feature of the planters was their remarkable progress. Between 1859 and 1860 they had eleven thousand sons and daughters in Southern colleges, while the enrollment of New England colleges was only four thousand. The income of the higher institutions in the South was $700,000, while that of New England was $268,000. They also boasted of many prominent scholars, such as Francis Lieber, who was a professor at the University of South Carolina; Mr. Le Conte and Joseph Senat, who were great geologists and who were also professors at the University of South Carolina; Messrs. Ruffner, Wiley, Yansey, and Manly, prominent Southern educators; and many notable statesmen who went forth from the Southern universities. Does it not seem natural, then, that the Southern planters, who were so charming and so progressive, should dominate the political and social life of the South?

No picture of the planter, however, is "able to be free from the warm, underlying color, the object upon which his progress rested advantageously"—slavery. The attractive life of the planter was made possible by the fact that he had hundreds of slaves to perform the manual labor. The power of the master over the slave was very similar to that of a master over an indentured apprentice in Europe. Both the apprentice and the slave were bound for a term of years, the slave being bound for life. In both cases the master regulated and controlled the person and had absolute enjoyment of his labor. The prominent difference in their power was that the master of a slave could sell him to another, and had the right to sell his child born during slavery, while the master of an indentured apprentice could not so treat him. In both cases the master was an absolute despot.[9]

Since the master, although making the rules of the plantation, was frequently absent, and since the enforcement of the rules and the severity of the labor depended upon the overseer, it is helpful to know the general character of this important power in order to understand the labor of the slaves. He was usually ignorant, high-tempered, and brutal. Patrick Henry has described him as a most "abject, degraded, and unprincipled man." Such men usually worked the Negroes to the limit, having a Negro driver go with each gang of slaves in order to secure the utmost labor. In the light of these facts, it is easy to understand how the slaves might be mistreated, in spite of the benevolent intentions of the master. Yet the overseers were not wholly blamable for their cruelty, inasmuch as they were assured of work only as long as they pleased the master, who judged them by the good behavior of the slaves, the general condition of the plantation, and the size and quality of the crop. Calhoun has truthfully said that by displaying too great an interest in the size of the crop, the master unconsciously encouraged cruelty by the overseer.

As to the general severity of the work, writers differ. Rhodes, in his history of the United States, says that the slaves presented a picture of sadness and fear, and that they toiled from morning until night, working on an average of fifteen hours a day, while during the picking season on the cotton plantations they worked sixteen hours and during the grinding season on the sugar plantations they labored eighteen hours daily. On the other hand, Murat, in his history of the United States, says that the work of the slaves was less strenuous than that of the free workers of the North, that they worked from sunrise till three o'clock in the afternoon, resting two hours at noon and receiving Sunday as a holiday and a half holiday on Saturday, and that they received many privileges, such as farming a small piece of land for themselves and selling its products. According to him, the slaves were supremely happy and contented. Which of these views is correct, it is difficult to say, for it is doubtless true that some slaves were driven to the extreme, while others enjoyed a comparatively easy life. When it is remembered, however, that, since the Constitution forbade the importation of slaves after 1808, the price of slaves had steadily risen, it is safe to conclude that the work was no more severe to the slaves than was agricultural life to the whites in the North, for it was advantageous to the owner to keep the slave in good health as long as possible, and this was not to be accomplished by overworking him.

The family life of the Negro was regulated by the planter, who, in return for the service of the slave, provided him with food, clothing, shelter, and all the necessities of life. This part of slave life is very sad. "A slave, his wife, and their children, around that charmed centre, a family table, with its influence of love, instruction, discipline, humble as they necessarily would be, yet such as God has given them, are too seldom seen."[10] Negroes were married only that slaves might be bred for the master to sell. The Negro families ranged from fifteen to twenty-five children. A certain man in Virginia said that he was fortunate "because his women were uncommonly good breeders; he did not suppose there was a lot of women anywhere that bred faster than his; he never heard of babies coming faster than they did on his plantation; and every one of them, in his estimation, was worth two hundred dollars, as Negroes were selling then, the moment they drew breath."[11] Many people purchased Negro women because they were good breeders, making large fortunes by selling their children. This compulsory breeding naturally crushed the maternal instincts in Negro women. One month after the birth of a child, it was taken to a nursery and cared for by a servant until it was sold, while the mother worked in the field. Thus she neither fed, clothed, nor controlled her child, and consequently the usual love between mother and child was absent. This is well illustrated in the case of a certain slave mother, who, when dying, was asked how she felt about leaving her children and who replied: "O missis, you will take care of them; I don't mind them." It has been truthfully said that the most appalling feature of slavery was the lack of family life suffered by the Negro.

The Negroes lived in huts near the large house, which were usually log cabins with board floors and good chimneys and which were generally comfortable, but which, because of filth and indolence, presented a foul and wretched appearance. Indeed, the appearance of the slave himself was unfavorable. Olmsted describes him as "clumsy, awkward, gross, elephantine in all his expressions and demeanor." The clothing of the slave was of every variety, from the "smart mulatto lady's maid, who wore the still fresh dress that had been her mistress's, down to the pickaninny of three, five, or eight years of age, who went as nature made him."[12] The little Negroes usually wore only a shirt that reached to their knees, while the grown ones received two pairs of shoes, a new suit of clothes, and a hat each year.[13] Their food, as well as their clothes, varied according to the master, generally consisting of cornmeal, bacon, and molasses, while on some plantations they were allowed wheat flour, seasonal vegetables, and even chicken.[14] It is reasonable to judge that the living of the slaves was not very high, for it was to the interest of the master to bring the food and clothing of the slaves down to the lowest cost.

The education of the slaves was very displeasing to the planter. North Carolina, South Carolina, Georgia, Alabama, and Louisiana passed laws forbidding slaves being taught to read or write, although North Carolina slaves could be taught arithmetic. It was said that if they were educated they would read abolition papers and would be discontented. On the other hand, some of the planters contended that they should be taught to read in order that they might understand the Bible. The majority of Negroes, however, were illiterate. As to their religious education, there was much consideration. Southern people were very pious and orthodox in their faith and usually baptized their slaves, taught them the catechism, and then had them confirmed. Their favorite text, however, was "Servants obey in all things your masters." One can not blame the planter for his attitude towards the education of the slave; for, after all, his chief aim was to obtain the utmost work from him, and what educated man free to read and think for himself would really be willing to work as a slave for another?

The question which next presents itself is: "How could anyone justify such a system by which one man is enslaved to the other, sacrificing his right to life, liberty, and happiness that another might prosper?" In the first place, the planter argued that the Negroes were naturally inferior to the white race and could not enjoy the intellectual pursuits; for they had always been savages, having lived in savagery in Africa before taken into captivity and, even in the nineteenth century when freed in Hayti, returning to that state of civilization. From this fact it was argued that, inasmuch as the Negroes belonged to an inferior race, it was only natural that men should enslave them and that they should be controlled by their superiors. Chancellor Harper said: "It is the order of nature and of Heaven that the being of superior faculties and knowledge, and therefore of superior power, should control and dispose of those who are inferior."

The planter argued, secondly, that the Negro was happy and contented in slavery; for he was secure, working for the master, and in return receiving good care all of his life. He was relieved of all worry of sickness or old age, for he knew his master would have to care for him. In time of business depression it was not he who suffered, but the master. On the other hand, the free worker of the North labored for his employer during the best part of his life and then, when no longer able to work, or during business depression, was turned away and obliged to suffer from lack of care. It was maintained that the assertion that the Negro was not happy when he might be whipped was "pathos misapplied." If a man hired a white laborer who robbed him, he dismissed the worker, who was then sentenced to prison, thus disgracing his family, which then suffered from lack of support. On the other hand, a master could not discharge his slave, but whipped and corrected him. After the whipping the Negro felt no bad consequence and his family did not suffer from his wrong doings. It was asserted that the slave was happy and loved his master as a father, "looking up to him as his supporter, director, and defender." Dew inquired: "Why, then, since the slave is happy and happiness is the great object of all animated creation, should we endeavor to disturb his contentment by infusing into his mind a vain and indefinite desire for liberty, a something which he can not comprehend and which must inevitably dry up every source of his happiness?"

But the chief argument advanced was that slavery was the price of prosperity and progress of the South. The North had a moderate climate because of the sea breeze and elevation, and thus white men were able to till the soil, while the intense heat of the South rendered it impossible for the white man to work in the fields and made a large supply of black men necessary. As Harper said, "The products of slave labor furnished more than two-thirds of the materials of our commerce, employed in transporting and exchanging; and among the slave-holding States is to be found the greater market for all the productions of their industry, of whatever kind. The prosperity of those States, therefore, and the civilization of their cities have been for the most part created by the existence of slavery." In addition, slavery released the planter from manual labor and gave him more time to cultivate his mind, and thus the Southern planter was highly educated, cultured, and refined. In the mind of the planter, slavery was "the defence of human civilization." Students of economics, however, saw that it was an evil which had to pass away.

FRANCES L. HUNTER

FOOTNOTES:

[1] *Muzzey, History of the United States, p. 304.*

[2] *Ingle, Southern Sidelights, p. 18.*

[3] *Ibid., p. 18.*

[4] Dodd, *Cotton Kingdom, p. 71.*

[5] *Ibid.*, p. 72.

[6] *Rhodes, History of the United States, Vol. I, p. 361.*

[7] *Ingle, Southern Sidelights, p. 45.*

[8] *Ibid.*, p. 40.

[9] *DeBow, Industrial History of the United States, Vol. II, p. 303.*

[10] *Adams, Three Months in the South, p. 82.*

[11] *Rhodes, History of the United States, Vol. I, 317.*

[12] *Hart, Slavery and Abolition, p. 100.*

[13] Dodd, *Cotton Kingdom*, p. 75.

[14] *Hart, Slavery and Abolition, p. 100.*

THE EVOLUTION OF THE NEGRO BAPTIST CHURCH

The freedom and local democracy of the Baptist Church enabled the Negroes to participate in the affairs thereof much earlier than they were so indulged in the other denominations. Pioneer Negro preachers and churches, therefore, first appeared in the Baptist Church. The development of the attitude of the Baptist Church toward the Negro, however, has been by cycles. The relations of the two races in church matters differ widely from what they were years ago. Members of both races formerly belonged to the same congregation, which in the beginning in this country ignored social distinctions. They have since then undergone radical changes to reach the present situation in which they have all but severed connection with each other.

In the beginning, the attitude of the so-called Christian whites toward the early Negro preachers was that of hostility. This opposition, however, did not come from the Baptists themselves, but from the master class. George Liele in the West Indies, Andrew Bryan in Georgia, and David George in Canada had much difficulty in their pioneer work, suffering many indignities and hardships. Andrew Bryan was whipped in a cruel and bloody manner but triumphed over persecution by his bold declaration that he was willing to die for Jesus. Rev. Mr. Moses, working in Virginia about this time, was often arrested and whipped for holding meetings. Others were excommunicated, but such opposition could not stay the progress of the work, for these pioneer preachers finally succeeded. This is attested by the resolution of the white Baptist Association expressing deep regret on the occasion of the death of Andrew Bryan.[1]

When the Baptists had won a standing after the grant of toleration in the United States and Negroes began to connect themselves with them, the status of the blacks in the Baptist Church had to be determined. Was the Negro to be a mere member in the back seat or a participant in the work of the Church? Under the labors of inspired white men thousands of Negroes were converted, baptized, set apart as churches, and instructed in all things which pertain to a life becoming the gospel of Christ. White persons, on the other hand, have been converted through the preaching of Negroes, and a few Negroes, even in the Southland, have been pastors of white Baptist churches. Speaking of the resignation of Mr. Thomas Armistead, who was pastor of the Portsmouth Church, in Virginia, until 1792, Robert B. Semple, in his *History of the Baptists of Virginia*, remarks: "After his resignation the church declined greatly. They employed Josiah Bishop, a black man of considerable talents, to preach to them. This, as might have been expected, could not answer in Virginia."[2]

Another instance of the same character is related by Mr. Semple, in connection with the Pettsworth or Gloucester Church. In his statement in regard to the death of Rev. Robert Hudgin, their first pastor, he observes that "This church continued to prosper moderately until Mr. Hudgin's death. They were then left without any person to go in and out before them. They at length did what it would hardly have been supposed would have been done by Virginians; they chose for their pastor William Lemon, a man of color." "He also died after several years. Since then," remarks Mr. Semple, "they have been destitute of stated ministerial aid." Here, then, is a man of color, who was pastor of a white Baptist Church in Virginia to the day of his death, covering a period of "several years."[3]

There is still another case, in which the order of things is reversed, and this the most remarkable in the history of the South. In 1798 there appeared in southwest Mississippi a colored Baptist preacher, Joseph Willis, a mulatto, who being duly licensed was very zealous to exercise his gift as a minister. In 1804 he crossed the Mississippi River and began a work into which he put a half century of earnest endeavor. After preaching at Vermillion and Plaquemine Brulé for eight years, amidst hardships and bitter persecutions, unaided and alone, and sacrificing a small fortune in the struggle, he was able, with the aid of visiting ministers, to constitute the first Baptist Church at Bayou Chicot. Other churches, the fruits of his labors, soon sprang into being, and in 1818 the Louisiana Baptist Association was constituted, with these churches as a nucleus. Joseph Willis was pastor of the church at Bayou Chicot for a number of years. As moderator of the Louisiana Baptist Association he was honored and respected—indeed, beloved and spoken of as "Father Willis." That a Negro should have the honor of giving to Louisiana its first mixed Baptist church and of being the pastor of that church—that a Negro was the first moderator of Louisiana's first white Baptist association,[4] and rendered the denomination fifty years of service, causes us greatly to marvel in these days of race division and race antipathy.

The Negro members of white Baptist churches of this country were, as a rule, permitted to worship with their white brethren within certain fixed limits. The gap between them, however, tended to widen. Later they were allowed another hour for worship, with large bounds and privileges. Still later they were provided with all the privileges of the Baptist meeting house under the restrictions of the white churches to which they belonged. The master class gradually reached the position of separating the races in worship, but for the security of slavery they deemed it wise to hold the Negroes as members of the white churches.

It was argued that, in all nature, living creatures move instinctively in groups after their kind, and that the Negro and the white man, left to themselves, do the same thing, as is evidenced by the fact that the black slave was ever offending against the institution of slavery by holding religious services after his own liking where only his own people were present and shared in the devotion. In this manner the master justified himself in segregating his slave in the house of God and pointed to the Court of the Gentiles, in the Temple of Jehovah, in confirmation of the righteousness of his act. But for some reason the untutored black slave was never entirely at home in the white man's church, with its special place for Negroes. He knew that the master could be at ease in any part of his church edifice. It was all his and he moved about through its aisles as a free man, but the slave was limited in his privileges, and was counted a good man only as he kept within the limits assigned him.

When the Negroes in the white Baptist churches of the South became very numerous, services for their special benefit were held in the church edifices, usually in the afternoon, by the pastor and other persons who felt a deep interest in them. In these meetings the colored members of the church not only enjoyed the freedom of the place for the time being, but often listened with great satisfaction to the exhortations of one or more of their own brethren who spoke by permission from the floor and not from the pulpit platform. These Negro exhorters were encouraged to exercise a measure of spiritual oversight in the midst of their brethren and so help the church and pastor in caring for the flock. The segregated group, in a separate church edifice, meeting for worship at the same hours as the parent body, gave rise to the separate church altogether, with a white ministry. In this way many of the largest and most progressive Negro Baptist churches of the South had their beginnings amid the vicissitudes of life peculiar to a land of human bondage. The African Baptist Church of Richmond, Virginia, under the direction of Dr. Robert Ryland, the white president of Richmond College, is a case in evidence.

Still another type of Negro Baptist church arose where there was no parent church of white persons in control of the offspring. There were churches of this character in Virginia, Georgia, South Carolina, the British West Indies, Canada, and in far-off Africa, before the close of the eighteenth century. In these churches the members were of the black race. In Virginia and in Georgia churches of this class as well as others were admitted to membership in the oldest and best white Baptist associations, in which they at one time were given considerable attention.[5] It is worthy of note that Negro Baptist churches of this type were the first Negro Baptist churches in all the land and preceded by many years the first Negro churches of other denominations in America.

These churches, moreover, soon established themselves in spite of opposition, for they were accepted by the Baptist associations. The Negro Baptist Church organized at Silver Bluff, South Carolina, in 1773 or 1775, probably had no such connection, nor did that of George Liele in Savannah, established not long thereafter; but the Negro Baptist Church of Williamsburg, Virginia, sought membership in the Dover Association in 1791 and was accepted. This church, according to John W. Cromwell, who is himself a Methodist, was founded in the year 1776. In 1815 the Gillfield Baptist Church, of Petersburg, Virginia, a Negro congregation, united with the Portsmouth Association, an organization of white Baptists. Shortly after doing so this church invited the association to hold its approaching annual meeting with the Gillfield Baptist Church. The "invitation was accepted and the church appointed a committee to rent stables and to buy feed for the delegates' horses." Richard Kennard, from whose church record we quote, adds: "A committee was also appointed to furnish blacking and brushes with which to clean the delegates' boots and shoes, and to see to the general comfort of the delegates." We agree with Mr. Kennard in the reflection: "At that age there did not seem to be as much prejudice among Christians or as much separation as since."[6]

The second step in the development was that of expansion abroad. There had been planted Negro Baptist churches, like the First African Baptist Church of Augusta, Georgia, in 1793, and Amos's Church at New Providence, Bahama Islands, British West Indies, in 1788. George Liele carried the work of the Baptists into Jamaica in 1784; and David George extended it to Nova Scotia and New Brunswick and finally into Sierra Leone about the same time. In this connection it may be remarked that because a Baptist church can arise and continue to exist as a self-originating, self-governing body without any consent or approval from without, the work of the denomination rapidly expanded. White ministers fully ordained to the ministry Negro Baptists, Negro Episcopalians and Negro Presbyterians and inducted them into pastorates, at a time when the Methodist Episcopal Church in America was not at first inclined to do so. This denomination, therefore, brought about that condition which resulted in the setting up of an independent African Methodist denomination under Peter Spencer in 1812, of another under Richard Allen in 1816, and still another under James Varick in 1820.

It should be remarked, moreover, that all Negro Baptist churches, except those in the South, which came out of white churches during slavery, had Negro pastors. Yet whatever their differences, Negro Baptists and white Baptists in America constituted one family until after the Civil War. Indeed there has never been any formal separation of the two groups. Each has simply followed the race instinct, in an age of freedom, while the one group cooperates with the other, North and South.

There were Negro Baptist churches in the South for more than a quarter of a century before they began to be constituted in the North, and about a half century before the first church of the kind was planted in the West. When in 1805, moreover, the first African Baptist church was organized at Boston, Massachusetts, it was not only the first Negro Baptist church in the North, but was also the only independent Negro church north except the St. Thomas Episcopal Church of Philadelphia, which had a Negro rector. The Boston African Baptist church had for its pastor a Negro, the Rev. Thomas Paul, a man of such intelligence and piety, such commanding presence and pleasing address, that pulpits everywhere in Massachusetts and in his native State of New Hampshire, were open to him, both before and after he became a minister in that city.

In the course of time Negro Baptist churches tended to associate among themselves, as they developed power independently of the white churches. There were in the South during the Negro's enslavement, however, no Negro Baptist associations which embraced their churches in any State or in any considerable part of a State; for all Negro Baptist churches were associated with white Baptist churches in the South. The "Richmond African Baptist Missionary Society," which was constituted at Richmond, Virginia, in 1815, was no exception to the rule. Lott Cary,[6] the chief spirit in that organization, and Mr. William Crane, a white merchant, its corresponding secretary, were members of the same church—not a Negro Baptist church, for there was no organization of the kind in Richmond at the time. Lott Cary was converted under the preaching of a white pastor. At the hands of that white pastor he was baptized, into the fellowship of the white church of which that pastor was the spiritual leader Lott Cary was received, and from that white church, the First Baptist Church of Richmond, Virginia, Lott Cary went to plant the standard of Christ on the shores of Africa.

Negro Baptist associations in this country were the achievements of free men on free soil. The Providence Association of Ohio, organized in 1833, and the Wood River Association of Illinois, organized in 1838, led the way. The colored Baptist churches of the North and East organized in 1840, and the abolition of slavery as an American institution resulted in the nation-wide formation of Negro churches, local associations, State conventions, and larger groups. In 1866 a national convention which merged the forces of the North and South, the East and West, under the significant name, "The Consolidated American Baptist Missionary

Convention," was organized. Its chief work was in the South and confined to the period of Reconstruction. In 1873 the West revived its organization under the name, "The Baptist General Association of the Western States and Territories," and the Northern churches did likewise in 1875 in the formation of "The New England Baptist Missionary Society." Each enlarged its borders until the two embraced the greater part of the whole country. In 1880 the Negro Baptists of the country formed their first national society to do work in foreign lands exclusively. The organization constituted at this time took the name, "The Baptist Foreign Mission Convention of the United States."

In 1886, at St. Louis, Missouri, the National Baptist Convention was formed, and the work of this organization was subsequently so modified that in it is unified all the national and international church work in which Negro Baptists of America were engaged. These efforts toward organization, however, were not altogether satisfactory, for the Baptists soon developed a factional struggle in regard to the question as to independent action or cooperation with the American Baptist Foreign Mission Society and the American Baptist Home Mission Society. In 1897, in the Shiloh Baptist Church, Washington, D. C., the Lott Cary Baptist Foreign Missionary Convention was formed by certain churches in the Atlantic States which looked with disfavor on the independent mission work as conducted by the Foreign Mission Board of the National Baptist Convention. Composed chiefly of men and women who were educated in the schools of the American Baptist

Home Mission Society, this organization has from the first cooperated with Northern Baptists in the prosecution of its work.

At Chicago in 1915 there arose a more serious division in the forces of the National Baptist Convention as the result of differences of opinion in regard to the ownership of the Convention in the lands and chattels of its Publishing Board. As a result of these differences there have developed two groups of colored Baptists in this country, engaged in similar work, and each claims to be the National Baptist Convention—the original and only National Baptist Convention of Negro Baptists in America.

One of the results of the association of Negro churches has been education. Negro Baptists in a land of slavery were not supposed to be versed in the knowledge of books. But inasmuch as master and slave were instructed out of the same inspired writings Sabbath after Sabbath, the slave quite frequently was as familiar with the Bible as his master. Ignorance and illiteracy are not one and the same thing. An unlettered people may be learned in the word of God, and being made wise unto salvation, may present to the world no mean type of Christian life. Apart from the knowledge received through the regular preaching of the gospel by the best preachers of the Southland, it was not unlawful to impart verbal instruction to slaves, in Sunday-school exercises and, under other circumstances, in regard to any number of things which have to do with conduct and character and human comfort, so long as nothing was said to endanger the institution of slavery. But some Baptists appear to have given some measure of literary training to Negroes attached to their churches. Andrew Bryan, in one of his letters to Dr. John Rippon of London, England, in 1800, speaks of the fact that certain white friends in Savannah, Georgia, had purchased a man of color of many excellent qualities, the Rev. Henry Francis, and had given him his freedom that he might be a teacher to his people. Bryan himself then opened a school for the slaves on his plantation outside of Savannah. George Liele established a school in connection with his church in Jamaica, hoping to develop the minds of his communicants that he might properly edify their souls.

The First Baptist Church (white), Richmond, Virginia, moreover, conducted a school for the literary training and instruction of its Negro members. For several years Lott Cary was a student in this institution. The church at Williamsburg, Virginia, which was a Negro Baptist church from its beginning, that is, from 1776, must have done something for education, for it kept correct church records, in the handwriting of its own members. Many of the Negro Baptist preachers of the South, moreover, obtained some degree of scholarship by private instruction and so won the respect of the people among whom they lived. The close of the Civil War brought together a group of scholarly men, from the North and West, men of purpose and consecration, preachers of great power who were an inspiration to their less cultured and less scholarly brethren in the South, and these invaded our Southland to help forward the new order of things in the churches as well as in civil life.

To-day the Negro Baptists of America have more than 20,000 churches, with about two and a half million members and church property valued at more than forty million dollars. They are conducting orphan schools, homes for the aged poor, and institutions of learning, and are as zealous as ever in sending the gospel to people in foreign lands. Great has been the progress of Negro Baptists in America, but that progress was due in very great measure to Northern philanthropy during a quarter of a century after the Civil War and is promoted also to-day by the good will of Southern Baptists who have put at the disposal of Negro Baptists in the South thousands of dollars. But the greatest glory of Negro Baptists is the spirit of self-help and heroic sacrifice in the endeavor to help others, and that spirit is now everywhere prevalent.

WALTER H. BROOKS

FOOTNOTES:

[1] The resolution was: "The association is sensibly affected by the death of the Rev. Andrew Bryan, a man of color, and pastor of the first colored Church in Savannah. This son of Africa, after suffering inexpressible persecutions in the cause of his Divine Master, was at length permitted to discharge the duties of the ministry among his colored friends in peace and quiet, hundreds of whom, through his instrumentality, were brought to the knowledge of the truth as it is in

Jesus. He closed his extensively useful, and amazingly luminous course, in the lively exercise of faith, and in the joyful hope of a happy immortality." See Benedict's *History of the Baptists.*

[2] *Semple, History of the Baptists in Virginia, p. 355.*

[3] *Semple, History of the Baptists in Virginia, p. 356.*

[4] *The Negro Year Book, 1918–1919, p. 236; Benedict, History of the Baptists, 376.*

[5] By way of comparison, be it further remembered, that the founder of the African Methodist Episcopal Church was originally a member of the St. George Society, of Philadelphia, Pennsylvania, and he and others withdrew from that body of white persons in 1787; but it was not until 1794, that Bishop Francis Asbury constituted the Bethel A. M. E. Church at Philadelphia, which claims to be the oldest Negro Methodist church in the country. The Zion Church, of the African Methodist Episcopal Zion connection, New York City, was founded in 1796, while the first church of Negro Episcopalians, the St. Thomas Church, Philadelphia, was planted by Bishop William White in 1794. The Lombard Street Presbyterian Church, Philadelphia, the oldest organization of Negro Presbyterians in America, was constituted in 1807, and not until 1829 was the first church of Negro Congregationalists, the Dixwell Avenue of New Haven, Conn., constituted.

[6] *Richard Kennard's History of the Gillfield Baptist Church, p. 16.*

[6] Let me quote here a paragraph from Sprague's *Annals of the American Pulpit*, Vol. VI, p. 583, (Ed. 1860, published by Robert Carter and Brother, New York.) The paragraph appears in an article which the publisher takes from *Taylor's Memoirs.—Missionary Heroes and Martyrs.*

"In 1850, the late Rev. Eli Ball of Virginia, visited all the Liberian Baptist Missionary Stations, as agent of the Southern Baptist Missionary Convention, and, with considerable difficulty, ascertained the spot where Lott Cary was buried. The next year, a small marble monument was sent out, and placed over the grave, with the following inscription:—

"On the front of the monument was—

LOTT CARY
Born a slave in Virginia,
1780,
Removed from Richmond to Africa, as a
Missionary and Colonist,
1821,
Was Pastor of the First Baptist Church,
and an original settler and defender
of the Colony at Monrovia.
Died Acting Governor of Liberia
Nov. 10th, 1828.
His life was the progressive development of an
able intellect and firm benevolent heart,
under the influence of
Freedom and an enlightened Christianity;
and affords the amplest evidence of the capacity

of his race to fill with dignity and usefulness
the highest ecclesiastical and political stations.
Of a truth God is no respecter of persons,
But hath made of one blood all nations of men.

On the reverse—

Lott Gary's self-denying, self-sacrificing labors,
as a self-taught Physician, as a Missionary and
Pastor of a Church, and finally as
Governor of the Colony,
have inscribed his name indelibly on the
page of history,
not only as one of Nature's Noblemen, but
as an eminent
Philanthropist and Missionary of Jesus Christ.

'Aye, call it holy ground,

The place where first they trod;

They sought what here they found,

Freedom to worship God.'"

That is, indeed, a remarkable utterance, coming from the Southern Baptist Missionary Convention, in the year 1851.

EARLY NEGRO EDUCATION IN WEST VIRGINIA

The early education of the Negro in West Virginia falls in three periods.[1] During the first period, it was largely restricted to such efforts as benevolent whites were disposed to make in behalf of those Negroes who had served them acceptably as slaves. This period, therefore, antedates the emancipation of the Negroes. Because of the scarcity of the slave population of Western Virginia, the 14,000 slaves scattered among the mountainous counties came into helpful contact with their masters, among whom the institution never lost its patriarchal aspect. Although it was both unlawful and in some parts of West Virginia unpopular to instruct Negroes, these masters, a law unto themselves, undertook to impart to these bondmen some modicum of knowledge. Upon the actual emancipation in 1865, when all restraint in this respect was abrogated, benevolent white persons, moved with compassion because of the benighted condition of Negroes, volunteered to offer them instruction. The first teachers of the Negroes in West Virginia, then, were white persons. The Negroes of Jefferson, Greenbrier, Monroe, Summers, Kanawha, Mason, and Wood counties still point with pride to these white friends, who by their indefatigable work as teachers blazed the way in a field which to Negroes had been forbidden.

During the next period there came into these same parts the Union soldier, followed and sometimes accompanied by the missionary teachers sent out by the Freedmen's Relief Commissions of the North and by the Freedmen's Bureau. The efforts of the Union soldier could not be crowned with signal success for the reason that they were sporadic and this volunteer was not in every case well prepared for such service. The greatest impetus was given the cause when missionary teachers appeared in the State. Having the spirit of sacrifice which characterized the apostles of old, they endured the hardships resulting from social proscription and crude environment. With the funds which they secured from the agencies which they represented and which they could raise among the poor freedmen and their few sympathetic white friends, these teachers of the new day built or rented shanty-like school-houses in which they proclaimed the power of education as the great leverage by which the recently emancipated race could toil up to a position of recognition in this republic. The educational achievements of this class of teachers were significant, not so much because of the actual instruction given, but rather on account of the inspiration which set the whole body of Negroes throughout the State thinking and working to secure to themselves every facility for education vouchsafed to the most highly favored element of our population.

The third period in the early education of Negroes in West Virginia was reached when these pioneer teachers had wrought well enough to enable the Negroes to help themselves. Because of the rapid development of this industrial State and the consequent influx of Negroes from other commonwealths, however, the number of Negro teachers produced on the ground proved inadequate to the demand for instructors among the increasing and expanding Negro population of West Virginia. There went out to the other States the call for help, which was answered largely by workers from Virginia, Maryland, and Ohio. Virginia did not have many workers to spare, but from Baltimore, where, because of the liberal attitude of the whites toward the education of Negroes prior to the Civil War, a considerable group of Negroes had been trained, came a much larger number of volunteers. From Ohio, however, came as many as were obtained from both Virginia and Maryland, for the reason that, although the Negroes were early permitted to attend school in Ohio, race prejudice had not sufficiently diminished to permit them to instruct white persons in public schools. Looking out for a new field, their eyes quickly fell on the waiting harvest across the Ohio in West Virginia. Some of these workers from adjacent States, moreover, served the people not only as teachers but also as ministers of the gospel. They were largely instrumental in establishing practically all of the Methodist and Baptist churches in the State, and while they taught school during the week, they inspired and edified their congregations on Sunday.

The beginning of the education of the Negroes in West Virginia at public expense was delayed inasmuch as its first constitution, although it made provisions for free schools, did not extend the facilities of the same to the freedmen. In the report of the State Superintendent of Public Schools in 1864, therefore, he complained that the Negroes had been too long and too mercilessly deprived of this privilege. "I regret to report," said he, "that there are not schools for the children of this portion of our citizens; as the law stands I fear they will be compelled to remain in ignorance. I commend them to the favorable notice of the legislature."[2]

In 1866, therefore, the legislature enacted a law providing for the establishing of public schools for Negroes between the ages of six and twenty-one years. These schools had to maintain an average attendance of sixteen pupils or be closed. As Negro communities were not very large and the number of such children small, some of them scattered throughout the State were denied the opportunity to acquire an education. This law, therefore, was amended in 1867 so as to authorize local boards of education to establish a school whenever there were more than fifteen Negro children between the ages of six and twenty-one.[3]

The attitude of the State approved separation of the two races in the schools, but the first two laws bearing on Negro schools did not make this point clear. Upon revising the constitution in 1872, therefore, it was specifically provided that whites and blacks should not be taught in the same school.[4] Thereafter, however, the whites and blacks sometimes used the same school-houses. As the term consisted of only four months of twenty-two school days each, the whites would open school in September and vacate by Christmas, when the Negroes would take charge.

No further changes were made in the school law until 1899, when it was amended to the effect that the trustees in certain districts should establish one or more primary schools for Negro children between the ages of six and twenty-one years, and that said members of boards of education should establish such Negro schools whenever there were at least ten Negro pupils who resided in their district, and for a smaller number, if it were possible to do so.[5] This gave impetus to the movement for more intensive education among Negroes throughout their communities. Often Negro children in groups of only four or five were thus trained in the backward districts, where they received sufficient inspiration to come to larger schools for more systematic training.

THE FIRST EFFORTS IN NORTHERN WEST VIRGINIA

Parkersburg enjoys the distinction of having established in this State the first school for Negroes supported by private funds. Having a desire to provide for their children the facilities of education long since denied to members of their race, a group of progressive Negroes met in Parkersburg in January, 1862, to translate their idea into action. Among these persons were Robert Thomas, Lafayette Wilson, William Sargent, R. W. Simmons, Charles Hicks, William Smith, and Matthew Thomas. They organized a board, which adopted a constitution and by-laws by which they were to be governed in carrying out this plan. They then proceeded to establish a subscription school requiring a tuition fee of one dollar a month of those who were able to pay; but poorer children were admitted free of charge. At this time there was a certain stigma attached to the idea of educating one's children at the expense of others or at the expense of the commonwealth. Persons able to pay for the instruction of their children were, therefore, willing to do so that they might not have a reputation for dependency or delinquency.[6]

The teachers first employed in Parkersburg were Sarah Trotter and Pocahontas Simmons, persons of color and Rev. S. E. Colburn, a white man. The number of pupils enrolled in the first year approached forty. To encourage Negroes in that city to avail themselves of their opportunity for their enlightenment, these teachers moved among the people from time to time, pointing out the necessity for more extensive preparation to discharge the functions of citizenship then devolving upon Negroes in their new State of freedom after the Civil War.[7]

Parkersburg enjoys also the distinction of having established the first free school for Negroes in the South. The work of the school organization of 1862 had been so well done that it was easily possible to interest school officials in the extension of school privileges to Negroes. The Parkersburg *Weekly Times* of June 7, 1866, carried a notice to the effect that the first public free school for the Negro children of the city of Parkersburg, West Virginia, had been opened in the school ward lately removed. "All colored children over six years of age and under twenty-one, as the law directs," continued the editor, "are at liberty to attend and are requested to do so." Rev. S. E. Colburn was the teacher. The private school then came to an end.[8]

It does not appear that the Reverend Mr. Colburn remained for a long time in this school, for at the close of the session in 1866 we have a record of an exhibition in Bank Hall under the charge of T. J. Ferguson. Ferguson was a versatile character among the Negroes at that time, participating extensively in politics during the reconstruction period, and contending for the enlargement of freedom and opportunity for their race. The next man of consequence after Ferguson was J. L. Camp, who served the system for eleven years. He passed among his people as a man of high character, and is remembered today as one of the most successful and inspiring workers to toil among the lowly in West Virginia. The Negro schools could then be turned over to teachers of the race who, having availed themselves of the opportunities for education, had become equipped for service among their own people. With the further organization of the public school system of Parkersburg, the Negro school was brought under the direction of the local superintendent of schools and given the same sort of instruction and inspection as that provided for the white schools. In the course of time the work developed from a primary into an intermediate and then into a grammar school.

Parkersburg is unique again, moreover, in having the first high school for Negroes in the State. This advanced phase of public school work was added in 1885, and the first class was graduated in 1887. For a number of years the Negro schools were housed in a frame building of two rooms, which was somewhat enlarged in 1883. This, moreover, has been followed by the erection of a brick structure with the modern conveniences for public schools, facilitating especially high school instruction, which under former conditions was handicapped. A new building known as the Sumner High School was constructed there in 1886, and A. W. Pegues, a graduate of the Richmond Institute, was made its first principal. He showed himself a studious man of intellectual bearing, but after serving in Parkersburg one year he resigned to accept a chair in Shaw University in North Carolina. He has since been made the head of the Deaf and Dumb Asylum of that State.[9]

Following Professor Pegues came T. D. Scott, who served in this high school five years, reorganizing the work and enlarging the curriculum. When he resigned in 1892 he became an instructor in natural science at Wilberforce University, of which he was an alumnus. Carter Harrison Barnett, a graduate of Dennison University, became principal in 1892 and served one year. Then came John Rupert Jefferson, who took charge of the institution in 1893, a position which he has successfully filled until the present time with the exception of one year when he was supplanted by Mr. B. S. Jackson, an alumnus of Howard University, who at the close of his first year's service gave way to Mr. Jefferson.[10]

Clarksburg followed in the wake of Parkersburg and soon bestirred itself in the direction of the education of Negro youth. The first school was established there in 1867, with an enrolment of thirty pupils under the direction of Miss Joe Gee. For her time she was well-prepared woman, using up-to-date methods, and was very successful in the work there for two and one-half years, at the expiration of which she married. Her successful work was due in no small measure to the cooperation of Mrs. Mary Rector, Mrs. Phyllis Henderson, Mr. Fred Siren, Jr., and Mrs. Harriet Beckwith. They did not own the school property, but conducted the work in a one-room ramshackled structure. Another group of ambitious Negroes established a school at Glen Falls, in the same county, in 1872, with Noe Johnson as the teacher.

Steps were soon taken to provide better educational facilities for Negroes in Clarksburg. On July 15, 1868, the Board of Education of that city accepted a bid of $1,147 to erect a one-story brick building to be used as a Negro school-house. This structure was completed and occupied by the end of the school year 1870. After the school had been better housed, the work was professionally organized and thereafter intelligently supervised to standardize instruction.

In the beginning of this new day the schools were successful in having a number of popular principals to serve them efficiently. Among these may be mentioned Charles Ankrum, a pioneer teacher, who was principal of the school from 1870 to 1873, J. A. Riley, a man of the same type serving from 1873-1874, G. F. Jones, a man of little more preparation than that of his predecessors, from 1874 to 1876, W. B. Jones, an honest worker, from 1876-1878, and M. W. Grayson, who served the system well from 1878 to 1889, doing much to lay the foundation upon which others built thereafter.[11]

The first Negro principal at Clarksburg, with extensive preparation as judged by the standards of today, was J. S. Williams, a graduate of Morgan College, who was the head of this school from 1889 to 1891. Mr. C. W. Boyd, a normal school graduate of Wilberforce University, served the system one year, that is, from 1891 to 1892, after which he became a teacher in the Charleston Negro Public Schools of which he is now the head. Then came Mr. Sherman H. Guss, the first Negro to receive a degree from Ohio State University. He made a special study of the needs of the school, forcefully presented them to the educational authorities, enlarged the school's facilities, and developed there a high school which ranks today as one of the best in the State. In 1901 Mr. Guss resigned to become instructor in Latin at the West Virginia Colored Institute, where he is still employed. He was followed by J. W. Robinson, a man of liberal and specialized education, who endeavored to maintain a high standard and to extend the influence of the Negro schools, adding much to develop an intellectual atmosphere through the enlargement of the school library and other accessories. After toiling in this city for a number of years he taught at St. Albans. He then accepted the principalship of the high school at Northfork, during his incumbency of which he has served as a member of the Advisory Council to the State Board of Education of West Virginia.

Weston did not lag far behind the other towns in making some provision for the education of Negroes.

During the early years immediately following the Civil War, a white man of philanthropic tendency named Benjamin Owens taught a Negro school in an old church located not far from the head of Main Street extended in Weston. A local historian believes also that one Doctor Gordon's daughter taught in the same school. It does not appear that Owens was a man of exceptional intellectual attainment, but he had well mastered the fundamentals of education when working in the printing office of Horace Greeley in New York, where he learned to manifest interest in the man far down, and to make sacrifices for his cause. His work was so successful that the school was later established as a public institution supported by the State.

The next pioneer to lend a helping hand was George Jones who, after serving the Negroes in Weston as a teacher for a number of years, abandoned this field for a much larger work as a minister. Then came Misses Hattie Hood, Grace Rigsby, and Anna Wells, who taught in this school one or two years each. There appeared next W. P. Crump, who is referred to as the first Negro teacher of exceptional ability to toil in Weston. He did much to develop the school and exerted a beneficent influence upon the people. After serving them as instructor for a few years, he abandoned the work for a more lucrative employment elsewhere. The next teacher of importance was Mr. Frank Jefferson who also toiled successfully in these parts. Inasmuch as the salary at that time was unusually low compared with the compensation offered in other parts, he eventually gave up that work for other service.[12]

About 1898 there came Mr. L. O. Wilson, a man of scholarship, who later became a leader of power and influence throughout the State of West Virginia. He reorganized the school, improved the methods of instruction, and supplied it with a library. He endeared himself to the people here, as he did wherever he was known; and, although he was several times offered higher salaries elsewhere, he preferred to toil among the people of Weston for less compensation. The results which he obtained, while laboring among these people, stand as a monument justifying the sacrifice which he made to serve them.[13]

The next school of importance in this part of the State was that of Piedmont, since then designated as the Howard School. Educational efforts began in this section about six years after the Civil War. Prior to that time the few Negroes coming into Piedmont were too migratory to necessitate any outlay for their education. Some efforts were made to secure their education through private instruction in the fundamentals, and a little progress therein was noted. Years later there came such substantial friends of education as the Barneses, the Masons, the Thomases, the Biases, and the Redmons. There was no organized effort to establish a real public school, however, until the year 1877, when one John Brown, being influential with one Mr. Hyde, then President of the Board of Education, induced him to provide a school-room and hire a teacher for the instruction of the Negroes. The following persons, since known as Mrs. Emma Stewart (Mason), Miss Mary Thomas, Mr. John Brown, Jr., Miss Alice Brown, and Mr. Harry Bias, presented themselves as the first students of this school. One Mr. Ross, a white man, was the first instructor. The next teacher of this school was a white man, and he was followed by a member of his own race.

The early history of this school published in 1919 states that the attendance was regular and that after three years of conducting a private school the board of education formally established this as a public school in the year 1880, with Mrs. Steiglar, a white woman, as instructor. The school was still held in the private building which has since been occupied by the Williams, Redmon, and Taylor families of that vicinity. After this school was conducted thus for about ten years, there came a change which marked the epoch of progress in education in Piedmont. This was the time when the white teachers were exchanged for those of Negro blood, who having more interest in their race, and treating the pupils with more sympathy, achieved much greater success than their predecessors. This school has since been much developed under the direction of Mr. H. W. Hopewell and Miss M. Brooks.[14]

The early schools of Shepherdstown, Martinsburg, Harper's Ferry, and other places nearby in West Virginia were in the beginning largely private, and even when established as public schools accomplished little more than their predecessors until they received an impetus from without. The first stimulus came from Miss Mann, a niece of the great educator, Horace Mann. She was sent by the Christian Commission to Bolivar, near Harper's Ferry, to open a Negro school, which in spite of militant race prejudice she maintained a year.[15] Then came the establishment of Storer College by that philanthropic worker for the uplift of the Negro race, Rev. Nathan C. Brackett, a graduate of Dartmouth College, who had during the last year of the Civil War been attached to the Christian Mission of Sheridan's army in Virginia. Fortunately the agents of the Freedmen's Bureau in charge of the educational work among Negroes designated him as the superintendent of such schools to be established in the Shenandoah Valley. While he was thus organizing and directing the education of the Negroes in this section, Mr. John Storer, of Sanford, Maine, expressed a desire to set aside a fund of ten thousand dollars for the establishment of an institution of education for the freedmen on the condition that an equal amount should be raised by other persons within a specified period. As there was an increasing interest in the uplift of the freedmen throughout the country at this time, it was an easy matter to meet this condition with a similar contribution from another quarter. The additional funds came largely from the Free Baptists, in the principles of which this institution had its setting when established.

The work was begun, by special arrangement with the Federal agents, in dilapidated houses recently abandoned by the Union troops at Harper's Ferry. With the cooperation of friends the buildings were secured through the influence of James A. Garfield, then a member of Congress, and William Fessenden, then United States Senator from Maine. Mr. and Mrs. Brackett opened this school in October, 1867, with nineteen earnest students. Since then it has become a power for good, a factor in the development of actual Christian manhood and womanhood. For a number of years it was the only graded school for Negroes in the State of West Virginia, and had to supply many of the first teachers and ministers in West Virginia and even in the adjacent portions of Maryland and Virginia. The towns nearby caught the spirit of the uplift of the Negro from what was being done for the race in Storer College. This institution, of course, had its opposition; but wherever there was a helpful attitude toward the Negro, the work which it was doing in spite of its difficulties stood out as a shining light.[16]

Many of the early teachers of Storer College spent a part of their time working among Negroes in nearby communities. Mrs. Annie Dudley, a white woman connected with that institution, taught the first school at Shepherdstown. She had about twenty-five students and conducted a night and a day school. She was a well-educated, sympathetic woman who did much to lay the foundation for the Negro public school which was established there in 1872. The next popular teacher in the Eastern Panhandle was William B. Evans, who successfully taught in Shepherdstown, Keyser, Martinsburg, and Bolivar for forty-two years. His wife, Mrs. M. E. L. Evans, after beginning in Virginia, taught ten years at Storer, Summit Point, Smithfield, and Bolivar. William Arter taught thirty-two years at Kabletown, doing excellent work. The most prominent teacher that Shepherdstown had was John H. Hill. He graded the work of the school and endeavored to standardize instruction. He is still remembered in that community for the efficient work which he did. He was finally succeeded by Alexander Freeman when Mr. Hill became an instructor in the West Virginia Colored Institute, of which he later became principal.

About the same time the influence of Storer College was felt in Charles Town, the county seat of Jefferson County, where there was another settlement of Negroes. The first teacher of whom we have a record was one Enos Wilson, a Negro. He was a man of fair preparation through self-instruction. He had much enthusiasm in his work, exerted an influence for good, and won the respect of his people. In achieving his success he had the cooperation of Mr. William Hill, the grandfather of J. H. Hill. Although not well informed himself, William Hill believed in education and religion, and supported all uplift movements then taking shape among the Negroes.

Following Enos Wilson, who later became an instructor in another field, came L. L. Page, who building upon the foundation made by his predecessors rendered unusually valuable service. Like his predecessor he was a very good man and an enthusiastic worker. The people waited upon his words, answered his summons to social service, and supported him in his efforts to promote their general welfare. This is evidenced by the fact that he served his community acceptably about twenty-five years. He was succeeded by Phillip Jackson, who found the school sufficiently well developed to necessitate the employment of three teachers.

Not far away from this point Mrs. Emma Hart Brady opened a large school at Kearneysville, in Jefferson County, in 1869. She was a popular teacher for that day, used modern methods, and successfully instructed 80 or 90 students there for two terms. This school today, as it was then, is overcrowded and in need of better facilities.[16a]

Speaking generally, however, one must say that the education of the Negro in the Eastern Panhandle of West Virginia today is, after all, much more backward than in other parts. A good example of noble effort in behalf of the Negro was given, and the spirit with which workers should address themselves to the task was furnished by the founders and graduates of Storer College, but they were not supported by public sentiment among the whites of that section. Glancing at the map of West Virginia, one can readily see that the Eastern Panhandle is geographically a part of Maryland and Virginia, states which have not as yet been converted to the wisdom of making appropriations to Negro education equally as large as those providing for the education of the whites. The ardor of the successors of these early enthusiastic workers in that section, therefore, was dampened, and the results which they obtained fell far short of the aspiration of these pioneers to remake these freedmen that they might live as the citizens of a free republic.

A mere glance at the Negro schools in the northern section will show that these beginnings were confined to the Baltimore and Ohio railroad and its branches. There were not many Negroes living in the other northern counties of the State. In 1878, Moundsville in Marshall County welcomed a Negro woman, of Smithfield, Ohio, who taught its Negro public school. She had a fair preparation and rendered valuable service with the cooperation of such patrons as Mrs. Rollen, William Love, and Thomas McCoy. Because of the small Negro population in this town, however, this school has not rapidly developed, although the work of the teachers employed there has been efficient, as has been evidenced by their well-prepared eighth-grade students who have done excellently in more advanced schools.[17]

A little farther north, in Wheeling in Ohio County, Negro education had a better opportunity. Wheeling is geographically a part of Pennsylvania, and its attitude toward education has been determined to a large extent by the impetus given the cause in that progressive commonwealth. The spirit of fairness in dealing with the man far down in urban communities nearby, moreover, has been reflected to a certain extent in the policies of the educational authorities of Wheeling in dealing with the Negro. At an early date the Negroes of Wheeling were provided with elementary schools. Referring to the increasing interest in Negro education in 1866, State Superintendent White said: "An excellent school has been started in Wheeling and a few are reported in other places. The school-house in Wheeling cost about $2500. The school is conducted by a teacher of their own color and the behavior and scholarship of the pupils are worthy of imitation."

Here, as in the case of most Negro schools near the

Ohio River and even in the central portion of the State, their first teachers came from Ohio, where they had the opportunity to attend the high schools and even colleges of high order, although they were not able to over-ride the race prejudice which barred them from the teaching corps in that free State. In Wheeling, moreover, the salaries paid were much more inviting than in many towns of West Virginia, and that city could easily employ the best equipped Negro teachers, who in the beginning came largely from Ohio.

The Wheeling school, then, fortunate in having the service of such teachers, developed about as rapidly as possible under the circumstances of a limited Negro population; for Wheeling is not in a Negro section, and the industrial aspect of the city not being inviting to Negro workers, the population of color did not rapidly increase. Because of the small enumeration thereby resulting, more extensive facilities could not be provided even when the board of education was favorably inclined. In 1897, however, when the pupils of all of the grades reached about three hundred, the city established the Lincoln High School, which had its development under the late J. McHenry Jones. He called to his assistance well-equipped teachers and succeeded in offering to the Negroes of that city practically the same course of study taught in the white high school, though at times some classes were too small to justify instruction in certain phases of specialized work.[18]

Blazing the Way in the Central Counties

A more extensive movement for the education of the Negroes was taking place during these years in the central part of West Virginia, following the line of the Chesapeake and Ohio Railway and the New and Kanawha Rivers. This work did not arouse equal interest in all of the counties along these routes, but in Greenbrier, Monroe, Summers, Fayette, Kanawha, Cabell and Mason Counties, reached a point of development deserving mention. It can be readily observed that this progress in education resulted largely from the early settlements of Negroes in the east-central counties of the State and from the influx of Negro laborers into the New and the Kanawha valleys to work on the salt works, and later from the migration of Negroes to the coal mines opened along the Chesapeake and Ohio and the Kanawha and Michigan Railroads. Negro schools, with such few exceptions as those at Marshes, in Raleigh County, at Madison and Uneeda in Boone County, at Red Sulphur Springs in Monroe County, and at Fayetteville in Fayette County, were unsuccessful when removed from those important thoroughfares.

The earliest teaching of the Negroes in the east-central counties of the State came as a result of the sympathetic interests of benevolent slaveholders who, living in a part of a State with a natural endowment unfavorable to the institution of slavery, failed as a whole to follow the fortunes of the slaveholders near the Atlantic Coast, and, hoping to see the ultimate extinction of the institution by gradual emancipation, gave the Negroes an opportunity for such preparation as they would need to discharge the functions of citizenship. Immediately after the War, when there was no public opinion proscribing such benevolence, sympathetic white persons privately instructed Negroes here and there. Such was the case at White Sulphur, long since known as a summer resort, attracting from afar persons of aristocratic bearing who, coming into contact with the Negro servants whom the resort required, not only proved helpful to them by way of contact, but gave them assistance in realizing limited educational aspirations. The private school in White Sulphur finally gave place to one established by the district. It had the support of the best white citizens of the community and was maintained largely by the enterprise of progressive Negroes seeking to provide for their children all facil-ities for education offered elsewhere. About the same time, that is, in 1866, the Freedmen's Bureau had a school in Lewisburg, under the direction of one Miss Woodford. After serving the people well for a year or two, this institution gave place to a public school.[19]

In Ronceverte, where the Negro population increased more rapidly and where these persons of color made more economic progress than in the case of White Sulphur, Negro education had a better chance. After passing through the stage of such private instruction as white persons interested in the man far down felt disposed to give, an actual school was opened in the early seventies with an enrolment of thirty pupils. The first teacher was Mr. Robert Keys of Charleston, West

Virginia. Mr. Keys was well prepared for that time and served there creditably for two years. Mr. Keys had the support of such well-known families as the Crumps, the Capertons, the Gees, the Petersons, the Eldridges, the Browns, the Eubanks, the Williamses and the Hayneses. There served also Miss Carr of Harrisonburg, Virginia, and Benjamin Perkins of Lewisburg, West Virginia. Mr. Robert D. Riddle was also one of the early instructors. Mr. Riddle retired from teaching several years ago, but is still living in the city of Ronceverte, where he has distinguished himself as a successful truck farmer. Some years later Rev. R. D. W. Meadows, who has for a number of years served as a missionary in West Virginia, labored as a teacher in these parts, leaving a favorable impression on the system. The school was first taught in the small one-room house privately owned. When it increased in later years, it was found necessary to divide it so as to teach a part of the school in the Negro Baptist Church until the larger building could be provided. It is now a well-graded and junior high school with many modern facilities.[20]

Union, in Monroe County, was not unlike the other large settlements of this section having considerable Negro population. There was at times even as early as 1855 a healthy sentiment in favor of the improvement of the few slaves there, and this was not lost after the Civil War had ended. So general was the interest in behalf of the Negroes that this proved to be a most favorable community. Union was one of the first towns in that section to establish a public school for Negroes. At first there was some difficulty in having well prepared

Negro teachers in the county itself; for one John Didell, a white man, was the first teacher of the public school. He had the support of such respectable Negroes as Julius Smalls, Andrew Bailey, Malinda Campbell, Henry Campbell, James Clair, Christopher Whitlock, and Charles Campbell. Two of the products of this school are Miss Charlotte Campbell and Bishop M. W. Clair of the Methodist Episcopal Church.[21] Among those who came in later to stimulate the first efforts of the teachers were Mrs. Leota Moss Claire, now a resident of Charleston, West Virginia, and J. M. Riddle who, after having taught at Sinks Grove in Monroe county and preached for several years in various parts of West Virginia, engaged in the ministry in Ohio and later went to California, where he is now serving as a State Missionary of the Baptist church.

In Summers County, the large settlement of Negroes was at Hinton. This place had a Negro school of fifteen pupils as early as 1878, with one T. J. Trinkle as instructor. He was a man of limited education, but prepared to help those who had not made advancement in the fundamentals. What he lacked in education he made up in moral influence, and his career is still remembered as a success. The cause of education among Negroes of Hinton was fearlessly supported by E. J. Pack and C. H. Payne, once a teacher in a rural district in this county himself and later a minister and a public servant in this country and abroad. The school in Hinton began in a one-room structure rented for four months, the length of the school term. Teachers were paid at the rate of $15, $25 and $30 a month for third, second, and first grade certificates respectively. It has recently developed into a well-graded school having a junior high school running nine months, with teachers paid at the rate of a combined monthly salary of $600.

The Negro public school experienced a later development in Fayette County than in the case of the counties nearer to the eastern border of the State or nearer the Ohio River; for, unlike those parts which had a larger number of slaves than the central and northern counties, Fayette County never before the eighties had Negro groups in sufficiently large numbers to warrant an outlay in education at public expense. The beginning of Negro education in this county was consequent upon the migration of Negroes to the coal fields. Many of them were interested in education and became its best patrons. Among those were Samuel Morgan, A. W. Slaughter, J. H. Shelton, J. D. Shelton, Aaron Chiles, Thomas Chiles, Randal Booker, Thomas Bradley, Oliver Jones, Ballard Rotan, Anderson Rotan, R. J. Perkins, Aaron Calloway, Mat Jordan, Henry Robinson, S. H. Hughes, Wellington Henderson, John Carrington, James Caul, George Moss, and Pleasant Thomas.

The first school established in Fayette County was that at Montgomery, in 1879. It was opened by H. B. Rice, a pioneer teacher in Kanawha Valley who had completed his education at Hampton Institute. For three years Mr. Rice taught in one room of the home of Thomas H. Norman, an intelligent and progressive Negro who, realizing the importance of education as a leverage in the uplift of his people, early made sacrifices for the establishment of this school. The school was then taught in a shanty. Inasmuch as at the end of one year, that is, by 1883, the Negro population had rapidly increased, this uncomfortable building was very much over-crowded and the school had to be divided so that part of it could be taught in the Baptist church nearby, until it secured better quarters. Among the teachers who toiled in this district were Mrs. A. G. Payne, Mrs. Anna Banks, Misses Sadie Howell, Julia Norman, Annie Parker, M. E. Eubank, Mrs. F. D. Railey, Mr. George Cuzzins, Mrs. M. A. W. Thompson, Miss L. O. Hopkins, Miss Lizzie Meadows, Mr. J. W. Scott, Miss Rebecca I. Bullard, Miss Mattie Payne Trent, Mrs. Lola M. Lavender Mack, Miss Nellie M. Lewis, Miss Ida M. King and Mr. H. H. Railey. The last mentioned not only attained distinction as the principal of this school, but so impressed his constituents as to be elected to the West Virginia Legislature.[22]

The impetus given to education at Montgomery was productive of desirable results in other towns in Fayette County. The second Negro school to be established in Fayette County was that Quinnimont in 1880. A storm of protest made the life of the teacher almost intolerable, although he was a white man. The schoolhouse had to be guarded, but Rev. M. S. G. Abbot taught it two years. Then came Mr. R. D. Riddle, mentioned above in connection with the school at Ronceverte.[23]

At Eagle, not far from Montgomery, there settled groups of Negroes sufficiently large to necessitate educational facilities for their children. A large one-room school followed and this had not been established very long before it was necessary to employ two teachers.

Among the prominent laborers in this field were Mrs. Mary Wilson-Johnson and Mrs. A. G. Payne. This work experienced most extensive growth under the direction of Miss A. L. Norman, Miss M. E. Shelton and Mr. A. C. Page.

There soon followed schools at Fire Creek, Hawk's Nest, Stone Cliff, Nuttallburg, Sewell, Fayetteville, and elsewhere in Fayette County. Prominent among the teachers serving in these towns were D. W. Calloway, A. T. Calloway, Miss L. E. Perry, Mrs. Lizzie Davis, Miss Bertha Morton, Mr. James Washington, Mrs. F. Donnelly Railey, Mrs. H. C. A. Washington, Mrs. J. B. Jordan-Campbell, C. G. Woodson, and Mrs. E. M. Dandridge. These teachers did not generally serve a long period in any one place, as there was a difference in salary in various districts and the best teachers usually sought the most lucrative positions; and sometimes, in the battle for bread and butter, the rather keen competition in certain districts led to the periodical dismissal of teachers without justifiable cause.

To those mentioned above, however, is due the credit for the development of the Negro schools in Fayette County. This is especially true of Mrs. E. M. Dandridge, who doubtless had a more beneficent influence in Fayette County than any teacher of color who toiled there. She taught for twenty-five years at Quinnimont, where she was not only a teacher but a moving spirit in all things promoting the social, moral, and religious welfare of the Negroes of her own and adjacent communities. She was fortunate in having a natural endowment superior to that of most persons and enjoyed, moreover, educational advantages considered exceptional for most Negroes of that day. She still lives to continue a noble work well begun and to complete a useful career in the same county where she cast her lot years ago.

For almost a generation earlier than this, Negro education had been launched with much better beginnings in the county of Kanawha. There were no free schools in West Virginia until 1866, but as in the case of several other settlements in the State, private schools were conducted for Negroes immediately after their emancipation. There had come into the county of Kanawha Rev. F. C. James, an Ohio Negro, the father of C. H. James, the wealthy wholesale produce merchant of Charleston. This pioneer was a man of fundamental education and unusual native ability. He opened at Chapel Hollow, or Salines, two and one-half miles from Malden, in 1865, probably the first Negro school in the Kanawha Valley. He thereafter taught elsewhere and later became the founder of the First Baptist Church of Charleston. The following year Miss Lucy James from Gallia County, Ohio, opened the first Negro school in Charleston. Among the first patrons were Matthew Dillon, Lewis Rogers, Alexander Payne, Lewis Jones, Perry Harden, Julius Whiting, and Harvey Morris. Mrs. Landonia Sims had charge of the school one year also. At this time Rev. Charles O. Fisher, a Methodist Episcopal minister of Maryland, had a private and select school which was later merged with the free public school. Between 1866 and 1869 Rev. J. W. Dansberry, another Methodist Episcopal minister from

Baltimore, Maryland, belonging as did Mr. Fisher to the Washington Conference, served also as a teacher while preaching in this State. The Simpson M. E. Church, their main charge, was being developed during these years and was in 1867 housed in a comfortable building on Dickinson and Quarrier Streets. Mr. C. O. Fisher was a well-educated man, but Mr. Dansberry depended largely on natural attainments.

Rev. I. V. Bryant, who has toiled for many years in the Ohio Valley as a Baptist minister, started his public career as a teacher at Baker's Fort school, about two and one-half miles from Charleston. Rev. Harvey Morris, another minister, opened a public school at Sissonsville in 1873, Rev. J. C. Taylor another at Crown Hill in 1882, and not long thereafter this school was attended by such distinguished persons as Mrs. M. A. W. Thompson and Dr. A. Clayton Powell of New York City. This work in Kanawha County was accelerated too by the assistance from the Freedmen's Bureau which sent to this section C. H. Howard, brother of Gen. O. O. Howard, the head of the Freedmen's Bureau, to inspect the field, and later sent one Mr. Sharp to teach in Charleston.[24]

One of the first schools in Kanawha County was organized at Malden. Immediately after the Civil War this town had a much larger and more promising Negro population than the city of Charleston. Many Negroes had been brought to Kanawha County, and after their freedom many others came to labor in the salt works. This private school at Malden was conducted by Mr. William Davis, the first teacher of Booker T.

Washington, who a few years before had come from Halesford, Virginia, to Malden.

Mr. Davis's career is more than interesting. He was born in Columbus, Ohio, November 27, 1848, remained there until his thirteenth year, spending parts of the years 1861, 1862, 1863 in Chillicothe. During these years he mastered the fundamentals of an English education. He moved back to Columbus in the fall of 1863. On December 18th of that year Mr. Davis enlisted in the Union "Light Guard," called "Lincoln's Body Guard," at Columbus. He served in the army eighteen months and was discharged at Camp Todd Barracks, Washington, D. C., June 24, 1865. He then returned to Columbus and after remaining there about a month went to Cincinnati, from which he proceeded to run on a boat from Gallipolis to Charleston for about a month.

About this time the people of Malden, under the wise guidance of Lewis Rice, a beloved pioneer minister, better known among the early Negroes of the State as Father Rice because of his persistent efforts in behalf of religion and education, had decided to establish a school for the education of their children. Mr. William Davis thereupon abandoned his work on the boat and became the teacher of this private school, established at Malden in the home of Father Rice, in 1865. As the school had to be conducted in the very bed-room of this philanthropist, it was necessary for him to take down his bed in the morning and bring in the benches, which would be replaced in the evening by the bed in its turn. The school was next held in the same church thereafter constructed, and finally in the schoolroom provided at public expense, as one of the schools of the county.

About the only white person who seemed to give any encouragement to the education of Negroes at Malden was General Lewis Ruffner. It seems, however, that his interest was not sufficient to provide those facilities necessary to ease the burden of this pioneer teacher. When we think, however, that out of this school came such useful teachers as William T. McKinney, H. B. Rice, and one of the world's greatest educators, Booker T. Washington, we must conclude that it was a success.

Mr. Davis's worth as a teacher rapidly extended through the Kanawha Valley. He was chosen by the authorities of Charleston to take charge of their Negro schools in 1871, when it was just a two-room affair. In this field, however, Mr. Davis had been preceded as mentioned above by noble workers in behalf of the Negroes. Building upon the foundation which other Negroes had laid, he soon had a school of four instead of two rooms, and before he ceased to be principal it had increased to five, with a well-graded system, standardized instruction, and up-to-date methods. His early assistants in this work were Charles P. Keys, P. B. Burbridge, Harry Payne, James Bullard, and William T. McKinney.

Mr. Davis received some cooperation from a few white persons, the chief one of whom was Mr. Edward Moore of Pennsylvania, the father of Spencer Moore, now a bookseller in the city of Charleston. Mr. Edward Moore taught a select school for Negroes and helped the cause considerably. Mr. Davis served about twenty-four years as principal, although he was a member of the teaching staff for a much longer period, serving altogether forty-seven years.[25]

Because of the unsettled policy of the Charleston public schools they changed principals every year or two, to the detriment of the system and progress of the student body. Rev. J. W. Dansbury served for a while as principal, and H. B. Rice, who entered the service as an assistant in 1888, became principal some time later and served about four years. Mr. Davis, who had been demoted to a subordinate position, was then reinstated, but not long thereafter came Mr. C. W. Boyd, who had rendered valuable service in Clarksburg and had later found employment in the public schools of Charleston. He succeeded Mr. Davis as principal. At the close of one year, however, Mr. Rice was reinstated and served for a number of years, at the expiration of which Mr. Boyd again became principal and remained in the position long enough to give some stability to the procedure and plans of the system and to secure the confidence of the patrons of the schools. Some of the valuable assistants serving during this period were Mr. William B. Boss, Miss Blanche Jeffries, Mrs. Fannie Cobb Carter and Byrd Prillerman, whose career as a teacher includes a period of short and valuable service in the Charleston public schools.[26]

At what is now Institute, in Union district, there was established in the fall of 1872 another Negro school, opened on the subscription basis in the home of Mrs. Mollie Berry, née Cabell. Mrs. Berry was the first teacher of this school. The building is occupied at present by a

Mr. James and owned now by Mrs. Berry's daughter, Mrs. Cornie Robinson. In the spring of 1873, Mr. William Scott Brown, who had by marriage connected himself with the Cabell family, was elected trustee in the Union district, and by his efforts a Jenny Lind one-room building, small and creditably furnished, was erected on a lot purchased by the board of education from Mrs. Cabell for twenty-five dollars, on the site now occupied by the family of Mr. Solomon Brown of Institute. The trustees chose Mr. Samuel Cabell as the first Negro public school teacher of the district. The method of qualifying as a teacher was purely perfunctory, as a license to teach was easily obtained by nominal examination. The term was four months.[27] The line of teachers from 1886 may be traced from records of the board of education of the district. Short tenure of office for a few years seems to have been the rule until the recent years dating from 1918. It is the opinion of Mr. W. A. Brown and others of the old system that the quality of the local school has grown better. The establishment of the West Virginia Collegiate Institute at this point is considered the greatest factor contributing to such development.[28]

The next school of consequence established on Kanawha River was the Langston School of Point Pleasant, in Mason County. This institution was organized in 1867 by Eli Coleman, its first teacher. He toiled for seven years in the one-room frame structure at the end of Sixth Street. At the very beginning the enrolment was sixty-four, some of the students being adults. The school continued as an ungraded establishment for a number of years, working against many handicaps, until the independent district was established and provided better facilities. This school then had a board of five trustees, three whites and two Negroes, and was incorporated into the city system by the Board of Education and placed under the supervision of the Superintendent of the Point Pleasant Public Schools.

Some of the early teachers following Mr. Coleman were J. H. Rickman, later principal of the colored school in Middleport, Ohio, P. H. Williams, Mrs. Lillie Chambers, Florence Ghee, Fannie Smith and Lida Fitch. In 1885 the school had grown sufficiently to justify the employment of two teachers. These were then L. W. Johnson as principal and Miss Hattie C. Jordan as his assistant. Mr. Johnson served until 1890 when he was succeeded by Miss Lola Freeman as principal with Samuel Jordan as assistant for one year. The Board of Education then secured the services of J. E. Campbell as principal. Under him the school moved into a five-story brick structure vacated by a white school when better quarters for the latter had been provided. The Negro school was then named the Langston Academy in honor of John Mercer Langston, a Negro congressman and public official of wide reputation. Miss Iva Wilson of Gallipolis succeeded Mr. Campbell as principal, with Miss Jordan as assistant. Later there came as principal Mr. F. C. Smith, A. W. Puller, and Ralph W. White, and finally the efficient and scholarly Isaiah L. Scott, a promising youth cut off before he had a chance to manifest his worth to the world.[29]

Somewhat later than this, another group of Negro

schools developed in Cabell County, the first and most important being in Guyandotte and Barboursville. These schools followed as a result of employment of Negroes on the Chesapeake and Ohio railroad, terminating in the seventies at the Ohio River, where it gave rise to the city of Huntington, West Virginia, laid out in 1870. Most of these Negroes, prominent among whom were James Woodson, Nelson Barnett, and W. O. James, came from Virginia. The first school established near Huntington was opened in the log house on Cemetery Hill, one and a half miles east of the town and a little west of Guyandotte. The Negro school enumeration was so small that the two towns had to cooperate in maintaining one school.

The teacher first employed was Mrs. Julia Jones, a lady who had most of the rudiments of education. Some old citizens refer to James Liggins as the first teacher in this community. In this precarious status of stinted support the school did not undergo any striking development during the first years. Not until 1882, some years after the school had been removed to Huntington itself, was there any notable change. The first impetus which marked an epoch in the development of this school came with the employment of Mr. and Mrs. W. F. James, products of the Ohio school system. They were for their time well-prepared teachers of foresight, who had the ability to arouse interest and inspire the people. Mr. James at once entered upon the task of the thorough reorganization of the school and by 1886 brought the institution to the rank of that of the grammar school, beginning at the same time some advanced classes commonly taught in the high schools. He was an earnest worker, willing to sacrifice everything for the good of the cause. While thus spending his energy as a sacrifice for many he passed away respected by his pupils and honored by the patrons of the school. His wife continued for a number of years thereafter to render the system the same efficient service as the popular primary teacher upon which the success of the work of the higher grades largely depended, until she passed away in 1899.

The school then had the services of Mr. Ramsey and Mr. J. B. Cabell who seemingly gave some impetus to the forward movement. Another epoch in the history of the school was reached when W. T. McKinney became principal in 1891. With the cooperation of the leading Negroes of the city he succeeded in inducing the board of education to build on the corner of Sixteenth Street and Eighth Avenue the Douglass High School, which in its first form, prior to the making of certain additions, consisted of a well-built six-room school costing several thousand dollars. Mr. McKinney added the high school course and in the year 1893 graduated the first class of three. Following Mr. McKinney there served the system efficiently as principals C. H. Barnett from 1890 to 1900, C. G. Woodson from 1900 to 1903, and R. P. Sims from 1903 to 1906. J. W. Scott, who succeeded Mr. Sims, is today principal of this school, ranking throughout the State as one of its foremost educators.

Following along the line of Wayne County there soon appeared a school at Ceredo and another at Fort Gay, just across the river from Louisa, Kentucky. Under Mrs.

Pogue, a woman of ambition and efficiency, this school accomplished much good and exerted an influence throughout that county. A number of students trained through the sixth, seventh, and eighth grades later attended schools in other parts and made good records because of the thorough training they first received. At Fort Gay in this same county, however, no such desirable results were achieved because of the small Negro population, the inability to secure teachers for the small amount paid, and the tendency on the part of local trustees there to change their teachers. Mrs. Cora Brooks Smith, a graduate of the Ironton High School, who toiled there a number of years, and Miss Susie Woodson, an alumnus of the Douglass High School of Huntington, West Virginia, who also labored in the same field, should be given at least passing mention in any sketch setting forth the achievements in education among the Negroes in Wayne County.

THE STRIVINGS IN SOUTHERN WEST VIRGINIA

In southern West Virginia there were at first few schools for Negroes, inasmuch as the small Negro groups here and there did not warrant the outlay. What instruction such Negroes received prior to 1888 was largely private. That year an epoch was marked in the development of the southern portion of the State by the completion of the main line of the Norfolk and Western Railroad, opening up one of the largest coal fields in the United States. As the discontented Negroes of Virginia and

North Carolina were eager for industrial opportunities in the mining regions of the Appalachian Mountains, these coal fields attracted them in large numbers. Bluefield, which developed in a few years from a barren field in 1888 to a town of almost ten thousand by 1900, indicates how rapidly the population there increased. Other large centers of industry, like Elkhorn, Northfork, Welch, and Keystone, soon became more than ordinary mining towns.

When these places had worn off the rough edges of frontier settlement and directed their attention to economic and social welfare, they naturally clamored for education. The first school for whites was established in Bluefield in 1889 and one for the Negroes, with Gordon Madson as teacher, followed in 1890. Prominent among the pioneering teachers in Bluefield were Mr. A. J. Smith and Mrs. L. O. McGhee, who began their work in a one-room log building in the suburbs of the town. About the end of the nineties there were Negro schools in most of the important mining towns along the Norfolk and Western Railroad between Bluefield and Williamson.

The Negro school in Bluefield had an interesting history. The school, of course, was poorly equipped and the teachers were not then adequately paid, but they continued their work two sessions of five months each. In the third year the school was moved to another town called Cooperstown where it was housed in a two-room building more comfortable than the first structure, but not a modern establishment. As it was situated in crowded quarters, the children had no playground. Several years thereafter, the work was continued by Mr. Patterson and Mrs. E. O. Smith. When, however, a large Negro population settled in North Bluefield it was necessary to provide there a two-room building between them. In this school-house taught Mr. P. J. Carter with an enrolment of about thirty pupils. Not long thereafter the building in the suburb of Cooperstown was burned. Two additional rooms were then annexed to that of North Bluefield, but before that could be occupied it was also destroyed in the same way. The Board of Education then opened a school, in a building used first as a bar-room, then as a pool-room, and finally as a courthouse. Thereafter an old store-room was used for four years.

There were then four teachers in Bluefield, Mr. H. Smith, Mr. T. P. Wright, Mesdames Lane, and E. C. Smith. In time Mr. Wright and Mr. Smith were replaced by Miss H. W. Booze, Mr. W. A. Saunders and Mr. R. A. McDonald. Mr. Saunders remained for one year and then was followed by Mr. G. W. Hatter who was in his turn succeeded by Mr. R. F. Douglass, who served as principal four years. Mr. Douglass had the board of education appropriate funds for a six-room building and increase the corps of teachers to five. By raising funds in the community through entertainments and the like, the teachers purchased a library of 100 volumes. In later years Mr. Douglass was followed by Mr. E. L. Rand, a graduate of Lincoln University.

At Keystone in 1890 Mr. J. A. Brown opened its first Negro school with an enrolment of about twenty-five. He was a man of fair education, but could not accomplish very much because the term was only three months in length. The school was held in one of the private houses belonging to the coal company and later in the church. In subsequent years there was very much development in the right direction, which proved the quality of the teachers employed in the school. Among these were Rev. J. Whittico, Mrs. Josephine D. Cannady, Mary A. McSwain, and Maggie Anderson. This school was later combined to form the Keystone-Eckman graded school, and now has an eight months' term and well-qualified teachers.[30] A school had been established at Eckman in 1893 by James Knox Smith.

In November, 1892, one Moses Sanders at Northfork opened a school with an enrolment of twenty. He had only a rudimentary education. He served at Northfork for three terms using methods considered fair for that time, and his work, as a whole, was regarded as successful. He had there the support of such a useful person as Henry Glenn, now a member of the board of education.[31] This school has later developed into a standard elementary graded school and a junior and senior high school of more than one hundred students. It has done well under the reorganization and direction of the efficient J. W. Robinson.

HIGHER EDUCATION OF NEGROES

It did not require much argument to show that the schools could not make much progress without some provision for developing its own teaching force. The

State Superintendent was early authorized, therefore, to arrange with some school in the State for the professional training of Negro teachers. For a number of years the State depended largely upon such normal training as could be given at Storer College at Harper's Ferry. The reports of the State Superintendent of Schools carried honorable mention from period to period of the successful work being accomplished there under the direction of Dr. N. C. Brackett, which work was the only effort for secondary education for Negroes in the State at that time. This was given an impetus by a measure introduced in the legislature by Judge James H. Ferguson of Charleston, providing for an arrangement with Storer College by which eighteen persons as candidates for teachers in this State should be given free tuition at that institution. As this school was in the extreme northeastern section of the State and was geographically a part of Maryland and Virginia, however, the Negroes of the central and southern portions of Virginia soon began the movement for the establishment of a Negro school providing for normal instruction nearer home. Mr. William Davis and his corps of teachers in Charleston, West Virginia, were among the first in West Virginia to direct attention to this crying need. Impetus was also given the movement by the rapid development of higher grades in Point Pleasant, Saint Albans, Montgomery, Lewisburg and Eckman, necessitating better trained teachers. In the summers of 1890, 1891, and 1892, Byrd Prillerman and H. B. Rice undertook to supply this need by conducting a summer school in the city of Charleston. Still further stimulus came later from the establishment of promising high schools in Parkersburg, Wheeling, Clarksburg, Huntington, and Charleston.

During this same period, however, a systematic effort was being made to interest a larger group in the more efficient training of Negro leaders. The Baptists of the State, led by C. H. Payne, undertook to establish a college in West Virginia. Payne toured the State in behalf of the enterprise, setting forth the urgent need for such an institution and showing how this objective could be attained. Rallying to this call, the people of the State raised a sum adequate to purchase a site, which was soon sought by authority of the Baptists of the State. They selected the abandoned building and grounds of Shelton College, overlooking Saint Albans. Because of race prejudice, however, the people of that town started such a protest that the owners of the property were induced not to sell the site for such an unpopular purpose.

A more successful effort, however, was soon made. Talking with Superintendent Morgan about the necessity for higher education for the Negroes of West Virginia, Byrd Prillerman obtained from this official the promise to support a movement to supply this need. Superintendent Morgan furthermore directed Prillerman to Governor Fleming to take up with him the same proposal. The Governor was in a receptive mood and informed Prillerman, moreover, that this problem could be more easily solved than he had at first thought, for the reason that such an institution could be so established as to benefit by the Morrill Land Grant Act intended to subsidize, with funds from the proceeds of public lands, institutions largely devoted to instruction in Agriculture. Like the Negro Baptists of the State, Governor Fleming thought of purchasing Shelton College in St. Albans; but inasmuch as that place was not available the State government had to take more serious action. As Governor Fleming said he would give his approval to a bill for the establishment of such an institution, the only problem to be then solved was to find persons to pilot such a measure through the legislature. Superintendent Morgan outlined the plans for this legislation. He showed how necessary it was to secure the support of Mr. C. C. Watts and Judge James H. Ferguson. Byrd Prillerman used his influence in securing the support of Mr. Watts and C. H. Payne induced Judge Ferguson to lend the cause a helping hand. These gentlemen framed the measure which, after some unnecessary debate and unsuccessful opposition from friends of Storer College, they piloted through the legislature in 1891 as a measure establishing the West Virginia Colored Institute.

The first head of this institution was James E. Campbell, a graduate of the Pomeroy High School. After laying the foundation and popularizing the work to some extent in the central portion of the State, Campbell resigned and was succeeded by J. H. Hill, who rendered very efficient service until 1899, when he was succeeded by J. McHenry Jones, under whom the school considerably expanded. Following him came Byrd Prillerman, a man beloved by the people of West Virginia. He had already been a successful teacher of English in this school. He then served the institution as president for ten years, emphasizing the high ideals of Christian character as the essentials in the preparation of youth. In 1915 a collegiate course was established at this institution and its name was changed to that of the West Virginia Collegiate Institute. In 1919 Byrd Prillerman was succeeded by John W. Davis, under whom the institution is progressing with renewed vigor in its new field as a reorganized college furnishing facilities for education not offered elsewhere for the youth of West Virginia.

The influx of Negroes into the southern counties of the State, which necessitated the establishment of many elementary schools, caused at the same time a demand for the extension of the facilities of pedagogic training of the advanced order provided in the West Virginia Colored Institute, which was not at first easily accessible to the people of southern West Virginia. Acting upon the memorials, praying that this need be supplied, the legislature established the Bluefield Colored Institute in 1895. Mr. Hamilton Hatter was made the first principal and upon him devolved the task of organizing this institution. After serving the institution efficiently until 1906 he retired, and was succeeded by Mr. R. P. Sims, who had formerly been an efficient and popular assistant under Mr. Hatter at this institution. Mr. Sims has acceptably filled this position until the present time.

THE WEST VIRGINIA TEACHERS' ASSOCIATION

To promote education and to encourage interest in their particular work the Negro teachers of the State soon deemed it wise to take steps for more thorough cooperation of the whole teaching corps of West Virginia. White and Negro teachers were then admitted to the same teachers' institutes and in certain parts were encouraged to participate in the general discussions; but believing that they could more successfully cooperate through organizations of their own, the teachers in Charleston, in 1891, appointed from their own reading circle a committee to organize a State Teachers' Association. This committee was composed of H. B. Rice, P. B. Burbridge and Byrd Prillerman. The meeting was invited by Byrd Prillerman, as secretary, to meet at the Simpson M. E. Church in Charleston. More than fifty teachers and race leaders attended. Inasmuch as H. B. Rice, the chairman of the committee, was absent on account of illness, P. B. Burbridge, whose name was second on the list of the committee, called the meeting to order, and delivered the address of welcome. William T. McKinney of Huntington was elected temporary chairman. The Association was then permanently organized by naming Byrd Prillerman its first president and Mrs. Rhoda Weaver its first secretary. Among the most important addresses was that of C. H. Payne, an influential and educated minister then engaged in religious and editorial work at Montgomery, and that of B. S. Morgan, State Superintendent of Public Schools. Others attending the meeting were Dr. W. T. Merchant, Mrs. E. M. Dandridge, Mrs. M. A. Washington-Thompson, F. C. Smith, and J. R. Jefferson.[32]

The second meeting of this Association assembled according to arrangement in Parkersburg, West Virginia. The work of the Association had by this time been taken more seriously by the teachers throughout the State. They adopted a constitution with a preamble which stated that the aim of the Association was "to elevate the character and advance the interest of the profession of teaching, and to promote the cause of popular education in the State of West Virginia." An address was delivered by State Superintendent of Schools B. S. Morgan, and papers were read by Mrs. E. M. Dandridge of Quinnimont, Miss Blanche Jeffries of Charleston, Miss Coralie Franklin of Storer College, and Principal J. E. Campbell of the West Virginia Colored Institute. Among the persons attending but not appearing on the program were C. H. Barnett, who had been recently graduated by Dennison University in Ohio; C. H. Payne, then well known in the State of West Virginia; Dr. W. S. Kearney, a graduate of the medical college of Shaw University, then beginning his practice in Huntington; J. R. Jefferson, F. C. Smith and O. A. Wells. Booker T. Washington was at this time made an honorary member. Byrd Prillerman was unanimously elected president.

The third annual meeting of the Association was held at Parkersburg, West Virginia, in 1893. For some reason there were not many teachers present. It was held at the Baptist Church of that city, with President Byrd

Prillerman presiding. The address of welcome was delivered by Mr. J. R. Jefferson, to the words of whom Mr. C. W. Boyd of Charleston responded. At this meeting Principal J. E. Campbell of the West Virginia Colored Institute was made president of the Association, with C. W. Boyd, J. R. Jefferson, Miss Mary F. Norman as vice-presidents, Miss Clara Thomas as secretary, Miss E. D. Webster as treasurer, and Mrs. Susie James as historian. Two of the most prominent persons participating in this meeting were J. McHenry Jones, then principal of the high school in Wheeling, and J. H. Hill, an instructor in the West Virginia Colored Institute.

The fourth annual meeting assembled at Montgomery. J. E. Campbell being absent, Professor C. W. Boyd presided. The meeting to a certain extent was a successful one. A Thanksgiving sermon was preached by Dr. C. H. Payne. Dr. H. F. Gamble read a paper on "Science in Common School Education." The Association took high ground by adopting a resolution urging a compulsory school law. A committee consisting of C. W. Boyd, Rev. G. B. Howard, J. W. Scott, John H. Hill, and Byrd Prillerman, was appointed to urge the State to make an appropriation for the teaching fund of the West Virginia Colored Institute. Byrd Prillerman was again elected President and Miss Fannie Cobb was chosen secretary.

The fifth annual meeting of the Association was held at Hinton. An important feature of the meeting was the method of entertainment, in that the citizens of Hinton gave the teachers a free banquet. Still more significant was the address delivered by Dr. J. E. Jones of the Richmond Theological Seminary. Byrd Prillerman, the President, himself delivered an important address giving valuable facts as to the conditions of the schools of the State, evoking widely extended comment. The most prominent persons attending were J. H. Hill, Principal of the West Virginia Colored Institute, G. B. Howard, Miss Mary Booze, W. T. McKinney, and Miss G. E. Fulks.[33]

The sixth annual meeting was held in Charleston in the House of Delegates, November 26-27, 1896. This was the largest and most interesting meeting hitherto held. Welcome addresses were delivered by C. W. Boyd of the Garnet High School, Mr. George L. Laidley, Superintendent of the Charleston Public Schools, and Governor W. A. McCorkle. Responses to the words of welcome were delivered by J. H. Hill, principal of the West Virginia Colored Institute, Hamilton Hatter, principal of the Bluefield Colored Institute, and C. H. Payne. Other prominent persons who attended the meeting were Honorable V. A. Lewis, P. F. Jones, Colonel B. W. Byrne, Professor A. L. Wade, J. R. Jefferson, Rev. D. W. Shaw, Dr. G. W. Holley, P. B. Burbridge, Dr. H. F. Gamble, Dr. L. B. Washington, Mrs. E. M. Dandridge, Mrs. M. A. W. Thompson and Mrs. Byrd Prillerman. Officers elected were: President, Byrd Prillerman; Vice Presidents, J. R. Jefferson, Mrs. E. M. Dandridge, C. W. Boyd; Secretary, Miss Mary J. Jones; Treasurer, Mrs. M. A. W. Thompson; Historian, Mr. George L. Cuzzins.

After this meeting of such unusual interest and unexpected success, the West Virginia Teachers' Association reached its purely pedagogic setting. It ceased to be the organization concerned with the general social uplift, of all, and thereafter restricted its program largely to educational matters. This was due not so much to any desire on the part of the teachers to discontinue cooperation with the clergy, but rather to direct attention primarily to the problems of education. Ministers, thereafter, figured less conspicuously in the conventions, except so far as their interests were coincident with those of the teaching body.

There have been twenty-eight sessions of the Association held at Charleston, Huntington,[34] Parkersburg, Hinton, St. Albans, Bluefield, Institute, Kimball, and Harper's Ferry. The session which was scheduled for Clarksburg in 1900 was called off because of the outbreak of small-pox just before the time for the session to be convened.

Eleven well-known persons have served as president of the Association. Byrd Prillerman served nine terms, C. W. Boyd one, J. R. Jefferson one, J. W. Scott three, H. H. Railey one, Hamilton Hatter one, R. P. Sims two, E. L. Rann two, J. W. Moss two, A. W. Curtis two, John F. J. Clark two, and H. L. Dickason, the present incumbent, two. Those who have served as secretary are Miss Rhoda E. Weaver, Miss M. Blanche Jeffries, Miss Clara Thomas, Miss Fannie C. Cobb, Miss Mary J. Jones, and Miss C. Ruth Campbell, and Miss H. Pryor.

Among the prominent persons who have addressed the Association are Hon. C. H. Payne, Ex-Governor George W. Atkinson, Ex-Governor William A. McCorkle, and State Superintendents B. S. Morgan, Virgil A. Lewis, James Russell Trotter, and M. P. Shawkey. Among other distinguished persons have been Dr. J. E. Jones, Prof. George William Cook, J. McHenry Jones, Prof. Kelly Miller, Dr. W. E. B. Dubois, Prof. William Pickens, Mr. William A. Joiner, Dr. Carter G. Woodson, Miss Nannie H. Burroughs, John W. Davis, and Dr. J. E. Gregg.[35]

C. G. WOODSON

FOOTNOTES:

[1] This study was undertaken at the suggestion of President John W. Davis, of The West Virginia Collegiate Institute. He appointed a committee to collect the facts bearing on the early efforts of workers among the Negroes in West Virginia. The members of this committee were C. G. Woodson, D. A. Lane, A. A. Taylor, S. H. Guss, C. E. Jones, Mary E. Eubank, J. S. Price, F. A. Parker, and W. F. Savoy.

At the first meeting of the committee, C. G. Woodson was chosen Chairman and at his suggestion the following questionnaire was drawn up and sent out:

A QUESTIONNAIRE ON NEGRO EDUCATION IN WEST VIRGINIA

PLACE.....................

1. When was a Negro school first opened in your district?

2. What was the enrollment?

3. Who was the first teacher?

4. Was he well prepared?

5. How long did he serve?

6. Were his methods up-to-date or antiquated?

7. Did he succeed or fail?

8. Who were the useful patrons supporting the school?

9. What was the method of securing certificates?

10. What was the method of hiring teachers?

11. What was the method of paying teachers, that is, did the school district pay promptly or was it necessary to discount their drafts or wait a long period to be paid?
12. Did the community own the school property or was the school taught in a private home or in a church?

13. What has been the progress or development of the school?

14. What is its present condition?

15. What persons in your community can give additional facts on Negro education?

Name.........................

From the distribution of these questionnaires there were obtained the salient facts of the early history of the pioneer education among Negroes in the State. A number of names of other persons in a position to give additional information were returned with the questionnaires. These were promptly used wherever the information needed could not be supplied from any other source. Members of the committee, moreover, visited persons in various parts and interviewed them to obtain facts not otherwise available. Wherever it was possible, the investigators consulted the available records of the State and county. In this way, however, only meager information could be obtained.

The most reliable sources were such books as the annual Reports of the State Superintendent of Public Schools, the History of Education in West Virginia (Edition of 1904), and the History of Education in West Virginia (Edition of 1907). Such local histories as the Howard School of Piedmont, West Virginia, and K. J. Anthony's Storer College were also helpful.

At the conclusion of this study, President John W. Davis made the celebration of Founder's Day, May 3, 1921, a convocation for rehearsing the early educational history of the State. Most of the living pioneers in this cause were invited to address this meeting, as they would doubtless under the inspiration of the occasion, set forth facts which an ordinary interview would not evoke, and thus it happened.

Of those invited Mrs. E. M. Dandridge, one of the oldest educators in the State, Mr. S. H. Guss, head of the Secondary Department of The West Virginia Collegiate Institute, and President Emeritus Byrd Prillerman responded with forceful addresses. Mrs. Dandridge gave in a very impressive way a brief account of education in Fayette County. Mr. Guss delivered an informing address on the contribution of the early teachers from Ohio, and President Emeritus Prillerman expressed with emphasis a new thought in taking up the rise of schools in the State and the organization and growth of the West Virginia Teachers' Association. Prof. J. S. Price, of the West Virginia Collegiate Institute, showed by interesting and informing charts the development of the Negro teacher and the Negro school in West Virginia.

At the conclusion of all of these efforts the facts collected were turned over to C. G. Woodson to be embodied in literary form. Prof. D. A. Lane, of the Department of English of The West Virginia Collegiate Institute, also a member of the committee, read the manuscript and suggested a few changes.

[2] Report of the State Superintendent of Public Instruction, 1864, p. 31.

[3] *History of Education in West Virginia (Edition of 1907)*, p. 274.

[4] See West Virginia Constitution.

[5] *History of Education in West Virginia (Edition of 1907)*, p. 274.

[6] *History of Education in West Virginia (Edition of 1907)*, p. 268.

[7] *Ibid.*, 269.

[8] *The Parkersburg Weekly Times,* June 7, 1866.

[9] These facts were obtained from local records.

[10] *History of Education in West Virginia (Edition of 1907)*, pp. 269-270.

[11] These facts were obtained from the local records, from Mr. S. H. Guss and from Mr. D. H. Kyle, both of whom served as teachers in Clarksburg.

[12] *History of Education in West Virginia (Edition of 1907), pp. 273-274.*

[13] These facts were obtained from local records.

[14] *History of the Howard School, Piedmont, West Virginia, 1919, passim.*

[15] This fact is stated in a letter of J. E. Robinson.

[16] *History of Education in West Virginia (Edition of 1907), pp. 264-266; and Storer College, Brief Historical Sketch, by K. J. Anthony.*

[16a] These facts were obtained from Mrs. Brady's daughter.

[17] Facts obtained from a former teacher at this place, Freida Campbell.

[18] *History of Education in West Virginia (Edition of 1907), p. 243.*

[19] Facts obtained from local records.

[20] These facts were obtained from the teachers and oldest citizens of the town, who actually participated in these early efforts.

[21] These facts were supplied by Mary Campbell, an old citizen of Union.

[22] *History of Education in West Virginia (Edition of 1904), Negro Education in Fayette County.*

[23] Facts obtained from old citizens and former teachers.

[24] These facts were obtained from old citizens and from local records. See also J. P. Hale's *Trans-Allegheny Pioneers*, 385.

[25] This is largely Mr. Davis's own statement verified by several other authorities and by local records.

[26] These statements are supported by the records of the Board of Education of Charleston.

[27] In the summer of 1874 there was circulated among the teachers of this school a petition in behalf of Miss Bertha Chapelle, who was chosen to teach the second term of the high school. In this way the last month of the session was taught with but one scholar attending. In the year 1875 Miss Mollie Berry was chosen to teach this school, and she was followed in 1876 by Mr. Frank C. James, who had taught previously the first public school in the county at Kanawha City, in 1866. He was succeeded in 1877 by Mr. Pitt Campbell, who was followed by Mrs. Bettie Cabell in 1878. She was in turn succeeded by Mr. Brack Cabell the following year. In 1880 the school was moved to the site now occupied by the two-room village school, and was called the Piney Road School. Mr. J. B. Cabell was chosen teacher for the first year.

In 1881 Miss Emma Ferguson was selected teacher.

Miss Ferguson, now Mrs. Emma Jones, is still an active teacher. In 1882 Miss Addie Wells taught this school. She was followed by Miss Annie Cozzins. In 1884 W. C. Cabell was in charge. He was succeeded in 1885 by Otho Wells and he by Mrs. Julia Brown in 1886.

[28] These facts were obtained from old citizens and from local records.

[29] For a more detailed account, see the History of Education in West Virginia, pp. 272-273.

[30] These facts were obtained from local records.

[31] These facts were obtained from J. W. Robinson, the principal of the school.

[32] The following resolutions adopted at the meeting of the Teachers' Association in 1891 were suggestive:

1. That all persons of high literary standing, who are not teachers, be admitted as honorary members.

2. That we highly commend the committee of arrangements for their success in bringing together so many teachers and professional persons, and for making the meeting of so much importance and interest.

3. That we recognize in the death of Prof. W. B. Ross, A.M., who died at his post at Greenville, Texas, August 20, 1891, the loss of one of our ripest scholars and most efficient educators.

4. That we tender our thanks to Hon. B. S. Morgan, State Superintendent, for the interest he manifested in the Association and the able address he delivered before us.

5. That the Summer School for Teachers, as has been taught by Professors H. B. Rice and Byrd Prillerman, has been a means of elevating the standard of our teachers, and should be continued.

6. That we indorse the action of the State Legislature in establishing the West Virginia Colored Institute, and that we will do all in our power to make this school a success.

7. That we make *The Pioneer* the official organ of the Association.

8. That we tender our thanks to the Pastor and Congregation for the use of this Church, and also to Mr. I. C. Cabell for his valuable services as organist.

The Committee was composed of J. R. Jefferson, Mary M. Brown, Dr. W. T. Merchant, C. H. Payne, Miss Luella Ferguson and Atty. M. H. Jones.

[33] This account of the early meetings of the West Virginia Teachers' Association is found in the Twelfth Biennial Report of the State Superintendent of Schools of West Virginia, 1895-1896, pp. 111-113.

[34] At the Huntington meeting in 1892 an original poem on Thanksgiving Day was read by Miss Leota Moss. The poem was written by Paul Lawrence Dunbar for this special occasion at the request of Byrd Prillerman, the president. The price paid Dunbar for this service was $2.00.

[35] The more recent record of the West Virginia

Teachers' Association was given by Byrd Prillerman, who served that body nine terms as president.

THE FIRST NEGRO CHURCHES IN THE DISTRICT OF COLUMBIA

The early Negro churches in the District of Columbia were Methodist and Baptist. The rise of numerous churches of these sects in contradistinction to those of other denominations may be easily accounted for by the fact that in the beginning the Negroes were earnestly sought by the Methodists and Baptists because white persons of high social position at first looked with contempt upon these evangelical denominations; but when in the course of time the poor whites who had joined the Methodist church accumulated wealth and some of them became aristocratic slaveholders themselves, they assumed such a haughty attitude toward the Negroes that the increasing race hate made their presence so intolerable that the independent church movement among the Negro Methodists and Baptists was the only remedy for their humiliation. The separation of the Negro Methodists was made possible at a much earlier date in the District of Columbia, when Richard Allen had set the example by his protest against discrimination in the Methodist church, of Philadelphia, which culminated in the establishment of the distinct Negro denomination, and also when the Zionites in New York City, led by James Varick, had separated from the Methodists there for similar reasons. It was not until the time of the critical period of the slavery agitation, however, that practically all of the Protestant churches provided separate pews and separate galleries for Negroes and so rigidly enforced the rules of segregation that there was a general exodus of the Negroes, in cities of the border States, from the Protestant churches.[1] The District of Columbia had the same upheaval.

The records show that among the Methodists the alienation developed sooner than in any of the other churches. "As early as 1820," according to an investigator, "the colored members of the Ebenezer Church on Fourth Street, East, near Virginia Avenue, erected a log building in that vicinity, not far from the present Odd Fellow's lodge, for their social, religious meetings and Sabbath school. About the same time some of the leading members among them, George Bell and George Hicks, became dissatisfied with their treatment, withdrew, and organized a church in connection with the African Methodist Episcopal church. At first they worshipped in Basil Sim's Rope-walk, First Street east, near Pennsylvania Avenue, but subsequently in Rev. Mr. Wheat's school-house on Capitol Hill, near Virginia Avenue. They finally purchased the old First Presbyterian Church at the foot of Capitol Hill, later known as the Israel Bethel Colored Methodist Episcopal Church. Some years thereafter other members of the old Ebenezer Church, not liking their confined quarters in the gallery, and otherwise discontented, purchased a lot on the corner of C Street south and Fifth Street east, built a house of worship, and organized the "Little Ebenezer Methodist Episcopal Church."[2]

About the year 1825 a third colonization from the original Ebenezer Church took place. One grievance among others was that the Negro members were dissatisfied with their white pastors because they declined to take the Negro children into their arms when administering the rites of baptism. In 1839 this alienation developed into an open rupture, when thirteen class leaders and one exhorter left the mother church, and, after purchasing a lot on the Island, erected a house and formed a Negro church, independent of the Methodist Episcopal body, under the name of the Wesley Zion Church, and employed a Negro preacher. Among the prominent men in this separation were Enoch Ambush, the well-known schoolmaster, and Anthony Bowen, who for many years was an estimable employee in the Department of the Interior.[3] Mr. Bowen served as a local preacher for forty years, and under his guidance St. Paul's Negro Church on the Island was organized, at first worshipping in E Street Chapel."[3a]

The white Methodists of Georgetown elbowed their Negro membership out of their meeting house, but for fourteen years, that is, until 1830, they kept no written church records except a list of this one sold to Georgia, another to Carolina, a third to Louisiana, and others to different parts—annals befitting the time and place, and a searchlight on conditions then prevailing at the National Capitol and elsewhere south of the Mason and Dixon line. In 1830 the membership was large and much spirituality was manifested. White ministers of more than local note were anxious to serve these people. At the instance of one of them, Mr. Roszel, the church was first called Mount Zion Methodist Episcopal Church, because it was located on a hill. The feasibility of having Negro ministers to preside over Negro churches was proposed in 1849 and was a fruitful theme for several years.[4] In fact, it was due to this effort that the organization of Union Wesley A. M. E., the John Wesley, and Ebenezer Churches followed. John Brent, a member of Mt. Zion, led in the first named movement, and Clement Beckett, another reformer, espoused the organization of Ebenezer in 1856, as a church "for Negroes and by Negroes."[5]

The beginnings of the Israel Colored Methodist Episcopal Church centered around the evangelical activity of David Smith, a native of Baltimore, the most energetic of individual forces in the organization of the first African Methodist Episcopal Church in the city of Washington. The presence of a Negro preacher was objectionable to many Negroes themselves. As early as 1821 Mr. Smith was assigned to Washington but his coming was the signal for personal attack, and he was mobbed by members of his own race, communicants of the Methodist Episcopal Church, who were opposed to the African Methodists. He persisted, however, and having secured an old school house for $300, entered upon his work with such zeal and energy that he commanded success. Among the men and women active in the first efforts were Scipio Beans, George Simms, Peter Schureman, George Hicks, Dora Bowen, William Costin, William Datcher, William Warren and

George Bell, one of the three colored men who fifteen years before had erected a building for a Negro school.

Israel promptly became a member of the Baltimore Conference, one of the oldest conferences of the African Methodist Episcopal Church. The first Negro conference to meet in Washington was held in Israel during the administration of Andrew Jackson. Its assembly caused a sensation and gave the church and the denomination a standing surpassing that of all other Negro churches in the community. It was also largely through the personalities of the ministers in charge of Israel that its influence on its congregation and through them on the community must be judged. Among those in the period of its African Methodist affiliation were David Smith, Clayton Durham, John and William Cornish, James A. Shorter, Daniel A. Payne, Samuel Watts, Jeremiah R. V. Thomas, Henry M. Turner, William H. Hunter, George T. Watkins, James H. A. Johnson, and finally Jacob M. Mitchell, the last of the African Methodist Episcopal pastors at Israel. Smith and Durham were colleagues of Richard Allen; William Cornish was in the antislavery struggle; Hunter and Turner served as chaplains in the Union Army; and Payne, Wayman, Shorter and Turner became bishops of the African Methodist Episcopal Church.

The career of Bishop Payne is widely known, but some incidents in his pastorate deserve emphasis. Under a prevailing law he had to secure a bond of one thousand dollars before he could remain in the District of Columbia and officiate as a minister. The building being without pews and the people too poor to buy them, Payne, who had learned the trade of a carpenter, bought tools, threw off his coat, and, with the aid of the society furnishing the lumber, in a few weeks seated the basement of the church. The first Negro ministers' union in Washington was organized by Bishop Payne, the other two members being John F. Cook of the Fifteenth Street Presbyterian Church and Levi Collins of Wesley Zion.

It was during the Civil War, however, that the influence of Israel was at its maximum. Then it was that the intellectual genius, the fiery pulpit orator, the daring and unique Henry McNeal Turner, was not only a conspicuous preacher but preeminent as a national character. These were stirring times. All eyes were on Washington. Israel Church played a leading part in the drama. Here the members of Congress, prominent among whom at the time were Benjamin F. Wade, Thaddeus Stevens and Henry Wilson, addressed the Negro citizens on the dominant issues of the day, buoying them up in the midst of their darkness and gloom. At this time the Israel Lyceum was an institution not unlike the Bethel Literary Association of thirty years later, that drew the most intellectual men to listen to lectures, participate in discussions, and read dissertations on timely topics.[6]

In reckoning the influence[7] of this church the individuals whose place was in the pew must not be forgotten. The minister passes from church to church; the layman remains. In hurried review there comes to mind Alethea Tanner, who rescued the church when it was about to be sold at auction. There were George

Bell and Enoch Ambush, who operated in this church basement a large school which was maintained for thirty-two years. Honorable mention belongs here also to Rev. William Nichols whom, because of his high ideals, Bishop Payne, in his *History of the African Methodist Episcopal Church from 1816 to 1856*, classed as "a man of more than ordinary intelligence firmly opposed to the extravagent zeal and rude manners which characterized so many of the leading men of his denomination." He was the "veritable hero who had aided the martyred Torrey in covering the escape of many slaves from the District of Columbia to Canada and who when by accident he learned that suspicion rested on him the fear of arrest was so great on his mind as to induce the paralysis which led to his (Nicoll's) sudden death."[8]

Some years later a sermon preached at Israel by Bishop John M. Brown, to whom the writer was a listener, deeply stirred the congregation. At the time I did not understand what caused the tumult until I learned from Rev. James Reid, a local preacher, that the church was negotiating for another lot on which to erect a new building, and the contention was whether the title to the new site should be held in trust for the congregation or for the denomination. The people contended that the property should be held in trust for them; the bishop, on the other hand, maintained that it should be in the name of the trustees of the denomination. The people were insistent and won their contention. A step further was the repudiation of the appointment made for them by the bishop, and the severance of their relations with the A. M. E. church made them independent. After a short interval Israel joined the Colored Methodist Episcopal Church, which had been set apart in 1870 by the M. E. Church, South.[9]

During these years the Asbury Methodist Episcopal Church was also in the making. Certain records show January 15, 1836, as the date of the organization of the Asbury Aid Society. These workers were originally a part of the Old Foundry Church. When this congregation augmented so that the gallery occupied by the Negro membership became too congested for their accommodation, it became necessary to find more suitable quarters. The old Smothers School House on H Street near Fourteenth was rented for their use, but it, too, became inadequate, making the purchase of ground on which to build an immediate necessity. Thomas Johnson, Lewis Delaney, and Benjamin M. McCoy were constituted the building committee that secured from William Billings the lot on which the church was ultimately built. The Foundry Quarterly Conference, under whose authority they were functioning, elected trustees and a building committee to secure funds and pay for the building, but no regular church organization was immediately effected. These communicants remained under the sole management and control of the Foundry Church until the organization of the Washington Conference in the Civil War. Originally there were two Negro preachers, one a deacon, the other a licentiate, and two exhorters in these early days. There were three stewards, two black and one white.

These constituted the officiary and were members of the Foundry Quarterly Conference.

After the Annual Conference of 1841, when there were, according to the stewards' records, 423 Negro members, an appeal was made to the Quarterly Conference of the Foundry for a preacher to take more direct supervision of the church. By order of the bishop, Rev. James M. Hanson, a supernumerary of the Foundry Church was appointed to take the charge of Asbury as its regular minister. Though a separate charge, Asbury was not a separate station, and it continued in subordination to the Foundry Church. After Hanson's appointment, regular weekly meetings were established, but the white leaders did not seem to succeed, for four of them had by this time resigned. In 1845 there was but one white leader remaining, and he did not meet regularly with the Negro leaders.[10] Again in 1851, therefore, there was an appeal to the presiding bishop and elders of the Baltimore Annual Conference (white) praying for a separate establishment,[11] and the request was finally granted in the Civil War.

Union Bethel (Metropolitan) A. M. E. Church was organized July 6, 1838, as a branch of Israel A. M. E., with Clayton Durham as pastor, assisted by John Cornish. They met in a little house which stood in the rear of one Mr. Bolden's residence on L Street near Fifteenth Street. William H. Moore took charge in 1840, after which regular appointments annually followed. In 1841 there served one Mr. Moore, who was reappointed, and in 1842 Edward Waters began an incumbency of two years. In 1844 Adam S. Driver became pastor and remained two years. He was succeeded in 1847 by Thomas W. Henry. In 1848 Alexander Washington Wayman, whose name frequently figures in the history of the church and denomination, appeared on the scene, followed in 1850 by W. H. Moore. In 1851 Wayman returned to Union Bethel and remained two years. In 1853 John R. V. Morgan, destined to occupy a unique figure because of his oratorical ability, was pastor. Savage L. Hammond, who was appointed in 1854, served also the next year.[12]

The first work towards the erection of the present Metropolitan African Methodist Episcopal Church, first known as Union Bethel, was begun by John W. Stevenson, who was transferred from the New Jersey Conference and appointed by Bishop D. A. Payne for the specific purpose of erecting the new building. He entered upon his work with great zeal and alacrity, but pursued methods which, though adapted to or suitable in the localities in which he had hitherto labored with such phenomenal success, occasioned much friction and disgust in Washington. He catered to elements that would relegate the more cultured and progressive classes to the background, yet he secured among the conservatives loyal support. At the end of his first year, however, the spirit of rebellion was rife. A delegation of the discontented element called on the presiding bishop to state their grievance and effect the removal of the irrepressible minister, but Bishop Payne was inexorable. He did not even give an actual hearing to the petitioners, although they were personally known to him to be some of the most faithful adherents of

African Methodism. The next step was open rebellion. Meetings were held by the dissatisfied group and in the month of June more than a hundred and fifty persons, after the question of forming a new religious organization had been carefully canvassed, agreed to sever their connection with their spiritual mother and raise their "Ebenezer" elsewhere. Notwithstanding this opposition within and without, however, the old edifice was pulled down and work on the new building was immediately begun.

The corner stone was laid in September, 1881, with appropriate ceremonies under the auspices of the Masons. During the work on the building, which was continued up to the fall of 1885, services were held in the Hall on M Street diagonally opposite the square to the west. By the end of Stevenson's second year, he had, by his characteristic methods, alienated so many of those on whom he had relied mainly for support that Bishop Payne, now disillusioned, was as bitter against Stevenson as he was blindly his champion the year before.[13] Stevenson was removed, but there were those who still believed in his leadership. He refused to accept the appointment given him and organized the Central Methodist Church with dissentients formerly members of Union Bethel. James A. Handy was appointed Stevenson's successor at this juncture, yet there was considerable opposition even among those regarded as his firm personal and political friends.[14] The building was finally completed. By a vote of the African Methodist Episcopal Conference in 1872 the name was changed from Union Bethel to Metropolitan.

The same forces tending toward separation were at this time at work also among the Negro Baptist members in the white churches. This was the case of the First Baptist Church (white) organized in 1802. Its Negro members worshipped at first on the basis of equality with the whites, but this came to an end when the Negro members were assigned to the gallery, just as other churches of this time were gradually segregating them. When the new white Baptist Church, which was afterward sold and converted into a theater later known as Ford's Theater, was built on Tenth Street, the Negro communicants were given the gallery, but this was not satisfactory to the majority, who chafed under the new arrangement. O. B. Brown, the pastor, however, tried under the circumstances to treat the Negro members with as much charity as his prejudiced members would permit, as he was a kind-hearted man and did not believe in distinction on account of color. When the Tenth Street Church was occupied in 1833, therefore, these discontented members bought the old church on the corner of 19th and I Streets, Northwest, which is still held by that congregation and known throughout the country as the Nineteenth Street Baptist Church.

This was the first church of the denomination among the Negroes of the District of Columbia. It was organized August 29, 1839, by Sampson White, a Negro, assisted by John Healy and S. P. Hill, white pastors of Baltimore, and Moses Clayton, a Negro minister, who was the founder and pastor of the first Negro Baptist church of Baltimore. The original members were William Bush, Eliza Bush, Lavinia Perry and Emily Coke. The accession of Sampson White and wife increased the membership to six. None of these had been members of any church in the District of Columbia. They held letters from churches elsewhere, and so were free to form a church of their own in this city. But the white Baptist church, which had worshipped at 19th and I Streets, Northwest, from the year of their organization, from 1802 to 1833, had many Negro members who worshipped at 19th and I Streets for six years before Sampson White organized his small congregation.

These Negro members of the white church, being separated in worship from their white brethren, and having become sole owners of the house of worship which formerly they and the whites owned as members of the white church, wished to be organized as a separate body. This was refused. Sampson White, therefore, organized the First Negro Baptist Church of Washington, with persons not of the Washington white church, and thereby secured the recognition of his church by the leading white and Negro Baptists of Baltimore. In less than sixty days he had it in the oldest and best known white Baptist connection in America, the Philadelphia Baptist Association. This accomplished, Sampson White's little group received into their body all of the Negro members of the white church, except about twenty-three. These additional members made this a congregation ten times the size of the original body. This larger group, too, was in possession of the property at 19th and I Streets, at the time that the founders received them as members, and having been in possession of the property from the time it was sold to the Negro members of the First Baptist Church, white, these Negro Baptists, thereafter worshipping as the First Negro Baptist Church, insisted that the property was theirs, while the few colored members of the white church, who did not leave the parent body, claimed the property as belonging to them. This led to a law suit which lasted for years, but finally all the Negro members of the First Baptist Church, white, cast in their lot with the members at 19th and I Streets, and the trustees of the white church kindly released all claim in behalf of Negro members of that body, and rendered the deed clear.[15]

The first pastorate of Sampson White was short. He was followed by William Williams. Under his labors the membership increased almost to two hundred. But the latter part of his incumbency was not peaceful and William Bush, and others of the church withdrew. After casting their lot with the white Second Baptist Church near the Navy Yard, these seceders, along with others, were constituted the Second Negro Baptist Church of this city, with H. Butler, a former member of the church at 19th and I Streets, as pastor.

Following William Williams came Martin Jenkins as a supply. In 1849 Gustavus Brown became pastor, remaining for a short while. He was succeeded by Sampson White, who, serving the congregation a second time, remained with the church until 1853. Chauncey A. Leonard was the next pastor, and after him Samuel M. Madden. At the close of the Civil War, D. W. Anderson became pastor and for seven years labored for the good of his church. During his ministry in Washington the church added to its membership a thousand or more, chiefly as the result of the additions to this city from the Negro population of the ex-slaves of the South. But D. W. Anderson, as a man of great heart, labored for all Washington. Under his leadership the Metropolitan and Vermont Avenue Baptist churches were organized. The Nineteenth Street Baptist Church building which had been altered and improved from time to time, before his pastorate, was demolished and a new edifice erected in 1871. In 1872, D. W. Anderson passed to his reward and the church erected a marble shaft in the Harmony Cemetery to mark the place where his remains lie.

Anthony Binga, Sr., of Canada, followed D. W. Anderson, but his pastorate was short. His successor was Jesse Boulden, of Mississippi, who occupied the pulpit for about four years. During his pastorate thirty members withdrew, and formed the Berean Baptist Church. Sometime before this, the Salem Baptist Church had been constituted with members from the churches of which Anderson, Binga and Boulden had been pastors.[16]

The pastorate of Dr. Walter H. Brooks is the outstanding one in the history of the church, extending from November 12, 1882, until the present writing, the third decade of the twentieth century. During his ministrations more than 3,500 have joined the church, 1,500 of whom were personally baptized by him. The financial condition of the church places it among the best managed churches in the country, although it has at times assumed heavy obligations in making improvements and in rebuilding. During the pastorate of Dr. Brooks a number of ministers and preachers have gone forth from the Nineteenth Street Baptist Church. Dr. J. L. Dart, the founder of an important education and missionary work in South Carolina, was ordained at this church. Dr. James R. L. Diggs, pastor of Trinity Baptist Church, and head of important educational work in Baltimore, is of this congregation, having been baptized and ordained by Dr. Brooks. E. E. Rick, of Newark, N. J., was ordained from the Nineteenth Street Baptist Church. James L. Pinn is a product of this body, and Dr. Brooks was influential in securing for him his first charge. John H. Burke, pastor of Israel Baptist Church, came up under Dr. Brooks, as did also Joseph Lee, of Arlington, Virginia, and James L. Jasper, of Brentwood, Maryland. But none of these products of the Nineteenth Street Baptist Church have done a better work than Miss Jennie Deane, the founder of the Manassas Industrial School, in Virginia, and Miss Nannie H. Burroughs, the founder and promoter of the National Training School for Women and Girls, Lincoln Heights, Washington, D. C. Nor should Mrs. Laura Queen be forgotten, for by her labors the doors of Stoddard Baptist Home were first opened.[17]

The Fifteenth Street Presbyterian Church, the next to be established, was formally organized November 21, 1841, in a little frame school house located on H Street near 14th Northwest. The moving spirit in this undertaking was John F. Cook.[18] He had been received as a licentiate by the Presbytery of the District of Columbia on the twenty-first of October of that same year. Eighteen persons took part in this organization. Of these John F. Cook and Alfred A. Cook had been official members of the Union Bethel, now the Metropolitan African Methodist Episcopal Church. The pioneer members came from the First, the Second, and the Fourth Presbyterian Churches of the city and one from the Shiloh Church of New York, of which the Rev. Theodore S. Wright was pastor. The reasons why they desired the establishment of an independent church were clearly set forth in a series of resolutions which were not unlike those which occasioned the organization of other Negro churches. The new society was received into the Presbytery May 3, 1842, when in session at Alexandria, Virginia, then a part of the District of Columbia. John F. Cook was installed as the first pastor July 14, 1855. Under his pastorate the church prospered, increasing its membership to 125.

The successor of Mr. Cook was William T. Catto of Philadelphia, the former pastor of the First African Presbyterian Church of the country. Others to occupy the pulpit as supplies and pastors were Benjamin T. Tanner, subsequently a bishop of the A. M. E. Church, William B. Evans, Henry Highland Garnet, J. H. Muse, J. Sella Martin, John B. Reeves, during his connection with Howard University, Dr. Septimus Tustin, George Van Deurs, a Swede, and John Brown, a Scotchman. The last mentioned incumbent was succeeded by the Rev. Francis J. Grimké, who has served longer than all other pastors combined, and with marked success. During the first years of the ministry of Mr. Grimké, which began in the spring of 1878, there was great spiritual awakening as the result of his forceful preaching.

The church has had a high record for its Christian ideals and its public spirit. It has always stood for the best things, morally and spiritually, in the life of the community. It has always been ready to aid in every worthy cause. During the period immediately preceding the Civil War, and in the days of the reconstruction, it divided honors with the Israel Church as a place of popular assembly and referendum. In 1918 it sold its old edifice on 15th Street between I and K Streets, where it had worshipped for seventy-five years, and is now located in a beautiful and commodious structure on the corner of R and Fifteenth Streets.

The next significant effort was made by the Baptists. Persons dismissed from the Nineteenth Street Baptist Church for the purpose of organizing another body began in the year 1848 the existence of the Second Baptist Church, under the leadership of H. H. Butler, a licentiate. The next year Jeremiah Asher, a native of Connecticut, became the first pastor and remained for two years. Mr. Asher was a typical New Englander of superior education and high ideals. In 1850 Gustavus Brown assumed charge of the new body when it worshipped on B Street, Southwest, between Sixth and Seventh, in a broom factory, and subsequently at 9th and D Streets, Northwest, over Ryan's Grocery Store. In 1853 H. H. Butler was recalled and formally ordained as pastor. He remained with the church until his death in 1856, when Sandy Alexander was asked to accept this charge. A permanent home was then bought on the present site where the congregation has worshipped ever since. Mr. Alexander continued for five years until his health compelled him to retire. In 1861, Caleb Woodyard became pastor and remained for two years. During this period conditions were such that progress was not steady and this led to the recall of Mr. Alexander, under whose direction a strong organization was effected. Following him, came Chauncey A. Leonard and next John Gaines. Then followed Madison Gaskins, whose service was characterized by alternating conditions, a lawsuit, a fire and new organizations branching therefrom as Mount Carmel, Mt. Olive in the Northeast, and Rehoboth in the Southwest.[20]

The African Methodist Episcopal Zion Churches of Washington, D. C., grew out of the efforts of their denomination, founded by James Varick, Peter Williams, William Miller, Abraham Thompson, Christopher Rush and others, in New York City, in 1796. These fathers early extended their work through New England, western New York, central and western Pennsylvania. In 1833, their first church was founded in South Washington, then known as the Island. It was established as the Metropolitan Wesley African Methodist Episcopal Zion Church, on D Street, Southwest, Washington, D. C. The first pastor was Abraham Cole, who took charge in 1833. The persons organizing this church were originally members of the Ebenezer M. E. Church, located on D Street, Southeast. They drew out of this organization because their pastor, a white man, held slaves. The Wesley Metropolitan African Methodist Episcopal Zion Church, its officers contend, was the first independent church in the District of Columbia organized by colored people. The first public school for the training of Negro youth was held in this church. Hanson Brooks was the secretary of the first organization.[21]

The establishment of the Union Wesley, the second church of the Zionites, in Washington, the progressive body, of which Dr. E. D. W. Jones was pastor, was very interesting. This church was organized in 1848 by Bishop J. J. Clinton, who afterwards became a bright star in the African Methodist Episcopal Zion Church. The organization took place in the residence of Gasoway Waters in Georgetown.[22] He had been sent to Georgetown as a missionary and started his labors in this organization of a few persons determined to become independent of the white Methodists.

They began the construction of a church with the help of such men and women as Charles Lemon, Charly Wilson, Eliza Wilson, William Crusoe, George Brown, Mary Brown, William Sewall, Margaret Waters, and Eliza Johnson. After having been organized for a little while, they bought a lot on the corner of what is now known as 28th and O Streets, Georgetown.[23] Things seemed favorable in the beginning, but the enemies of the church were busy those days putting temptation in the path of the Negro and betraying him unto his enemies. Bondmen, according to the slave code, were not allowed to meet or hold any kind of meeting unless a white man was present. Nor were they allowed to be out after ten o'clock at night without a pass, or to have two or more congregate on the street at one time. If they did any of these things, they thereby violated the sacred laws of bondage and suffered imprisonment and persecution. Thus handicapped in their worship, they, like Paul and Silas, prayed for a deliverer, and he came in the person of a young lawyer from Philadelphia, who had taken up the cause. By his earnest endeavors in their behalf, they were released without being sentenced to jail or whipped. But, nevertheless, they were driven out of Georgetown, across Rock Creek, and into Washington, where they worshipped for a while in the house of William Beckett on the corner of 23d and L Streets.

A short time afterwards they bought the lot where this church now stands and built thereon a frame chapel which was contemptuously called the Horseshoe Church. After they had been there but a short time, there was a funeral at the chapel one day. Across from the chapel the Hibernian fire company was stationed. While the funeral services were being held in the chapel, two of these firemen came across the street and while one of them got inside of the hearse the other one got up on the driver's seat and drove all around the streets, while the people were out looking for the hearse. When they came back, the one who was inside got out and said that he was Lazarus risen from the dead. This act so inflamed some of the white gentlemen that they had the firemen arrested and prosecuted. These two impious gentlemen became so indignant because of their arrest that they set fire to the chapel and burned it to the ground. These communicants, being homeless again, went back to the house of William Beckett on L Street and commenced to rebuild. This time they succeeded in erecting a brick building, a portion of which stands today.

The John Wesley African Methodist Episcopal Zion Church was organized in 1849 at the home of John Brent on Eighteenth and L Streets. Among the founders were John Brent, W. H. Johnson, John Brent, Jr., William V. Ingram, Arnold Bowie, Charles Wilson, Joseph Conner, Edward Curtis, and Gilbert Joy. These communicants then purchased property on Connecticut Avenue and built thereon a simple frame building into which they moved in 1851.[24] This church finally bought the old Berean Baptist Church property on Eighteenth Street, under the pastorate of Dr. B. J. Bolding, in 1902.

The ministers who pastored the congregation while it worshipped in Connecticut Avenue were Abraham Cole, J. B. Trusty, N. F. Turpin, J. H. Hamer, H. F. Butler, Nathaniel Stubbs, Sampson Talbert, S. T. Jones, John V. Givens, S. T. Henry, G. W. Bosley, S. S. Wales, J. W. Smith, J. P. Thompson, Jesse Cowles, W. A. Cypress, J. A. Williams, J. B. Small, B. J. Bolding, R. H. G. Dyson, D. H. Anderson, R. A. Fisher, J. J. Clinton, and J. H. McMullen. Those who served the body in Eighteenth Street were Rev. L. W. Kyles, W. A. Blackwell, P. H. Williams, C. C. Alleyne, and Dr. William C. Brown. John Wesley Church has had at different times six pastors, who later were elected to the bishopric. These were Bishops Sampson Talbert, J. J. Clinton, J. P. Thompson, S. T. Jones, J. B. Small and John Wesley Smith, all of whom are deceased. Among the officers of the church may be mentioned Gilbert L. Joy, who was made secretary of the Trustee Board in 1864, and served thirty-two years in that capacity. He had the enviable record of being a trustee of this church for forty-three years, a longer period than that of any other person connected with it, and he is still an active member.

The awakening of John Wesley A. M. E. Zion Church, characterized by the selling of its property on Eighteenth Street to purchase at the same time the edifice on Fourteenth and Corcoran Streets for $61,000, is significant. It is the most important event in the history of Zion Church in Washington. The Zion Church long needed a larger representative edifice in this city. This advanced step was taken, and under the leadership of Dr. W. C. Brown and Dr. W. O. Carrington the progress of the congregation has been epochal.

The Galbraith African Methodist Episcopal Zion Church was founded in 1859. That year five members of Zion Wesley, under the leadership of Samuel Payne, withdrew and organized a church in a small house on L Street between Third and Fourth Streets. They subsequently built a house of worship near New York Avenue. Robert H. G. Dyson who had been active as a class leader and chorister in Zion Wesley, became the first pastor. It developed from its little frame church on L Street, Northwest, into a larger congregation in the modern structure on its present location, under N. J. Green, the pastor in charge. This church has figured conspicuously in the religious, moral and civic uplift of the city. It has been served by an array of prominent ministers, chief among whom are J. Harvey Anderson, J. S. Coles, Wm. Chambers, J. B. Colbert, H. P. Kyler, William Dixon, S. L. Corrothers, George C. Clement, and

William D. Battle. During Mr. Battle's administration the church was relieved of its long-standing debt and the well begun work was steadily developed.[25]

The next efforts in the District of Columbia were of the Baptists. Albert Bouldin, who began public prayer services near Fourth and L Streets in 1857, was a prominent influence in the organization of the Third Baptist Church.[26] On June 20, 1858 there was held a council of ministers at which were present G. W. Sampson, Chauncey A. Leonard, A. Rothwell, Lindsey Muse, Evans Stott, Henry H. Butler, Sandy Alexander, and L. Patten. There were also the following laymen: Joseph Pryor, Joseph Alexander, N. Nookes, Henry Scott, John Minor, Charles Alexander, and Austin Robinson. The trustees were William B. Jefferson, Joseph Alexander, Henry Scott, Charles Alexander, Vernon Duff, and Henry Nookes, who assisted in effecting the organization and served it as the first deacons.

In 1863 there was secured on Fourth and L Streets a lot on which the people began to erect their meeting house. On account of disputes, four years afterward it became necessary to look elsewhere, and William B. Jefferson became the controlling spirit. Then a lot was purchased on Franklin Street between Fourth and Fifth at a cost of $1,198.50. In September, 1871, the church was dedicated. Rev. D. W. Anderson, at that time pastor of the Nineteenth Street Baptist Church, delivered the sermon. After a lapse of thirteen years, August 2, 1884, another lot situated on the corner of Fifth and Que Streets was purchased.[27] The next forward movement was toward the erection of a new building which was completed July 1893 at a cost of $26,000 and dedicated the fifth Sunday of July 1893.[28]

There soon followed another significant undertaking. After preaching regularly to four persons for four years, Sandy Alexander organized on October 5, 1862, the First Baptist Church of West Washington. Two of the four pioneer members were from churches in Fredericksburg, Virginia. Dr. G. W. Sampson, president of Columbian College, subsequently Columbian University, now the George Washington University, was of great service to Mr. Alexander in this work of the organization of this church. The church was first located on the corner of Greene and Beale Street, Georgetown, where it remained one year, after which a lot was purchased at the corner of Dumbarton and 27th Streets and a large frame building was first constructed at a cost of $15,000.[29] From this church there have been regularly organized the Macedonia, the First Baptist Church of Rosslyn, Virginia, and the Memorial Baptist Church in Maryland.

The Baptists were at the same time receiving recruits from another source. In June, 1862, while a destructive war was being waged by the Southern States against the Union, warning was given that a terrible siege was to be started against the city of Fredericksburg, Virginia. This news caused between three and four hundred members of the Shiloh Baptist Church of that town to leave for Washington as a place of refuge. After arriving there many tearful eyes were turned toward the dear old church of their childhood and riper years, where "many a pleasant hour had been enjoyed, and it was only natural for these fellow church members to plan for a place where they might once more gather in prayer and praise God for their deliverance from the ravages of war."[30] Home gatherings were frequent among these refugees and in this way the organization of the present church was effected.

Shiloh Baptist Church, like many other churches, had its beginning in a Sunday School.[31] The constant meeting of these seekers after the truth served to keep a number of them in close touch with each other and intensified the desire for a church of their own. They then began to meet in each other's houses for prayer and for conference upon the subject and soon resolved to have a Shiloh Baptist Church in Washington, since they could not return to Shiloh Church in Fredericksburg. It was at one of these prayer meetings in the bedroom of Henry D. Peyton in an old brick house on K Street, between 26th and 27th Streets, in Georgetown (now West Washington) that Shiloh Baptist Church of Washington had its beginnings in September, 1863.[32]

Having formed the church, the founders sent a communication to the various Baptist churches of Washington, both white and black, asking that a council be called to consider the propriety of recognizing them as a regularly constituted Baptist church. The Negro Baptist churches gave these petitioners no encouragement and sent no delegates to the council, but the white Baptist churches sent a number of their members, deacons, and pastors, as delegates, who met in the First white Baptist church, located at that time on 13th Street between G and H Streets, Northwest, at eight o'clock Wednesday evening, September 23, 1863, and formed a recognition council. Dr. G. W. Sampson, pastor of the First Baptist Church and President of Columbian College, was chosen Moderator, and John S. Poler, clerk. After approving the credentials of the delegates the Moderator stated the purpose of the meeting. He further stated that the council had also been asked to examine William J. Walker as to his fitness and qualification for the gospel ministry, and if found worthy to ordain him, as the church had called him as its pastor and recommended his ordination.[33] It was so ordered and done by the council.

The church continued to meet in the homes of the members, but it grew so rapidly that it soon became necessary to secure larger quarters. The little frame building on the north side of L Street, between 16th and 17th Northwest, was then bought, and the church moved into it and remained there until 1868. The church prospered greatly and soon outgrew its first meeting house. Steps were then taken to purchase a site and erect a building sufficiently large to accommodate the growing membership. The present lot was secured, and in 1868 a commodious frame structure was erected thereon and used until 1883, when the church tore down the frame building and erected upon the same spot the present brick edifice.

William J. Walker, the first pastor, played a large part in building up the Baptist denomination in the District of Columbia and adjoining States. He organized four churches in Washington, namely, Zion Baptist, Enon Baptist, Mt. Zion Baptist and Mt. Jezreel Baptist churches, and two churches in Virginia, all of which are strong and prosperous organizations. He also founded the Baptist Sunday School Union and the Woman's Baptist Home Mission Society.

For a year or more after the death of William J. Walker the church remained without a pastor. During the greater part of this time William H. Scott served as supply, and it was while he was serving the church that the Walker Memorial Baptist Church was formed out of the members who drew out of Shiloh. Dr. J. Anderson Taylor became pastor in 1890 and remained with the church until near the close of 1906. During his ministry the church greatly increased in membership, and enlarged its building at a cost of $10,000. When Dr. Taylor gave up the pastorate of the church about 200 members withdrew from Shiloh and formed the Trinity Baptist Church and called him to take charge thereof. Shiloh Baptist Church, then, has been divided twice within twenty-three years. In spite of these handicaps, however, the church has prospered financially, numerically and spiritually. Dr. J. Milton Waldron took formal charge of Shiloh Baptist Church on the 6th of June 1907 and has labored with success in edifying his congregation and extending the influence of the church.[34]

While the organization of Shiloh Church was being effected in the northern section of Washington, there was in the southwest also another group from Fredericksburg. This effort resulted in the establishment of the Zion Baptist Church. They first organized a Sunday and day school in Jackson's School House on Delaware Avenue and L Street, Southwest.

Their next movement was the organization of a church, September 12, 1864, with nine members. They bought what was then known as Simpson's Feed Store on the present site of the church, and remodeled this building in 1867; William J. Walker was its founder and first pastor. In January, 1869, William Gibbons of Charlottesville, Virginia, became the pastor and under his temporal and spiritual oversight the church flourished. The first church edifice was dedicated in 1871 and for twenty-one years was used by the congregation. In 1891 the present structure was built at an expenditure of $35,000. The membership at the forty-eighth anniversary was 2,310, the largest at the time in the District of Columbia. Up to the close of the nineteenth century they raised annually on an average of $8,000 for current expenses. Their present pastor, William J. Howard, has a unique record as being one of the best known ministers and men in the city, regardless of denomination, and with a character beyond reproach.[35]

The Metropolitan, formerly known as the Fourth Baptist Church, was organized May 1863 by a few holding letters from the Nineteenth Street Baptist Church during the pastorate of Duke W. Anderson, and by a few members from other churches. Henry Bailey was the first pastor of the new group. In 1865 there took place a division of this body which resulted in the establishment of the Fifth, now the Vermont Avenue Baptist Church. The organization was effected in a mission building which stood in the intersection of what is now E Street and Vermont Avenue. Two contending parties, both claiming to be the Fourth Baptist Church, were then engaged in presenting their rival claims. Four church councils were held before it was established which one had the right to bear the title Fourth. Robert Johnson took charge in 1870, seven years after the original movement. Under him the establishment prospered.

Four buildings have been used as church edifices in the history of this congregation, the mission building referred to above, the barracks, a relic of the Civil War, and a frame structure on the site of the present edifice, which at that time of its dedication in 1884 was valued at $60,000; but today the valuation, conservatively speaking, may be placed at $175,000. From 1865 to 1890 the membership was about 2,000, 1,100 of whom were baptized by Robert Johnson. The first Washington Baptist Convention composed of churches principally of the District of Columbia requested in September, 1890, that the church be called the Metropolitan. The congregation formally agreed to bear the title and since then Metropolitan has been its legal as well as its popular name.

After securing the services of Dr. M. W. D. Norman, who came from Portsmouth, Virginia, in 1905, the progress of the church has been such as to merit fully the title Metropolitan. On his assumption of the pastorate, a large floating and bonded indebtedness rested on the church. This has been discharged and modern improvements of electricity and steam heating at the cost of $15,000 have been provided. Yet there is not a dollar of indebtedness and the membership has increased to 5,748.

The following ministers have been ordained by the Metropolitan Baptist Church: Charles H. Parker, W. Bishop Johnson, John A. Pryer, Edward B. Gordon, Anderson Hogan, Luke D. Best, William Richardson, William Johnson, E. R. Jackson, John Braxton, John Mercer, Noah Grimes, Levi Washington, and W. L. Hill.[36]

The Baptist church on Vermont Avenue between Q and R Streets was originally established as the Fifth Baptist Church, June 5, 1866, by the pious J. H. Brooks, with seven members. He built a frame structure which was afterward replaced by a more comfortable brick building. Under him the congregation grew and in 1884, when he died the church had a membership of 1,800. He had served his people well, impressed the community with his worth, and passed to his reward loved not only by his own members but by the Christian people throughout the city.

He was succeeded by Dr. George W. Lee, who came to this church from North Carolina where he had served successfully as a pastor. Dr. Lee was installed in 1885 and served a quarter of a century, passing away on February 6, 1910. There were several important achievements during his pastorate. In 1890, at a cost of about $25,000, he remodeled the building left by J. H. Brooks and changed the name to Vermont Avenue Baptist Church. Being a great preacher and pastor noted for his originality and his ability to master the situation, he soon attracted a large following and increased the membership of his church almost to 4,000. He easily became a man of national reputation and in his travels abroad so impressed the people wherever he went that he developed into an international character.

Dr. Lee was noted especially for three significant elements in his character. Near to his heart was the promotion of African missions in keeping with his deep sense of charity. He was always a friend of the poor and, being such, emphasized more than any other duty of the church that of supporting missionary work in Africa. As a result the Vermont Avenue Baptist Church did more for this purpose than many other churches of the District of Columbia combined. He was always disposed, moreover, to help the under man in the struggle with his uncharitable accusers and traducers. When a minister was under fire, he usually stood by the unfortunate, if there was any possible chance to save him for the good of the service. He made himself, too, a patron of young men aspiring to the ministry, raising money for their support by impressing upon the people the importance of educating them. In this connection he trained and helped to support Dr. James E. Willis, who was baptized, licensed and ordained to preach under Dr. Lee. Through contact the one became attached to the other so that the younger imbibed the spirit of the other.

Dr. Willis became his successor in 1911. At first many of the members questioned his ability to fill such a position so that there developed much trouble in the congregation and much anxiety among the people at large. There followed a schism which resulted in litigation in the courts and the secession of a group of members who established the Florida Avenue Baptist Church, now in the charge of Dr. Taylor. Dr. Willis, however, was established as pastor with the support of a large majority of the members of the church. He filled the position with such distinction and attracted to him such a following of willing workers that the church prospered under him as it did under his predecessor. In recognition of his valuable services the congregation gave him a trip to the Holy Land at a cost of $3,000. It then purchased adjoining property upon which it erected a monument to Dr. George W. Lee.

According to a recent report rendered by the clerk and treasurer, the congregation has during the pastorate of Dr. Willis raised more than $68,000 for general expenses and $1,850 for their Old Folk's Home. This does not by any means account for the amount raised for charitable purposes, which include home and foreign missions. The support given needy members and institutions of learning, traveling ministers, and the like, has amounted approximately to $35,000 or $40,000. The church, moreover, has been very generous in the support of home missions, a duty decidedly emphasized by Dr. Willis in contradistinction to the inclination of Dr. Lee, who emphasized foreign missions.[36a]

Baptists in another part of the city were planning an additional organization. The First Baptist Church of South Washington was organized on Sixth Street between G and H Streets, Southwest, in 1866. Alfred Bolden was the first pastor. Two buildings have been erected on the present site. One Mr. Lee afterward served as the pastor until the coming of Henry C. Robinson, who exhibited energy that promised a bright future. Early in the history of the church, as an outcome of an internal agitation, however, 54 excluded members organized the Virginia Avenue Baptist Church and were afterward joined by others, thus weakening the parent organization; but in 1891 the property was valued at $25,000 and the church had a membership of 500.[37]

Another Baptist church soon resulted from a secession. In 1873 William Shanklin, Peter Gray, Abraham Blackmore, Edward Montague, and Catherine Wilson left the Fifth Baptist Church, now the Vermont Avenue Baptist Church, and formed, with their friends, Mt. Jezreel. Since then it has grown to be the largest Negro Baptist church in Southeast Washington, though it is also the youngest. The church, when first formed, was located on Van Street. It grew rapidly, and soon was able to buy desirable property on the southeast corner of Fifth and E Streets and begin the erection of its present handsome church edifice. In 1888 the building was finished and it was dedicated the first Sunday in November of that year, when Dr. Robert Johnson, of the Metropolitan Baptist Church, preached the dedicatory sermon. Its membership numbers about 300 people, and the church is in a very prosperous condition.[38]

The organization of another Baptist church soon followed. In September, 1876, there was organized on Nichol's Avenue, Hillsdale, the Bethlehem Baptist Church by Henry Scott, its first pastor. It was an outgrowth from the Macedonia Baptist Church organized nine years before by Sandy Alexander, of the First West Washington Church. The first officers were William Singleton, Carle Matthews, James Flood, Richard Harrison, Mack McKenzie, Cornelius W. Davis, David Simpson, Armstead Taylor, and Leonard Peyton. [39] The second minister, William H. Phillips, served with considerable success for six years when he was called to the Shiloh Baptist Church in Philadelphia, where he died.[40]

A new church was soon to evolve as a result of another stir among the Baptists. The succession of the pastorates of Dr. Anthony Binga, Sr., and Jesse Bolden to that of Dr. D. W. Anderson did not satisfy an important element of the 19th Street Baptist Church, which for fifteen years had given that church moral and financial support. Steps to organize a new church were therefore taken. In the preliminary stages of the separation there was much opposition. Nevertheless, they organized May 7, 1877, at the residence of William H. A. Wormley, 1126 16th Street, Northwest, and were recognized by a council of Baptist churches which met at the residence of L. C. Bailey, 1022 Nineteenth Street, June 5, 1877.[41] With twenty-two members this determined body went pluckily to work. In the first place, they were fortunate in securing for their pastor a man who for thirteen years voluntarily served the flock without salary. For twenty-five years, 1877 to 1902, they worshipped in their church on 18th Street, which was erected within six months of organization for the sum of $19,000. The church grew from 22 to 200. It is a fair estimate that $50,000 was received from all sources during this period. In 1902 they sold this church to the John Wesley A. M. E. Zion for $19,500 cash. After vacating their building and meeting in Odd Fellows Hall they erected their present building at 11th and V Streets, which they have paid for in full. The successor to Mr. Wm. Waring was Dr. W. A. Creditt.[42] Then came Dr. J. M. Waldron, who in 1892 was succeeded by Rev. Mr. D. F. Rivers, who still abides as a potent factor in the life of the Washington people.

After the Civil War Negroes became attracted to denominations in which they had never sought membership because of their close attachment to the Methodists and Baptists. From just such a divergence from the old order resulted the organization of the Lincoln Memorial Temple Congregational Church, on the northeast corner of 11th and R Streets, Northwest. This church was organized in the parlor of F. S. Presbrey, publisher of *Public Opinion*, January 10, 1887, with Rev. S. P. Smith as its first pastor. Lincoln Temple is the outgrowth of the Colfax Industrial Mission founded by members of the First Congregational Church, prominent among whom was John W. Alvord. It later became the Lincoln Mission. In addition to the Sunday School feature should be mentioned the industrial work, as classes in domestic science and domestic art were conducted there. For a time this mission constituted the first church home for Negro girls in the country. Among its founders were R. S. Smith, William H. Jackson, Theodore Clark and wife, Otwina Smith, Miss Booker, Hiram Ball, a Mrs. Jackson of Chicago and a Mr. Shorter. The Lincoln Mission Sunday School, with an attendance running at times to 700 and more, was a part of the work of the charitable organizations of the North engaged in missions and education in the South among the freedmen. As such it was one of the institutions of the city in Sabbath School work, with music especially popular. This school enjoyed the fostering care of the American Missionary Association, which appointed a minister to conduct religious services and a woman to work in the homes of the people. The teachers of the Sunday School were of both races. The whites were drawn from the First Congregational Church and Negroes were mainly students from Howard University.

During the operation of these two instrumentalities, the thought that the work of the school could be made more effectual and permanent by the organization of a church first took tangible form in the years of Mr. Smith's ministrations, and the church grew steadily and surely. Rev. George W. Moore became pastor on June 1, 1883. His work was a thorough success, due in no small measure to the personality of his wife, Ella Sheppard Moore, who had been pianist of the Fisk Jubilee Singers and with them had circled the globe. Dr. Moore resigned in 1893. Subsequent pastors have been Rev. Eugene Johnson, A. P. Miller and Sterling N. Brown. Dr. Brown was followed by Rev. Emory B. Smith, an enterprising young man who has brought the church to the very foremost in all the activities of religious work.[43]

The Plymouth Congregational Church was the direct outcome of dissatisfaction of many members of Union Bethel, now the Metropolitan Church, at the arbitrary action of Bishop Daniel A. Payne in the matter of the appointment of the Rev. John W. Stevenson as pastor of Union Bethel Church and the refusal to remove him. For these reasons 63 members decided to withdraw from the African Methodist Episcopal denomination and organized themselves in the Shiloh Hall on L Street, near 16th, Northwest, as the First Congregational Church of Washington in the District of Columbia. William T. Peele, who for several years had been a local preacher and class leader at Union Bethel Church was one of the number—in fact, the leader of the recalcitrant communicants. Church services for the new congregation were held in the meeting place of the Salem Baptist Church on N Street near 17th. Here they could meet only in the afternoon on Sunday. Other quarters were then secured on 18th Street near L and M Streets. On October 5, 1881, the name of the new organization was changed to that of the Plymouth Congregational Church of Washington. Their leader, William T. Peele, was then regularly ordained and installed as their pastor by Dr. Holmes of Baltimore, assisted by Dr. J. E. Rankin, then pastor of First Congregational Church, Dr. William Patton, President of Howard University, W. W. Hicks, and S. P. Smith. The church attached itself to the New Jersey Association of Congregational Churches at the fourteenth annual meeting held in the First Congregational Church in April, 1882. The church then purchased at a cost of $4,500 a site at the southeast corner of 17th and P Streets, on which it built by 1887.

William T. Peele, to whom this body rallied as its first pastor tendered his resignation July 26, 1888, and for several months the church was without a pastor. Dr. Sterling N. Brown of Cleveland, Ohio, entered upon the pastorate April 1, 1887, and rendered a most successful service. Under his guidance they evolved steadily from Methodism to Congregationalism.

Dr. Alexander C. Garner became the next pastor in 1896 and for twenty-five years led the church both temporally and spiritually. The church has been honored by his being chosen to represent the Congregationalists at national gatherings. The entire church mortgage debt was cancelled during Dr. Garner's incumbency, when all the churches were making strenuous and successful efforts to the same end. In fact, his successful career had much to do with his call to the direction of the growing spiritual interests of the Congregationalists in Harlem in New York.[44]

Some Negroes, too, had begun to look with more favor upon the Protestant Episcopal church. As early as 1866 cottage meetings were held by C. H. Hall, rector of the Epiphany, with the assistance of J. Vaughn Lewis, rector of St. John's Church. This movement went to the extent that steps were taken looking to the establishment of a church and the purchase of a lot on which an edifice was to be built. At this juncture Mrs. Parsons, a communicant of St. John's parish, donated a lot for the purpose on 23d Street, and Secretary of War E. M. Stanton contributed a frame building in 1867. From 1867 to 1873 several white clergymen officiated, but the selection of a colored minister to take charge of the work was indispensable. Efforts to this end soon followed. Among the clergymen considered were

William H. Josephus, a talented West Indian, and William J. Alston, who had been rector of St. Phillip's in New York and of St. Thomas in Philadelphia. John Thomas Johnson, a progressive Negro citizen who in the reconstruction times was Treasurer of the District Government, began on behalf of a number of interested people a correspondence with Dr. Alexander Crummell with a view to securing him as the spiritual leader of these Episcopalians. This effort resulted in bringing Dr. Crummell to Washington in June, 1873.

The people almost instantaneously rallied to Dr. Crummell's support and the outcome was the determination to build a church. A sinking fund association, composed of young people from different sections of the city, and in which other denominations were represented, was a most active factor. The enthusiasm was intense. The corner stone was laid in 1876 at Fifteenth and Sampson Streets, near Church Street, and work on the new building went rapidly on. Dr. Crummell meanwhile traveled extensively throughout the North and East for funds in aid of the new movement. Such was his success that the first services in the new building were held there on Thanksgiving Day, November 27, 1879.[45]

With the opening of St. Luke's a new opportunity presented itself at St. Mary's, where the congregation under the administration of Mr. O. L. Mitchell developed into an institutional church. It was consecrated December 11, 1894, by Bishop William Paret, then of Maryland, assisted by Bishop Penick and Dr. W. V. Tunnell, of Howard University, who preached the sermon. St. Mary's is one of the most beautiful of churches.

The rise of Negro Catholic churches in the District of Columbia as well as throughout the United States has been less extensive for the reason that not very many Negroes have been attracted to this denomination because of its ritualistic appeal, and those who have become adherents to the Catholic faith have been treated with so much more of the spirit of Christ than they have been by other sects, that the tendency toward independent church establishments has not been so pronounced. Early in the history of the District of Columbia Rev. Leonard Neale, the Archbishop of Georgetown, his brother, the Rev. Francis Neale of the Holy Trinity Church, and Father Van Lomell, pastor of the same church in 1807, were all friends of the Negroes, showing no distinction on account of color in the establishment of parish schools and the uplift of the people. The same policy was followed by Father De Theux, who in 1817 succeeded Father Macelroy, who established a Sunday School and labored with a great deal of devotion to bring them into the church. The Catholic Church was free in all of its privileges to all persons regardless of color. This was especially true of St. Patrick's Church under its founder, Father Matthew, who permitted the poorest Negro to kneel at the altar side by side with the highest personages in the land. The same was observed in St. Aloysius Church and in St. Mary's Church at Alexandria. The Catholics were the last to change their attitude toward the Negro during the critical antislavery period of the thirties, forties, and fifties, when the Protestant churches practically excluded the Negroes from their Sunday Schools and congregations. This explains why the Negro Catholics organized in the District of Columbia during the early period only one Catholic church of their own, St. Martin's, although the Negro Catholics constituted a considerable part of the Negro population.

The actual separation of the Negroes in the Catholic Church did not take place until the Civil War itself necessitated certain changes to meet the special needs of the Negroes in their new status. The establishment of St. Augustine's Church, however, somewhat antedated this. Before the organization of this church there was established a school meeting the special needs of the Negroes on L Street, and out of that developed the organization of this church in 1863. The moving spirit in this undertaking was Father Charles J. White, who was then pastor of St. Matthew's church in which the Negroes had always felt free to worship. Early in 1863 he purchased a lot on 15th Street between L and M and built there a two-story structure with the assistance of colored members from the various churches of the city and especially from those of St. Matthew's. Among those participating in the launching of this new church were the following: Miss Mary Harrison, Mr. Isaac Landic and wife, Mrs. Jane Smallwood, Mrs. Henry Warren and family, Mr. and Mrs. William Henry Smith, the Misses Mary and Sara Ann Smith, Mr. William T. Benjamin, Mr. Bazil Mullen, Mr. John West, Miss Agnes Gray, Messrs. William H. Wheeler, Henry Jackson, Henry Neal and family, James F. Jackson and family,

Mrs. Frances Madison, and the Misses Eliza Ann Cook, Mary T. Smith, Eliza Hall, and Jane Teagle.

In the course of time there were so many accessions to the church that more space was needed. In 1865, therefore, a frame building was added at the time that the church was under the patronage of Martin de Porrers, a colored lay brother of the order of St. Dominic, who had labored in South America. Dr. White was still the pastor, with Martin de Porrers officiating at most of the services. In the course of time it was necessary to seek other assistants, who were supplied by the Society of Jesus at Georgetown College in the person of Fathers Kelly and Cleary.

After the Civil War Archbishop Spaulding, then in charge of the diocese, saw the opportunity and the challenge of the church to meet the many needs of the freedmen who without spiritual guidance might morally retrograde. He therefore called for other workers to offer their lives as a sacrifice to a noble cause. In Italy at this time there was Father Barroti, who after having equipped himself for missionary work prepared to carry the Gospel message to the Chinese. In 1869, however, he was persuaded to go to the more inviting field of the freedmen in the United States. After some further instruction in English and other matters essential to the equipment for service among these people, he took charge of this Negro congregation in 1867. He immediately succeeded in securing the cooperation of the Negroes and the respect of the community. He passed among them as a man of Christian virtue and an apostle to the lowly. His following so rapidly increased that it was soon necessary to add wooden buildings to the original structure and to purchase additional property for a new building in 1869. To finance these undertakings he had the cooperation of Father Walters in St. Patrick's.

The new structure, planned to cost about $100,000, was begun in 1874 and completed and dedicated in the midst of impressive ceremonies in 1876. At first it was thought best to place this church under the patronage of the Blessed Martin de Porrers. According to the regulation of the church law, however, whereas a chapel could be designated in honor of an ecclesiastic, a parish church could not be thus dedicated, but must be named for one of the Saints. It was then decided to name it for St. Augustine, Bishop of Hippo in Africa. Upon the completion of this structure the Negro Catholic congregation was given a new standing in the community and in the United States.

In 1881 the death of Father Barroti marked an epoch in the history of this church. For some time there was serious doubt as to how the congregation could secure the services of some one so well equipped as this sacrificing churchman. Fortunately, however, the zealous Fathers of St. Joseph, an order established in England for the special benefit of the Negroes, came to take up the task. Thoroughly devoted to their work and believing in the uplift of the Negroes to a plane of equality with the whites, these Fathers caused the white Catholics much trouble by imposing upon those visiting St. Augustine's the same restrictions that some of the Catholic churches after the Civil War began to impose upon Negroes worshipping elsewhere. Chief among these may be mentioned Fathers Michael J. Walsh as rector, with Father Girard Wiersma and Father Francis P. Kerrick as associate pastors. Later he had such assistants as Father Burke and Father Hohlman. The successor of Father Walsh was the Rev. Paul Griffith, with Father G. A. Dougherty as assistant and later an additional assistant in the person of the Rev. Father H. Bischoff. Father Olds succeeded Father Griffith, having as his assistant Father O'Connor and Father Mihm. As the church had the cooperation of Archbishop Spaulding in his day, it was similarly assisted by Archbishop Baily and especially so by Archbishop Gibbons, later Cardinal. Among the teachers who made possible the increasing membership by their valuable work in the parochial school of the church should be mentioned Miss Mary Smith, later Mrs. W. F. Benjamin, Mr. Ambrose Queen, and Miss Eliza Ann Cook.[46]

Negro Catholics living in East Washington and worshippers at St. Peter's and St. Joseph's churches, desirous of having a church of their own, were responsive to the labors of Father James R. Matthews, assistant pastor of St. Peter's. He was a native of Johnstown, Pennsylvania, had studied at St. Charles College and St. Mary's Seminary in the diocese of Maryland, and was ordained a priest in 1886. He worked so assiduously and energetically for the new congregation here at Washington, which was then known as St. Benedict's, that a site for their building was purchased on the corner of 13th and C Streets, Southeast, about the middle of April, 1893. The work of excavation was begun on the last day of July and the corner stone was laid on the 24th of September of that year. Less than eight months afterward the church was complete and ready for public worship. An imposing parade, participated in by uniformed white and Negro Catholic societies of Baltimore and Washington, was a feature of the occasion. Cardinal Gibbons dedicated the Church as St. Cyprian.[47]

JOHN W. CROMWELL

FOOTNOTES:

[1] This dissertation was written from facts obtained from these churches and their pastors and verified by reference to books and newspapers. The most important source was the *Special Report of the U. S. Commissioner of Education on the Schools of the District of Columbia*, pp. 197 *et seq.*

[2] *Special Report of the United States Commissioner of Education on the Schools of the District of Columbia,* pp. 195–197.

[3] *Special Report of the United States Commissioner of Education on the Schools of the District of Columbia.*

[3a] After the Civil War "Little Ebenezer" entered upon a new career. The white pastors who up to this time had been serving this congregation were replaced by ministers of color, the first one being Noah Jones. About 1874 the property of the church was transferred from the white church to the local organization.

Placed upon this advantageous basis, the success of this congregation soon entitled that church to rank among the leading Negro churches of the city. C. G. Keyes built the first church edifice. Under C. G. Walker, who came later, there were added so many more new members that a new building was necessary to accommodate the congregation. Then came W. H. Draper, Alexander Dennis, and finally Dr. M. W. Clair. Using the plans devised by Dr. M. W. Clair, now Bishop of the M. E. Church, John H. Griffin built the edifice which is today used by the Ebenezer Church. This church was later served by W. T. Harris, E. W. S. Peck, and more recently by the efficient S. H. Brown and W. H. Dean, who did much to promote the religious life and expand the work of the present flourishing congregation now under the direction of J. W. Waters.

[4] From records preserved by Miss H. H. Beason.

[5] The time for radical changes was approaching when the political discussions of the time were affecting Washington and all elements of its population. It was not until the Civil War was in its third year that Mt. Zion felt the change, and this was by the organization of the Washington Annual M. E. Conference in 1864. Had it not been effected at this time, it is doubtful if the M. E. Church would have been able to make much headway in Virginia with the Negro members who up to that time were counted a part of the M. E. South, worshipping in the same edifice as the whites and under such conditions as to give rise to little or no friction. The Civil War was in its last year, and there had been no opportunity before this time for the M. E. Church to secure Negro

members to any extent. The A. M. E. Church, moreover, had already got a foothold in Norfolk and Portsmouth where the Union armies had triumphed, as early as 1862, and in 1865 the A. M. E. Zion Church secured a large following with valuable property in Petersburg.

Bishop Levi Scott, who organized the Washington Conference, was not concerned primarily for such churches in Baltimore as Sharp Street, Asbury, and Mt. Zion in Washington, but he was looking beyond the Potomac. At any rate he organized with four members and in 1864 sent to Mt. Zion Rev. John H. Brice, who thus became their first Negro pastor. Mt. Zion then had a membership of 317. Rev. Mr. Brice was reappointed in 1865. He was succeeded in 1866 by Rev. N. W. Carroll, whose career as an aggressive minister is that of one of the very first in his denomination. Rev. Mr. Carroll served three years and was an elder when his successor, Rev. Henry R. Elbert, was appointed in 1869.

Following Mr. Elbert came Rev. G. T. Pinkney, under whose administration the planning of a new structure first took form, and $1,500 for the purpose was deposited in the Freedmen's Bank. Rev. Mr. Pinkney was succeeded by Rev. George Lewis, who raised $1,600 for the building fund. Then came the Rev. Benjamin Brown, one of the useful pastors of the Negro church, a man whose reputation was coextensive with the confines of the Washington Conference, which at that time included Virginia and West Virginia as well as Maryland and the District of Columbia.

The desire for a new edifice increased, and the people

contributed liberally. At the time of the suspension of the Freedmen's Bank in 1874 the church had on deposit $2,500. The effect of the failure of the bank was most disastrous. There was a cessation of effort for a time, but under the magnetic and masterly leadership of Rev. Mr. Brown the people rallied, and $624 was collected in one day toward the new building. The time had come for a forward movement. The members were called together March 24, 1875. The question of rebuilding was discussed thoroughly and with but ten dissenting votes the proposition was endorsed and the trustees, thus empowered, undertook the purchase of a lot on Twenty-ninth Street, between Dunbarton and O Streets, from Mr. Alfred Pope, one of their number, for $25.

The work on the new edifice was begun. Meanwhile Rev. Mr. Brown was reappointed and the cornerstone was laid, the ceremony being performed by the Good Samaritans. Then came Rev. R. A. Read, who subsequently became pastor at Asbury. Rev. James Dansbury followed Mr. Brown and gave a good account of himself. In 1880 Rev. James D. S. Hall, an eloquent preacher, who had done very creditable work in different parts of the country and who had served successfully in the A. M. E. Church as well as in the M. E. Conferences, was appointed. His appointment was the signal for new life. The cornerstone was relaid, this time under the authority of the Masons. The next morning the building when only five feet high was discovered on fire. Dissatisfaction crept in the flock, lawsuits followed, and there was formed a separate A. M. E. body, with Rev. James T. Morris as its first pastor. Mt. Zion kept on nevertheless, and the first services were held in the new structure October 30, 1880, although the building was without roof or plaster. The subsequent history of Mt. Zion until the close of the nineteenth century was notable for its steady progress.

[6] In 1869 a bill passed both houses of Congress to transfer the authority of the separate management of the Negro schools to the white board. The colored people became alarmed. Israel Church opened its doors for a mass meeting and under the leadership of John F. Cook a strong protest against the legislation was voiced. The other churches were asked to follow and endorse the stand taken at Israel. They did so; the President, Andrew Johnson, refused to sign the bill and the schools remained intact under Negro management until 1900.

[7] Israel was the church above all which made itself an example for other independent churches in Washington. Mt. Zion in Georgetown had been acting as an organized church since 1816. Until 1830, however, it had no records. It had no Negro pastor for forty-eight years and no trustees until 1866.

[8] *Payne, History of the A. M. E. Church, p. 38.*

[9] Some of the strongest men in that denomination were sent to Israel. Charles Wesley Fitzhugh, Charles H. Phillips, R. S. Williams, N. S. Cleaves, and S. B. Wallace were among the number. Phillips, Williams, and Cleaves became bishops, while Dr. Wallace, who died while pastor in 1895, was certainly one of the foremost pulpit orators in any of the Negro churches, without exception, during the nineteenth century.

[10] From the records of this church.

[11] At this time there were eighteen classes at the Asbury and a membership of about 640. A financial report for the year ending March 30, 1850, shows receipts of $829.17½. Ten years later the stewards' financial report gives $798.01. At the dedication of Asbury in 1869 a review of its history was given by Benjamin McCoy, who was the most influential personage in the history of this church. He was a colleague of John F. Cook, Sr. An extract from a report submitted by him is very interesting, showing for the building the amount of the debt of the old Asbury, $15,354.97, on which $11,610.97 was paid Downing and Brothers, $3,744 to Rogers and Cissil, $1,257.48 paid to Morsell and Dearing, leaving a balance of $2,486.52.

[12] The order then follows: W. H. Waters, 1856; John J. Herbert, 1857; Michael F. Sluy, 1858; Alexander W. Wayman, 1859; Daniel W. Moore, 1860-1861; James A. Handy, 1864 (6 weeks); James D. S. Hall, 1864, 1865; James A. Handy, 1866, 1867; Richard A. Hall, 1868, 1869; Daniel P. Seaton, M.D., 1870, 1871; Daniel Draper, 1872, 1873; Richard A. Hall, 1874; Joseph S. Thompson, 1875, 1876; George W. Brodie, 1877, 1878, 1879; Rev. John W. Stevenson, 1880, 1881.

Union Bethel finally became the Metropolitan Church in 1881. James A. Handy served in 1882, 1883, 1884; after which came Rev. George T. Watkins, 1885; Theophilus G. Steward in 1886 and 1887, and John T. Mitchell in 1888 and 1889.

[13] The organization of the Bethel Literary and

Historical Association by Bishop Payne in the early autumn of 1881 was an event worth chronicling because of its immediate influence on the individual church, the community, the denomination and the entire country. For twenty-five years the Bethel Literary in the fall and winter seasons was recognized as an intellectual clearing house. In distant communities the reflex influence was just as unmistakable because of the newspapers, whose Washington correspondents did not fail to register the utterances and the discussions which the Literary occasioned.

[14] Union Bethel became the Metropolitan A. M. E. Church by order of the General Conference of 1872, affirmed by that of 1876 and reaffirmed by its successor in 1880.

The church building is 80 x 120 with a sub-basement for domestic purposes and a basement above grade containing lecture, Sunday School, library, and class rooms. The cost was $70,000 on ground, the assessed valuation of which at the time of the erection of the edifice was $25,000. The cornerstone was laid in 1881. The basement was opened for divine worship November 8, 1885, and dedicated by Bishop A. W. Nayman, Dr. J. A. Handy, Dr. B. W. Arnett, and Dr. G. T. Watkins, pastor. On the completion of the main auditorium services were first held Sunday, May 30, 1886. When dedication features extending one week took place, John A. Simms, Andrew Twine, William Beckett, John Shorter, George C. Brown, James Washington, Walter F. Hyson, George R. Dalley, and J. T. Harris were the trustees.

In 1886 the new edifice was dedicated with elaborate exercises. T. G. Steward was the first pastor to serve in the new building. After an administration of two years he was succeeded by Dr. John G. Mitchell. John W. Beckett followed Dr. Mitchell in 1889 and remained three years. In 1873 John T. Jenifer, who bears the distinction of being a member of the first graduating class of Wilberforce University, was appointed and served three years. He was succeeded in 1896 by John Albert Johnson, who served a term of five years with unusual success. Daniel J. Hill followed J. Albert Johnson and remained two years. Oscar J. W. Scott, who followed in 1903, filled out three terms and was serving his fourth when he received an appointment as Chaplain in the 24th United States Infantry to succeed Chaplain T. G. Steward. John H. Welch, named to succeed J. W. Scott, served two years and was appointed for the third when he suddenly passed away to the intense sorrow of his congregation. Dr. Isaac N. Ross began in 1909 an incumbency of five years.

In 1914 Dr. C. Harold Stepteau succeeded Dr. Ross and remained for three years. Dr. Stepteau was succeeded in 1917 by Rev. Carlton M. Tanner. He at once bent his efforts toward the reduction of the debt which had handicapped the progress of the church for a generation. Such was his success that within two years he accomplished what had been regarded as an impossible task. The event was made an occasion for great rejoicing, culminating in a thanksgiving service Monday evening, January 27, 1919, which included among other features an address by the pastor, Dr. Tanner, one by the presiding Bishop, John Albert Johnson, and an original poem by Dr. Robert E. Ford. The most spectacular number was the burning of the fourteen thousand dollar mortgage deed in the presence of the vast audience, the taper being applied by a committee of elderly members who had been connected with the church for a score or more of years.

[15] One has said that not long thereafter they employed as temporary pastor the Rev. Mr. Nickens, whose coming being unacceptable to some members of the congregation, caused about thirty to secede, organizing a church by themselves. These seceding members were expelled and, as the church property was deeded to the members of the church, there ensued a controversy as to the title of the church, which for a number of years was in litigation between the mother church and her offspring. See the *Special Report of the United States Commissioner of Education on the Schools of D. C.*, 311.

[16] During his school days Rev. Harvey Johnson of Baltimore was a follower of the Nineteenth Street Baptist Church.

[17] This account was given by the present pastor of this church, Dr. W. H. Brooks.

The deacons during Dr. Brooks's pastorate have included some of the foremost men in the community. Such men are William Coke, who was a deacon in 1840, John H. Beale, Nathaniel Gilmer, Henry Jarvis, Linsey Muse, Albert Parker, William P. Pierre and William Syphax, while among the trustees will be recalled

Carter A. Stewart, Charles Lemos, David Clark, William B. Brooks, W. A. Johnson, Edgar Ball and John H. Hunter. Among the local churches either directly or indirectly originated in the Nineteenth Street Church are the Vermont Avenue, the Metropolitan, Berean, Pilgrim of Brentwood, Salem and Israel Baptist Churches.

[18] The following persons constituted the church: John F. Cook, David Carroll, Jane Noland, Mary Ann Tilghman, Clement Talbert, Lydia Williams, Elizabeth Carroll, Ann Brown, Charles Bruce, Basil Gutridge, Clarissa Forest, John Madison, Catherine Madison, Ann Chew, Ruth Smith, Emily Norris, Maria Newton, Alfred Cook and Eliza Stewart.

[19] *See F. J. Grimké's Anniversary Address on the Occasion of the Seventy-fifth Anniversary of the Fifteenth Street Presbyterian Church.*

[20] A statement verified by the present pastor, Dr. J. L. S. Holloman.

In 1883 Dr. William Bishop Johnson accepted the call to the pastorate which, notwithstanding its nearly forty years of struggle, had been reduced to a membership of less than one hundred. During Dr. Johnson's pastorate a church edifice was erected in 1895 at a cost of $75,000, one of the largest and most imposing in the city. An outstanding feature of Dr. Johnson's administration was the organization of a Sunday School Lyceum in 1885 which was one of the most popular literary organizations in the Capitol, meeting Sunday afternoons, when there were discussions of some foremost topic by representative thinkers of both sexes and races.

Notable among the presidents of the Sunday School Lyceum were Mr. Jesse Lawson, Mr. R. D. Ruffin, and Mr. R. W. Thompson, the newspaper correspondent. Johnson died in 1917 mourned by the congregation and community as one of its leading preachers. Through his administration of the affairs the church became one of the best known throughout the country because of the organizing abilities of the pastor and his unusual ability. In 1917 the church called as pastor Dr. J. L. S. Holloman of Winton, North Carolina. During his four years of service the church has been practically freed of debt and has entered on a new era of progress.

[21] The present building was erected about 1886, by Dr. R. H. G. Dyson. The present pastor is Rev. H. J. Callis, who easily takes rank in the city as one of its leading public-spirited influences.

[22] This story is taken largely from records preserved by Mr. B. J. Grant, one of the oldest members of this church.

[23] At the present time this plot of ground is covered by the Ebenezer A. M. E. Church.

[24] Two years later they erected another story, which remained intact until the church was sold. The remodeling and addition cost $1,100. This property proved to be very valuable, as they decided after many years to make it one of its most fashionable thoroughfares. Bought for almost a pittance, this property had advanced in value to such an extent that the business interests offered a high price for it and it was sold.

[25] A new edifice is being favorably considered to accommodate the growing congregation. A building fund has been started for this purpose.

[26] This account was taken from the records of the Third Baptist Church.

[27] There were elected the following officers in 1885: W. C. Laws, Joseph Jones, Henry Hughes, James H. West, Daniel Lewis, Moten Waites, and Joseph Montgomery. P. H. Umbles officiated during the vacancy of the pulpit occasioned by the death of Mr. Jefferson, which occurred in October, 1885.

On March 19 James H. Lee of New Bedford, who had formerly been connected with the Third Baptist Church, was called to the pastorate. He accepted and preached his inaugural sermon May 9 and was installed on May 30. During the first seven years of his administration 242 members were received by baptism, 49 by letter, 62 by experience, 59 by restoration. In the same period 24 were dismissed by letter, 65 excluded and 117 lost by deaths. A debt of $3,475.55 was paid during this period including balance due on site. The collections aggregated $28,729.

[28] The following officers were then in charge: Deacons W. L. Laws, Daniel Lewis, Joseph Jones, Joseph Montgomery, James H. West, Henry Hughes, and Moten Waites; and Trustees Alexander Peyton, Henry C. Bolden, William Reynolds, Ottowa Nichols, Richard Basey, George Duff and Dennis Johnson. After the death of Rev. James H. Lee, Rev. Mr. Bullock became the pastor.

[29] James L. Pinn is the present pastor, having served since September, 1916.

[30] Records of the Shiloh Baptist Church.

[31] About a year before the church was organized a number of Baptists, who with their children afterward formed the church, met in a little shanty situated at that time on the south side of L Street, just across from the present church house, and under the direction of J. McCleary Perkins, a white Union soldier, formed a Sunday School. The members of this Sunday School were largely adults of African descent, while the teachers were from both races. The Bible was the book from which morals and religion were taught, and Webster's blueback speller was the constant companion of children and parents while they were learning to read the Word of God. James H. Payne succeeded Mr. Perkins as Superintendent of this school, and six months thereafter John M. Washington succeeded Payne. These two men alternated as superintendents of this Sunday School for ten or twelve years, and worked together faithfully until they succeeded in building up a flourishing institution.

[32] Those who were in the original company that founded the church were Washington Whitlow, John J. Taylor, J. Mason Wilson, George Armstead, Edward Brook, Clement Morgan, Henry Frazier, Henry D. Payton, Griffin Saunders, Alfred Pendleton, James H. Payne, James G. Semple, Jane Brown, Elizabeth Morgan, Annie Armstead, Lucy Davis and Rev. William J. Walker.

[33] The Moderator then informed the members

of Shiloh that the Council was ready to hear their statement, whereupon Henry Frazier, the senior deacon of the newly formed church, gave a history of the organization and prosperity of Shiloh Baptist Church in Fredericksburg, from which the members forming the new church had come. William J. Walker, who had been associated with the Fredericksburg church for about twelve years, presented some interesting facts, and added: "These brethren, who have been driven from their homes and scattered among strangers, long to be gathered into a church, that they may worship God unitedly as they formerly did." Thereupon A. Rothwell offered the following resolutions which were unanimously passed:

"Resolved, That we recognize with devout gratitude the good hand of our Heavenly Father, in delivering these, His children, from the fetters of bondage, so that they may freely serve Him, and more perfectly learn His Way, and we tender to them our cordial Christian sympathies, as well as our prayers and our aid, in maintaining their church organization.

"Resolved, also, That we heartily approve the proposition of the brethren to be recognized as a church, based upon the Christian doctrines and principles which are the foundation of our denomination, and that we will cheerfully cooperate in the services appropriate to the recognition of the Shiloh Baptist Church of Washington, D. C."

The following were the officers of the newly formed church: Deacons Henry Frazier, Clement Morgan,

James G. Semple, Edward Brook, James H. Payne, Henry D. Payton and Alfred Pendleton; Trustees William J. Walker, Edward Brook, John J. Taylor, James H. Payne, Griffin Saunders, Washington Whitlow and Henry D. Payton; John J. Taylor, church clerk, and J. McCleary Perkins, Superintendent of the Sunday School.

William J. Walker, the first pastor of Shiloh Baptist Church, was a native of Fredericksburg, Virginia. He was born of free parents and was about 72 years of age at the time of his death, in 1889. He was a printer by trade, and enjoyed considerable educational advantages for the times in which he lived. He was a wise leader, an untiring worker, and a faithful and able minister of the gospel.

[34] This is a condensed account furnished Dr. J. M. Waldron.

[35] These facts were obtained from the church records.

[36] A statement verified by the present pastor.

[36a] A statement made by the clerk of the church.

[37] A statement made by a number of old members of the church.

[38] The records of the church.

[39] Their first meeting house was erected with a seating capacity of 300 at a cost of $800; the second, which would seat 500, cost $2,000. With their more than 150 membership they raised $1,000 annually and expended $850 on current expenses.

[40] These are facts given by the officers of this church.

[41] J. W. Parker, pastor of the E Street Baptist Church, was moderator, and Lalmon Richards, of the North Baptist Church, was clerk of this council. The organization consisted of twenty-two members, 10 men and 12 women: James Storum, Wormley, White, Harrod, Denney, Bailey, John Pierre Randolph, Rowe, Page, Mrs. Wormley, Mrs. Anderson, widow of D. W. Anderson, Eliza Jackson, Mary Jackson, Thompson, Pierre, Denney, White, Farley, Bailey and Watson.

[42] This is an abridged statement verified by the church itself.

[43] This is based on a statement made by this church.

[44] This account is based on the records of this church.

[45] These facts were obtained from the records of the church.

[46] These facts as to Negro Catholics were taken from records in the form of a church monthly newspaper in the possession of Dr. John F. Smith.

[47] The sermon was delivered by Dr. O'Gorman. The edifice is an imposing structure of Potomac blue stone, granite basement with trimmings of Baltimore County marble. A slate roof crowns the building, the elevation to the apex of the roof being 56 feet. The facade is broken at the corner with a square tower standing with its top about 113 feet from the ground. Three wide doors open from the street approached by ten stone steps so constructed as to make them easy to ascend

or descend. The church will seat 600 persons and cost about $40,000. In connection with its religious activities St. Cyprian's has a parochial school and academy located on 8th and D Streets, five blocks west. This is the gift of one Miss Atkins, one of the most thrifty of Negro women of the community, who had been a student at St. Francis Academy in Baltimore.

DOCUMENTS

THE EXPERIENCE OF A GEORGIA PEON—MY ESCAPE FROM BONDAGE[1]

It was on a faraway plantation, where the big bell rang out the call to work, and the overseer shouted at the top of his voice, "All in line." For twenty-seven years I was one among the groups that must hearken to the call of the big bell.

Some years ago the owners of these plantations agreed among themselves to let the colored people have schools, with the understanding that no one should be admitted as a pupil who was old enough to work. So I found myself among those who had to work. I hardly know how the thought came into my mind that I wanted to go to school, for there was no talk of schools around the fireside, but for some cause that I cannot explain I became possessed with the longing for an education. I did not know what for, but, with all my heart, I wanted to go to school.

There were ten of us in our family, including our father. Our mother departed into the beyond when we were very small. Our father was an easy-going man. Any way would do for him. Whatever *was* was right. Whenever I told him that I wanted to go to school he would answer, "You know what the boss says." But I would reply, "Father, he can't *make* me stay here." That was to him a piece of foolishness and he would turn away and say nothing more. At last I saw that I must do my own thinking and plan my own way of leaving. For ten years school was my chief thought. Every day I saw myself turning from the old plantation to what was for me the land of freedom and opportunity.

It was years before the opportunity came. One night I said to my father, "I am going to leave on the first day of May if it costs me my life." For the first time he seemed to realize that I was in earnest. Then he said, "If you leave me you will travel in my tears." That was a horrible thought to me so I did not leave then nor until several more years had gone by, ten in all from the time I first began to think about school.

Finally, one night I said to him: "This is the third and last time I shall tell you I want to go to school. You hindered me for years by telling me that I would be travelling in your tears. That will not answer any longer." When he saw that the blaze had never died out he said: "My son, these may be right thoughts that have come to your mind and their power may lead you to a good end, yet they may be the ruin of you. I would rather follow you to your grave than see you captured and brought back to be punished by these hateful laws they have on these plantations. God will change things after a time and then it may be you can go to school in safety." I saw then that my poor father wanted me to go to school but was afraid I would be punished if I did, as he had known others to do. I said I was going to risk it anyway. As the appointed time drew near he was very sorrowful. Never shall I forget the night of parting. After he had pronounced a benedirection upon me he said: "May you ever be happy."

I had really started upon my journey. I had a sack of gingerbread which I did not want to bother with but that my dear sisters persuaded me to carry with me. When daylight appeared I knew it would not be safe to keep the road so I planned out a road of my own. When I came to the spring into which Ponce de Leon had plunged to regain his lost youth I sat down and ate all the bread I could and left the rest. How often afterwards I wished for it!

Not long after I left Ponce de Leon spring I heard the plantation dogs coming after me. "What shall I do now?" was the question. When they had nearly reached me I hid behind a tree and then dashed off as if I saw game ahead. They soon recognized me and became my fast friends.

We slept in the same bed under the same guardian stars. Every night I would thank God for their voiceless sympathy. I shared my meals with them. When I bought crackers I would eat but a few of them and give the rest to my dumb companions. But I saw at last that I must get rid of the poor creatures somehow, although the thought almost broke my heart. When I reached the Mississippi I lashed two logs together and sent my companions out hunting. Then I sailed away on the raft I had made across the Father of Waters. When they returned I looked back and saw them running alongside of the river where they could see me, willing to die with me. I broke down in tears and could not look back any more, because I would have gone back and died with them.

For hundreds of miles I made a path where no human foot had ever trod. I swam rivers and made harbors where no boat had ever landed. At last I reached Texas. For many days I travelled without seeing any house. At night I was afraid of being destroyed by some wild beast, so I would climb a tree and stay awake until morning. But none of these things moved me for I had ten years' study of my journey and whatever it might bring, even death. Coming to a little town I found work with one of my race. I thought all colored people were like those on the plantation so I told my employer everything and from what plantation I came. He said I had taken the right step. Imagine my surprise therefore when I discovered that I was captured! It almost broke my heart. Rather than go back to the old plantation I would suffer death. I pulled away from my captors and ran with all my might. My pretended friend was ahead trying to overtake me but I soon freed myself in a large swamp. This taught me a lesson I did not have to go to school to learn, I found out that some among my own race would put me to death for a dollar and I learned to keep my mouth shut.

When I reached Chattanooga, the nights were so cold I saw I could no longer lie out. For many months I had not slept in a bed, nor eaten a cooked meal. My clothes were those I wore away from home and they were what you can imagine they would be. I did not know how to go about getting a job. Finally I found a good place and before long was earning enough to make me comfortable. But one day when I was out in town I saw a drummer who had sold goods to the store on our plantation, for many years. He recognized me and called out, "The boss is going to break your head, nigger, if he gets you!" This ended my happy home. I had not yet learned to get on a train but with my same dependence I soon ran away to Knoxville. Writing to a certain place from there I learned of my father's death. These were dark days for me. I was strolling about in the cold world without home or friends. I would often ask myself, "What am I living for when there is no heart beating for me?" I began to drift with the current and even thought I would take to drinking. Then the thought came to me that I would be a coward to come so far and then give up. I arose with this thought and determined to act like a man. I entered school in Morristown Tenn., thinking that all my troubles were over. I made low grade with small children. It seemed funny to them to see a man who knew so little. I was there about four months and was beginning to lose my fear when one day I saw the same drummer again. When he caught sight of me he called out, "Hello, nigger, I thought you were in New York!" Never will sinner tremble in the presence of the Almighty as I did in the presence of that drummer. But he seemed only delighted in spending some time talking with me. He said one of my sisters and several other hands from the plantation had run away and the boss thought I was the cause of it all, and, he added, "If that old man gets his hand on you, they'll take you some night and skin you alive. I told him I saw you in Chattanooga and he said he would make me a present of $200 if I would let him know where you were if I should see you again. But I would not do you that way for anything. I'll tell you what I will do for you, however. I'll get you a good job up North where you can go to school. I would not stop here." I replied "All RIGHT!" As he was going away he threw me a quarter saying, "Get you a drink, old boy!" I lifted my hat and scraped back my foot as I thanked him for the money. But I was not so easily fooled at that time. I knew just what such sweet talk meant. I saw that it was my move. I had learned then to get on the train. I left Morristown that night and next morning was in Lexington. Being afraid to stay I went to Wilberforce, Ohio, then to Frankfort but finally came back to Lexington again. By that time I had found out that my boss could not carry me back to the plantation, as its laws were not so large in the world as I had thought. I found out that if I violated the laws of the State I could not be carried back without the consent of the Governor of Kentucky. I entered Chandler School without money but happy. For the first time I wrote to my old Miss telling her I was in Lexington in Chandler School. She answered with sweet words about my going to school, and said the boss had spoken kind things about me before he passed away.

The kind teachers of Chandler did their best to unfold those twenty-seven years of ignorance. I had almost to bite the dust to stay in school but I stayed there. I have studied many days hungry—walking the streets after-noons trying to find work for a little to eat.

Since I have been in Lexington I have often been asked, "What do you want with so much education?" Out of those same lips I have heard other students praised for going to school. I did not let this discourage me. Dr. J. E. Hunter, Rev. E. A. Clarke, and Kelly Robinson will ever have my heart-felt gratitude for the kind words of encouragement they gave me. We little realize what a word of encouragement means to one who has lived the life I have.

FOOTNOTES:

[1] This narrative was obtained by the editor. It relates an incident which took place between Wrightsville and Dublin, Georgia, in 1903. There is abundant evidence that many other cases of this have been and may be found in the United States.

COMMUNICATIONS

This letter contains at least one important fact showing the development of racial relations in the United States since the establishment of the independence of this country.

FEBRUARY 8, 1916.

MR. C. G. WOODSON,
  EDITOR, THE QUARTERLY JOURNAL OF NEGRO
  LIFE AND HISTORY,
  2223 12TH ST., NW.,
  WASHINGTON, D. C.

Sir:

Referring to your letter of the 4th instant, in which you express a desire to be furnished with information showing the number of negro soldiers who served in the Revolutionary War, their names, if possible, and some information concerning the regiments in which they served, and in which letter you also make inquiry as to whether such records are accessible to some member of your staff for making the necessary research, I am directed by the Secretary of War to inform you as follows:

A cursory examination of the Revolutionary War records on file in this Department has resulted in the discovery of information here and there concerning the services of colored men in that war, but there is no index indicating where records of such services may be found and in order to ascertain data showing the names, organizations and numbers of such colored men it would be necessary to make an extended search of the entire collection of Revolutionary War records in the custody of this Department. Even after making such an extended search the results would be doubtful because the War Department records afford but little information showing whether Revolutionary War soldiers were white or colored.

No attempt has ever been made by the War Department to compile information regarding the numbers or names of colored men in the Revolutionary War or the designations of the organizations to which they belonged, and owing to the limited clerical force allowed by law, the Department cannot undertake any compilation, which, as already explained, would in any event necessarily be incomplete and unsatisfactory.

Historical investigators of recognized standing are permitted to have access to the War Department records under certain conditions, but the Revolutionary War records have become so worn and dilapidated by reason of lapse of time and long use thereof that access thereto is permitted only under exceptional circumstances. Inasmuch as those records are very incomplete and afford scarcely any information bearing upon the subject in question it is not seen that any useful purpose can be served by granting permission to search those records for the data desired.

Many of the States that had troops in the Revolutionary War have published rosters of such troops. These rosters can probably be readily consulted in the Congressional Library, and it is believed that they afford the most promising source for obtaining the information sought

Very respectfully,

H. T. McCain,
The Adjutant General

The following sent out some time ago under the frank of Congressman Goldfogle may have some historic value:

When the Jamestown Exposition Bill was under consideration by the Committee on Industrial Arts and Expositions of the House of Representatives, at Washington, Congressman Henry M. Goldfogle, of New York, a member of the committee, took a very keen and lively interest in securing an appropriation of a hundred thousand dollars for a Negro exhibit.

On the day the Committee finally revised the bill and voted on it, Congressman Goldfogle was suffering intensely from carbuncles, and was about to undergo a surgical operation. Despite this, he went to the committee meeting, and there moved the insertion of the provision for the appropriation for a Negro exhibit.

Some members of the committee who were not favorable to the project and others who were quite indifferent to it urged the Congressman to allow the matter to remain in abeyance, saying that it might be taken up at some future time. Judge Goldfogle, however, insisted there was no time like the present and that the colored men and women of the country ought to have an opportunity to show through means of the proposed exhibit the remarkable progress that they had made since the days when they emerged from slavery. In the course of his remarks to the Committee, he said that he came of a race that had been oppressed and which centuries ago had been in slavery, and that had he lived forty years after the children of Israel had passed out of the house of bondage, he would have been thankful and grateful had anyone given his people an opportunity to show the progress they had made as free men.

Congressman Goldfogle called attention to the testimony that had been given during the hearings before the Committee of the great advancement made by the colored people in every avenue of life from the time of their emancipation, and the credit that was due to many of the men and women of the Negro race who had shown themselves worthy of the freedom that happily this country accorded them.

After quite a spirited debate, in which Judge Goldfogle warmly espoused the cause of the colored man, the Committee, by a majority of one vote, inserted the appropriation provision; and thus, mainly through the efforts of this New York Congressman, who has not a single colored vote in his district, the Negro exhibit was established at the Jamestown Exposition.

BOOK REVIEWS

A Social History of the American Negro. By Benjamin Brawley. Macmillan Company, New York, 1921. Pp. 420.

As Negro history has been so long neglected, it will require some time to develop in this field the necessary standard to secure a distinction between the significant and insignificant and between truth and fiction. On account of the emphasis which has been recently given to this study, many novices lacking especially the historical point of view have entered this field because it is so productive that it is an easy task to write a work therein. Benjamin Brawley whose chief preparation and efforts have been restricted to English is one of these novices. Among his first efforts were *A Short History of the American Negro* and *The Negro in Literature and Art.* In neither of these works does he exhibit the knowledge required by the standards of present day historiography. This more recent work although more extensive than the others has no better claim to its being called history.

There can be no question as to many valuable facts contained in this work, but it lacks proportion, style, and accuracy. The book begins with a study of African origins based largely on Wiener's *Africa and the Discovery of America* and upon Lady Lugard's *Tropical Dependency.* He next takes up the Negro in the Spanish exploration but has little or nothing to say about the Negroes in connection with other explorers. His treatment of the development of the slave trade and of the introduction of slavery shows a slightly improved conception of his task. In his discussion of the Negroes in the colonies, into which he works servitude and slavery, the Indian, the mulatto, the free Negro, and efforts for social betterment, he presents a veritable hodgepodge. Passing then to the study of the estrangement from Great Britain, the participation of the Negro in the Revolutionary War, and the effect of that movement upon the Negro's social and political situation, he exhibits no scientific grasp of the status of the Negroes during the eighteenth century or of what they were thinking and doing. The treatment of the new West, the South, and the West Indies, which follows this portion of the book is merely certain generalizations which may be obtained from an average knowledge of American history and from such topical discussions of the Negro history as may be found in B.A. Johnson's *History of the Negro Race* or in John W. Cromwell's *The Negro in American History*. In his discussion of the Indian and the Negro there is an effort which serves to direct attention to a neglected aspect of our history, that is, to figure out the extent to which the races were associated and the race admixture which resulted from such contact.

Coming nearer to our day to take up the discussion of the Missouri Compromise, the abolition agitation, and the constitutional debate on slavery, Mr. Brawley shows his inability to develop his subject for he merely draws a few facts first from one field and then from another to fill out certain topics in the book without correlating them in such a way that the reader may be able to interpret their meaning. He has endeavored not to write a history but to summarize what other persons are now publishing as selected topics in this field. In other words, he has added to the unscientific history of the Negro, which has hitherto appeared in the so-called text books on Negro history, facts culled from various sources but so improperly used as not to develop the subject.

The chapter on Liberia should have been incorporated into the treatment of colonization or made a supplementary chapter in the appendix of the book. Placed in the middle of the work, it has been necessary to repeat certain facts which could have been stated elsewhere once for all. The same is true of his treatment of the Negro as a national issue, and of social progress, which he takes up the second time as topics inadequately developed in the earlier stages of the treatise. In his discussion of the Civil War, the Emancipation, the Reconstruction, and the Negro in the new South, he says very little which is new. Under the caption *The Vale of Tears*, he drifts almost altogether into opinion as he does also in the case of the *Negro in the New Age* and the *Negro Problem*. Judging, then, from the point of view of an historian, one must conclude that this work does not meet any particular want and that so far as the history of the Negro is concerned the publication of it will hardly result in any definite good. Mr. Brawley does not know history.

William Lloyd Garrison. By JOHN JAY CHAPMAN. Moffat, Yard and Company, New York, 1913. Pp. 278.

This is a revised edition of a work of a similar name by this author, published in 1913 by Moffat, Yard and Company, New York. After having written the first edition the author made further investigation and had other reflections which led him to think and to see things from a different angle. He was impressed, moreover, with the fact that, being now further removed from the Civil War, persons have learned to think more seriously with regard thereto and to consider the value of the deeds of the participants therein in a more sympathetic manner. This work, however, has not been so very much enlarged; for it has only eighteen pages more, but unlike the first edition it has an index. Hoping, however, to give the subject of this sketch a larger place in American history and to popularize the story of his career this revised edition has been given to the public.

The work is not set forth as a scientific study. It is rather an abridged account which may be read without much difficulty by the average student in quest of concise opinion concerning one of the most important American characters figuring in that great crisis between 1830 and 1860. On reading this work, one receives the impression that the author has done his task very well. It borders somewhat on hero worship, however, as is evident from the use of the following language: "If one could see a mystical presentation of the epoch, one would see Garrison as a Titan, turning a giant grindstone or electrical power-wheel, from which radiated vibrations in larger and in ever larger, more communicative circles and spheres of agitation, till there was not a man, woman, or child in America who was not a tremble." He says further: "We know, of course, that the source of these radiations was not in Garrison. They came from the infinite and passed out into the infinite. Had there been no Garrison they would somehow have arrived and at some time would have prevailed. But historically speaking they did actually pass through Garrison: he vitalized and permanently changed this nation as much as one man ever did the same for any nation in the history of the world."

The book gives a good background and then dramatically stages Garrison as a striking figure. Next follows a dramatic presentation of the antislavery struggle with pen pictures of the participants. The story finally reaches the crisis when Garrison stood as a central figure. The work contains a retrospect and a prospect, an excellent account of the man in action, the Rynders Mob, Garrison and Emerson, and foreign influence. The story closes with a summary and an impressive epilogue. Although not a scientific treatise it certainly furnishes stimulus to further study, and when a student thus interested has read it, he will desire to study one of the larger biographies of this distinguished man.

The Education of the South African Native. By CHARLES T. LORAM. Longmans, Green and Company, London, 1917. Pp. 340.

This is a treatise written by a South African brought up among the natives. He was once a Fellow in Teachers College of Columbia University. At the time of writing this book he was serving as an inspector of schools in Natal. The study, however, was undertaken as a doctoral dissertation at Columbia.

Observing the shortcomings of writers on Africa, this author endeavors to make a step ahead of them. He feels that they have dealt too much with ethnology, and with the descriptions of customs and habits. He does not think very much of the books primarily devoted to a discussion of the conflicting opinions on craniology and psychology of the natives. Taking up his own chosen task, however, he found it rather difficult because the government has had no definite policy of native education, and when there has been a policy among the four important South African governments there does not appear to be any uniformity of effort. No one, moreover, has undertaken to give the problem of the uplift of the natives adequate treatment.

The author desired to make his work scientific but it appears that he had not prosecuted this study very far before he found that important facts were lacking and that in making his conclusions and suggestions he would have to rely upon faith that what he may surmise may in the future prove to be true, although some modification may be necessary. Taking up this problem of education, however, he made use of the reports of the government departments, reports of school officials, books, pamphlets, articles in periodicals, statistical and experimental investigations, personal experience, and the experiences of his colleagues. While the work for the lack of some scientific treatise blazing the way suffered from so many handicaps that it could not be thoroughly scientific, it is the nearest approach to it and must be considered the best authority in this field until superseded.

The work begins with a consideration of such scientific topics as race contact in its larger aspects, the native problem and its proposed solution, serving as a sort of introduction to the essential portion of the work. The chief value of the book lies in its consideration of why the natives should be educated, the early missionary enterprises, the present status, elementary, industrial and higher education of the natives, a comparison of the achievements of native education with that of European, the basis for reconstruction of the native system, the educational budget, and proposed changes.

The work is generally readable but grows a little dull in certain statistical portions. The table of contents is detailed, but the book could have been considerably improved had an index been added. On the whole, the volume is a justification of some change in the political status of the Negro for the good of all. South Africa cannot in its own interest neglect the uplift of the natives, if it would promote the social and economic progress of the whole group. The one element cannot be elevated or kept up while the other is being held down. Persons interested in education of belated peoples and in the missionary enterprises should avail themselves of this volume.

From Slave to Citizen. By CHARLES M. MELDEN. The Methodist Book Concern, New York and Cincinnati, 1921. Pp. 271.

This is a work written by one who has spent sixteen

years as an educator of Negroes in the South. His experience there was sufficient for him to learn the Negro and his needs and he writes in the vein of one speaking as having authority. Because of his long service among the Negroes, the author has doubtless caught the viewpoint of the aspiring members of the race. He aims, therefore, to present the Negro's claim for recognition as a man, as a member of the human family with the implied rights and privileges belonging to him.

The book presents a definite program. It proceeds on the basis that, in a democracy, citizenship with its duties and its privileges must in the long run be recognized. He does not feel that democracy means the wiping out of racial preferences but the recognition of racial gifts and endowments. The author considers it an injustice to hold the Negro to the standards of democracy without training him to meet the responsibility. He considers it unfair to require every individual of the race to reach a prescribed standard before any of that group shall be recognized. It is, therefore, a plea for treating the Negroes as individuals and not as a single group, for fair treatment will not lead to amalgamation in as much as Christianity has not been known to promote that.

The chief remedy for the evils of racial conflict, according to the author, is cooperation. This must be brought about through growth and development from the contact of the two races on the higher plane of Christian service. Men must learn to work together without surrendering their fundamental connections.

They must confer on all matters pertaining to economic welfare. This means that the white man must give the Negro a chance for initiative and leadership in the program of cooperation rather than the eternal super-imposed leadership from without. In the language of Bishop W. P. Thirkield, who wrote the introduction to this work: "The Negro must be offered not crutches but a spirit of cooperation to make him strong that he may stand on his feet and walk."

It is evident then that this book is primarily concerned with the solution of the race problem. Yet written by a man who for years lived in the South, it presents a point of view which will be of value to the historian. From such topics as citizenship, social and legal discrimination, disfranchisement, and mob law, the historian will learn much by observing how these things impressed this worker in the South and his reaction on them. Valuable information may be obtained also from the discussion of the work of the Christian teacher in the South, the mission school, and the silent protest in the form of the exodus. There are valuable statistics in the chapters presenting the progress in education, advancement in wealth, achievement in social uplift, attainments in literature and art, and the record of the Negroes in the World War. The last part of the book concerned with the currents and counter-currents, the grinding of the mills of the gods and a possible modus vivendi will decidedly interest the social worker but will not concern very much the student of history. On the whole, however, this volume is a valuable historical document which the student of Negro life must read to be well informed as to what the Negro has been doing in the South during the last generation and what others have been doing for him.

NOTES

The annual meeting of the Association, held at Lynchburg on the 14th and 15th of November, was the most successful conference hitherto held by this organization. The proceedings appear elsewhere in this number.

At this meeting Prof. John R. Hawkins, for years a member of the Executive Council, was elected President. A new Secretary-Treasurer, Mr. S. W. Rutherford, was also elected. Mr. Rutherford is a well-known business man in Washington. The Executive Council was reconstructed to make it national. The following persons were added thereto: Bishop R. A. Carter, R. R. Church, John W. Davis, Clement Richardson, and R. C. Woods. Most of the former members of the Executive Council were retained.

The Associated Publishers, Incorporated, Washington, D. C., have brought out C. G. Woodson's *History of the Negro Church*. A review of this work will appear in the next number. Another work, the *Negro in Our History*, will be published some time in March.

The Journal of Negro History has received for review Mason and Furr's *With the Red Hand of France*, an account of a regiment of Negro soldiers in France with the American Expeditionary Force.

A group of intelligent Negroes in North Carolina have formed a state historical society to preserve the records of the race in that commonwealth.

Dr. C. G. Woodson, the Director of the Association is now making a study of slavery from the point of view of the slave himself. He has sent out a searching questionnaire from which some results are being obtained. He is also consulting local records and documents left by slaves themselves and by those in a position to know their attitude toward the institution. The cooperation of all interested in unearthing the truth is earnestly solicited.

Professor A. A. Taylor, of the West Virginia Collegiate Institute, is now making a scientific study of the influence of the Negro congressmen on the legislation of Congress and on the general policy of the country. He will appreciate any facts which may not be covered by the public documents and books available.

Duffield and Company of Boston have published a new edition of Benjamin Brawley's *The Negro in Literature and Art.*

PROCEEDINGS OF THE ANNUAL MEETING OF THE ASSOCIATION FOR THE STUDY OF NEGRO LIFE AND HISTORY, HELD AT LYNCHBURG, NOVEMBER 14 AND 15, 1921

The morning session of the annual meeting of the Association on the 14th at the Virginia Theological Seminary and College was called to order by the Director, C. G. Woodson, who briefly traced the history of the organization showing how it had gradually gained influence and power and reached the position which it now occupies as a national organization of concern to the people of both races throughout the country. The Director then introduced Professor Charles H. Wesley of Howard University, who delivered a most instructive and inspiring address on the value of Negro History. After a few remarks by Dr. R. C. Woods, a number of persons expressed their interest in the Association by becoming members.

At two o'clock in the evening, the business session of the Association was held. From the Executive Council, there was presented a recommendation for the following amendments to the constitution, which, after some discussion, were adopted by the Association:

That Article IV be amended so as to change "twelve" to "fourteen," and to incorporate after the words "business committee" therein the words "to fix salaries of employees." This article would then read as follows:

The Officers of this Association shall be a President, a Secretary-Treasurer, a Director and Editor, and an Executive Council, consisting of the three foregoing officers and fourteen other members elected by the Association. The Association shall have three trustees, who ex-officio shall be the President, Secretary-Treasurer, and the Director and Editor. It shall also appoint a Business Committee to fix salaries of employees, to certify bills, and to advise the Director and Editor in matters of administrative nature. These officers shall be elected by ballot through the mail or at each annual meeting of the Association.

That Article V be amended so as to read as follows:

The President shall preside at all meetings of the Association and of the Executive Council. He shall be ex-officio a trustee of the Association, a member of the Business Committee and a member of all standing committees. He shall perform such other duties as may be required of him from time to time by the Executive Council or by the Association.

In case of the absence of the President or his inability to act, his duty shall be performed by the Secretary-Treasurer, who in that event shall exercise any of the above mentioned powers of the President. In case of the absence of both the President and the Secretary-Treasurer, the duty of the President shall be performed by the Director and Editor, who in that event shall exercise any of the above mentioned powers of the President.

The Secretary-Treasurer shall attend all meetings and keep a full account of their proceedings in a book to be kept for that purpose. He shall through his Assistant keep a full and accurate account of receipts and disbursements of the Association in books belonging to the Association and shall deposit all monies and other valuable objects in the name of this Association in such depositories or safety vaults as may be designated by the Business Committee. He and his Assistant shall be required by the Executive Council to give bond as the Executive Council may designate. The Secretary-Treasurer shall be ex-officio a trustee of the Association, and a member of the Business Committee.

The Director and Editor shall be the executive of the Association when it or the Executive Council is not in session. He shall devise plans for the collection of documents, direct the studies of members of the Association, and determine what matter shall be published in the Journal of Negro History. He shall employ a business manager and clerk, the last mentioned to serve also as the Assistant to the Secretary-Treasurer. He may employ other assistants for administrative work and upon the approval of the Executive Council may employ specialists to prosecute the research to be undertaken by the Association. The

Director and Editor shall be ex-officio a trustee of the Association, and a member of all standing committees except the Business Committee.

The Executive Council shall have charge of the general interests of the Association, including the election of members of the Association on recommendation of the Director, the calling of meetings, the collection and the disposition of funds.

The report of the Director was read and adopted as was also the report of the Secretary-Treasurer, which was referred to an auditor. Important extracts from these reports follow.

The work of the Association has been successfully promoted. In some respects the Association has merely maintained its former status. Considered from another point of view, however, a decided advance in several ways has been noted. In the fields in which the work has advanced the progress has been so significant that the year through which the Association has just passed has been the most prosperous in its history.

The subscription list of the Journal of Negro History does not show a large increase for the reason that it became necessary more than a year ago to raise the fee from one to two dollars a year and the current strin-gency in the money market has borne so heavily upon teachers, and students to whom this publication must appeal, that they have been unable to give it more liberal support. Among the subscribers and members, however, there has been manifested a deep interest in the matter published and a keen appreciation of its value in the uplift of the Negro.

The membership of the Association for the same reason has about remained the same as that of last year. The interest of the members in the work and the value of the direction of the Association to them, however, have both unusually increased. This interest has culminated in the organization of clubs under the supervision of the Director, who through them has been able to give considerable stimulus to the work in remote parts of the country. Among the clubs thus organized should be mentioned those of San Antonio, Louisville, Chicago, Baltimore, Washington, Philadelphia, Brooklyn and New York. Classes doing the same work under the instruction of teachers have been formed in most of the accredited Negro secondary schools and colleges. The work of such classes at the West Virginia Collegiate Institute, the Virginia Theological Seminary and College, Hampton Institute, Morehouse College, Atlanta University, Paine College, Lincoln Institute in Missouri, and the Kentucky State Normal School has been helpful to the Association in its prosecution of the study of Negro life and history.

With the cooperation of these friends and through travel the Director has been making a study of *Slavery from the Point of View of the Slave*. This has been done through questionnaires filled out by ex-slaves and former masters, through the collection of documents, and the study of local records. This study, however, is just beginning and will require much more time for completion. The Director expects to finish at an earlier date his studies of the *Free Negro* and the *Development of the Negro in the Occupations.*

The most significant achievement of the Association has been the success of the Director in increasing the income of the Association to about $12,000 a year. This substantial uplift has come in part from a large number of Negroes, who now more than ever appreciate the value of their records and the importance of popularizing the study thereof. A large number of Negroes have made small contributions and as many as forty have given the Association $25 each this year. Through the strong endorsement of Dr. J. F. Jameson and other noted historical scholars the Director secured from the Carnegie Corporation the much needed appropriation of $5,000 a year for each of the next five years. With this income the Association has paid all of its debts except that of the bonus of $1,200 a year promised the Director for 1919-1920 and 1920-1921. Besides, the Association has been enabled to employ a Business Manager and to pay the Director a regular salary that as soon as practicable he may sever his connection with all work and devote all of his time to the prosecution of the study of Negro Life and History.

The details as to how the funds thus raised have been expended appear in the following report of the Secretary-Treasurer:

NOVEMBER 12, 1921.

The Association for the Study of Negro Life and History, Washington, D. C.

Gentlemen: I hereby submit to you a statement of the amount of money received and expended by the Association for the Study of Negro Life and History, Incorporated, from September 30, 1920, to November 12, 1921.

Receipts		Expenditures	
Subscriptions	$913.96	Printing and Stationery	$5,731.53
Memberships	126.00	Petty Cash	709.90
Contributions	8,239.50	Stenographic Service	1,134.60
Advertisements	255.15	Rent and Light	438.61
Rent and Light	198.61	Miscellaneous	86.10
Books	75.40	Salaries	1,225.00
		Traveling Expenses	77.21
Total	$9,808.62	Total	$9402.95
Balance on hand Sept. 30, 1920.	48.86	Balance on hand November 12, 1921	454.53
	$9,857.48		$9,857.48

Respectfully submitted,

SECRETARY-TREASURER.

Upon the recommendation of the committee on nominations the officers of the Association were, in keeping with the custom of this body, elected by a motion to the effect that the Acting Secretary be instructed to cast the unanimous ballot of the Association, for those recommended by the committee on nominations, that is, for John R. Hawkins as President, for S. W. Rutherford as Secretary-Treasurer, for C. G. Woodson as Director and Editor, and as members of the Executive Council the three foregoing officers together with Julius

Rosenwald, George Foster Peabody, James H. Dillard, Bishop R. A. Carter, R. R. Church, Albert Bushnell Hart, John W. Davis, Bishop John R. Hurst, A. L. Jackson, Moorfield Storey, Bishop R. E. Jones, Channing H. Tobias, Clement Richardson, and R. C. Woods.

The evening session of the 14th was held at the Eighth Street Baptist Church where were assembled a considerable representation of the members of the Association and a large number of persons seeking to learn of the work and to profit by the discussion of the Association. Dr. R. C. Woods, President of the Virginia Theological Seminary and College, presided. The first speaker of the evening, Dr. W. H. Stokes of Richmond, Virginia, delivered a well-prepared and instructive address on the value of tradition. His aim was to encourage the Negro race and other persons interested in its uplift to do more for the preservation and study of its records. The next speaker of the evening was Professor J. R. Hawkins, Financial Secretary of the African Methodist Episcopal Church. He delivered a very forceful and informing discourse on the history of the Negro Church. How the church has figured in the life of the Negro; how it has been effective in promoting the progress of the race; and what it is doing to-day to present the case of the Negro to the world and offer him opportunities in other fields were all emphasized throughout this address. Dr. R. T. Kerlin, former Professor at the Virginia Military Institute, was then introduced. He briefly spoke about the importance of acquainting the white race with the achievements of the Negro, and showed that his task was not, therefore, to appeal to the Negroes, themselves, but to the white people, who too often misunderstand them.

The morning session of the 15th at the Virginia Theological Seminary and College was called to order by the newly elected President, Prof. John R. Hawkins. The Director, Dr. C. G. Woodson, was then introduced. He showed how the Negro is a menace to the position of the white man in trying to maintain racial superiority. The significant achievements of the Negro in Africa and this country were passed in rapid review to show how untenable this position of the white man is and how unlikely it can continue in view of the fact that the Negro is accomplishing more now than ever before in the history of the race. Professor John R. Hawkins then delivered a brief address showing how the development of the schools and the maintenance of the proper school spirit through teachers and students can be made effective in the social uplift of the race. President Trigg of Bennet College then followed with impressive remarks expressing his interest in the cause and his confidence in those who are now doing so much to preserve the records of the Negro and to popularize the study of them throughout this country and abroad.

There was no afternoon session of the Association except a brief meeting of the Executive Council, to which the public was not invited. The conference closed with the evening session at the Eighth Street Baptist Church, where a large audience was addressed by Dr. I. E. McDougle, of Sweet Briar College, Dr. E. Crooks, of Randolph-Macon College, and Professor Bernard Tyrrell of the Virginia Theological Seminary and College. Dr. McDougle briefly discussed Negro history as a neglected field, showing that it is generally unexplored, and introducing an abundance of material which may be discovered with little effort. He spoke, moreover, of Negro History as a neglected subject, giving statistical information as to the places where the subject is now being taught and the manner in which such instruction is offered. Dr. Crooks spoke for a few minutes on self-respect as a means by which the race may develop power. He unfortunately, however, drifted into a discussion of certain phases of the race problem and disgusted his audience by advancing ideas with which, as he was informed, Negroes cannot agree. Professor Tyrrell then delivered a scholarly address on Negro ancestry and brought forward from his study of ancient history and especially that of Africa, facts showing that the Negro race has made a record of which it may well feel proud. He explained, moreover, how historians since the early days have become prejudiced against the proper treatment of the achievements of Africans and have endeavored to convince the world that the record of the race is not significant.

This meeting on the whole was a success, above and beyond that of any other hitherto held. The attendance was large, the enthusiasm ran higher, and the financial support secured far exceeded that of other meetings. There was expressed a general interest in the plans for the future prosecution of the work and the intention to give it more support that it may be extended in all of its ramifications throughout this country and even abroad.

187

THE JOURNAL OF NEGRO HISTORY

VOL. VII—APRIL, 1922—No. 2

NEGRO CONGRESSMEN A GENERATION AFTER

The period of reconstruction which followed the Civil War presented to the statesmen of that time three problems of unusual significance. These were: what should be the status of the eleven Confederate States; what should be done with the leaders of the Confederacy; and finally, what should be the rôle to be played by the several millions of freedmen? In the effort to deal effectively with these problems the Thirty-ninth and Fortieth Congresses adopted a reconstruction policy which provided for the readmission of the formerly rebellious States to the Union, the imposition of political disabilities upon many former Confederates, and the bestowal of citizenship and suffrage upon the freedmen. Upon the enlarged electorate the reconstruction of the States was undertaken.

That the freedmen, comprising in many communities a preponderance of voting power, should elect to public office ambitious outstanding men of their race was expected. At that time, therefore, Negroes attained not only local and State offices of importance, but also sat in the United States Congress. Indeed, during the period from 1871 to 1901, the latter year marking the passing of this type of Congressman, twenty-two Negroes, two of whom were senators, held membership in Congress. It seems, moreover, that men like Menard of Florida,

Pinchback of Louisiana, Lee and others, though unable to prove their contentions, were, nevertheless, contestants with good title.

This situation, no less unique than it was interesting, has become the source of interminable debate. It has been contended that because of the ignorance of the blacks, in letters, in manners, in business, and in the affairs of State, it was a serious mistake to enfranchise them, thus making possible for a period however brief their virtual direction of the political affairs of some of the Southern States. Consistent in principle, historians of this conviction have viewed with abhorrence the seating of black men in the highest legislative assembly of the land. Not all men, however, have concurred in this opinion. There were those who had precisely the opposite view, basing their argument on the necessity of the plan of reconstruction effected, in order to preserve to the Union the fruits of its victory.

The merits of that reconstruction are not here, however, at issue. Of far greater import for our consideration is the single fact that Negroes were thereby sent to Congress. Did the Negroes elected to Congress justify by their achievements their presence there? To what extent did they give direction to the thought and policies which were to govern and control in this nation? Manifestly an impartial judgment in this matter may be most adequately arrived at by the setting up of certain criteria of excellence expected to inhere in Congressmen and measuring by these the achievements of these functionaries. Considering the matter in this light, therefore, the following questions are advanced as bearing a direct relationship to the services of these Congressmen. First, what of their mental equipment to perform the tasks of law makers? Second, as measured by their experience in public positions of trust and by their grasp of the public questions at that time current, to what extent did they show capacity for public service? Third, in what directions were their chief interests manifested?

EVIDENCES OF MENTAL EQUIPMENT

Regarding the Negro Congressmen in the light of the standards already referred to, we shall first make inquiry as to their mental fitness to function as law makers. Broadly considered, they may be divided into two groups: first, those who possessed but limited education; second, those who were college bred.

Among the men comprising the first group, certain common characteristics are noticeable: first, they were mainly members of the earliest Reconstruction Congresses, beginning with the Forty-first, in which Negroes held membership, and were therefore but little removed from slavery; second, some of them were born of slave parents or had been, themselves, slaves; third, others were brought up in communities which expressly prohibited the establishment of educational institutions for Negroes; and fourth, all of them, by dint of severe application in later years, secured, prior to their election to Congress, a better education than rudimentary instruction. The members of this group were twelve in number, including Long[1] of Georgia; De Large,[2] Rainey,[3] Ransier,[4] and Smalls[5] of South Carolina; Lynch[6] and Bruce[7] of Mississippi; Haralson[8] and Turner[9] of Alabama; Hyman[10] of North Carolina; Nash[11] of Louisiana; and Walls[12] of Florida.

As many as ten of the twenty-two Negro congressmen were men of college education. This training, however, varied widely in scope and purpose. Two men of this group became ministers of the gospel. One of them, Richard H. Cain[13] of South Carolina, was trained at Wilberforce University, Xenia, Ohio, whence he left in 1861, at the age of thirty-six years, to begin a career in his chosen field; the other, Hiram E. Revels[14] of Mississippi, was educated at the Quaker Seminary in Union County, Indiana. Prior to their election to Congress, both of these men attracted wide attention as churchmen. Cain was for four years the pastor of a church in Brooklyn, N. Y., after which his congregation sent him as a missionary to the freedmen of South Carolina. Senator Revels, on the other hand, was widely known as a lecturer in the States of Indiana, Illinois, Ohio, and Missouri. For some time he preached in Baltimore, taught school in St. Louis, and among other things, organized churches and lectured in Mississippi. The wide experiences of both gentlemen offered to them unusual opportunities to develop the power, keenness of insight, and knowledge of human nature so essential to the leadership of men.

To some of these future Congressmen, the profession of teaching seemed more attractive than the ministry.

Three of the number were destined to become educators. One of them, Henry P. Cheatham[15] of North Carolina, attended the public and private schools near the town of Henderson, and was later graduated with honor from the college department of Shaw University. Immediately thereafter, in 1882, he was elected to the principalship of the Plymouth State Normal School, where he served until 1895. The second member of this group, George W. Murray[16] of South Carolina, won by competitive examination a scholarship at the reconstructed University of South Carolina. There he remained until 1876, his junior year, when by the accession to power of an administration unfriendly to the coeducation of the races, he was forced to withdraw. For many years thereafter, Murray was engaged as a teacher in the schools of his native county.

John Mercer Langston[17] of Virginia, the third member of the group of educators, was graduated, in 1849, at the age of twenty, from Oberlin College. Four years later, in 1853, he completed the work of the theological department of that school. Because of his ripe scholarship, moreover, unusual honors were conferred upon him by several American colleges and universities, and he was the recipient of several honorary memberships in scientific and literary institutions and associations of foreign countries. Indeed, there have sat in Congress few men of greater mental power and energy than John Mercer Langston.

Of the twenty-two Negroes who have sat in Congress, five were members of the legal profession. One of these men represented Alabama, two South Carolina, and two

North Carolina. Robert Brown Elliott, the first member of this group of legally trained leaders, was perhaps the most outstanding and certainly the most brilliant of the Negroes who have served in Congress. Elliott[18] entered the High Hollow Academy of London, England, in 1853, at the age of eleven years. In 1859, he was graduated from Eton College. Later, he studied law and was admitted to the bar, where he practiced for some time before the courts of South Carolina. This superior training of Elliott no doubt contributed in large measure to his eminence in debate, which was so often manifested during the memorable sessions of the 42nd and 43rd Congresses.

James T. Rapier[19] of Alabama, one of the really brilliant men in this group, acquired a liberal education, after which he studied law and practiced in his native State. Another member of the legal group was James E. O'Hara[20] of Enfield, North Carolina. Following his academic training which was received in New York City, O'Hara studied law, first, in North Carolina, and later at Howard University in Washington. In June, 1871, he was admitted to the bar of his State.

Two others of this group were Miller and White. The first one, Thomas E. Miller,[21] of Beaufort, South Carolina, attended the free public school for Negroes in his native city. In 1872 he was graduated from the Lincoln University in Pennsylvania. Later, Miller read law, and in 1875 was admitted to practice before the Supreme Court of his State. The second of these two, George Henry White[22] of North Carolina, studied first in his native State and later at Howard University.

While there he pursued concurrently courses in liberal arts and in law. In January, 1879, he was admitted to practice before the Supreme Court of his State.

THEIR PUBLIC SERVICE PRIOR TO MEMBERSHIP IN CONGRESS

Perhaps the most accurate method whereby one's capacity for the performance of any service may be measured is that which seeks, first, to establish the experience of the individual in the performance of the identical or similar services, and second, to evaluate the degree of skill with which the individual, at a given time, performs the particular service. Regarded in this light, therefore, we subject the Negro Congressmen to this test: As measured by their experience in public positions of trust and confidence and by their grasp of the great public questions at that time current, to what extent did they show capacity for public service?

The first part of our query lends itself to solution without difficulty. Indeed, one may with great ease establish the fact that, with but few exceptions, these men, prior to their election to Congress, had held public offices of honor and trust. A case in point is that of John Mercer Langston[23] of Virginia. While never a member of a State legislature, Langston was, nevertheless, brought often into other public service. Indeed he early attracted attention in Ohio by his service as a member of the Council of Oberlin and by his record in other township offices. Langston served as dean of the Law Department of Howard University, and in 1872 became Vice-President and Acting President of that institution. In 1885 he became President of the Virginia Normal and Collegiate Institute. He served, moreover, as Inspector-General of the Bureau of Freedmen, a member of the Board of Health of the District of Columbia, Minister resident and Consul-General to Haiti, and Charge d'Affaires to Santo Domingo. His election to Congress, therefore, was the crowning achievement of a lifelong public career.

Hyman,[24] O'Hara,[25] Cheatham,[26] and White,[27] all of North Carolina, had held public office prior to their election to Congress. Hyman and White had each been members of the State Senate, the former for six years, from 1868 to 1874, while O'Hara and White had each served in the lower house of the legislature. Hyman had been a delegate to the Constitutional Convention of 1868, moreover, while O'Hara, who had also served as chairman of the Board of Commissioners of the County of Halifax, had been a delegate to the Constitutional Convention of 1875. For the eight years from 1886 to 1894, White served as prosecuting attorney for the second judicial district of the State, while Cheatham, the fourth member of the North Carolina delegation, had held but one office, that of Register of Deeds for Vance County.

It is especially significant that each one of the Negro Reconstruction Congressmen from South Carolina, namely Cain,[28] De Large,[29] Elliott,[30] Rainey,[31] Ransier,[32] and Smalls[33] were members of the State Constitutional Convention of 1868. Two of them, Cain and Rainey, had been formerly State Senators; Smalls had served two terms in the Senate and four in the House; while each of the others had been members for one term or more in the lower branch of the legislature. Ransier, moreover, had held, prior to his election to Congress, the high office of lieutenant-governor of the State; Elliott had served as adjutant-general, and Smalls had held successively the offices of lieutenant-colonel, brigadier-general and major-general in the State militia.

Of the two South Carolinians who served in Congress after the Reconstruction, Thomas E. Miller[34] was for four terms a member of the lower chamber of the State legislature and for one term a member of the Senate. Furthermore, he was for one term a school commissioner of his county, and received also his party's nomination for the office of lieutenant-governor of the State. Indeed, of the entire South Carolina group, Murray, alone, seems to have been elected to Congress without previously having held public office.[35] Jefferson F. Long,[36] of Georgia, was not unlike Mr. Murray in that the former had never held public office. In this, his experience differed from that of Walls, of Florida, who had been a member of the Florida State Senate.

Alabama sent to Congress three Negroes, Turner,[37] Rapier,[38] and Haralson.[39] Of these men Haralson alone had had experience in the legislature prior to his election to Congress, having served in both branches of that body. Turner was elected in 1868 to the city council of Selma. Later he became tax collector of

Dallas County, but because of his inability to secure honest men as assistants, resigned the office. The third member of this group, James T. Rapier, served as an assessor and later as a collector of internal revenue in his State.

The two Negro United States Senators, Hiram R. Revels[40] and B. K. Bruce,[41] both of Mississippi, and Representative John R. Lynch[42] of the same State, had all served in public office before they were sent to Congress. Senator Revels had held several local offices in Vicksburg, while Senator Bruce, before he came to the Senate, had been sheriff, a member of the Mississippi levee board, and for three years the tax collector of Bolivar County. John R. Lynch, on the other hand, had served not only as justice of the peace, but also two terms in the lower house of the legislature, during the latter one of which he was the Speaker of that body. Unlike the Congressmen from Mississippi, Nash[43] of Louisiana held office for the first time when his state elected him a representative to Congress.

Accessible records and impartial and unbiased historians support the contention that with a few exceptions the record of these Negro functionaries was honorable. Corrupt government was not always the work of the Negro. In the chapter on reconstruction in his *The Negro in Our History*, C. G. Woodson states that local, state, and federal administrative offices, which offered the most frequent opportunity for corruption, were seldom held by Negroes, but rather by the local white men and by those from the North who had come South to seek their fortunes. In many respects selfish and sometimes lacking in principle, these men became corrupt in several States, administering the government for their own personal ends. "Most Negroes who have served in the South," says he, "came out of office with honorable records. Such service these Negroes rendered in spite of the fact that this was not the rule in that day." New York, according to the same authority, was dominated by the Tweed ring, and the same white men who complained of Negro domination robbed the governments of the Southern States of thousands of dollars after the rule of the master class was reestablished.

NEGRO CONGRESSMEN IN ACTION

With the facts concerning the earlier experiences of these Congressmen in public life a matter of record, attention may now be centered upon the second aspect of the question of their capacity for public service—namely, that of their reactions to the great public questions of their day. Perhaps this topic may be most properly treated first by determining what were the problems of greatest public moment during the period in which these men were in Congress. From the year 1871—the period of service of the first Negro in Congress—throughout the first year of the administration of Rutherford B. Hayes, there were brought prominently before the public mind the questions of reconstruction, economic, social, and political, in the North and West as well as in the South. The exploitation of the public domain in the West, the development of transcontinental railroads and other means of communication, the plea for sound money, the economic regeneration of the South, the proper adjustment of the social relations between the two races living in that section, and the readjustment of political control in the former Confederate States were the great issues upon which, during this period, the attention of the nation was focused.

In the solution of some of these problems the Negro was intimately involved. What was to be his place in the scheme of social adjustment in the South? What part was he to play in the economic regeneration of that section? How and to what extent should he maintain the political power delegated to him by the war amendments? Indeed, of utmost importance to the Negro was the proper solution of three perplexing problems: first, to secure to themselves the civil rights so freely exercised by other groups in the nation; second, to obtain national funds to aid education; third, to determine whether their former masters should be relieved of their political disabilities. It was to the solution of these problems, therefore, that the Negro Congressmen of that period especially addressed themselves.

The problem of civil rights, however, did not immediately take precedence. With the passage by Congress, in 1875, of a measure known as the Civil Rights Bill, which was supplementary to measures of the same sort previously enacted, the Negroes of the country were accorded the rights granted by the Constitution to all other citizens of the United States. The subsequent approval of this bill by the president, and the well-known policy toward the Southern States then adopted, served to remove from the fore of American politics the various issues arising from the larger problems of the social and political reconstruction of the South.

Economic questions then had more opportunity for consideration. A new era in the nation's development was ushered in, and with it came new issues and new policies. The question of the exploitation of the public domain in the West and that of transcontinental railway construction had long been before the nation and still remained, but in lieu of the others of the earlier period, there arose also such questions as the free coinage of silver, the bimetallic monetary standard, tariff for protection or for revenue only, and the Chinese immigration. Despite the new character of the great problems before the public forum, and of the consequent relegation to a minor position of national importance the problems of reconstruction in the South, the issues of peculiar interest to the Negro were not so aptly settled. Indeed, it is to the discredit of the Supreme Court of the United States that in all cases coming before that body in which there was at issue a right granted by the Constitution to the freedmen, efforts were made to evade the real issue, or to interpret the laws so as to contravene the intent of the framers of the Constitution.[44] To urge the protection of the Negro in his exercise of the rights and privileges granted by the Constitution, to secure the enactment of laws with the purpose to secure to him a greater measure of opportunity for social advancement, to oppose the enactment of laws proposing to retard such progress, to stimulate a healthy public opinion favorable to the Negro's cause, to protest against every injustice, great or small, meted out to him, became, as never before, the imperative duties of the Negro members of Congress. Whatever other time and energy remained might be directed towards the solution of the other important issues before the public, but for the most part, the Negro Congressmen were of necessity compelled to defend those interests peculiar to the freedmen. The petitions which these Congressmen presented, the resolutions which they offered, the amendments which they proposed, the bills which they introduced or supported, and the issues which they discussed or debated, will enable one to ascertain to what extent these men viewed aright the needs of their constituents and of the nation. Because of the constitutional right of all citizens to petition Congress for a redress of grievances, however, Congressmen have, in general, considered it a duty to present to Congress the petitions of their constituents, whatever their nature may be. An examination of these, therefore, does not always assist in the effort to determine the interests of a statesman. The sole justification for their consideration in this case is the fact that they have formed, in many instances, the basis of the resolutions, motions and bills which were subsequently introduced.

While petitions of varying natures were presented by all of these legislators, three classes, particularly, claimed the attention of practically every one of them. These petitions sought the relief either of an individual or of an institution suffering from some misfortune of the war, made application for a pension, or requested the adjustment of a claim. Of greater significance, however, were the petitions which, while not so generally popular, led often to the introduction of legislative measures. Conspicuous among these were those seeking to remove the political disabilities of former secessionists, those praying that undesirable laws or privileges be abrogated, those advocating the passage of bills, those praying an investigation of the political methods used in certain States, those directing attention to conditions which merited legislative enactment, those praying an appropriation by Congress for the construction of public buildings, the promotion of public works, and the making of local improvements, and those endorsing movements for the good of the body politic.

One of the first problems of reconstruction that claimed the attention of the Negro Congressmen arose from the measures proposing to grant amnesty to the former Confederates who, by a provision of the Fourteenth Amendment to the Constitution of the United States, had been declared ineligible to vote and to hold office. In reference to this matter, Jefferson F. Long, a representative from Georgia to the Forty-first Congress, spoke in a manner reflecting the attitude of many of the Negro Congressmen who were to follow him. His forceful protest maintained that any modification of the test oath as then administered, having the purpose to bring about a general removal of political disabilities, would effect the subjugation of the loyal men of the

South to the disloyal. It would, moreover, appear to the Ku Klux Klan to be an indorsement of their campaign of lawlessness, depredation, and crime, fostered and abetted by the men whose political disabilities it was then being sought to remove.[45]

Speaking on the enforcement act, on which he stated first his own position and later that of the Republican Party in his State, Revels, the Senator from Mississippi, said: "I am in favor of removing the disabilities of those upon whom they are imposed in the South just as fast as they give evidence of having become loyal and of being loyal. If you can find one man in the South who gives evidence of the fact that he has ceased to renounce the laws of Congress as unconstitutional, has ceased to oppose them, and respects them and favors the carrying of them out, I am in favor of removing his disabilities; and if you can find one hundred men that the same is true of, I am in favor of removing their disabilities. If you can find a whole State that this is true of, I am in favor of removing the disabilities of all its people."[46]

Revels at that time had reasonable grounds for supporting amnesty, but conditions soon changed. Speaking in the 42nd Congress as it regarded the enforcement of the 14th Amendment, Rainey felt that too much amnesty had led to the murderous activities of the disloyal after they had reached the point of acquiescing. He said:[47] "If the Constitution which we uphold and support as the fundamental law of the United States is inadequate to afford security to life, liberty, and property—if, I say, this inadequacy is proven, then its work is done, then it should no longer be recognized as the magna charta of a great and free people; the sooner it is set aside the better for the liberties of the nation." Another member of the 42nd Congress, Robert C. De Large of South Carolina, while speaking on the bill for the removal of political disabilities, made it quite clear that he would not support the bill unless the gentlemen for it would support a measure to protect the loyal people of the South.[48]

Notable among the speeches on the question of amnesty was that made by Elliott protesting against a bill to this effect by Beck of Kentucky. Contending that the men now seeking relief were responsible for the crimes perpetrated against the loyal men of the South, Elliott maintained that the passage of the bill would be nothing less than the paying of a premium on disloyalty and treason at the expense of those who had remained loyal. Pointing out the cause of their disfranchisement, he demanded in the name of the "law-abiding people of his constituency, whites as well as Negroes," the rejection of this bill and the protection of those whose "only offense was their adherence to the principles of freedom and justice."[49] That the proposed bill was defeated[50] was perhaps in some measure due to his masterful arraignment of its purposes.

Contemporaneous with the question of amnesty, and lasting throughout the thirty years during which Negroes served in Congress, the problem of securing civil rights for the freedmen or of protecting them in the exercise of such rights demanded, to a greater extent than any other, the energy and efforts of the

Negro Congressmen. Indeed, but few of the men of this group failed during their careers in Congress to register their opinions on this all-absorbing matter.

Remarking at length on the Georgia bill,[51] Senator Revels spoke out fearlessly in the defense of his race. He defended the Negroes against charges of antagonism and servile strife, lauded the conduct of Negro soldiers in the Civil War and the part they played in saving the Union. He called attention to the loyalty of the Negroes in protecting the white women and their homes, with the knowledge that the masters were engaged in the prosecution of a war the success of which would have meant permanent bondage to the blacks. He asserted that the Negroes bore toward their former masters no revengeful thoughts, no hatreds, no animosities. He recounted the iniquities of the bill then before the body, prayed the protection of those whose rights were thereby threatened, and appealed to Congress to give to the reconstructed State such direction and support as would best meet its most imperative needs.

The discussion of the civil rights bill gave rise to one of Robert Brown Elliott's greatest speeches.[52] Arising to defend the bill, he proceeded to refute the proposition advanced by Beck of Kentucky and supported by Stephens of Georgia, that Congress had no power to legislate against a plain discrimination made by State laws or customs against any person or class of persons within its limits. In reference to the decision of the Slaughter House Cases of Louisiana, which the gentlemen had advanced in support of their thesis, Elliott pointed out the difference in principle between the issues there involved and those at hand. In the former case the court held the act in question to be "a legitimate and warrantable exercise of the police power of the State in regulating the business of stock landing and slaughtering in the city of New Orleans and the territory immediately contiguous." In this case, however, the evils complained of comprehended "the exclusion of certain classes of persons from public inns, from the saloons and tables of the steamboat, from the sleeping-cars on railways, and from the right of sepulchre in public burial-grounds."

The Supreme Court, Elliott contended, has recognized two classes of citizenships, state and national, but nowhere is there denied to Congress the power to prevent a denial of equality of rights, whether those rights exist by virtue of citizenship of the United States or of a State. It followed, therefore, that it is within the authority of Congress to see that no State deny to one class of citizens or persons, rights which are common to other citizens, unless it can be shown to be for the good of all, or pursuant to the legitimate exercise of its police power. Rejecting such classification of the case at hand and pointing out from the decision of the Slaughter House Cases the express recognition of Congress to pass such a bill as the one then under discussion, he concluded that the Constitution warranted the passage of the bill, the Supreme Court sanctioned it, and justice demanded it.[53] Elliott submitted also a resolution directing the Judiciary Committee to report a civil rights bill.[54]

The civil rights of the Negroes constituted the general

theme of the remarks made by Alonzo J. Ransier, a representative from South Carolina in the Forty-third Congress. In the first instance he spoke in refutation of the allegements of certain members of the opposition to the effect that the mass of Negroes did not want civil rights. Ransier sought mainly to show, by the presentation[55] of data in form of resolutions from Negro bodies and conventions, the intense desire of the race for civil rights. During the course of these remarks, Ransier served notice of his intention to offer to the civil rights bill an amendment to prevent the disqualification of competent citizens for service as jurors in any court in the nation because of "race, color, or previous condition of servitude." The amendment would provide also for the repeal of all laws, statutes, and ordinances, national or State, which were devised to discriminate against any citizen on account of color by the use of the word "white."[56]

The civil rights of the Negro found nowhere a more ardent champion than James T. Rapier, a representative from Alabama in the Forty-third Congress. In a speech on the measure supplementary to the civil rights bill, Rapier made a lucid analysis of the anomalous position then occupied by the Negro in the United States. Pointing out that Negroes were accorded political rights without the civil, he deplored the whole situation and challenged the truth of the statement that America is the asylum for the oppressed. Averring that the problem was national in scope, he asserted the constitutional authority of Congress to solve it. Denying the contentions of Alexander H. Stephens, of Georgia, Rapier deplored the apparent inability of that gentleman to comprehend the new order ushered in since the formerly sat in Congress. Stephens, he said, maintained the ideals of the old South. Thus, despite the decision of the war that national rights are paramount to those of the States, Stephens urged that it is the prerogative of the States to confer civil rights upon the Negro, and contended that such action should be left to the States. He thereby offered no constitutional objection to the bestowal of civil rights upon the Negro, but advanced a principle, the acceptance of which would forever preclude his enjoying them. To this proposition Rapier could not assent. That the Negro was considered to possess no rights under the Constitution, he maintained, was fully demonstrated by Kentucky and other Southern States, in which they were denied the privilege of testifying in court against a white man, were refused the right to education by the destruction of their schools and the visitation of violence upon their teachers, and were prevented by the Ku Klux Klan from exercising their right of suffrage. Such actions, he insisted, were in conflict with the contention that the States would eventually confer upon Negroes civil rights. In conclusion he declared that the Negro had earned all the rights that he then exercised as well as those enjoyed by other citizens, that the current conditions constituted a stricture on the fair name of America, and that the solution of the problem lay in the immediate passage by Congress of the Civil Rights Bill then being considered.[57]

Not unlike his colleagues, Richard H. Cain, a

representative from South Carolina to the Forty-third and Forty-fifth Congresses, gave to the matter of civil rights much of his time and energy. Replying in part to Vance of North Carolina, Cain denied that the Civil Rights Bill, if passed, would be without the limits of the Constitution or that it would enforce "social equality," maintaining that the regulation of that condition was without the province of legislation. Cain asserted that the Negroes of South Carolina did not enjoy, in public places, all the "rights, privileges and immunities" accorded to other citizens and showed that the admission of Negro students to the University of South Carolina had not effected its destruction. He did not believe that the passage of the bill would alienate from the Negroes the white men of the South who were then friendly to them. Cain reviewed, furthermore, the history of the part played by the Negro in the economic and industrial development of the nation, pointed out the importance of giving to him, in every State, the best possible school facilities, asserted the right of the Negro by statutory enactment to his full civil liberties, and insisted that in the name of justice he should demand for himself all the rights, privileges and immunities accorded to other citizens.[58] Conforming in principle to the doctrine that he had pronounced, Cain introduced before Congress a bill supplementary to the Civil Rights Act.[59]

Much of the energy of James E. O'Hara, a representative from North Carolina, in the Forty-eighth and Forty-ninth Congresses, was directed toward the protection of the Negro in the exercise of his civil rights.[60]

During the course of his remarks on the bill to regulate interstate commerce, he offered an amendment to the effect that any person or persons having purchased a ticket to be conveyed from one State to another, or paid the required fare, should receive the same treatment and be offered equal facilities and accommodation as are furnished all other persons holding tickets of the same class, without discrimination. In support of this amendment, he asserted the constitutional right of Congress to regulate commerce between the States, and that the action contemplated by his amendment came within the scope of this constitutional power. Denying that it was class or race legislation, he maintained that it was in line with the enlightened point of view of the age. The amendment was passed.[61] His opponents, however, were not sufficiently progressive to leave his victory intact.

A defense of the civil rights of the Negro was brought prominently to the fore in the Fifty-first Congress. In his remarks on the affairs of South Carolina,[62] Thomas E. Miller, a representative from that State, declared that the Negroes of South Carolina were suffering from several distinct causes. Among these causes he named lynch law, the petty system of theft which deprived them of the fruits of their daily toil, and injustice in the courts in which they had no rights where their interests and those of the whites conflicted. He demanded for them trial by jury, pay for their work, and the assurance that their lynchers would not become also their legislators. These considerations, he maintained, were of invaluable importance to the country. Miller, furthermore, deplored the action of the Governor of his State, which refused State aid to Negro schools and caused to be closed certain white colleges which had the courage to consider, in a sane way, the so-called Negro problem.

In the Fifty-fifth and Fifty-sixth Congresses, the questions of the protection of the Negroes in the exercise of their civil rights demanded virtually the entire attention of George H. White, who was at that time the sole Negro member of Congress. Among his many protests of discrimination, appeals for just treatment, and discourses on the upright character of his race, there were no speeches more significant nor more prophetic than his arraignment of the apathetic manner with which Congress had greeted his bill, designed "to give to the federal government entire jurisdiction over all cases of lynching and death by mob violence." If, he declared, the nation is to avoid the state of anarchy and moral decay to which conditions were then rapidly leading, there remained no alternative, save the enactment, by some future Congress, of a law to constitute lynching a federal offense.[63]

EDUCATION

Despite the great significance attached by many of the Congressmen to the civil rights of the Negroes, that of the education of the freedman was considered hardly less important. One of the first Negro Congressmen to commit himself on this problem was Rainey of South

Carolina. That he had the proper grasp of the educational needs of his country is shown by his forceful speech made for national aid to education. He contended that the natural result of this mental improvement will be to impart a better understanding of our institutions, and thus cultivate a loyal disposition and lofty appreciation for them. "The military prowess and demonstrated superiority of the Prussians, when compared to the French, especially in the late war [The Franco-Prussian War]," said he, "is attributable to the fact that the masses of the former were better educated and trained than those of the latter. The leavening spirit of the German philosophers has apparently pervaded all classes of the population of that empire."[64]

The same problem of the education of the Negroes evoked from Walls, of Florida, an opinion replete with sound judgment on the matter. Replying to the objection of McIntyre, of Georgia, that the establishment of a national education fund would interfere with States' rights, Walls conceded, first, that the Constitution confers upon the States all those rights neither expressly delegated to the Federal Government nor prohibited to the States, and second, that one of those rights is the power of regulating common schools; but he doubted the applicability of that principle in this instance. The enemies of progress in the South, he maintained, opposed the education of the masses both of Negroes and whites because of its tendency to liberalize these people. He assigned this policy, therefore, as the motive underlying the opposition of McIntyre to the establishment of a national education fund. He rejected the proposition advanced by McIntyre that the $300,000 appropriated by the legislature of Georgia, of which the Negroes are entitled to a portion, would be shared by them. Continuing, Walls pointed out the activities of the Ku Klux Klan, and the burning of Negro homes and of their schools as inconsistent with the contention that they would receive a fair distribution of the school fund. He reviewed, moreover, the history of the free school movement in Florida and Georgia, assigning the cause of its failure. Concluding his speech with a summary arraignment of the policy of that time, he urged not only the establishment of a national education fund but also of a national education system as constituting the sole assured method whereby the poor whites and Negroes of the South might secure proper educational facilities.[65]

Walls, moreover, submitted a resolution calling for a statement relative to the public lands granted for school purposes, and thereafter introduced bills for the purpose of making large grants of the public lands to schools.[66] Contemporary with Walls in the Forty-third Congress, R. H. Cain shared with him great concern over the question of educating the masses. In the Forty-fifth Congress, he proposed a measure,[67] somewhat similar to one previously submitted by Jere Haralson, to establish an educational fund and to apply the proceeds of the public lands to the education of the people.[68]

PROTECTION OF LOYAL CITIZENS

The protection of the loyal people of the South claimed also the attention of Negro Congressmen. When, therefore, the House had under consideration the bill to enforce the 14th Amendment, Robert C. De Large made eloquent remarks replying to Cox of New York, who had denounced the "ignorant" rulers of South Carolina for their "rapacity," which in his opinion justified the activities of the Ku Klux Klan.[69] It was in the defense of the bill for the protection of life and property in the South[70] that Robert B. Elliott had occasion to speak. He showed that the argument upon the pending bill had proceeded upon a question of constitutional law, the opponents denying that its provisions were warranted by the Constitution of the United States, and questioning the data upon which the proposed bill was founded. The probable efficacy of the bill, as a measure of relief and protection for the loyal men of the South from the extraordinary system of oppression to which they were subjected, had not been assailed. Elliott, therefore, undertook to prove that the proposed bill was not obnoxious to the spirit of the Constitution, that it was founded on reason, and that in view of the state of affairs then existing in the South, it was, as a measure of protection, not only warranted, but imperatively demanded.

For his first task, Elliott was compelled to sustain the position that the government of the United States has the right, under the Constitution, to protect a citizen of the United States in the exercise of his vested rights as an

American citizen, by the exercise of direct force, or the assertion of immediate jurisdiction through its courts, without the appeal of the State in which the citizen is domiciled. Asserting the legal maxim that where power is given the means of its execution are implied, he sought to establish that the power had been given by Article IV of the Constitution, which imposes upon the Federal Government the duty to protect the States against domestic violence. He attempted, moreover, to establish by the authority of the preamble to the Constitution the violence of the "presumption that the majority of the people of a State may be oppressively subordinated to the minority." To support his own constructions of the Constitution, Elliott quoted Justice Story on this same issue, pointed out the inconsistencies in the argument of his chief opponent, defined within the meaning of the Constitution a republican form of government and thereafter affirmed that the bill in hand came within the limits of the Constitution.

Elliott had next to establish the validity of the facts upon which the proposed bill was founded. Little difficulty, indeed, was experienced in bringing forward convincing evidence. There were presented before the House numerous editorials from Southern newspapers showing the animus of the enemies of the Negro; the report of the partisan committees of Charleston in 1868; communications appearing in the Newberry, South Carolina, *Herald* of July 17 in 1868; the Ku Klux Klan order appearing in the Charleston *News* of January 31, 1871; and the printed allegements of leading unreconstructed Southerners, all of which tended to indicate to what extent violence had superseded law, and exactly how unsafe were the lives and property of the loyal people of the South. Elliott quite properly affirmed, therefore, the urgent need for the passage of the bill as a measure of relief and protection to those in the South, whose liberties had been assailed.

On the political conditions in the South during the decline of the Reconstruction régime many Congressmen spoke with seeming authority. Two speeches of note on Southern conditions were made, during the Forty-second Congress, by Robert Brown Elliott. On May 30, 1872, he addressed the House on the subject of the Ku Klux Klan. In this speech, he exposed the whole scheme of domination by violence as effected by that element of the Southern whites who would either "rule[71] or ruin the governments of the several States." The second speech followed remarks by Voorhees, of Indiana, on the misconduct in financial matters of the administration of South Carolina. Replying to the specific charge that his party had been guilty of an over-issue of bonds, Elliott reviewed briefly the financial history of his State for the period in question and, in conclusion, pointed out, first, that "in a legal sense an over-issue of bonds is an issue made in excess of such issue authorized by law," and second, that no act of the General Assembly of South Carolina had limited the extent of bonds to be issued in that State.[72]

An unceasing interest in the political conditions of the South was manifested by John R. Lynch of Mississippi throughout his three terms in Congress. He was quite active in proposing legislation relating to the Southern judicial districts of Mississippi, and he offered also an amendment to the federal election laws.[73] Remarks made by him comprehended discussions of such subjects as the political affairs of the South, reconstruction and restoration of white rule in Mississippi, and "the Southern Question."[74] In his analysis of the "Southern Question," Lynch attributed the condition of the South to certain underlying causes, namely: (1) "A continuous and unnecessary opposition of the impracticable element within the ranks of the Democratic Party to the system of reconstruction finally adopted by Congress, and a stubborn refusal on their part to acquiesce in the results of the War"; (2) "the persistent and uncharitable opposition of this same element—the element that had obtained control of the party organization and therefore shaped its policy—to the civil and political rights of Negroes"; and (3) "the methods of the so-called white-league whereby an armed military organization was maintained to effect a condition of white supremacy." Lynch, in concluding, appealed to the fairminded and justice-loving people of America to unite in a common effort to eradicate these evils and secure to the Negroes the rights that they so justly merited.

Referring to the same situation, Charles E. Nash, a representative from Louisiana to the Forty-fourth Congress, held to be unjustified the attacks upon the character of the white men and the integrity and ability of Negroes in the South, who had joined purposes to promote the principles of justice and of sectional harmony. Furthermore, he entered a general denial of the charge that liberty in Louisiana had been destroyed, and pointed out the need of a policy of cooperation between the whites and blacks, to the end that the education of both races might be fostered, that the indiscriminate and illegal killing of Negroes might be eliminated, and that the reign of terror effected by a union of the ruffian whites and ignorant blacks might be prevented. Nash then extolled the record of the party in power for its fairness to the Negro, and arraigned the attitude of the opposition to all measures designed to ameliorate the condition of the race. Concluding his remarks, Nash preached the sound doctrine that sectional animosities should be buried and that all units and sections of the nation should cooperate to the end that a greater, more humane and more powerful America might be evolved.[75]

The most comprehensive remarks of Smalls of South Carolina concerned the electoral vote and the policy of parties in his State.[76] In this he pointed out that ruffians had intimidated the black voters, had driven out the white, and had perpetrated crimes and election frauds to the end that the political control of the State might be recommitted to the hands of reactionaries. Concerning the frauds committed in the election held prior to the Forty-fourth Congress, facts and figures were presented in great detail to verify his contentions.

During his discussion of the proposal to investigate the frauds in the late election in Mississippi, B. K. Bruce, a senator from that State, came fearlessly to the defense of his State government. On this occasion, also, he put into the record valuable statistics showing the progress of the freedmen in Mississippi. The Negroes, he believed, had suffered on account of leadership, but they had, at that time, better leaders who, though not all educated, yet understood the duties of citizenship. Senator Bruce[77] believed that the thing needed was peace and good order at the South, but it could come only by the fullest recognition of the rights of all classes. The opposition would have to concede the necessity of change, not only in the temper, but in the philosophy of their party organization and management. The sober American judgment would have to obtain in the South, as elsewhere in the Republic, since the only distinctions upon which parties can be safely organized in harmony with our institutions, are differences of opinion relative to principles and policy of government; because differences of religion, nationality, race, can neither with safety nor propriety be permitted to enter into the party contests. The unanimity with which the Negro voters acted with a party was not referable to any race prejudice. On the contrary, the Negroes invited the political cooperation of their white brethren, and voted as a unit because proscribed as such. They deprecated the establishment of the color line by the opposition, not only because the act was unwise and wrong in principle, but because it isolated them from the white man of the South and forced them in sheer self-protection and against their inclination to act seemingly upon the basis of race prejudice which they neither respected nor entertained. As a class he believed they were free from prejudices and had no uncharitable suspicions against their white fellow citizens, whether native born or settlers from the Northern States. "When Negroes," continued he, "can entertain opinions and select party affiliations without proscription, and cast their ballots as other citizens and without jeopardy to person or privilege, they can safely afford to be governed by the considerations that ordinarily determine the political actions of American citizens." Senator Bruce asked, therefore, not for new laws, but rather for the enforcement of the old. Peace in the South could come, he believed, only by guaranteeing the protection of the law.

Replying in part to the remarks of Senator Colquitt, from Georgia, Miller, a representative from South Carolina in the Fifty-first Congress, spoke impressively on the subject, "Southern Affairs."[78] The colleague of Miller in this Congress, John M. Langston of Virginia, spoke at great length on the federal election laws, pointing out the need for an adequate legislation and its proper enforcement.[79] He offered, moreover, a measure directing an inquiry relative to the instructions of the Attorney-General concerning elections.

To the bill to repeal all statutes relating to supervisors of elections and special deputy marshals, George W. Murray, a member of the Fifty-third and Fifty-fourth Congresses, took vigorous exception. [80] Asserting that such action would have the effect of promoting the election frauds of the reactionaries in the South, and that already in the States of Louisiana, Mississippi, and South Carolina, a decided minority of the voting population of each Congressional district elected regularly the representative to Congress, he maintained that the present law should not only remain unchanged, but rather, be vigorously enforced. He introduced, moreover, measures designed to assure minority representation in federal elections[81] and to investigate the political conditions in the State of South Carolina.

INTEREST IN ECONOMIC PROBLEMS

Although not equally interesting to the Negro Congressmen as matters of political import, to not a few of them problems essentially economic in character, or at any rate, of economic significance, made a forceful appeal. Measures designed to provide superior facilities for the trade and commerce of their communities constituted, in some instances, the most valuable service rendered by these legislators.

With the interests of his constituency ever in mind, Benjamin S. Turner of Alabama, a member of the Forty-second Congress, proposed various measures to effect local improvements.[82] He urged a distribution of the public lands, proposed a bill to erect a public building in Selma, sought to increase the appropriation for rivers and harbors from $50,000 to $75,000, and made efforts to secure improvements in navigation in Alabama waters.

Of all the Congressmen, Josiah T. Walls of Florida was perhaps the most persistent in the effort to secure improvements for his district and State.[83] He introduced numerous bills to erect in his district custom houses and other public buildings, and to improve the rivers and harbors of his State. Walls introduced also bills to provide a lifesaving station along the coast of Florida, to amend an act granting right of way through public lands for the construction of railroad and telegraph lines through Florida, and to create an additional land district. He sought further to amend an appropriation bill to the end that $50,000 be made available for the establishment of a navy yard at Pensacola.

James T. Rapier, who succeeded Turner in Congress, continued, to some extent, the policy of the latter to secure local improvements.[84] Of two measures introduced by Rapier, one proposed to erect public buildings in his district, the other to make improvements in the rivers and harbors of the State. He succeeded in having enacted into law his measure to constitute Montgomery, Alabama, a port of entry.

The policy of John R. Lynch of Mississippi in the matter of local improvements[85] did not differ materially from that of Rapier. Lynch proposed measures for the construction of the Memphis and New Orleans Railroad, for the construction of public buildings and custom houses, and for the improvement of rivers within the State of Mississippi.

Smalls, of South Carolina, likewise concerned himself with the matter of local improvements.[86] He endeavored to secure an appropriation for the restoration of the Beaufort Library which was destroyed during the War. He proposed measures to establish in his district custom houses, docks, warehouses, a weather observation station, and other public buildings. He was interested also in the redemption of lands held by direct taxes and sought to promote a measure for the construction of telegraph lines in the State. Similarly concerned was James E. O'Hara of North Carolina, whose chief measures for improvements[87] embraced bills to erect public buildings in his district, and to improve the rivers and harbors in his State. Murray, of South Carolina, was some years later advocating the exemption of the Young Men's Christian Association from taxation and the relief of cyclone sufferers in Beaufort, South Carolina.

The Negro Congressman, too, had an interest in the more important economic questions. On the question of the tariff several Congressmen expressed opinions. In the Forty-second Congress, Josiah T. Walls sought to amend the tax and tariff bill relative to certain commodities produced in the State of Florida.[88] He favored a tariff for protection as opposed to one for revenue only. During a similar discussion, in the House, John R. Lynch, a member of the Forty-seventh Congress, urged a protective tariff[89] for cotton, lumber, and sugar. His argument was that the cotton producers of the South were in favor of a protective tariff. When its producing class (meaning labor) was slave, when all of its products were exported, when all of its wants were supplied from without, and when cotton was its only interest, the South favored cheap labor and free trade. At this time, however, labor was free as distinguished from slave, and it therefore added to the cost of production, while jute, sugar, rice, lumber, and manufactures in the embryonic stage, shared with cotton the interests of producers. These changed conditions, he maintained, demanded for the South a policy of reasonable protection.

Regarding protection as a panacea for all the economic ills of the South, Lynch asserted that it would foster the growth of industries, permit the manufacturing interests to develop, and prevent the recurrence of a situation in which the whole output of raw material is shipped to a foreign market and sold at a price fixed by market, whereas goods manufactured from this same raw material are shipped to the South and sold at a price dictated by the sellers. He said, moreover, that a protective tariff would effect a decrease of American imports in cotton goods and at the same time an increase of employment among the folks at home. With reference to tariff on sugar and lumber, Lynch held that the South needed diversified industries, that the investment of capital in the South was essential to a diversification of industries, that a reasonable interest must be guaranteed to attract the capital, and that inasmuch as protection afforded the only way whereby the interest could be assured, protection for these industries was nationally demanded.

Any consideration of the merits of the arguments advanced by Lynch must not overlook the fact that protection has been the policy of the nation during its periods of remarkable growth. Two arguments largely supported this policy. In the first place, it was early conceived that protection was essential to the development of infant industries; in the second, the belief was accepted that to an agricultural country a home market is the only guarantee of a regular market. Because, however, of the unprecedented growth of the country and its final achievement of economic independence, other reasons were sought to support the protective policy. It was contended, therefore, that the high wages paid in the United States would discourage producers from introducing new industries which, without protection, must compete on equal terms with the products of low waged Europe. Finally, it was pointed out that the owners of great wealth must suffer tremendous loss of capital if protection were withdrawn from certain industries, compelling them to compete on equal basis with the industries of like kind of foreign countries.

In addition to these economic arguments, moreover, a political argument was not lacking. Ambitious statesmen have ever dreamed of a policy with which to cement the bonds that unite the different sections of the country, making them mutually dependent and, at the same time, independent of Europe. Protection, it was said, would do this. In full justice to Lynch, therefore, it must be said that his doctrine, whether or not sound, was not without basis. His firm stand for a protective tariff conformed to the policy that has recently controlled in the nation.

Sometime thereafter, White, in the Fifty-fifth Congress, had occasion to speak on the Wilson Tariff Law enacted in 1893. This measure[90] he held to be responsible for the unemployment among mill workers in his community and the loss of contracts by the Southern producers. He advocated, therefore, protection for the industries and labor of America against the pauperism and cheap labor of foreigners.

Several other subjects of economic character were discussed by the Negro Congressmen. During his terms in the Forty-eighth and Forty-ninth Congresses, James E. O'Hara discussed at length the measure on labor arbitration.[91] Shortly thereafter, in the Fifty-first Congress, John M. Langston made informing remarks on the shipping bill.[92] Presenting in support of his position communications from the chambers of commerce of the principal cities of his State urging his support of the pending bill, facts and figures exhibiting recent progressive development of trade in Newport News, and information showing the growing dependence of world trade upon the development of an American merchant marine, he urged the passage of the shipping bill, with legislation to subsidize an American marine that would assist this nation to recover her former position upon the sea. While pointing out causes underlying the decadence of the merchant marine, he enumerated also the conditions which at that time favored its certain development.... He was, therefore, committed to a vigorous prosecution of any constructive plan leading in that direction.

In the Fifty-second Congress, H. P. Cheatham logically discussed the anti-option bill,[93] a measure defining "options" and "futures," imposing special taxes on dealers therein, and requiring such dealers and persons engaged in selling specified products to obtain a license to do so. Speaking in the behalf of the agricultural class of people whom he represented, Cheatham set forth the disastrous economic effects that dealing in "futures" and "options" has always had on the farming class in fixing the price of cotton and other commodities. As a measure contemplating an adjustment of this most portentous evil in the industrial life of the nation, he urged the passage of the bill then under consideration.

RACIAL MEASURES

In the case of some of the Negro Congressmen measures designed either to promote the welfare of their race or to give publicity to its achievement commanded precedence over all others. Many offered petitions and bills providing especially for the benefit of Negroes. Benjamin Turner, of Alabama, secured from the Federal Government several thousands of dollars in payment of a claim for damages to his property during the Civil War. In the Fifty-first Congress, Thomas E. Miller submitted two measures in the interest of his race.[94] The first proposed the establishment of a home for indigent freedmen, and the second sought to authorize the erection of a monument in commemoration of the Negro soldiers who fought for the Union in the Civil War.

The World's Columbian Exposition received much consideration during the first session of the Fifty-second Congress. Henry P. Cheatham,[95] a representative from North Carolina, during the course of his remarks on the Negro race urged that Congress make provisions for exhibiting, at that fair, the facts and statistics of the progress that the Negro had made during his thirty years of freedom. He deplored the fact that "politics" had crept into the amendment designed to effect his purpose and urged its acceptance as a matter of encouragement and justice to a numerically significant group of the American people. Cheatham proposed, also, a measure which sought to have printed the historical record of the Negro troops in the wars in which they had participated.

The welfare of the race was often reflected in the remarks of George W. Murray, a Congressman from South Carolina. When, in the Fifty-third Congress, there arose, in connection with the proposal that federal aid be extended to the Atlanta Exposition,[96] the question of the progress of the Negro race, Murray favored such an exposition because, he declared, it would offer opportunity to have registered the facts and statistics of the Negro's achievement since emancipation. As evidence of the inventive genius of his race, he submitted to Congress at this time a list of patents which had been granted by the government for the inventions of Negroes. Murray spoke briefly of what the Negroes were doing and thinking and, in conclusion, gave to the effort for federal aid his unqualified endorsement.

Measures proposed by George H. White, a representative from North Carolina to the Fifty-fifth and Fifty-sixth Congresses, tended mainly to promote the social welfare of his race.[97] One of these was a resolution for the consideration of a bill to provide a home for aged and infirm Negroes. His other measures of this sort were bills to pay the wages of the Negro Civil War-time employees withheld by the War Department, to incorporate a "National Colored American Association," and to provide for the exhibit of the educational and industrial progress of the Negro at the Paris Exposition of 1900. Few measures of this type could become law.

VARIOUS INTERESTS

Many problems miscellaneous in character interested the Negro Congressmen. Indeed, early in the Forty-second Congress, Josiah T. Walls[98] supported a measure which proposed to appropriate $3,000,000 to aid the centennial celebration and international exhibition of 1876. Sometime later, moreover, he urged the recognition of the belligerent rights of Cuba. In the Forty-fourth Congress, John A. Hyman, of North Carolina, offered a measure to provide relief for the Cherokee Indians, who had returned to the "Nation West"[99] while the measures of his colleague, Jere Haralson[100] of Alabama, comprised such objects as the amendment of the revised statutes of the United States, the relief of the Medical College of Alabama, and the payment of war claims. During his three terms in Congress, John R. Lynch maintained interest in a wide range of subjects. He spoke at length on a bill "to provide and regulate the counting of votes for President and Vice President and the decision in the disputed election of R. B. Hayes.[101] He opposed the bill to repeal the act providing for the pay of Congressmen,[102] but supported a measure to appropriate funds for the establishment of a national board of health.[103]

In the Forty-fifth Congress, R. H. Cain proposed a measure to establish a line of mail and emigrant steam and sailing vessels between certain ports of the United States and Liberia.[104] His colleague, Robert Smalls, was a man of wider interests.[105] Among his various remarks, there must be noted those on the District of Columbia liquor traffic, interstate commerce, and the army reorganization bill. In the latter instance, he attempted to have inserted into the bill an amendment providing for the merging of enlisted men into military units without distinction as to race or color.

In the Senate, B. K. Bruce was afforded opportunity to debate the issues of the day. While most active in offering bills and resolutions, he nevertheless spoke forcefully on several matters of greater than ordinary import. He spoke out fearlessly against the bill restricting Chinese immigration,[106] and while discussing the Indian bill,[107] he took high ground, showing that we had failed in our selfish policy toward the Indian—a policy by which the breeding of hatred and discontent had kept him a fugitive and a vagabond—and emphasized the necessity for the government to do something to civilize the Indian. There must be a change in the Indian policy "if they are to be civilized," said he, "in that the best elements of their natures are to be developed to the exercise of their best functions, so as to produce individual character and social groups characteristic of enlightened people; if this is to be done under our system, its ultimate realization requires an adoption of a political philosophy that shall make the Indians, as individuals and as a tribe, subjects of American law and beneficiaries of American institutions, by making them first American citizens, and clothing them as rapidly as their advancement and location will permit, with the protecting and ennobling prerogatives of such friendship."

In support of his resolution, proposing to admit as a Senator from Louisiana P. B. S. Pinchback, Mr. Bruce spoke out, cogently presenting the facts as he saw them, contending that the gentleman had been regularly elected and that the National Government would, by declaring his election irregular and not expressive of the will of the people, repudiate the very government that it had recognized.[108] Pinchback was not seated, but the records show that his title was as sound as that of scores of senators whose right has never been questioned.

B. K. Bruce had another good claim to statesmanship. During his incumbency in Congress the question of the improvement of the navigation of the Mississippi and the protection of life and property from the periodical inundations of that stream was of much concern to the whole country. As a spokesman for the State of Mississippi and a statesman seeking to provide facilities for interstate and foreign commerce, B. K. Bruce fearlessly advocated that the Federal Government should appropriate funds to undertake this improvement. He repeatedly offered bills and amendments to this end and endeavored to secure the support of the leaders of Congress to pilot these measures through that body. While the results which Senator Bruce obtained were not proportionate to the effort which he made, he paved the way for other promoters of this enterprise, who have been more successful. Subsequent history shows the importance of this national task and demonstrates the statesmanlike foresight of Senator Bruce in championing its cause.[109]

General remarks by James E. O'Hara comprehended discussion of the bills on oleomargarine and the payment of pensions.[110] Towards the former he was opposed, while in the latter he urged that white persons and Negroes be paid according to the same standard. George H. White sought to amend the bill to provide a government for Hawaii.[111] He gave some attention also to the debate on the civil service law.[112] Concerning it he held that the administration of the law had been subversive of the principles of appointment by merit. Indeed, in his opinion, its failure warranted either a return to the spoils system or the adoption of a new policy, by which there would be established in each department of the government a bureau with the duty of determining the fitness of each applicant for a position in that department.

A Critical Survey

It appears, then, these two general types of legislation, the one proposing local improvements, the other seeking social justice for the Negro race, were preeminent in the measures proposed by the Negro Congressmen. On the other hand, however, most of these measures, regardless of merit, met in general one of three fates: they were either sidetracked in committee, reported adversely, or defeated after debate in open session.

The character of measures proposed by these Congressmen has been the subject of much adverse criticism. Not a few persons have considered as weakness the tendency to propose measures relating to local improvements, and those racial rather than national in character. The records of Congress show, however, that the motives impelling the Negro Congressmen to propose the type of legislation stated differed in no wise from those underlying similar actions of other Congressmen. Discussing the service of Congress, Mr. Munro, in his *Government of the United States*, says: "First among the merits of congressional government as it has existed in the United States for over one hundred and thirty years, is the fidelity with which law-making has reflected the public opinion of the country."[113] Mr. Munro further says that while Congress has not always been immediately responsive to popular sentiment, it has seldom failed to act when there has come to it an "audible mandate" from the whole country.

If, therefore, the Congress as a whole must be somewhat immediately responsive to the expressed public will, what, indeed, is the precise course of action that a representative, as a matter of policy, must pursue?

He is regarded, in the first instance, as representing not his State, but rather a particular Congressional district of his State. His tenure of office runs for but two years, at the expiration of which he must submit to his constituents not a record of constructive statesmanship, based upon his fealty to measures of national or international importance, but rather one alleging the skill with which he has protected the peculiar interests of his district. That he has sought to obtain a new customs house, has opposed a tariff for revenue only, has defended the principle of bimetallism, not indeed in relation to the wider demands of the nation, but because of the particular demands of his constituency, are matters of great practical import to him, for upon these depends the approval or the rejection of his record. The Congressman who aspires to longevity of service is apt, therefore, to determine his proposal and defense of measures of legislation largely, if not wholly, by the expressed opinion of those whom he represents. Regarding the Negro Congressmen, therefore, in the light of the practices common to all Congressmen, there can be offered no valid criticism of the character of their legislation. The records of Congress show that these functionaries were, as a matter of policy, interested in their constituents, and that they promoted legislation for general advancement for the reason that the circumstances of the people whom they represented warranted legislation of that sort.

For the tendency of some of the Negro Congressmen to propose legislative measures which were racial in character, two reasons are conspicuously obvious. In the first place, these men regarded themselves the official spokesmen of their race. The power conferred upon them they believed to be evidence of the expectation and confidence of the Negroes in them to secure for the race civil rights, economic opportunity and political preferment. They found, moreover, that legislation granting to Negroes their civil rights failed often to protect them in the exercise of those rights. For such protection, then, these Congressmen had often to contend. These personal, ever present, inherent duties permitted these Congressmen neither time nor energy for the preparation of legislative measures of other types.

Another reason for restricting their efforts to local measures or those peculiar to their race was the rule of politics that all honor for the formulation of national measures must attach to the seasoned veterans in Congress. This custom has become so well established as to be traditional. It could not have been expected that the Negro members, then, should take the lead in Congressional legislation. They faithfully cooperated with the leaders of Congress and generally voted for measures considered productive of the greatest good of the country.

Why did the Negro Congressmen fail to have their measures enacted into law? The path of a bill is fraught with difficulties. The well-known journey through the committee, through both houses of Congress, to the conference and to the President, but few bills complete. Many bills of the Negro Congressmen died of this natural cause. Others because of lack of merit were reported adversely from committee; still others reported favorably could not withstand the Congressional debate. A few that survived the whole ordeal became laws.

There were two preeminent causes for the failure of some of these bills. The Negro membership in any Congress, in the first place always an exceedingly small minority, was never a determining factor in the passage of a measure proposed by one of this particular group. Secondly, the objects of the suspicion of their party colleagues,[114] and regarded by them as an experiment in the legislative program of the nation, these men were not generally able to secure for their measures sufficient white Republican votes. Considered from this point of view, the failure of these measures is in no wise an evidence of the lack of ability and statesmanship.

Of them, James G. Blaine, a Republican leader of fifty years ago, has spoken in a most praiseworthy manner. Conceding the right of the Negroes to sit in Congress and attesting the success of their activities there, he asserted that "they were as a rule studious, earnest, ambitious men, whose public conduct—as illustrated by Mr. Revels and Mr. Bruce in the Senate, and by Mr. Rapier, Mr. Lynch and Mr. Rainey in the House—would be honorable to any race."[115]

ALRUTHEUS A. TAYLOR

FOOTNOTES:

[1] Jefferson F. Long was born in Crawford County, Georgia, March 3, 1836. Some time thereafter he moved to Macon, Bibb County, where, under the direction of his owner, he learned the tailor's trade. Prior to his election to the third session of the Forty-first Congress, Mr. Long conducted, in Macon, a thriving business as a merchant tailor. His patronage, which consisted largely of that of whites, was much decreased after his term in Congress, due no doubt to their resentment of his activities in politics. Mr. Long was a good speaker, a Christian gentleman, and a man of many fine qualities. Upon his death in Macon, February 4, 1900, his loss was mourned alike by whites and Negroes.—Chaplain T. G. Stewart, *Fifty Years in the Gospel Ministry*, p. 129.

Letter from Mrs. A. L. Rucker, Atlanta, Ga., daughter of Mr. Long. October, 1921.

[2] Robert C. DeLarge was born at Aiken, South Carolina, March 15, 1842. He received only a limited education and chose to pursue the occupation of farming. He entered politics in 1868, held several local and State offices, was elected to the Forty-second Congress, and on February 15, 1874, became a trial justice at Charleston.—*Biographical Congressional Directory*, p. 497.

[3] Joseph H. Rainey was born of slave parents at Georgetown, S. C., June 21, 1832. He received a limited education. After following the trade of a barber, he was compelled, in 1862, to work on Confederate

fortifications. From this work he escaped, going to the West Indies, where he remained till the end of the war. Upon his return to the United States, he entered politics. He served in the 42nd, 43rd, 44th, and 45th Congresses, and died at Georgetown, S. C., August 1, 1887.—*Biographical Congressional Directory*, p. 757.

[4] Alonzo J. Ransier was born at Charleston, South Carolina, January 3, 1836. He received a limited education, entered politics, and held various offices. In 1868, he was a presidential elector, casting a vote for Grant and Colfax, while four years later he was a delegate to the Republican National Convention. He served as a member of the 42nd Congress and died at Charleston, S. C., August 17, 1882.—*Biographical Congressional Directory*, p. 759.

[5] Robert Smalls was born a slave at Beaufort, South Carolina, April 5, 1839. Debarred by statute from attending school, he availed himself of such limited educational advantages as he could secure. In 1851, he moved to Charleston, worked as a rigger, and thereafter led a seafaring life. In 1861, he became connected with the *Planter*, a steamer plying in the Charleston Harbor as a transport, which he took over the Charleston bar in 1862 and delivered with his services to the commander of the United States blockading squadron. He was appointed a pilot in the Quartermaster's Department of the United States Navy, and remained in the service till 1866, and meanwhile rose to the rank of Captain. In 1868 he entered politics and was later elected to the 44th, 45th, 47th, 48th, and 49th Congresses. In the State militia of South Carolina, he held successively the

commands of lieutenant-colonel, brigadier-general, and major-general, the latter terminating with the reorganization of the militia in 1877. Mr. Smalls was a delegate to several National Republican Conventions. His last public office was that of collector of the port of Beaufort.—*Biographical Congressional Directory*, p. 803.

[6] John R. Lynch of Natchez, Mississippi, was born in Concordia Parish, Louisiana, September 10, 1847. He attended evening school at Natchez for a few months, and by private study acquired a good English education. He engaged in the business of photography at Natchez until 1869, when Governor Ames appointed him a justice of the peace. Mr. Lynch served in the 43rd, 44th, and 47th Congresses, and was elected to the 45th Congress, but was counted out. Later he served as Fourth Auditor of Treasury Department under President Harrison, and as a paymaster in the Volunteer Army during the Spanish-American War.—*Biographical Congressional Directory*, p. 662.

[7] Blanche K. Bruce of Floreyville, Mississippi, was born in Prince Edward County, Virginia, March 1, 1841. A man of limited education, he became, in 1869, a planter in Mississippi. Later he became a member of the Mississippi levee board, served in several local offices, and finally was elected, in 1875, to the United States Senate where he served till 1881. Mr. Bruce died at Washington, D. C., March 17, 1898.—*Biographical Congressional Directory*, p. 420.

[8] Jore Haralson was born a slave in Muscogee County, Georgia, April 1, 1846. He was emancipated in 1865,

after which he acquired through self-instruction a fair education. After moving to Alabama, he entered into the politics of that State. Mr. Haralson was elected to the 44th Congress, but failed of re-election to the 45th.—*Biographical Congressional Directory*, p. 557.

[9] Benjamin Sterling Turner was born a slave at Halifax, North Carolina, March 17, 1825. In 1830, he moved to Alabama, where by clandestine study he obtained a fair education. He became a prosperous merchant, was elected to several local offices, and to the 42nd Congress. He was defeated for the 43rd.—*Biographical Congressional Directory*, p. 849.

[10] John Adams Hyman was born a slave in Warren, North Carolina, July 23, 1840. He was sold and sent to Alabama, where he was emancipated in 1865. Returning to North Carolina, Mr. Hyman engaged in farming and acquired a rudimentary education. Entering politics in 1868, he was later elected to the 44th Congress. In June, 1877, he was appointed collector of internal revenue for the 2nd district of North Carolina.—*Biographical Congressional Directory*, p. 614.

[11] Charles E. Nash was a native of Opelousas, Louisiana. He was educated at New Orleans, later following the trade of bricklayer. In 1863, Mr. Nash served as a private in the Eighty-third Regiment United States Chasseurs d'Afrique. He was later promoted to sergeant-major and lost a leg in the storming of Fort Blakeley. He was elected to the 44th Congress, but defeated for the 45th.—*Biographical Congressional Directory*, p. 713.

[12] Josiah T. Walls was born at Winchester, Virginia,

December 30, 1842. He received a limited education, became a farmer, and in 1868 entered politics. Mr. Walls received a certificate of election as a representative from Florida to the 42nd Congress, but his seat was successfully contested by Silas Niblack. He was admitted, however, to the 43rd and 44th Congresses.—*Biographical Congressional Directory*, p. 864.

[13] Richard H. Cain was born in Greenbrier County, Virginia, April 12, 1825. In 1831, he moved with his father to Gallipolis, Ohio. Of limited education prior to his marriage, and having entered the ministry at an early age, he found it to his advantage, at the age of 35 years, to undertake formal study at a recognized school of learning. Following a career as clergyman, missionary, and politician, he was elected to the 43rd Congress and re-elected to the 45th. After his retirement from Congress, Mr. Cain, was elected the fourteenth bishop of the African Methodist Episcopal Church. He died in Washington, January 18, 1887. — *Biographical Congressional Directory*, p. 434.

[14] Hiram B. Revels was born at Fayetteville, North Carolina, September 1, 1822. Being unable to obtain an education in his own State, he moved to Indiana and there began study for the ministry. At the outbreak of the Civil War, Mr. Revels assisted in the organization of the first two Negro regiments in Maryland. Having made a record for service among his people in the central States, he went to Mississippi and there became interested in managing the freedmen's affairs. He was elected to several local offices and in 1870 was elected to fill an unexpired term in the United States Senate. After

his retirement from Congress, Mr. Revels served as president of Alcorn University at Rodney, Mississippi, and later as pastor of the African Methodist Episcopal Church at Richmond, Indiana. He died January 16, 1901, at Abeerden, Mississippi.—*Biographical Congressional Directory*, p. 763.

[15] Henry Plummer Cheatham of Henderson, North Carolina, was born at Granville, North Carolina, December 27, 1857. After acquiring a good education, he entered the teaching profession. Later he became interested in politics and was elected to the 51st and 52nd Congresses. His last public office was that of Recorder of Deeds of the District of Columbia.—*Biographical Congressional Directory*, p. 450.

[16] George Washington Murray was born of slave parents, September 22, 1853, near Rembert, Sumter County, South Carolina. At the age of eleven years, he found himself free, bereft of parents, completely dependent upon his own resources. His early life, therefore, was one of great trials and sacrifices. Possessed, however, of a determination to live and learn, young Murray availed himself of every opportunity to improve his meagre stock of knowledge. So well did he succeed that his first day in school was spent as teacher rather than student. In later life, he acquired a good education, entered into the service of the public schools of his county and was finally elected to the 53rd Congress. Mr. Murray was elected also to the 54th, but secured his seat only after a successful contest with a leading Democrat of his State.—*Biographical Congressional Directory*, pp. 711-712.

[17] John Mercer Langston was born in Louisa County, Virginia, December 14, 1829. He distinguished himself as an educator and won many honors in his field. Mr. Langston served also in many civic and political offices prior to his election to the 51st Congress. Due to the contest he was forced to make for his seat, Mr. Langston served actually a very short time in Congress. He died in Washington, D. C., November 15, 1897.—*Biographical Congressional Directory*, p. 643.

[18] Robert Brown Elliott was born in Boston, Massachusetts, August 11, 1842. He was educated in England, and upon his return to the United States entered into the politics of the State of South Carolina. Mr. Elliott was elected to the 42nd Congress and resigned before the term had expired; he was re-elected to the 43rd Congress and again resigned, this time to accept the office of sheriff.—*Biographical Congressional Directory*, p. 517.

[19] James T. Rapier was born at Florence, Alabama, in 1840. He was sent to Canada to be educated, and while there was given the opportunity to recite before the late King Edward VII, then Prince of Wales, who was at that time visiting the United States and Canada. Prior to his election to Congress, Mr. Rapier held several local offices in Alabama and also aspired to become Secretary-of-State. In this contest he was defeated by one Nicholas Davis, a white man. Mr. Rapier was a partisan in the split in the Republican Party in his State, aligning himself with one Spencer, a Republican leader of that date. Losing in this contest, he lost also his ability to win votes and so was defeated in his attempt

to seek re-election to the 44th Congress. Soon thereafter, Mr. Rapier gave his attention to farming and was highly successful as a cotton planter.—*Biographical Congressional Directory*, p. 760, and a statement of Thomas Walker, a local officer in Alabama during the reconstruction period.

[20] James E. O'Hara of Enfield, North Carolina, was born in New York City, February 26, 1844. He acquired a liberal education, read law, and entered into the politics of the State of North Carolina. After holding several local offices, he was elected to the 46th, 48th, and 49th Congresses, but was counted out in the former.—*Biographical Congressional Directory*, p. 722.

[21] Thomas E. Miller was born in Beaufort County, South Carolina, at Ferrybeeville, June 17, 1849. After acquiring a good education, he entered politics. Mr. Miller held many local and State offices, and was nominated by his party, in 1878, for the office of Lieutenant-Governor of the State. Due, however, to riotous actions of the Democratic party throughout the elections that year, the ticket was withdrawn. Mr. Miller was seated in the 51st Congress after a contested election with Col. William Elliott. In 1896, he was elected president of the State Colored College at Orangeburg, South Carolina.—*Biographical Congressional Directory*, p. 695.

[22] George Henry White of Tarboro, North Carolina, was born at Rosindale, North Carolina, December 18, 1852. He acquired a good education, practiced law, and entered politics. After serving in several local and State offices, Mr. White was elected to the 55th

and re-elected to the 56th Congress.—*Biographical Congressional Directory*, p. 877.

[23] Biographical Congressional Directory, p. 643.

[24] Ibid., p. 614.

[25] Ibid., p. 722.

[26] Ibid., p. 450.

[27] Ibid., p. 877.

[28] Biographical Congressional Directory, p. 434.

[29] Ibid., p. 497.

[30] Ibid., p. 517.

[31] Ibid., p. 757.

[32] Ibid., p. 759.

[33] Ibid., p. 803.

[34] Ibid., p. 695.

[35] Ibid., pp. 711–712.

[36] Letter from Mrs. A. L. Rucker, Atlanta, Ga., daughter of J. F. Long, Oct., 1921.

[37] Statement of Thomas Walker, Washington, D. C., a local officer in Alabama, during the Reconstruction Period.

[38] Statement made by Thomas Walker.

[39] Biographical Congressional Directory, p. 577.

[40] *Ibid.*, p. 763.

[41] *Ibid.*, p. 420.

[42] *Ibid.*, p. 662.

[43] *Ibid.*, p. 713.

[44] C. G. Woodson, *Fifty Years of Negro Citizenship*, JOURNAL OF NEGRO HISTORY, Vol. VI, p. 11.

[45] *Congressional Globe*, 41st Congress, 3rd Session, p. 881.

[46] "In regard to the State of Mississippi," continued Senator Revels, "I have this to say: The Republican Party now dominating there pledged itself to universal amnesty. That was in their platform; these speakers pledged themselves to it and the legislature redeemed that pledge, unanimously adopting a resolution asking Congress to remove the political disabilities of all the citizens of Mississippi, which resolution they placed in my hands, and made it my duty to present here, and which I have presented.

"Now I can say more, I believe, for the State of Mississippi, than I can say for any other of the lately insurrectionary States. I do not know of one State that is altogether as well reconstructed as Mississippi is. We have reports of a great many other States of lawlessness and violence, and from parts of States we have well-authenticated reports of this effect; but while this is the case, do you hear one report of any more lawlessness in evidence in the State of Mississippi? No! The people now I believe are getting along as quietly, pleasantly, harmoniously, prosperously as the people are in any of the formerly free States. I think this is the case, I do not think my statement exaggerates anything at all. Now, sir, I hope that I am understood. I am in favor of amnesty in Mississippi. We pledged ourselves to it. The State is for it."—*Congressional Globe*, 41st Congress, 2nd Session, p. 3520.

[47] *Ibid.*, 42nd Congress, 1st Session, p. 393.

[48] *Congressional Globe*, 42nd Congress, 2nd Session, p. 103.

[49] *Ibid.*, 42nd Congress, 1st Session, pp. 102-103.

[50] *Ibid.*, 102-103.

[51] *Congressional Globe*, 41st Congress, 2nd Session, p. 1287.

[52] *Congressional Record*, 43rd Congress, 1st Session, pp. 407-410.

[53] *Congressional Record*, 43rd Congress, 1st Session, pp. 407-410.

[54] *Congressional Globe*, 42nd Congress, 2nd Session, p. 3383.

[55] *Congressional Record*, 43rd Congress, 1st Session, pp. 1311-1314.

[56] *Ibid.*, p. 407.

[57] *Congressional Record, pp. 4782-4786.*

[58] *Ibid.*, pp. 565-567.

[59] *Ibid.*, p. 64.

[60] *Ibid.*, p. 64.

[61] *Congressional Record*, 48th Congress, 2nd Session, p. 297.

[62] *Ibid.*, 51st Congress, 2nd Session, p. 1216.

[63] *Congressional Record*, 56th Congress, 2nd Session, p. 1634.

[64] *Congressional Globe*, 42nd Congress, 2nd Session, p. 813; App., p. 15.

[65] Congressional Globe, pp. 808–810.

[66] *Ibid.*, 42nd Congress, 1st Session, p. 3655; 3rd Session, p. 220. *Congressional Record*, 43rd Congress, 1st Session, pp. 87, 88.

[67] *Congressional Record*, 45th Congress, 2nd Session, p. 1646; 44th Congress, 1st Session, pp. 2714, 3602.

[68] At a later date, Langston, in the Fifty-first Congress, introduced a measure for the establishment of normal and industrial schools for Negroes. These numerous measures were referred invariably to the Committee on Education and Labor, from which they were usually reported adversely to the House.—*Congressional Record*, 51st Congress, 2nd Session, p. 1650.

[69] In placing the responsibility with both parties, DeLarge said: "Mr. Speaker, when the governor of my State the other day called in council the leading men of the State, to consider the condition of affairs there

and to advise what measures would be best for the protection of the people, whom did he call together? The major portion of the men whom he convened were men resting under political disabilities imposed by the Fourteenth Amendment. In good faith, I ask the gentlemen on this side of the House, and gentlemen on the other side of the House, whether it is reasonable to expect that those men should be interested, in any shape or form, in using their influence and best endeavor for the preservation of the public peace when they have nothing to look for politically in the future? You say that they should have the moral and material interest of their State at heart, though even always denied a participation in its honors. You may insist that the true patriot seeks no personal ends in acts of patriotism. All this is true, but, Mr. Speaker, men are but men everywhere, and you ought not to expect of those whom you daily call by opprobrious epithets, whom you daily remind of their political sins, whom you persistently exclude from places of the smallest trust in the government you have created, to be very earnest to cooperate with you in the work of establishing and fortifying the government set up in hostility to the whole tone of their prejudices, their connections, and their sympathies. What ought to be is one thing; what in the weakness and fallibility of human nature will be is quite another thing. The statesman regards the actual and acts upon it; the desirable, the possible, and even the probable furnishes but poor basis for political action."—*Congressional Globe*, 42nd Congress, 1st Session, App., pp. 230-231.

[70] *Ibid.*, 42nd Congress, 1st Session, p. 376.

[71] *Congressional Globe*, 42nd Congress, 3rd Session, p. 4039.

[72] *Congressional Globe*, 42nd Congress, 3rd Session, App., p. 475.

[73] *Congressional Record*, 43rd Congress, 1st Session, p. 1121; 44th Congress, 1st Session, p. 206; 47th Congress, 1st Session, p. 3946.

[74] *Ibid.*, 44th Congress, 1st Session, pp. 3825-3826; 3781-3784; 5540-5543.

[75] *Congressional Record*, pp. 3667, 3668, 3669.

[76] *Ibid.*, 44th Congress, 2nd Session, App., pp. 123-136.

[77] *Ibid.*, 44th Congress, 1st Session, pp. 2100-2105.

[78] Miller pointed out the inherent weaknesses of the South, the insecurity of investment, violation of the right of property and of contract, the jeopardy of life, and over-assessment of taxes on property held by Northern Whites—as constituting the causes underlying the failure of investors to direct their monies to Southern enterprises. He discussed the amenability of the Negro to civilizing influences and the economic progress that the race had made since its emancipation from slavery. Miller asserted, moreover, that though these remarks might effect the loss of his seat in the next Congress, he conceived it his duty to his party and to his race to defend his people against the dastardly attack of one

who pretended to be its friend. *Congressional Record*, 51st Congress, 2nd Session, p. 2691.

[79] *Ibid.*, pp. 1479-1482; 1524.

[80] *Ibid.*, 53rd Congress, 1st Session, pp. 2158-2161.

[81] *Ibid.*, 54th Congress, 1st Session, p. 1868; 2nd Session, p. 320.

[82] *Congressional Globe*, 42nd Congress, 2nd Session, pp. 393, 2439, 2447, 2452.

[83] *Ibid.*, 42nd Congress, 1st Session, pp. 198, 178, 3793; 3rd Session, p. 220; 43rd Congress, 1st Session, pp. 87, 88.

[84] *Ibid.*, 43rd Congress, 1st Session, pp. 85, 320, 1333.

[85] *Congressional Globe*, 44th Congress, 1st Session, pp. 321, 1203; 47th Congress, 1st Session, pp. 4551, 6146.

[86] *Ibid.*, 44th Congress, 1st Session, pp. 442, 3754, 4857; 45th Congress, 2nd Session, p. 2706; 47th Congress, 1st Session, p. 6432; 49th Congress, 1st Session, p. 1218.

[87] *Ibid.*, 49th Congress, 1st Session, pp. 437, 1404, 3748, 4980, 4982, 5069.

[88] *Congressional Globe*, 42nd Congress, 1st Session, p. 3570.

[89] *Congressional Record*, 47th Congress, 2nd Session, pp. 2312, 2660, 2870-2871.

[90] *Congressional Record*, 55th Congress, 1st Session, p. 550.

[91] *Ibid.*, 49th Congress, 1st Session, p. 3049.

[92] *Congressional Record*, 51st Congress, 2nd Session, p. 3490.

[93] *Ibid.*, 52nd Congress, 1st Session, App., p. 508.

[94] *Congressional Record*, 51st Congress, 1st Session, pp. 10,707, 10,708.

[95] *Ibid.*, 52nd Congress, 2nd Session, pp. 4695, 5974.

[96] *Ibid.*, 53rd Congress, 2nd Session, p. 8382.

[97] *Congressional Record*, 56th Congress, 1st Session, pp. 166, 372, 594, 791; 2nd Session, p. 188; 55th Congress, 2nd Session, p. 3153.

[98] *Ibid.*, 43rd Congress, 1st Session, App., p. 250; pp. 27, 206. *Congressional Globe*, 42nd Congress, 1st Session, pp. 198, 178.

[99] *Congressional Record*, 44th Congress, 1st Session, p. 3340.

[100] *Ibid.*, 44th Congress, 1st Session, pp. 771, 2714, 2791.

[101] *Congressional Record*, 44th Congress, 2nd Session, pp. 1025-1026.

[102] *Congressional Record*, 44th Congress, 1st Session, pp. 118, 119.

[103] *Ibid.*, 47th Congress, 1st Session, p. 6898.

[104] *Ibid.*, 45th Congress, 2nd Session, p. 1646.

[105] *Ibid.*, 44th Congress, 1st Session, pp. 3457, 3467, 3468; 48th Congress, 2nd Session, pp. 316, 2057; 49th Congress, 1st Session, p. 1919.

[106] *Ibid.*, 45th Congress, 3rd Session, p. 1914.

[107] *Ibid.*, 46th Congress, 2nd Session, pp. 2195-2196.

[108] *Congressional Record*, 44th Congress, 1st Session, pp. 1444, 1445.

[109] *Congressional Record*, 45th Congress, 1st Session, pp. 245, 1750; 3rd Session, 1314, 1316, 2309.

[110] *Ibid.*, 53rd Congress, 2nd Session, p. 2399; 1st Session, pp. 1392, 1396.

[111] *Ibid.*, 56th Congress, 2nd Session, p. 3814.

[112] *Ibid.*, 55th Congress, 2nd Session, p. 541.

[113] *Munro, The Government of the United States, p. 297.*

[114] A Letter from John E. Bruce, Brooklyn, N. N., a man active during the Reconstruction. June 6, 1921.

[115] James G. Blaine, *Twenty Years of Congress, 1861-1881*, Vol. II, p. 515.

THE PRIORITY OF THE SILVER BLUFF CHURCH AND ITS PROMOTERS

In speaking of the beginning of Negro churches in the United States, those of the Baptist faith must not be forgotten. Nor must we err in thinking that the first churches of this faith were planted in the North. It is true that there were Negro Baptists in Providence, Rhode Island, as early as 1774,[1] and doubtless much earlier, but they had no church of their own. Indeed, there is absolutely no trace of Negro Baptist churches in the North prior to the nineteenth century. The oldest Negro Baptist churches, north of Mason and Dixon's Line, are the Independent or First African Baptist Church, of Boston, Massachusetts, planted in 1805; the Abysinnian, of New York City, established in 1808; and the First African, of Philadelphia, Pennsylvania, organized in 1809.[2]

Negro Baptist churches, unlike other Negro churches, had their beginning in the South, and at a somewhat earlier date. The first church of Negro Baptists, so far as authentic and trustworthy writings of the eighteenth century establish, was constituted at Silver Bluff,[3] on Mr. Galphin's[4] estate, a year or two before the Revolutionary War. It continued to worship there, in comparative peace, until the latter part of 1778, when the vicissitudes of war drove the church into exile[5]—but only to multiply itself elsewhere.[6] The work at Silver Bluff began anew with the cessation of hostilities, moreover, and was more prosperous than ever in 1791.[7]

Silver Bluff was situated on the South Carolina side of the Savannah River, in Aiken County, just twelve miles from Augusta, Georgia.[8] All there was of it, in September, 1775, seems to have been embraced in what William Tennett, of Revolutionary fame, styled "Mr. Galphin's Settlement."[9] Nevertheless, as it lay in the tract of the Revolutionary forces, and was for a time a center of supplies to the Indians, who had their habitation in that quarter, living in treaty relations with the colonists, Ramsey, Carroll, Drayton,[10] and others, give it a place on the map of South Carolina. Indeed, so identified was Silver Bluff with the Galphins, their interests and their influence, that by 1785 it was known far and near as Galphinton. Fort Galphin was there. Bartram, who visited it in 1776, says that Silver Bluff was "a very celebrated place," and describes it as "a beautiful villa," while the picture which Jones, in his history of South Carolina, gives of Silver Bluff, is animating, to say the least.[11]

David George, who was one of the constituent members, and the first regular pastor of the Silver Bluff Church, is our authority in regard to the early history of this flock. We make the following extracts from letters of his, published in London, England, in connection with other foreign correspondence, during the period from 1790 to 1793:

Brother Palmer,[12] who was pastor at some distance from Silver Bluff, came and preached to a large congregation at a mill of Mr. Galphin's; he was a very powerful preacher.... Brother Palmer came again and wished us to beg Master to let him preach to us; and he came frequently.... There were eight of us now, who had found the great blessing and mercy from the Lord, and my wife was one of them, and Brother Jesse Galphin.... Brother Palmer appointed Saturday evening to hear what the Lord had done for us, and next day, he baptized us in the mill stream.... Brother Palmer formed us into a church, and gave us the Lord's Supper at Silver Bluff.... Then I began to exhort in the Church, and learned to sing hymns.... Afterwards the church advised with Brother Palmer about my speaking to them, and keeping them together.... So I was appointed to the office of an elder, and received instruction from Brother Palmer how to conduct myself. I proceeded in this way till the American War was coming on, when the Ministers were not allowed to come amongst us, lest they should furnish us with too much knowledge.... I continued preaching at Silver Bluff, till the church, constituted with eight, increased to thirty or more, and 'till the British came to the city of Savannah and took it.[13]

The first clear conception of time, which we get from these extracts, in regard to the origin of the Silver Bluff Church, is where David George speaks of being left in sole charge, as Liele and Palmer might no longer visit Silver Bluff, lest in so doing, they should impart to the slaves of the settlement a knowledge, which, in the then prevailing conditions, would result in their personal freedom, and, consequently, in great financial loss to their masters. This undoubtedly was not later than November, 1775, when the Earl of Dunmore issued on American soil a proclamation of emancipation, in which the black slaves and the white indentured bondmen were alike promised freedom, provided they espoused the cause of England, in its struggle with the colonists. How well these slaves understood and appreciated the proffered boon, may be inferred from a letter which was written by Stephen Bull to Col. Henry Laurens, President of the Council of Safety, Charleston, South Carolina, March 14, 1776. In that letter he says: "It is better for the public, and the owners, if the deserted Negroes who are on Tybee Island be shot, if they cannot be taken."[14] By this means, as he informs us, he hoped to "deter other Negroes from deserting" their masters. According to Bull's representation, the Negroes along the Savannah River were abandoning their masters, and now going to the British in scores and hundreds, to the detriment of their owners, and the menace of the cause of American independence.

Now George Liele, although not a runaway slave, appears to have had some liking for the Tybee River, as a place of abode, and it is probable that when he could no longer visit Silver Bluff, and was not in camp with Henry Sharp (who had not only given him his freedom, but also taken up arms against the Revolutionists), he reported to Tybee Island to preach to the refugees there assembled. At any rate, when Liele appears in Savannah, Georgia, as a preacher of the Gospel, his biographer declares that "He came up to the city of Savannah from Tybee River."[15]

The next hint which we get from the statements of David George, in regard to the time when the Silver Bluff Church was planted, is where he says that George Liele preached at Silver Bluff both before and after the organization of the church. Happily, Liele himself refers to Silver Bluff as a place where he used to preach. Liele also informs us that he became a Christian about two years before the American Revolution, but did not immediately connect himself with a church; that when he did join, he became a member of Matthew Moore's church, in Burke County, Georgia; that he was a member of this church about four years; that his membership terminated with the evacuation of Savannah; that he preached at Yamacraw and Brumpton Land about three years; and that he went to Jamaica, in the West Indies, in the year of 1782.

Let us consider carefully these facts, with reference to time. The three years, which preceded 1782, were 1781, 1780, 1779. This brings us to the evacuation of Savannah by the Americans, within two days, as the British captured the city December 29, 1778. The four years which preceded 1779 were 1778, 1777, 1776, 1775. We understand from George Liele's statements concerning himself, therefore, that he became a member of Matthew Moore's church at the close of the year 1774, or the beginning of 1775, but was converted at the end of the year 1773, and let a whole year, or nearly so, pass before becoming a church-member.

It is probable that George Liele did not wait to be received into the fellowship of a church before going from plantation to plantation to tell his fellow slaves of the blessing of salvation which he had experienced. He may have thus declared the love of Christ, at Silver Bluff, as early as 1773, as Burke County, Georgia, in which he lived, is in part practically adjacent to Aiken County, South Carolina, in which was Silver Bluff. Accordingly, we are warranted in concluding that the Negro Baptist Church at Silver Bluff was constituted not earlier than 1773, nor later than 1775.

In making these deductions, we bear in mind that the year 1777 has been designated as the time of Liele's conversion, 1778 as the time when he united with Matthew Moore's church, and four years later, or 1782, as the time when his membership in that church ceased. In explanation of this view its advocates insist that the three years in which Liele preached at Brumpton Land and Yamacraw are included in the four years during which he was a member of Matthew Moore's church. According to this claim, the Silver Bluff Church could not have been planted earlier than 1777 nor later than 1778.

We do not share this view for good and sufficient reasons. When Liele, in 1779, went to Savannah to reside, during the British occupancy, he became separated from Matthew Moore's church and the people of Burke County, Georgia, for all time. With the British troops he entered Savannah, as the Americans had evacuated it at the very close of the year 1778. With the British he remained in Savannah during his three years stay in that city, and with one of their officers he left the country, in 1782, for Kingston, Jamaica, British West Indies, where he spent the remainder of his life. His four years of connection with Matthew Moore's church, therefore, must have preceded the year 1779, covering the time from the latter part of 1774 to the latter part of 1778.

As George Liele informs us that he became a Christian about two years before the American War, those who place his conversion in the year 1777 are compelled to reckon the beginning of the Revolutionary War from the year 1779. Errors are hard things to substantiate, and force men to choose between strange dilemmas. But, in explanation of this absurdity, it is claimed that the Revolutionary War did not make itself manifest in Georgia and South Carolina until about the year 1779, and the Negroes of Georgia and South Carolina, in speaking of it, would refer to that year as the beginning of the war. But as a matter of fact, the Revolutionary struggle in South Carolina and Georgia was manifest from the very first. Thus the biographer of Abraham Marshall, of Kiokee, Georgia, having informed his reader that the subject of his sketch was ordained to the work of the Gospel ministry on May 20, 1775, adds, "Just as he had chosen his life work, the Revolutionary War broke out, and Georgia became a scene of violence and bloodshed. During almost the entire struggle, the people were subject to the combined outrages of Britons, Tories and Indians."[16]

Thus, too, the biographer of Gov. John Houston's trusted slave, Andrew C. Marshall, writes, "The embargo having taken effect in Savannah at the opening of the Revolution, fifteen merchants of that city agreed to give him a purse of $225.00 if he would carry word to several American vessels that lay in a bay on the lower seaboard, in which achievement he was successful."[17] The expression, "the opening of the Revolution," in this passage, refers to the year 1775, and not to 1778-1779, for the British attacked the city of Savannah as early as March 3, 1776, and would have captured it if they had not been repulsed by the Americans.

The English agents, their American allies (the Tories), and the Cherokee Indians, who resided in the neighborhood of Silver Bluff and made it the commercial mart it was in colonial times, took up the cause of the British against the revolutionists from the very beginning of the war. Accordingly, William H. Drayton, of South Carolina, on August 30, 1775, urged the sending of foot-soldiers and mounted men to the vicinity of Augusta, Georgia, to protect the interests of the patriots, and chasten their foes.[18]

Eight days later, September 7, 1775, William Tennett, of South Carolina, wrote in his journal as follows: "Went ten miles to New-Savannah, where I had appointed a meeting of inhabitants, in hopes to draw an audience out of Augusta, from Mr. Galphin's Settlement, and Beach Island, but most of the men having marched with Mr. Drayton, and Mr. Galphin being from home, I had but few."[19] To this same neighborhood Col. Andrew Williamson led a large force of South Carolinians, in defense of the American cause, some time later, and General Griffith Rutherford, with 2,400 men, reinforced him, September, 1776.

In view of all these statements in regard to the time when the Revolutionary War began to make itself manifest in Georgia and South Carolina, we conclude that when George Liele says he was converted to Christianity about two years before the Revolutionary War, he refers to the year 1773, and his visits to Silver Bluff were at an end by the summer of 1775. We are, therefore, driven back to our first affirmation, namely, that the Negro Baptist Church at Silver Bluff, South Carolina, was organized not earlier than 1773, nor later than 1775.

The writers who have insisted that Mr. Liele united with Matthew Moore's church in 1778, and terminated that membership in 1782, have followed what is undoubtedly an erroneous inference. Liele said, "I continued in this church about four years till the 'vacuation.'" But as the expression seemed to Dr. Rippon indefinite in some particulars, he sought information from persons who were supposed to be capable of guiding him, and added five words to the statement of Liele, which made it read as follows: "I continued in this church about four years, 'till the 'vacuation'—*of Savannah by the British*."[20] Dr. Rippon carefully states that "Brother George's words are distinguished by inverted commas, and what is not so marked, is either matter compressed, or information received from such persons to whom application had been made for it."

It is easy enough to see how the inference was drawn,

for in one of his letters Liele says, "Our beloved Sister Hannah Williams, during the time she was a member of the church at Savannah, until the 'vacuation, did walk as a faithful, well-beloved Christian."[21] Here there is no room for doubt. Liele speaks in this case of the evacuation of Savannah by the British, July, 1782, but in the former instance the only evacuation of Savannah which harmonizes with the story of his own life, the events and circumstances of his time, and those of his associates, is the evacuation of Savannah by the Americans, December 29, 1778.

GEORGE GALPHIN—PATRON OF THE SILVER BLUFF CHURCH

The planter and merchant on whose estate the Silver Bluff Church was constituted is deserving of special mention in connection with the story of that people. We learn from White's *History of Georgia*, that George Galphin was "a native of Ireland, emigrated soon after manhood to America, and died at Silver Bluff, his residence, on the Savannah River, in South Carolina, on the second of December, 1782, in the seventy-first year of his age." N. W. Jones, in his history, quotes William Bartram as saying that George Galphin was "a gentleman of very distinguished talents and great liberality."[22]

The spirit of justice and kindness, it appears, was manifest in all his dealings with the peoples of the weaker races, who were daily about him. The red man and the black man alike saw in him a man of kindly soul. David George, who was ever a British subject, described his former master as an "anti-loyalist." N. W. Jones, speaking as an American, pronounced him a "patriot." Neither spoke of him except to praise. A master less humane, less considerate of the happiness and moral weal of his dependents, less tolerant in spirit, would never have consented to the establishment of a Negro church on his estate. He might have put an end to the enterprise in its very incipiency, but he did not. He fostered the work from the beginning. It was by his consent that the gospel was preached to slaves who resided at Silver Bluff. It was by his permission that the Silver Bluff Church was established. It was he who permitted David George to be ordained to the work of the ministry. It was he who provided the Silver Bluff Church with a house of worship, by permitting his mill to be used in that capacity. And it was he who gave the little flock a baptistry, by placing his mill-stream at their disposal on baptizing occasions. But we are satisfied that he had no conception of the far-reaching influence of these deeds of kindness.

The truth is, the Galphins appear to have been masters of the patriarchal type. Thomas Galphin, under whose beneficence the work at Silver Bluff was renewed in postbellum time, was, as we shall see, as much the benefactor and protector of Jesse Peter, as George Galphin had been of David George before, and during the earlier stages of the Revolutionary War.[23] Accessible records reveal the fact that John Galphin was an Indian interpreter and a friend of the Cussetahs. It is indeed suggestive that, in 1787, these Indians wished a Negro, whom John Galphin owned, to be a messenger with one of their men to the whites.

THE SILVER BLUFF CHURCH IN EXILE

With the fall of Savannah, at the very close of the year 1778, the Silver Bluff Church completed the first stage in its history. At that time Rev. David George, the pastor, and about forty other slaves, whom George Galphin had abandoned in his flight, went to Savannah, to find safety and freedom under the British flag. Later David George returned to South Carolina, and abode for a time in the city of Charleston. Thence, in 1782, he sailed to Nova Scotia, in company with not less than five hundred white persons, who were adherents of the British cause. In Nova Scotia he abode ten years, preaching to the people of his own race who had found their way into that portion of the continent, in large numbers, after abandoning their homes in the United States.

These labors were performed amid hardships and persecutions, but in faithfulness to God and suffering humanity. In prosecuting his mission, he preached in Shelburn, Birchtown, Ragged Island, and in St. Johns, New Brunswick. So pronounced was the opposition to his labors in New Brunswick, that he found it necessary to invoke the protection of the civil authorities. How well he succeeded in doing so, may be imagined from the subjoined statement:

"Secretary's Office, Fredericktown, 17th July, 1792, I do hereby certify that David George, a free Negro man, has permission from his Excellency, the Lieutenant Governor, to instruct the Black people in knowledge, and exhort them to the practice of the Christian religion. Jno. Odell, Secretary."[24]

It should excite in us no surprise that David George was opposed in his labors in his new home, for, as Lorenzo Sabine declares, "the original population of this Colony was composed almost entirely of the Loyalists of the Revolution."[25] They had not changed their views in regard to the rights of Negroes, by being removed from a land where the two races had hitherto sustained the relation of master and slave. The real surprise lies in the fact, that the secretary of the province was himself a preacher, a minister of the Episcopal Church, and a former resident of the State of New Jersey.

So effective were the arduous labors of David George that he is enrolled among the pulpit pioneers, in Bill's history of Canadian Baptists. He was certainly first to plant a Baptist church at Shelburn, as well as a number of feeble beginnings elsewhere. But Canada was only a temporary home to David George, and to others from the States. Accordingly, he took a colony of Negroes to Sierra Leone, British Central Africa, in 1782.

Of this distant colony, G. Winfred Hervey remarks: "The first settlers of Sierra Leone were what they needed to be, men of bravery. They consisted of about 12,000 colored men who had joined the British forces in the American Revolution. At the close of the war they were sent to Nova Scotia, but the climate proving too unfriendly to them, they were, in 1792, transported to Sierra Leone."[26] One of the first things that David George did, after reaching Africa, was to plant a little Baptist church, which was composed of Negroes from America who had arrived in their fatherland by way of Nova Scotia.

In order to stimulate in the English people an intelligent interest in the colony of Sierra Leone, and secure for the Baptist cause in Freetown the sympathy and aid of English Baptists, David George took a trip to London, England, shortly after establishing himself on the continent of Africa. It was this visit to the metropolis of the world which doubtless, more than anything else, facilitated the collection and publication of many facts then existing and ascertainable in regard to Negro Baptist preachers and their churches in the eastern and western hemispheres.

In visiting Europe, David George took with him letters of commendation from persons of recognized standing in England. John Rippon, the distinguished London divine, thus speaks of David George, after investigating his standing: "Governor Clarkson, in the most unreserved manner, assured me that he esteemed David George as his brother, and that he believes him to be the best man, without exception, in the colony of Sierra Leone."[27] Had the Silver Bluff Church done nothing more than produce this one earnest Christian man, this faithful preacher of Christ, this potent factor in the planting of a colony under the English flag, it would not have existed in vain, but it did more.

THE SILVER BLUFF CHURCH REVIVED

When peace had been restored, and the Revolutionary forces had been disbanded or recalled, Silver Bluff resumed once more the aspect of social distinctions between master and slave in colonial times. Once more, too, the Galphin place became a center of religious activities, and the Negro Baptists of Silver Bluff were more numerous than ever.

The man who was instrumental in resuscitating the work at Silver Bluff was Jesse Peter, who, according to an old custom of applying to the slave the surname of the master, was better known as Jesse Galphin, or Gaulfin. Having been connected with the Silver Bluff Church from the very first, and only separated from it during the Revolutionary War and the period of readjustment immediately thereafter, Jesse Peter was eminently fitted, at least in one particular, to take up the work at Silver Bluff which David George had abandoned in the year 1778. He knew the place and he loved the people. Silver Bluff was his home, and there he was held in high esteem. Moreover, he possessed what is essential to ministerial success everywhere, deep sincerity, seriousness of purpose, knowledge of the Bible, an excellent spirit, and the ability to deliver, with profit and pleasure, the message of the truth. Jonathan Clarke, and Abraham Marshall, who knew him personally, have left on record beautiful testimonials of his work and his worth.[28]

Why this young man, who had obtained his freedom by going to the British at the fall of Savannah,[29] in

1778, remained in America to resume the condition of a slave, after the Revolutionary War, is not known. It is known, however, that, unlike George Liele and David George, men of adventurous spirit, Jesse Peter was not a pioneering worker in strange fields. If, indeed, he ever traveled beyond Kiokee, Georgia, in the one direction, and the city of Savannah in the other, we have failed to note the fact. It is known, too, that he had an indulgent master, and it is possible that he preferred a state of nominal slavery, under his protection, to a probable state of want and hardship in a foreign land. Or it may be he was willing to die for the cause, and so deliberately entered again into the old condition of bondage in order to enjoy the privilege of preaching, where Liele and George had labored in other days.

It is to be presumed that Jesse Peter was regularly ordained to the work of the Gospel ministry. We take this view because he exercised the duties and privileges which ordination implies, without ever being called in question for doing so. His three years of association with Liele and George, in Savannah, during the British occupancy, moreover, afforded him ample opportunity to be publicly and regularly consecrated to his life-work. Certainly Abraham Marshall, of Kiokee, Georgia, would not have associated himself with Jesse Peter in the ordination of Andrew Bryan, of Savannah, in 1788, if Jesse Peter had not himself been ordained to the work of the ministry.

Conditions in the earlier stages of Jesse Peter's pastorate at Silver Bluff were such that he did not reside at his old home, but came and went as a stated visitor.

Accordingly, Jonathan Clarke, writing from Savannah, Georgia, December 22, 1792, says, "Jesse Peter (whose present master is Thomas Galphin), is now here, and has three or four places in the country, where he attends preaching alternately."[30] George Liele, writing from the West Indies, in 1791, had said to Joseph Cook, of South Carolina, "Brother Jesse Galphin, another black minister, preaches near Augusta, in South Carolina, where I used to preach."[31] Referring to him, George White speaks as follows: "On the 20th of January, 1788, Andrew, surnamed Bryan, was ordained by Rev. Abraham Marshall, and a colored minister named Jesse Peter, from the vicinity of Augusta."[32] Benedict, referring to Andrew Marshall, in the same connection, states that "he was accompanied by a young preacher of color, by the name of Jesse Peter, of Augusta."[33] From these testimonies, it is evident that Jesse Peter was a nonresident pastor of the Silver Bluff Church from 1788 to 1792, if not for a longer period.

During the first period of Jesse Peter's pastorate at Silver Bluff, another slave, who lived in that locality, began to preach. Andrew Bryan, writing from Savannah, Georgia, December 28, 1800, refers to him in the following manner: "Another dispensation of Providence has greatly strengthened our hands and increased our means of information: Henry Francis, lately a slave of the widow of the late Col. Leroy Hammond, of Augusta, has been purchased by a few humane gentlemen of this place, and liberated to exercise the handsome ministerial gifts he possesses amongst us, and teach our youth to read and write." He adds, "Brother Francis has been in the ministry fifteen years, and will soon receive ordination."[34] According to Andrew Bryan, Henry Francis was a half-breed, his mother being white, his father an Indian, but I find in a letter, written by another from the city of Savannah, May 23, 1800, that he is characterized as "a man of color, who has for many years served Col. Hammond, and has handsome ministerial abilities."[35]

The question easily suggests itself, was Henry Francis a member of the Silver Bluff Church when, in 1785, he began to preach? We infer that he was, from certain known facts as to his place of abode, and his opportunities for church membership. In the first place, he lived in the immediate neighborhood of Silver Bluff. William Tennett informs us that the Hammond place was in South Carolina, four miles from Augusta, Georgia and Lossing, Abraham Marshall, and others, that Silver Bluff was also in South Carolina, twelve miles from Augusta. It was easy, therefore, for Henry Francis to attend divine service at the Silver Bluff Church. In the second place, it was the custom of the slaves on the neighboring plantations to attend preaching at Silver Bluff during the pastorate of David George,[36] and the custom doubtless prevailed during Jesse Peter's pastorate. If Henry Francis attended church at Silver Bluff, he did only what other slaves of the neighborhood did. Furthermore, there was no other Baptist church, white or colored, in the neighborhood, for Francis to join. Marshall's church at Kiokee, Georgia, was twenty miles above Augusta, while Botsford's Meeting House, in the opposite direction, was "25 or

30 miles below Augusta."[37] In Augusta itself, there was no Negro Baptist church until 1793,[38] and no white Baptist church until 1817.[39] To our mind the conclusion is inevitable that Henry Francis, in 1785, was a member of the Negro Baptist church, at Silver Bluff, South Carolina.

In reaching this conclusion, moreover, we have been not a little influenced by the fact that when Henry Francis was formerly ordained to the ministry at Savannah, Georgia, seventeen years after he had commenced to preach, and when he was an officer in the Negro church at Savannah, the ordination sermon was not preached by Dr. Henry Holcombe, of the white church of that city, nor by Andrew Bryan of the First African, but by Jesse Peter,[40] pastor of the Silver Bluff Church. We can account for the deference shown Jesse Peter, on this occasion, only on the presumption that Henry Francis was converted, baptized, and licensed to preach at Silver Bluff, and that Jesse Peter was the instrument used in bringing these results to pass. It is evident, then, that the Ogeeche African Baptist Church,[41] on the Ogeeche River, fourteen miles south of Savannah, organized in the year 1803, is more indebted to the Silver Bluff Church for her first preacher and instructor of youth than to any other church.

Of Jesse Peter's ministry at Silver Bluff, as a resident pastor, we are not well informed. In a letter written from Kiokee, Georgia, May 1, 1793, Abraham Marshall speaks of him as follows: "I am intimately acquainted with Jesse Golfin; he lives thirty miles below me in South Carolina, and twelve miles below Augusta. He is a Negro servant of Mr. Golfin, who, to his praise be it spoken, treats him with respect."[42] Jesse Peter, then, was resident pastor of the Silver Bluff Church in the early spring of 1793. From another source we learn that the membership of the Silver Bluff Church, at this time, was sixty or more.[43]

THE CHURCH AT AUGUSTA

Here we lose sight of the Silver Bluff Church, just as the First African Baptist Church, of Augusta, Georgia, better known as the Springfield Baptist Church, comes into being. Jesse Peter had secured standing and recognition for the First African Church, at Savannah, Georgia,[44] and Henry Francis had been ordained for the Ogeeche Church by him and Andrew Bryan and Henry Holcombe. It was natural, then, that he would wish for his work at Silver Bluff the standing and recognition which had been secured for the work in and about Savannah, Georgia. In order to obtain this boon, and have his work in touch with that near the seacoast, it would be necessary to transfer its place of meeting from the State of South Carolina to the State of Georgia, where he had a friend, who was able to bring things to pass. It is in this way alone that we account for the beginning of the First African Baptist Church at Augusta at the very time when the Silver Bluff Church disappears. The curtain falls on the Silver Bluff Church, with Jesse Peter as pastor, when the church is reported as in a flourishing condition. The curtain rises, and again we see a flock of devoted Christians, with Jesse Peter as pastor, but they are twelve miles away from Silver Bluff, South Carolina, receiving from Abraham Marshall and another white Baptist minister the regulating touches which gave the body standing and influence as the First African Baptist Church, of Augusta, Georgia.

Here is what Benedict says of the body: "This church appears to have been raised up by the labors of Jesse Peter, a black preacher of respectable talents, and an amiable character. It was constituted in 1793, by elders Abraham Marshall and David Tinsley. Jesse Peter, sometimes called Jesse Golfin, on account of his master's name, continued the pastor of this church a number of years, and was very successful in his ministry."[45] If, as we presume, the Silver Bluff Church is still with us, in another meeting-place and under a new name, the oldest Negro Baptist church in this country today is that at Augusta, Georgia, having existed at Silver Bluff, South Carolina, from the period 1774-1775 to the year 1793, before becoming a Georgia institution.

THE FIRST AFRICAN BAPTIST CHURCH OF SAVANNAH, GEORGIA

The story of the Silver Bluff Baptist Church would not be complete without reference to the Negro Baptist Church at Savannah, Georgia, which existed before Andrew Bryan became a Christian. Neither E. K. Love, a recent pastor of the First African Baptist Church, nor

James M. Simms, of the Bryan Church, have intimated, in their respective histories, that Savannah had a Negro Baptist church before the 20th of January, 1788. Nevertheless, the fact remains that during the British occupancy—that is, from the year 1779 to the year 1782—there was at Savannah, Georgia, an African Baptist church.

If the Negroes of Savannah had been without a Baptist church from 1779 to 1782, it would have been strange indeed. For David George led a company of fifty or more fugitive slaves from Galphinton, South Carolina, into that city at the close of the year 1778, and this company, it is reasonable to infer, included a considerable part, if not nearly all, of the members of the Silver Bluff Church. Devout Christians who had enjoyed such privileges as slaves, and that for years, in South Carolina, would scarcely be satisfied without them in Georgia, as free men, when they had with them three preachers of the Gospel, David George, George Liele, and Jesse Peter, men of their own race and denomination, men from the vicinity of Augusta, who had figured in the planting and growth of the Silver Bluff Church.

We are glad that we have historical data which establish the fact that there was a Negro Baptist church in Savannah from 1779 to 1782, and that the Negro Baptist ministry, which had made itself felt at Silver Bluff for the centuries to come, was now embraced in the church at Savannah. But in this church, it will be seen, George Liele, the eldest of the trio, was the pastor, and not David George. George Liele, as servant of the British officer, who had given him his freedom, could secure for the church recognition and influence, at the hands of the military government then in possession of Savannah, which neither David George, nor Jesse Peter, could obtain. Liele was with a man who had influence with the British government. David George and Jesse Peter, as strangers and fugitives, were unknown to that government, and without influence. It is in this way that we account for the fact that George Liele, and not David George, was pastor of the church. Under ordinary circumstances, the Silver Bluff element, which probably included nearly the whole church at the beginning, would have insisted upon having their old pastor.

In seeking facts, which make it manifest that Savannah, Georgia, had a Negro Baptist church prior to 1788, we have consulted the testimony of persons who were connected with the church at the time, and that of persons of recognized standing who were contemporaneous with them and competent to testify. Joseph Cook, of Euhaw, Upper Indian Land, South Carolina, in a letter to Dr. John Rippon, London, England, dated September 15, 1790, uses the following language: "A poor Negro, commonly called Brother George, has been so highly favored of God, as to plant the first Baptist church in Savannah, and another in Jamaica."[46] As Hervey, Cox, Phillipo, and others who have noticed the missionary efforts of Negro Baptists in the West Indies, inform us that George Liele left the United States in 1782 and began preaching at Kingston, Jamaica, British West Indies, in 1784, it is evident from Cook's letter that the church which Liele planted at Savannah existed prior to 1782.[47] Cook is corroborated by F. A. Cox, who, in speaking of George Liele, in his history of the Baptist Missionary Society of England, states that "He had been pastor of a colored congregation in America." A paragraph which we take from the *History of the Propagation of Christianity Among the Heathen*, is of the same nature. It refers to the church of which Mr. Cook speaks, in this manner: "The first Baptist preacher in Jamaica was a black man named George Liele, who, though a slave, had been the pastor of a Baptist church in Georgia. He was brought to Jamaica about 1782." Liele, on his own behalf, testified that there was a Negro Baptist church in Savannah, Georgia, during the British occupancy, and mentions by name at least three of its members, who were not in this country, after the British withdrew their forces from Savannah, in 1782. In a letter to Joseph Cook, written from Jamaica, in 1790, Liele refers to one of these members in the following manner: "Also I received accounts from Nova Scotia of a black Baptist preacher, David George, who was a member of the church at Savannah."[48]

In a communication written in 1791 and addressed to the pastor of a London church, Liele refers to one of his Jamaica members in this style: "Sister Hannah Williams, during the time she was a member of the church at Savannah, until the 'vacuation, did *walk* as a faithful, well-behaved Christian."[49] In answer to questions in regard to Jesse Peter, Liele replied to his London correspondent as follows: "Brother Jesse Gaulphin, another black minister, preaches near

Augusta, in South Carolina, where I used to preach. He was a member of the church at Savannah."[50]

In the face of this testimony, coming from different sources and from parties widely separated from each other who had no motive to deceive, there is absolutely no room for doubt as to the fact that a Negro Baptist church existed in Savannah, Georgia, from 1779 to 1782.

As to what measure of prosperity attended the work of the Negro Baptist church at Savannah, Georgia, during the years 1779-1782, we are not informed. It was well that at a time when churches in some parts were going to pieces because of the ravages of war, this little flock remained intact. We infer, however, that it did a most blessed work. George Liele speaks in one of his letters of one "Brother Amos,"[51] who appears to have been a product of the Negro church at Savannah, or the older church at Silver Bluff, South Carolina. Amid the changes wrought in the closing days of the Revolutionary War, this Negro preacher had his lot cast in New Providence, Bahama Islands, British West Indies. According to George Liele, Amos had a membership of three hundred in 1791. Benedict informs us that Amos was in correspondence with his brethren in Savannah, Georgia, in 1812, and at that time the church at New Providence numbered eight hundred and fifty.

A Remnant of Liele's Church in Savannah After The Revolutionary War

What portion of the Savannah Church remained in America, after the evacuation of the city of Savannah by the British, in 1782, we are not able to state. But blessings and trials attended both that portion of the flock which went abroad and that which remained. Andrew Bryan, Hannah Bryan, Kate Hogg, and Hagar Simpson,[52] were among the last converts received into the fellowship of the Negro Baptist church at Savannah before the pastor, the Rev. George Liele, sailed for the West Indies in 1782. These and probably others, like Jesse Peter, remained in America after the restoration of peace between the United States and the "mother-country," and labored under Andrew Bryan, their new spiritual leader, for the continuation of the work which had been so blessed of God under the labors of George Liele.

From Liele's departure, in 1782, to the time of Andrew Bryan's ordination, in 1788, the little flock at Savannah, Georgia, was bitterly persecuted, but its work for resuscitation, and progress, was wonderful—wonderful because of the moral heroism which characterized it. It is reasonable to suppose, however, that much of the opposition to the church at Savannah from 1782 to 1787 was due to the circumstances in which it had come into being, and not to any real antipathy to the cause of Christ. For it must be borne in mind that it was a creature of the Revolutionary War, and of British origin, having been planted when the rightful people of Savannah were languishing in exile, or heroically struggling with the enemy in other parts of the country. Bryan and his associates were beaten unmercifully for their persistency in holding on to the work, but they were prepared to yield their lives in martyrdom[53] sooner than relinquish what George Liele had instituted. So it lived—lived amid the fires of persecution.

Jesse Peter, a member of the church under Liele, and, after the Revolutionary War, pastor of the church at Silver Bluff, saw what was needed to end this persecution, and proceeded to change the aspect of things. He was held in high esteem by the colonists, and Abraham Marshall, of Kiokee, Georgia, was his chief admirer and friend. Accordingly, he secured the services of Abraham Marshall in setting things aright. The church was organized anew, the pastor was ordained to the office of a Baptist minister, and the reestablished church, with its preacher, was brought into membership with the Georgia Baptist Association.[54] As Abraham Marshall was beloved by Georgia Baptists as no other man of the State, it was enough that this church should have his official approval and recognition. Referring to this new order of things, instituted on the 20th day of January, 1788, Marshall, the one associated with Jesse Peter in the undertaking, recognizes Jesse Peter as taking the initiative, when he says, "I assisted in the constitution of the church, and the ordination of the minister."[55]

So ended the second period in the history of this church, as the dawn of its new day began—a day in which the once-persecuted congregation could say:

"We enjoy the rights of conscience to a valuable extent, worshipping in our families, preaching three times every Lord's Day, baptizing frequently from ten to thirty at a time, in the Savannah, and administering the sacred supper, not only without molestation, but in the presence and with the approbation and encouragement of many of the white people."[56]

Let us recapitulate. We began with the church at Silver Bluff, South Carolina. We were next attracted to Canada, and then to far-off Africa by the labors of David George, the first regular pastor at Silver Bluff. Again we follow a portion of the Silver Bluff Church to Savannah, Georgia. In Savannah we see a church growing under the labors of George Liele, then we find Liele and Amos in the British West Indies, leading large congregations of Negro Baptists. Once more we turn our eyes homeward, and we are attracted to the church at Silver Bluff, South Carolina, to the church at Augusta, Georgia, and the church at Savannah, which, having endured the severest trials, rejoices in recognition and peace—the church of today.

WALTER H. BROOKS

FOOTNOTES:

[1] Benedict's *History of the Baptists* (edition, 1848), p. 454. Rippon's *Annual Baptist Register*, 1801–1802, p. 836.

[2] *Ibid.*, pp. 397, 577, 620. Compare with edition 1813, Vol. II, pp. 504, 509, 515.

[3] See Ramsey's *History of South Carolina*, Vol. I, p. 158, note 19, p. 159; Steven's *History of Georgia*, Vol. I, pp. 255-256; Gibbes' *Documentary History of American Revolution* (South Carolina), Vol. I, pp. 235-236 and 158-159; Furman's *History Charleston Baptist Association*, p. 77; Rippon's *Annual Baptist Register*, 1790-1793, pp. 445, 474, 477, 541; *State Papers, Indian Affairs*, Vol. I, pp. 15, 32, 35, 36; Lossing's *Field Book of Revolution*, Vol. II, p. 484; article on Henry Lee in Appleton's *Cyclopedia*, Vol. X, p. 487; *Light Horse Harry* in Larner's *History of Ready Reference*, Vol. V, pp. 32-74-5; *American Cyclopedia*, Vol. II, p. 378; N. W. Jones' *History of Georgia*, Vol. II, pp. 136-138; *Abraham Marshall* in Cathcart's *Baptist Encyclopedia*, Vol. II, p. 349.

[4] George and John Galphin, brothers, are mentioned in *State Papers, Indian Affairs*, Vol. I, pp. 32, 35, 36, 158, 159. Thomas Galphin is referred to in Rippon's *Annual Baptist Register*, 1790-1793, pp. 540-541. Milledge Galphin, according to Act of Congress, passed August 14, 1848, and statement of United States for 1850, set forth in Lossing's *Field Book of the American Revolution*, Vol. II, p. 484, received in settlement of his claim against the United States as heir of George Galphin, $200,000.

[5] For date of fall of Savannah, Dec. 29, 1778, Sir Archibald Campbell in Appleton's *Cyclopedia of American Biography*, Vol. I, p. 511, and for troubles at Silver Bluff, South Carolina, see Rippon's *Annual Baptist Register*, 1790-1793, p. 477, and compare with pp. 473-480 and 332-337. For conditions necessitating the exile of Silver Bluff Church, see letter of Wm. H. Drayton, written from Hammond's place near Augusta, Georgia, August 30,

1775, to the Council of Safety in Gibbes' *Documentary History of the American Revolution* (South Carolina), Vol. I, p. 162, and for distance from Silver Bluff see letter of Rev. Wm. Tennett, p. 236, and compare with note in Lossing's *Field Book of the American Revolution*, Vol. II, 484. See also Rev. Tennett's letter of September 7, 1775, for movement of men at Silver Bluff and surrounding country. Gibbes' *Documentary History of the American Revolution* (South Carolina), Vol. I, pp. 245-246.

[6] Rippon's *Annual Baptist Register*, 1791, p. 336, compare with 1790-1793, pp. 476-477.

[7] See Rippon's *Annual Baptist Register* for 1793, pp. 540-541. Compare with 1790-1793, pp. 544-545.

[8] Lossing's *Field Book*, p. 484; Steven's *Georgia*, Vol. II, pp. 255-256, etc., as above in note 3.

[9] Gibbes' *Documentary History American Revolution*, Vol. I, pp. 235-236; Furman's *History Charleston Baptist Association*, p. 77, and compare letters of George and John Galphin in *State Papers, Indian Affairs*, Vol. I, pp. 15, 35, 36, and G. No. 2, p. 32.

[10] Ramsey's *History of South Carolina*, Vol. I, p. 158.

[11] Steven's *History of Georgia*, Vol. II, pp. 255-256; article on Henry Lee, Appleton's *American Cyclopedia*, Vol. X, p. 487.

[12] But who was "Elder Palmer," the man who planted the first of this series of churches? David George states that he was a powerful preacher, and that he was pastor of a church some distance from Silver Bluff. We are

satisfied that the church alluded to was not in South Carolina, nor in Georgia, nor were the members of the church in question, nor its pastor, of African descent. It is our opinion that "Elder Palmer" was no less a distinguished person than Wait Palmer, the founder of the First Baptist Church of Stonington, Connecticut. It was possible that he should be the cause of this remarkable beginning of Negro Baptist churches in the United States, for he was living and active during and prior to the Revolutionary period, and long before.

Wait Palmer, of Stonington, Connecticut, moreover, was, as his biographer states, "an actor in the great New Light, or Separatist movement," and in this capacity he "preached often in destitute regions." Benedict testifies that "he became a famous pioneer in Virginia and North Carolina." But what is more, Mrs. Marshall, the mother of Abraham Marshall, of Kiokee, Georgia, was a sister of Shubal Sterns, and Shubal Sterns was baptized and ordained to the work of the ministry by Wait Palmer, at Tolland, Connecticut, in the spring of 1751. It was but natural that, in his zeal to preach Christ in destitute regions, Palmer would visit this Connecticut family and preach the gospel to any who might desire to hear it.

If it should be thought by some that no man would, in the circumstances, have gone on a preaching tour from Connecticut to South Carolina, it may be well to recall the fact that Rev. Abraham Marshall covered the ground in question, in the year 1786, travelling both ways on horseback, preaching nearly every day during the three months he was away from home. But Palmer was now in the South and not in the North, as Benedict states. No other Palmer, known to Baptists, fits the case like this friend of Shubal Stearns. We shall continue to assign to him the credit of the first Negro Baptist Church in America, until we can find another "Elder Palmer," whose claim is absolutely certain. See Rippon, *Annual Baptist Register*, 1790-1793, pp. 475-476; Catheart's *Baptist Encyclopedia*, II, 882.

[13] Rippon's *Annual Baptist Register*, edition 1790-1793, pp. 473-480, and compare article, Sir Archibald Campbell, in Appleton's *Cyclopedia of American Biography*, Vol. I, p. 511.

[14] See Bill's letter of March 12, and one of March 14, 1776; also March 26, 1776, printed in Gibbes' *Documentary History of the American Revolution* (South Carolina), Vol. I, pp. 266-273. Compare with letter in Vol. II, p. 62. See also Dunmore's Emancipation Proclamation issued in November, 1775, in Joseph T. Wilson's *Emancipation*, pp. 36-37.

[15] *Cyclopedia American Biography*, Vol. I, p. 511. Compare with Rippon's *Annual Baptist Register*, edition 1790-1793, pp. 332-333.

[16] Cathcart's *Encyclopedia*, Vol. II, p. 749, and compare article of John Houston in Appleton's *Cyclopedia of American Biography*, Vol. III, p. 273.

[17] Appleton's *Cyclopedia of American Biography*, Vol. IV, p. 219. Compare Vol. III, p. 273. See article, Savannah in Appleton's *American Cyclopedia*, Vol. III, p. 646.

[18] See Drayton's letter in Gibbes' *Documentary History of American Revolution* (South Carolina), Vol. I, p. 162, and for distance from Silver Bluff compare letter of Tennett, p. 235, note in Lossing's *Field Book of Revolution*, Vol. II, p. 484.

[19] Gibbes' *Documentary History of the American Revolution* (South Carolina), Vol. I, pp. 235-236, letter of Tennett, of September 7, 1775.

[20] Rippon's *Annual Baptist Register*, 1770-1773, pp. 332-337.

[21] *Ibid.*, 1790-1793, p. 344.

[22] White's *History of Georgia*, pp. 246-247; Jones, Vol. II, p. 137.

[23] *State Papers, Indian Affairs, Vol. I, G. No. 2, p. 32.*

[24] See Jonathan Odell, Appleton's *Cyclopedia of American Biography*, Vol. IV, p. 556; Rippon's *Annual Baptist Register*, 1790-1793, p. 481; Bill's *History of the Canadian Baptists*, pp. 26, 176, 653, 657. Compare with Rippon's *Annual Baptist Register* for 1798-1800, p. 336.

[25] Sabine's *American Loyalists*, Vol. I, p. 127. Compare pp. 122-123.

[26] G. W. Hervey, *Story of Baptist Missions in Foreign Lands*, p. 596. Compare article on Sierra Leone in Appleton's *American Cyclopedia*, Vol. XV, p. 32; also article on Nova Scotia, Vol. XII, pp. 524-525; See Rippon's *Annual Baptist Register*, 1790-1793, pp.

481-483. See also article on Sierra Leone in *The Earth and its Inhabitants*—Africa—Vol. III, p. 207.

[27] Rippon's *Annual Baptist Register*, 1790-1793, pp. 481-484.

[28] Rippon's *Annual Baptist Register*, 1790-1793, pp. 473, 544-545; 1791, p. 336; 1793, pp. 540-541.

[29] Joseph T. Wilson's *Emancipation*, pp. 36-38; Dunmore's Emancipation Proclamation issued 1775.

[30] Rippon's *Annual Baptist Register*, 1793, pp. 540-541.

[31] *Ibid.*, 1791, p. 336.

[32] *White's Historical Collections of Georgia, p. 316.*

[33] *Benedict's History of the Baptists, p. 170.*

[34] Rippon's *Annual Baptist Register*, 1798-1801, p. 367. Compare 263.

[35] *Ibid.*, p. 263.

[36] Rippon's *Annual Baptist Register*, 1790-1793, p. 476.

[37] Benedict's *History* (edition 1848), p. 723.

[38] Benedict's *History of the Baptists* (edition 1813), Vol. II, p. 193.

[39] Article on Augusta, Georgia, First Baptist Church of, Cathcart's *Baptist Encyclopedia*, Vol. I, p. 49.

[40] *James M. Simm's First Colored Baptist Church in North America, p. 57.*

[41] *Ibid.*, pp. 58-59.

[42] Benedict's *History of the Baptists*, edition 1813, Vol. II, p. 193, quoted from Rippon's *Annual Baptist Register*.

[43] Rippon's *Annual Baptist Register*, 1791, p. 336.

[44] White's *Historical Collections of Georgia*, p. 316; Benedict's *History of the Baptists* (edition 1848), p. 740. Compare with Rippon's *Annual Baptist Register*, 1793, p. 545. Benedict's *History of the Baptists*, edition 1848, p. 727, note 5, shows no white minister was present except Abraham Marshall, and he says here he "assisted in the constitution of the church, and the ordination of the minister."

[45] Benedict's *History of the Baptists* (edition 1813), Vol. II, p. 193.

[46] Rippon's *Annual Baptist Register*, 1791, p. 332.

[47] *Hervey's Story of Baptist Missions in Foreign Lands, pp. 611-612; Cox's History of the British Baptist Missionary Society, 1792-1842, p. 12. Phillipo, Jamaica, Past and Present; E. K. Love's History First African Baptist Church, p. 35; Brown, Propagation of Christianity among Heathen, Vol. II, p. 94.*

[48] Rippon's *Annual Baptist Register*, 1791, p. 336, and compare Rippon's *Annual Baptist Register*, 1790-1793, pp. 476, 481-483.

[49] *Ibid.*, 1791, p. 344.

[50] *Ibid.*, 1791, p. 336.

[51] Benedict's *History of the Baptists* (edition 1813), Vol. II, p. 206.

[52] *James M. Simm's The First Colored Baptist Church in North America, p. 15.*

[53] "Andrew Bryan, and his brother Sampson, who was converted about a year after Andrew was, were twice imprisoned and they with about fifty others, without much ceremony, were severely whipped. Andrew was inhumanly cut and bled abundantly; but while under their lashes he held up his hands and told his persecutors that he rejoiced not only to be whipped but would *freely suffer death* for the cause of Christ." *Baptist Home Missions in America*, 1832-1882, Jubilee Volume, p. 388.

[54] Benedict's *History of the Baptists*, edition 1848, p. 170. Compare with p. 723.

[55] Rippon's *Annual Baptist Register*, 1793, p. 545.

[56] Rippon's *Annual Baptist Register*, 1793-1801, p. 367. Compare with Clark's letter, 1790-1793, p. 540.

THE NEGROES IN MAURITIUS[1]

Mauritius was discovered by the Portuguese in 1505 and remained in their possession until 1598, when it was ceded to the Dutch, who gave it the name by which it is now known. Aside from erecting a fort at Grand Port, however, the Dutch did no more for the development of the colony than the Portuguese. The Dutch finally abandoned it in 1710 when the island was taken over by the French. Under the French the island was considerably developed, especially during the second half of the eighteenth century, and this new step, as the majority saw it, necessitated the introduction of slavery. During the Napoleonic Wars Mauritius was captured by England and was formally ceded by France in 1814.

The significant history of the Negroes in Mauritius, however, dates from the year 1723 when the East India Company of France, in order to promote agriculture in the Island, sanctioned the introduction of slaves, whom they sold to the inhabitants at a certain fixed price. This price was seldom paid at the moment of purchase, and, as many evaded payment altogether. Mahé de Labourdounais, the then Governor of the Colony, received instructions on this point, the execution of which made him unpopular among the inhabitants.[2]

The slave trade, at this period, was principally in the hands of those pirates who had formed a settlement at Nossibé (Nossé Ibrahim), on the northeast coast of Madagascar, where they had been received with kindness and hospitality by the natives. In return they excited a war between the tribes in the interior and those inhabiting the seacoast, and purchased the prisoners made by both for the purpose of conveying them for sale to Bourbon or Mauritius. If the prisoners thus obtained proved insufficient to the demands of the slave market, a descent was made on some part of the Island, a village was surrounded, and its younger and more vigorous inhabitants were borne off to a state of perpetual slavery.[3]

Harrowing as the scenes witnessed in such forays must have been, the slave trade from Madagascar to Mauritius was not accompanied with the same horrors as from the neighboring continent to America, if history be credited. Its victims were spared the toiling and harassing march from the interior and the horrors of being cribbed and confined for successive weeks beneath the hatches till they reached their final destination; and yet, of every five Negroes embarked at Madagascar, not more than two were found fit for service in Mauritius. The rest either stifled beneath the hatches, starved themselves to death, died of putrid fever, became the food of sharks, fled to the mountains, or fell beneath the driver's lash.

Mahé de Labourdounais was not the founder of slavery. The institution preceded his arrival. Slavery existed in Mauritius even under the Dutch régime. Of every eighteen slaves in the colony one died annually, so that if the traffic had ceased for eighteen years, at the end of that time the whole black population would have died out. From first to last Mauritius has been the tomb of more than a million of Africans. Their lamentable history is like the roll of the prophet, written within and without, and the writing thereof is mourning and lamentation.

Many became fugitives, and sometimes by daring adventure returned to Africa. In order to check the fugitive slaves, Labourdounais employed their countrymen against them, and formed a mounted police who protected the colonists from their incursions.[4] To preserve the inhabitants from famine, he introduced the cassava from the Island of St. Jago and the Brazils, and published an ordinance by which every planter was compelled to put under cultivation five hundred feet of cassava for every slave that he possessed. The planters, an ignorant and indolent race, used every measure to degenerate and discredit this innovation, and in some cases destroyed the plantations of the cassava by pouring boiling water on the root. The benefit conferred by this ordinance was later felt and appreciated when their crops were destroyed by the hurricanes or devoured by locusts. The cassava was immune from either of these casualties and was the usual article of food for the Negroes. Labourdounais instructed the slaves in the art of ship building, made them sailors and soldiers and found them highly useful in the expedition which he undertook against the English in India. He endeavored also to mitigate their sufferings from the enforcement of the regulations of the *Code Noir*.

After the dispersion of the pirates, the slave trade fell into the hands of European merchants or Creole colonists, who extended it to the adjoining coasts of Africa. The Mozambique Negroes were found more tractable than those of Madagascar, but Negroes were obtained from both points, according to the difficulties and exigencies of the traffic. The price paid by the French at Madagascar for a man or a woman from the age of thirteen to forty was two muskets, two cartridge boxes, ten flints, and ten balls, or fifteen hundred balls or seventeen hundred flints. In spite of the price the trade developed. In 1766 there were about 25,000 slaves and 1200 free Negroes in the colony. In 1799 there were 55,000 of the former class and 35,000 of the latter. In 1832 they were estimated at 16,000 free Negroes and 63,500 slaves. It seems difficult to account for the diminution among the free Negro population. Baron Grant de Vaux[5] states that to prevent the increase of this class it was enacted that no slaves should be liberated save those who had saved the lives of their masters. A kind-hearted master, however, could always give his slave an opportunity to save his life.

Slavery as it developed in Maritius falls in three epochs. During the earliest period the institution gradually took the form of a system somewhat like that of the bondage of the Hebrews, modified in the case of Mauritius, however, according to the requirements of the temper and habits of the natives and the situation of the planters. There was no regard for the comfort of the slaves and they tended to degrade to the lowest depths. Yet the slaves were not considered altogether as chattels, convertible at the will of their masters. In the second stage, however, the bondage of the Negro reached the darkest age of irresponsibility to law and cruelty absolutely intolerable. A few officials and planters protested, and travelers who saw the horror appealed for mercy in behalf of the unfortunate.[6] A change in the attitude of the planters toward the slaves was finally forced and characterized the third stage of slavery in Mauritius. These cruelties were mitigated largely by the agitation of *Les Amis des Noirs*, among whom were some of the most distinguished actors in the grand drama of the French Revolution. The leading reformers were the brilliant orators Mirabeau and Madam de Poivre, the wife of the deceased Intendant of the Isle of France. At a much earlier date, even under Labourdounais, under whose economic development of Mauritius slavery flourished, much was said about improving the condition of the slaves.[7] Yet it was not until the rule of De Caen that we observe actual efforts to provide for the slaves, such as better nourishment, religious instruction and legal marriage.[8]

The first attempt to emancipate the slaves was made by the leaders of the French Revolution, who, while they professed to discard Christianity as a revelation from God, deduced the equality of all men before God from the principles of natural reason.[9] The prohibition of slavery was rendered null and void by the planters of Mauritius and the members of local government, all of whom were slaveholders and opposed to any change. The only effect of the prohibition was to alienate the affections of the colonists from the mother-country, and to lead them to rejoice when Napoleon assumed the consular power and annulled the ordinance prohibiting slavery after the capture of the island by the British. The importation of slaves was prohibited under severe penalties.

As the execution of this law was vested in the local authorities, who had a direct personal interest in the continuance of this traffic, slaves were still imported in sufficient numbers to satisfy the wants of the planters. [10] It is true that trading in slaves was declared to be felony, that the two harbors of Port Louis and Matubourg were closed against their entrance, that a slave registry was opened in 1815, and that credulous Governors wrote to the home authorities that the Mauritians, far from wishing to renew this nefarious traffic, were filled with indignation at the remembrance of its horrors. All this may be true, but the slave trade was as brisk as ever, and the island swarmed with Negroes whose peculiar appearance and ignorance of the Creole language proved them to be of recent introduction.

No law can be executed unless it be in accordance with public opinion, and the feelings of the white Mauritians were altogether in favor of slavery. The illicit introduction of slaves was a felony by law, and yet, notwithstanding the notorious violations of this law, no one was ever convicted. The prisoner might have turned on the judge and proved his complicity in the crime. The only convictions that were obtained were in the case of offenders that were sent to England for trial. This statement will excite no astonishment on the part of those who are acquainted with the manner in which justice is still administered in Mauritius. The slave registry was opened in 1815, but the entries were so falsified that instead of checking slavery it threw its mantle of protection upon it.[11] Slaves were not introduced publicly at the two chief ports of the island from Africa, but the Seychelles Islands lay at a convenient distance, and slaves registered at the Seychelles were admitted into Mauritius without any questions being asked. The coral reef that surrounds the island could easily be passed and the slaves loaded in those light coasters that are used by fishermen. The governors were surrounded by functionaries who were slaveholders and who were therefore interested in supporting the traffic and screening the offenders from punishment, so that their reports, based on information received from these parties, were not entitled to much credit.

As to the feelings of indignation expressed by the colonists at the remembrance of the horrors of the slave trade, it is sufficient to remark that rogues are always louder in protestation of their innocence than honest men—that this change of feeling was too rapid to be sincere, and that truthfulness of character does not stand high in the code of Mauritian morality, to judge from the attitude of the white population.

In judging the treatment of the slaves in Mauritius, recourse must be had to those writers who visited or lived in the colony during the prevalence of slavery, and have given the world the benefit of their experience. These are St. Pierre, Soumerat and Baron Grant. St. Pierre spent several years in the island, and mingled freely with the inhabitants of all classes. The last was born in the island where his father had sought to retrieve his fortune after the failure of Law's Mississippi scheme. The pictures presented in the writings of St. Pierre might appear exaggerated, or prejudiced, if drawn by a foreigner; but it must be borne in mind that he describes only what he witnessed, and that his good faith has never been questioned.[12] He thus speaks of the importation and treatment of slaves:

"They are landed with just a rag around their loins. The men are ranged on one side and the women on the other with their infants, who cling from fear to their mothers. The planter, having examined them as he would a horse, buys what may then attract him. Brothers, sisters, friends, lovers, are now torn asunder, and bidding each other a long farewell, are driven weeping to the plantations they are bought for. Sometimes they turned desperate, fancying that the white people intended eating their flesh, making red wine of their blood, and powder of their bones. They were treated in the following manner:

"At break of day a signal of three smacks of a whip called them to work, when each betook himself with his spade to the plantation, where they worked almost naked in the heat of the sun. Their food was bruised or boiled maize, or bread made of cassava root, their clothing a single piece of linen. Upon the commission of the most trivial offence, they were tied hands and feet to a ladder, where the overseer approached with a whip like a postilion's and gave them fifty, a hundred, and perhaps two hundred lashes upon the back. Each stroke carried off its portion of skin. The poor wretch was then untied, an iron collar with three spikes put round his neck, and he was then sent back to his task. Some of them were unable to sit down for a month after this beating—a punishment inflicted with equal severity on women as on men. In the evening, when they returned home, they were obliged to pray for the prosperity of their masters, and wish them a good night before they retired to rest. There was a law in force in their favor called the *Code Noir* or the Black Code, which ordained that they should receive no more than thirty lashes for any offence, that they should not work on Sundays, that they should eat meat once a week, and have a new shirt every year; but this was not observed."[13]

Soumerat, who visited the island during the period of slavery, speaks of their treatment by their white masters in the following terms:

"I have known humane and compassionate masters who, instead of maltreating them, tried to mitigate their servile condition, but they are very few in number. The rest exercise over their Negroes a cruel and revolting tyranny. The slave, after having labored the whole day, sees himself obliged to search for his food in the woods, and lives only on unwholesome roots. They die of misery and bad treatment, without exciting the smallest feeling of pity, and consequently they never let slip any opportunity of breaking their chains in order to escape to the forests in search of independence and misery."

So miserable indeed was their condition that they welcomed death as a friend, and often committed crime in the hope of being executed.[14] Conditions decidedly improved in Mauritius, however, after the British took possession in 1814. The freedom of slaves was then agitated throughout the civilized world. The British interfered with slavery there in 1826, endeavoring to ease the burden of the bondmen. In 1829 the charter of the slave population was proclaimed. It provided for the religious instruction of the slaves, the recognition of the sanctity of the Sabbath, toleration in worship, the right of the slave to contract marriage, and prohibition of the separation of husband from wife or the mother from her children. Slaves were made competent to acquire stock and movable or immovable property. They were given power to dispose of property by will. Punishments were diminished and the way to elevation to civil power was opened.[15]

The end of this ordeal finally came. The British Emancipation Act was passed in 1833. From 1834 the traffic in human flesh ceased. In 1839 all slaves in Mauritius six years old and upwards became apprentice laborers and remained so until 1841 as regarded field laborers, and until 1839 for those unattached. There were then in the island 39,464 men and boys and 25,856 women and girls, in all 65,320. Knowing that the change in the status of so many inhabitants might interfere with the labor supply, the planters prepared for this contingency by importing coolies from Ceylon and India. By 1838 they had brought in 24,566 such natives, but because they had managed the importation so badly that many evils resulted therefrom, it was stopped by public protest. When the apprentices were freed in 1839, however, there followed such a scarcity of labor that the immigration of the Cingalese and Hindoos was reopened. So many have since then made their way to the island that they now constitute a substantial element of the colony. So much race admixture has followed, on the other hand, that observers sometimes refer to the Mauritians as creoles and coolies.

A. F. FOKEER

FOOTNOTES:

[1] For the leading facts of the life and history of Mauritius see the following: Charles Pridham's England's Colonial Empire (London, 1846); Le Premier Établissment des Neerlandais à Maurice; A Transport Voyage to the Mauritius and Back; Baron Grant, History of Mauritius or the Isle of France and the Neighboring Islands; Jacques Henri Bernardin de St. Pierre, A Voyage to the Island of Mauritius, the Isle of Bourbon, the Cape of Good Hope, etc. (London, 1775); Le Baron d'Unienville, Statistique de l'île de France et ses Dépendances (Paris, 1838); M. J. Milbert, Voyage pittoresque de l'île de France à Cap de Bonne Espérance et à l'île de Teneriffe (Paris, 1812); Adrien d'Epinay, Renseignements pour servir à l'histoire de l'île de France jusqu'à l'année 1810, inclusivement, précédés de notes sur le découverte de l'île sur l'occupation hollandaise; Henri Prentout, L'île de France sous Decaen, 1803–1810 (Paris, 1901); Patrick Beaton, Creoles and Coolies (London, 1858); Nicholas Pike, Subtropical Rambles in the Land of the Aphanapteryx (New York, 1873); and An Account of the Island of Mauritius and its Dependencies by a Late Official Resident.

[2] Adrian d'Espinay Renseignments, etc., 112–113; An Account of the Island of Mauritius, 19.

[3] Grant, History of Mauritius, 74.

[4] Grant, History of Mauritius, 74–75.

[5] Grant, History of Mauritius, p. 75, 1801.

[6] Pridham, England's Colonial Empire, I, 160.

[7] Beaton, *Creoles and Coolies*, 94–111; *An Account of the Island of Mauritius and its Dependencies by a Late Official Resident*, p. 19; Adrien d'Epinay, *Renseignments, etc.*, pp. 112–113.

[8] Henri Prentout, *L'île de France sous DeCaen*, 126.

[9] Pridham, p. 154.

[10] *Ibid.*, p. 156.

[11] Pridham, p. 157.

[12] Pridham, pp. 164, 165.

[13] Bernardin de St. Pierre, *A Voyage*, etc., pp. 100–105.

[14] Pridham, p. 161.

[15] *Ibid.*, pp. 175–175.

DOCUMENTS

LETTERS COLLECTED BY R. E. PARK AND BOOKER T. WASHINGTON

This is an extract from the publications of the Southern History Association, Spangenberg's Journal of Travels in North Carolina, 1752.[1]

Whoever comes to North Carolina must prepare to pay a poll tax. Poll tax is required from all white men, master or servant, from 16 years of age and on; all Negroes and Negresses pay poll tax from their twelfth year. Whoever marries a Negro, or Indian, a mixed blood—his children are liable to the fourth degree from the twelfth year on, and the female Indian or Negro is also taxable. Should this tax not be paid to the sheriff—by whom it is demanded, he is empowered to sell anything belonging to the delinquent party, he can seize at public vendue, and after keeping enough to pay his own fees and satisfy the tax he returns the remainder to the party.

When anyone wishes to marry he must go to the clerk of his county and deposit a Bond for fifty pounds, as assurance that there is no obstacle or impediment to his marying.

He then receives a certificate which he presents to the Justice, who gives him his license: he may then get married. The fees are 20 shillings for the clerk—five shillings for the Justice; 10 shillings for the Minister. Should the "Banns be published," however the license fee is not required. Should the marriage not be performed by the Minister, his fee must, nevertheless, be offered to him. Whoever marries a Negress, Indian, Mulatto or anything of mixed blood, must pay a fine of fifty pounds. Whoever marries such a couple must also pay a fine of fifty pounds.

If a slave or servant buys or sells anything without his master's knowledge and consent, the parties dealing with him shall not only lose three times the amount bargained for, but also pay a penalty of six pounds.

Whoever assists a slave to escape from his master, be it much or little, shall serve the master 5 years, as punishment.

The following is a letter from an investigator seeking in Ohio information concerning the Randolph slaves:

NOVEMBER 18, '08.

Dr. Park:—

The following is what I found in answer to your questions concerning the Randolph slaves in Ohio:

In Virginia, they lived in Charlotte and Prince Edward Counties on the Roanoke River.

They traveled overland, in wagons and carts from there

to Cincinnati and from Cincinnati, to Mercer Co., in Ohio by flat boats. The land which is said to have been bought for them was in Mercer Co.

The settlers of the Community were mainly Germans who would not allow the landing of the Negroes where they arrived there.

The Colony then moved down the Miami River, settled in camp in Miami County not far from the towns of Piqua and Troy.

They never got possession of any of the land supposed to have been purchased for them.

The citizens of Piqua held a mass meeting to discuss the condition of the Negroes in Camp, to decide upon some course of action in regard to them.

The decision was to find employment for them wherever they could and distribute them accordingly. Some were sent to Shelby County-Sidney, about 12 miles N. E. of Piqua—being the county seat. Several descendants live in this community yet.

Many remained in & about Piqua & Troy where there are still few of the old ones & many descendents. Some were sent into Indiana and other parts of Ohio. There were 385 of them.

The most noted of them is Mr. Goodrich Giles. His father was a member of the Colony. His mother belonged to another planter in Virginia & did not get to go.

Mr. Giles is without any question a Negro. He farms

& has succeeded at it. He owns 425 acres of land just out from Piqua not an acre of which is said to be worth less than one hundred dollars. He lives in a good roomy brick house, has good farm buildings, is supplied with farming implements and though old is still active— leading in his work.

His crop this year consists of about,

4500 bus. Corn
500 bus. Oats
1400 bus. Wheat
100 tons Hay with potatoes & other crops in smaller quantity but enough to do him.

He raises most of his meat. Has twelve horses & fifteen cows.

He is a good churchman, attends, counsels and pays. Believes in lodges & helps them too. His city property is said to be worth from $15,000 to $20,000. His obligations he says are very slight, well within his ability to handle. The best citizens of the community are loud in praise of him.

Mr. Fountain Randolph went up with the colony a boy. He is not very active now & has not prospered as Giles has, but lives in his own house of brick with four rooms I think, and is still respected by the community. He & Giles lead in trying to keep the descendents of the colony together & in the effort to get the land which it is claimed was bought for them.

Randolph still lives in Piqua. A son of his, John S.

Randolph was born there, educated in the city schools, and was called to Macon, Ga. several years ago to teach in the schools there, is reported to have done well, established a school at Montezuma, Ga. known as Bennett University. I have not had chance to look him up or his work.

A Miss Anna Jones born at Troy, O. is a descendent who has been prominent as teacher I was told. Mr. Fountain Randolph said she now lives & teaches at Wilberforce as Mrs. Coleman. I wrote Prof. Scarborough about her but have not heard from him.

Mr. Robert Gordon living at Troy is prospering in business and is greatly helped—says Mr. Randolph, by his wife who is one of the descendants.

Mr. Samuel White at Troy is a prosperous farmer owning his farm & is a successful Tobacco grower. He is a descendent.

Mr. Cash Evans is a prosperous barber in Piqua. He is one of the descendants & is said to own several houses there.

In the summer of 1901 Messrs Goodrich Giles & Fountain Randolph started what became known as "The Randolph Slave Society."

It grew out of a custom in Ohio of holding what they call "Family Reunions" one day in each year. This is a day of feasting and special amusement of some kind when all the members and relatives of a family from far and near are brought together and rejoice among themselves.

The day chosen is usually the anniversary of the birth of some member of the family when all others make special effort to cheer that one, bringing presents & greetings of various sorts.

Giles & Randolph being impressed with this, arranged for a picnic and invited all the members of the Randolph colony that could be reached and their descendents. A number came and spent the day pleasantly together. A permanent organization was effected. Mr. Fountain Randolph was made President & still holds that position.

That meeting and later ones attracted attention. The Newspapers got interested and began to write them up. The story of their going into Ohio, of the land which was said to have been bought for them in Mercer Co., and of the refusal of the settlers to permit them to occupy the land and more was set forth in the papers. Then lawyers began to talk with them about the lands. A colored lawyer named Henderson from Indianapolis was among the first to call upon them advising that the land could be secured. He was employed to look it up, He advised & secured the employment of a white lawyer, Mr. Johnson at Salina, O. in Mercer Co. to assist him in working out the matter. Mr. Johnson is said to have a certified copy of the Randolph will providing for the liberation of the slaves—their transportation into Ohio, the purchase of land for them, its distribution among them etc. How much money has been raised for the lawyers I could not find but some money has been raised & more probably will be.

Speaking of John Randolph the Master, old Mr.

Fountain Randolph said "my father said he had lots of peculiarities about him. He never sold a slave & never allowed them to be abused. He never sold any produce as corn, meat and stuffs used by the slaves without first enquiring of the slaves if they could spare it. He would say to the person wanting to buy "You must ask my slaves." "and my mother said:" continued Mr. Randolph "He would often go among his slaves, parents & children & pat them on the head saying 'all these are my children.' His chief body guard was a faithful slave called John White for whom some special mention & provision was made in the will."

This man went with the colony to Ohio, was respected by the others & treated by them just as if he had not been favored by the Master, says Mr. Randolph.

The master gave as his reason for not marrying that should he die—his heirs would want to hold the slaves or sell them and he wanted neither of the things to happen.

He often called the slaves together and asked which they preferred: "Freedom while he lived or after his death and they always said after his death."

Mr. Fountain Randolph has in his possession an old copy of "Life of Randolph of Roanoke" written by Hugh A. Garland, & Published in New York in 1850 by D. Appleton & Co. and Published in Phila. the same year by G. S. Appleton & Co. It is in two volumes. Mr. Randolph had both Vols. but loaned Volume I to the Indianapolis lawyer & has not been able to get it back.

The Randolph will is set forth in Vol. II from which I made the following notes:

Will 1st written in 1819 & left with Dr. Brockenbrough saying:

"I give my slaves their freedom to which my conscience tells me they are justly entitled. It has long been a matter of deepest regret to me that the circumstances under which I inherited them and the obstacles thrown in the way by the laws of the land have prevented my emancipating them in my life time which it is my full intention to do in case I can accomplish it. All the rest & residue of my estate (with exceptions herein after made) whether real or personal, I bequeath to Wm. Leigh, Esq., of Halifax, Atty at Law, to the Rev. Wm. Meade of Frederic and Francis Scott Key Esq., of Georgetown, D. C. in trust for the following uses and purposes viz:

1st To provide one or more tracts of land in any of the States or Territories not exceeding in the whole 4000 acres nor less than 2000 acres, to be partitioned & apportioned by them in such manner as to them shall seem best, among the said slaves.

2nd To pay the expense of their removal & of furnishing them with necessary cabins, clothes & utensils."

In 1821 another Will was written saying: 1st I give and bequeath to all my slaves their freedom—heartily regretting that I have ever been the owner of one.

2nd I give to my executor a sum not exceeding $8,000

or so much thereof as may be necessary to transport & settle said slaves to & in some other state or Territory of the United States, giving to all above the age of 40 not less than ten acres of land each.

Then special annuities to his "old faithful servants Essex & his wife, Hetty, same to woman servant Nancy to John (alias Jupiter) to Queen and to Johnny his body servant." In 1826 a codicil was written confirming previous wills. In 1828 a codicil to will in possession of Wm. Leigh Esq., confirming it as his last will and testament revoking any and all other wills or codicil at variance that may be found.

In 1831 on starting home from London another codicil adding to former provisions as follows:

Upwards of 2000 £ were left in the hands of Baring Bros, & Co of London & upwards of 1000 £ in the hands of Gowan & Marx to be used by Leigh as fund for executing the will regarding the slaves.

Respectfully yours,

The following account and the clipping attached thereto give an interesting story of the success and the philanthropy of a Negro:

I was born in Milledgeville, Ga. about the year 1867. My mother belonged to a white man by the name of Dr. Garner Edwards. My father belonged to a different family. About two weeks after I was born my mother died. She was still working for the same people who once owned her. She was much liked by them so they decided to keep her child and try and raise it. They taught me at home so when I went to school I knew how to read and write. They sent me to a school four or five years. Dr. Edwards had a son by the name of Miller or (Buck) Edwards. It was through him that I received my schooling as Dr. was old and Miller was the support of the house. After years Miller died and I had to stop school and go to work. I worked in a number of stores in Milledgeville and was always trusted.

My earnings I always carried them home and gave them to the white people. They never asked me for anything. They gave me all I made but I thought they needed it more than I, so that went on for a number of years. At this time I was about twenty years old so I told them I was going to Macon, Ga. to work. I secured work at the Central R. R. Shop. I worked on the yard a number of months. During that time I was called off the yard at different times to work in the office when some one wanted to get off. Finally I was given one office to clean up. My work was so satisfactory until I was moved from the shop to the car shed and was given a job of delivering R. R. Mail. I was promoted three times in two years. It was then where I became acquainted with a route agent. He boarded at the same house. We were often in conversation. He was telling me of a daughter he had in school. I told him I wanted to go but I was not able. He ask me did I know Booker Washington. I said no. He said well he runs a school where you can work your way through school. I told him I would like to go so he gave me the address. I wrote and received a little pamphlet. I was looking for a catalogue so I was much disappointed in getting this little book and said it was not much. But I decided to go and try. I did not have much money. I had been living high in Macon and spending all I made. I did not stay to make more but left in about four weeks after I received the first letter. I asked for a pass to Montgomery. It was given me. I arrived in Montgomery with 10 or 12 dollars. I said well I am going to school so I will have a good time before going so I got broke did not know any one, thought my trip was up. I walked up the street one morning. In passing a drug store I saw a young man inside. I step back a few steps to look again. I recognized it to be some one I knew some years ago so the first thing came in mind was to borrow enough money from him to take me to Tuskegee. After a long talk he asked me where I was going and what I was doing there, so now was my chance. I told him I was on my way to Tuskegee. He said it was a fine that he had worked up there. I told him I had spent all the money I had and wanted to borrow enough to get there which he very liberally responded. But before I saw him I begged a stamp and some paper and wrote to Mr. Washington that if he would send me the money to come from there I would pay him in work when I came. I received an answer from Mr. Logan stating that if I would go to work there it would not be long before I would get enough money to come on so I borrowed some money from that man and landed there with $3.40. The food was very poor so I soon ate that up. I was not satisfied at first and wanted to leave but I did not have any money and did not want to write home because I did not want my white people to know where I was until I accomplished something so I made up my mind that if all these boys and girls I see can stay here, I can too. So I was never bothered any more. I went to work at the brick mason's trade under Mr. Carter. They did not have any teacher at that time. Soon after Mr. J. M. Green came and I learned fast and was soon a corner man. I was a student two years and nine months. After that time I secured an excuse and left for home. I was very proud of my trade and all seemed to be surprised as no one knew where I was but my white people. I wrote to them once a month and they always answered and would send me money, clothes something to eat. They were very glad I had gone there and tried to help me in many ways when I got home. They had spoken to a contractor and I had no trouble in getting work. I worked at home about two years. Meantime I received a letter from Mr. Washington stating he would like for me to return and work on the chapel, which I did. At this time I was a hired man and not a student. I worked for the school five or six years. Within that time I had helped build two houses in Milledgeville Ga. and paid for them and bought me thirty acres of land in Tuskegee, Ala. I feel very grateful to the school for she has help me in a great many ways. I have always had a great desire to farm but I said I never would farm until I owned my land and stock.

So three years ago I bought some land and I am at the present time farming. I like it and I expect I will continue at farming instead of my trade. My white people are as good to me now as they were when I was a boy. I made it a rule not to ask them for anything unless I was compelled to but when I do they always send more that

I ask for. I will say that I did not know the real value of a dollar until I had spent 2 years and 9 months at Tuskegee. The teachings from the various teachers and the Sunday evening talks of Mr. Washington made an indellible impression upon my heart. I remember the first Sunday evening talk that I ever heard him. He spoke of things that were in line with my thoughts and I have tried to put them in practice ever since I have been connected with the school. There is one word I heard Mr. W. Speak 13 years ago that has followed me because I was taught the same words by my white people and they were not to do anything that will bring disgrace upon the school you attend. I was taught not to do anything that will bring disgrace upon the people that raised you. There are a number of other thoughts that I will not take time to mention for I have thanked him a thousand times for those Sunday evenings talks.

GARNER J. EDWARDS

The Republican—Springfield, Mass.—Dec. 6, 1902.

The Milledgeville (Ga.) *News* of November tells the following interesting story of one of the young colored men connected with Booker T. Washington's school at Tuskegee, in regard to the work of which Mr. Washington is to speak in the high school hall in this city the 10th:—

A case has come to the News which deserves more than a mere passing mention. The story deals with the prettiest case of loyal Negro's devotion and gratitude to his white benefactors that we ever knew of. When we refer to the incident as a story we mean that there is in it a good subject for a real story with a genuine hero. And every word of it is true; in fact, there is more truth in it than we feel at liberty to tell.

About 30 years ago Buck Edwards of this city picked up a very small and dark-colored boy and undertook, in his language, "to raise him and make something of him." Mr. Edwards clothed and fed the boy, and in a general way taught him many things. In return the boy was bright and quick, and rendered such return as a boy of his years could. His name was Garner, and in time he came to be known as Garner Edwards, which name I think he yet clings to.

In the course of human events, Mr. Edwards passed from the stage of life and went to reap the reward of those who rescue the perishing and support the orphans. After his death, Mr. Edward's sisters, Misses Fanny and Laura, continued to care for the boy, and raised him to manhood. Garner was proud of his family, "and was as faithful as a watchdog, honest at all times, and a great protection to the good ladies who were befriending him, and who were now also alone in the world without parents or brothers. When Garner grew into manhood he did not forsake the home that had sheltered him, but insisted that it was his home— the only home he knew—and that it was his duty and pleasure to aid in supporting it; and he did come to bear a considerable part of its expenses.

Garner learned to be a brickmason, and finally moved to Alabama. He became acquainted with Booker Washington, the great Negro Educator, and the acquaintance ripened into friendship. Washington aided Garner in getting work that would enable him to take a course in the school at Tuskegee and at the same time be self-sustaining. Here as in all other of his positions, Garner made a good record and won many honors. In the meantime he did not forget the folks at home, and his remittances to them were always punctual. After finishing school he married, but continued in the employ of the school and Booker Washington and is there yet.

Sometime ago Miss Laura had a fall and sustained a painful injury which confined her to her room. As soon as Garner heard of it he telephoned to Warren Edwards here to provide the best medical attendance possible, and to supply every want at his expense. Following the telegraph came his wife, a trained nurse, "to take care of his white folks," and she is here yet performing every duty with a devotion seldom witnessed. Garner wanted to come too, very much, but he sacrificed the pleasure to keep his salary doing, "because they might need something."

Garner paid the taxes on the old home for years, but in the meantime he has saved enough to buy him another home in Alabama. No one of any color could have been more faithful and appreciative, and such gratitude and devotion as this humble Negro has shown for his white benefactors is a lovely thing to behold in this selfish day. It is said that he never once presumed anything or forgot his place and the respect due to those around him.[2]

The following letter and list accompanying it explain themselves:

BELOIT, WIS. DEC. 28, 1906.

Dear Mr. Washington

In answer to your telegram for names of graduates and former students engaged in farming in Ala I send the following. I know there are others especially former students but I cannot now recall names. I will try to add to the list if possible.

I would say in regard to the Bowen sisters they have about 600 acres of land and look after the cultivation of it and some parts Cornelia and Katie care for directly actually raising a crop. McRae farmed last year at Louisville, Ala. the year just closing. Mr. W. A. Menafee has 200 acres of land at Alexander City. This he super-intendents by two visits each year. Those marked with a cross farm on their own land. Edwards and Barnes own land at Snow Hill which they farm by the labor of others. Whether they and Mr. Chambliss come under the head of farmers according to your idea you can decide.

I leave January 3 for Denmark, S. C. You can write me there till further notice.

YOURS

(SIGNED) R. C. BEDFORD

GRADUATES AND FORMER STUDENTS ENGAGED IN FARMING IN ALA.
Wholly Or in Part

*Cornelia Bowen '85 also teaches	Waugh, Ala.
J. T. Hollis '85 also teaches	Armstrong, Ala.
*Berry Bowen Campbell '84 also nurses	Waugh, Ala.
W. D. Floyd, teaches also	Hawkinsville, Ala.
Watt Buchanan 1889 farming wholly	Montgomery, Ala.
*Enoch Houser 1889 also teaches	Antangville, Ala.
William Chambliss 1890	Tuskegee, Ala.
*Davis Henry 1890	Bells Landing, Ala.
*Abner Jackson 1890	Newville, Ala.
John W. Perry 1890	Myrtle, Ala.
Abner Edwards 1890	Salem, Ala.
*J. H. Michael 1890	Mt. Meigs, Ala.
Robert B. Sherman 1890	Sprague Jc., Ala.
*H. A. Barnes 1893	Snow Hill, Ala.
*W. J. Edwards 1893	Snow Hill, Ala.
*N. E. Henry 1893	China, Ala.
Sophia Momen 1894	Notasulga, Ala.
*C. A. Barrows 1894	Snow Hill, Ala.
*S. F. Bizzell, has a store 1894	Hammac, Ala.
E. W. McRae 1894 also teaches	Louisville, Ala.
*Moses Purifoy 1894 also teaches	Evergreen, Ala.
*J. C. Calloway 1896 also teaches	Dawkins, Ala.
Geo. W. Henderson, preacher 1899	Hannon, Ala.
*Martin A. Menafee, Treasurer 1900	Alexander City, Ala.
George K. Gordon, Dairying 1902	Mobile, Ala.

FORMER STUDENTS

Katie Bowen also teaches	Waugh, Ala.
Benjamin Jones	Waugh, Ala.
Nelson Judkins	Cecil, Ala.
Gomine Judkins	Cecil, Ala.
Wm. Plato, also black smith	Waugh, Ala.
James Pinckett, carpenter	Waugh, Ala.
Ossie Williams	Waugh, Ala.
James Garrison	Waugh, Ala.
Nelson Garrison	Waugh, Ala.
John Mitchell also painter	Waugh, Ala.
*Wallace Campbell blacksmith	Fitzpatrick, Ala.
*R. T. Phillips blacksmith	

This is a letter from a Negro farmer in the south:

Isaac P. Martin—

Merryweather Co—near Stenson

Father belonged to Peter Martin near about 3 miles from where he was born—never did own any land. Went to work planting at 9—Worked 9 to 25—Had six or eight months schooling—Went one month in a year. School lasted about three months. Used Blue Back Speller got as high as Baker; Got as far as subtraction—Did not know anything outside of reading—Did not know what a newspaper was.

Father taught us to work corn, cotton sweet potatoes— He was a —— farmer—Had eleven children all worked—about 1880 they began to grow up and leave the farm—go on some other plantation—all married.

My older brother and all the younger children got more schooling Brother next younger—Payne's Institute Ga.—finished preaching in Americus Georgia. I had a cousin to come here—He wanted to buy —— here—He was interested in machine shop—He was down in Opelika. He met more boys on their way here, inquiring around to get down this far and get in.

I had saved up $200 in the bank. I was going to buy land. Went into day school a Preparatory about 800 or 900 students. The first work was in harness & shoe shop—Lewis Adams was in charge—I came there walking. I wanted to get away from the farm. Going around town I saw that everyone looked better than on the farm—I wanted to be something. Went in twice a year. We had plenty country churches. Rabbits, squirrels, ducks, possums—Geography, reading, Wentworth's Arithmetic. Miss Hunt and Miss Logan were one of my teachers. I read lots about Hiawatha. There was a number of little boys in the shop—they used to call me "Pop." They were ahead of me. Went to Blacksmith Shop. Worked about four months. Then went to work in Wheelwright. I learn a good deal about blacksmith and wood work. I find both these trade very handy.

I was here three weeks before I could eat in the dining room—had to go to restaurant—I was ashamed.

I was here only one term. Came in 1895—left in 96—Never came back until tonight. My mother sent for me—My mother was awful sick. My class was so low that I was ashamed to come back. I weighed 240 pounds. I went back home until 1898—on farm. I got to read my newspapers. I subscribed for the semi-monthly Atlanta Journal—I could read that.

I saw advertised and so much money paid out for wages—I thought I would go into business. I started grocery store and meat market—I had $2,500 made on farm. Father used to run us off the farm at 20 so I rented some land.

I was born 1870. I had been working for myself for years. 1898 I came to Birmingham. I failed in grocery business. "Credit." I made a lot of friends all over town. ································· They had lots of money but they owed a lot. It take lot to feed them. Took three years and little over to get all of money.

Worked for Tenn. Coal and Iron Co. I leased some land from the Republic Iron and Steel Co. Leased 64 acres outside of Pratt City and went to trucking. I bought two mules for $40. It was a sale. They were old run down mules. They were blind—I worked there until I grew something. Farm about a mile from Pretts. Paid $1.50 per acre—now I pay $7. The company would not sell. I peddle vegetables to people here—ran two wagons— now I run three. Got new feed for horses. By fall had lots of stuff. Married in 1900—year after went to Birmingham. Second year I was able to buy two good mules—Had two good wagons made. Fall of second year had another which made three. Running three now. I employ six people—3 men and 3 women all the time. I drive the wholesale wagon.

I raise between $3,500 and $4,000 worth of stuff each year. Have since the second year. I sell about $2,000 a year above expenses. Production increases every year. I learned all I know about trucking since then. I have fifteen head of cattle. Eight milking cows. I raise three crops. That is the highest. Third crop is not worth so much. 90,000 cabbages this year. Got the plants from South Carolina. I bought a piece of land in Oklahoma for $3,000 outside of 22 miles from Muskogee. Land rents now for $300. I own a lot in Red Bird. Have 2 children. 14 & and 17. They go to school.

Won county prize year before last—196 bushels—this year received State prize 200 bushels. Plant eight and ten acres of cotton, 14 acres corn. Raise all my fodder. Three-fourths acres of new sugar cane, 150 gals. of syrup. I make butter $30 per hundred. $40 retail. I take two or three little farm journals and take the bulletin.

These letters addressed to R. E. Park and to Booker T. Washington give information about the estate of John McKee:

Estate of }
JOHN MCKEE, }
Deceased. }

HON. BOOKER T. WASHINGTON,
Tuskegee Institute,
 Alabama,

Dear sir:

Your favor has been received and in reply thereto I would state that the State Appraiser fixed the valuation in Estate of the late Colonel John McKee as follows:

Gross valuation of Personal estate,	$ 71,644.29
Gross valuation of real estate in Pennsylvania,	271,188.33
Making together,	$342,832.62
Net valuation of the above,	$212,831.86

Of this $46,500. is in unimproved real estate from which, at this time, no income is derived.

In addition to the above the Estate owns the following from which no income (or but a nominal income) is derived:—a lot in Gloucester County, New Jersey, valued at One hundred Dollars ($100),—a large area of land in Atlantic County, New Jersey, known as McKee City, assessed for taxation at twenty-thousand six hundred and fifty Dollars ($20,650) and a tract of coal and mineral lands in Kentucky, which Colonel McKee always considered would turn out to be valuable and would eventually realize a considerable sum. It is assessed for taxation for 1909 at Seventy thousand Dollars ($70,000)—

In brief the testamentary directions of Colonel McKee are to accumulate the rents and income of his estate until the decease of all his children and grand-children, meanwhile improving (under certain conditions) his unimproved real estate. Upon the death of all his children and grand-children, the estate is to be made use of in the establishment and maintenance of a college for the education of colored and white fatherless boys.

VERY TRULY YOURS,

JOSEPH P. MCCULLEN
FEBRUARY 23, 1909.

MR. ROBERT E. PARK,
 Tuskegee Institute, Ala.,

Dear Sir:

Yours of the 13th inst., post marked the 16th inst., has been received. You state you would be glad to have any information I can give you about Mr. McKee, particularly in regard to the amount of the estate he left at the time of his death.

The value of Mr. McKee's estate has been variously estimated from $1,000,000 to $4,000,000. I am not able to give a more exact estimate, as I have not seen any inventory made by his executors. He owned more than 300 houses in this city, all unencumbered. He also owned oil and coal lands in Kentucky and West Virginia, and lands in Bath and Steuben Counties, N. Y. As to his personal characteristics, I would suggest that you see the Philadelphia Press of April 20, 1902. If you desire a more exact estimate of the value of his estate, I would suggest that you write Joseph P. McCullen, Jr., No. 1008 Land Title Building, this city.

YOURS TRULY,
T. J. MINTON.

The following letter from Colonel James Lewis to Booker T. Washington gives valuable information about

Thomy Lafon and incidentally about other persons in New Orleans:

NEW ORLEANS, LA., JANY. 25/09.

COLONEL JAMES LEWIS,
 Dear Sir:

In answer to your letter of 14th instant, will say that the delay in my answer was caused by my desire to obtain and furnish to you all informations regarding the late Mr. Thomy Lafon.

The baptismal records in the archive of the Cathedral at that time written in Spanish attest that the late Mr. Thomy Lafon was born in this city on December 28th, 1810. He died at his home, corner Ursulines & Robertson Streets, on December 23rd, 1893, at the ripe age of 83 years. His body rests in the St. Louis cemetery on Esplanade Avenue. He was a man of dignified appearance and affable manners. In early life he taught school; later he operated a small dry goods store in Orleans Street until near into 1850. He was never married. Sometime before the war of Secession he had started his vast fortune by loaning money at advantageous rates of interest and by the accumulation of his savings. Toward the close of his career he became attached to the lamented Archbishop Janssens and began his philanthropies. By the terms of his will, dated April 3rd, 1890, he provided amply for his aged sister and some friends, and wisely distributed the bulk of his estate among public charitable institutions of New Orleans. His legacy was appraised at $413,000.00 divided in securities and realty.

In recognition of his charity, the City of New Orleans, named after him one of its public schools.

Before his death he had established an asylum for orphan boys called the Lafon Asylum, situated in St. Peter Street between Claiborne Avenue & N. Derbigny Street. To this Asylum he bequeathed a sum of $2000, and the revenues, amounting to $275 per month of a large property situated corner Royal & Iberville Streets.

Other legacies were to the

Charity Hospital of New Orleans	$10,000
" " Ambulance Dept.	3,000
Lafon Old Folks' Home	5,000
Little Sisters of the Poor	5,000
Shakespeare Almshouse	
Catholic Institution for indigent orphans	2,000

and the following property:

1st. St. Claude St. bet. St. Philip & Ursulines Sts., valued at	$1500
2nd. Robertson St. bet. St. Philip & Ursulines Sts., valued at	2000
3rd. Burgundy St. bet. Hospital & Barracks Sts., valued at	2000
4th. Union St. between Royal & Dauphine Sts., valued at	2000
St. John Berchman Asylum for girls, under the care of Holy family	2000

and the following property:

1st. Burgundy St., No. 528, worth about	$1500

2nd. Dumaine St., Nos. 2129/31, worth about	2500
3rd. Galvez St., No. 828, worth about	1800
4th. Toulouse St., Nos. 726/28, worth about	2500
5th. Tulane Ave., No. 1402, worth about	4000
Asylum for old indigents, corner Tonti & Hospital Streets	15000

and the following property:

1st. St. Andrew St., 1536/38 valued at	$ 6000
2nd. Baronne St., No. 722 valued at	4000
3rd. Baronne St. Nos. 732/36 valued at	8000
4th. Canal & Villere Sts. valued at	6000
5th. Canal St., old No. 176 valued at	30000
An another cash	$ 2000
Society of the Holy Family, Orleans St.	10000
Straight University of New Orleans	3000
Southern University of New Orleans	3000
New Orleans University of New Orleans	3000
Society of Jeunes Amis, New Orleans	3000
Eye, Ear Nose & Throat Hospital	3000
Mother St. Clair of the Convent of the Good Sheperd	20000

All of which cash legacies were doubled.

Yours respectfully,

(Signed) P. A. Bacas

FOOTNOTES:

[1] This extract and the documents which follow were collected by Dr. R. E. Park.

[2] *The Springfield Republican, Dec. 6, 1902.*

BOOK REVIEWS

The History of the Negro Church. By CARTER G. WOODSON, Ph.D. The Associated Publishers, Inc., Washington, D. C. 1921. Pp. 330.

With due regard for the modern scientific methods of historiography, the author of this book has traced the rise and spread of institutionalized Christianity among American Negroes. He discusses such salient points as the early efforts of white missionaries to evangelize the heathen bondmen, the difficulties which beset their labors, the respective contributions of the white denominations, showing the Baptists in the lead, followed closely by the Methodists, with the Presbyterians, Catholics and Congregationalists in the rear. There are set forth the psychological, geographical and other reasons why the Negro was attracted more readily to the Baptist and Methodist denominations, the causes for the reactions of slave holders for and against the evangelization of the slaves, the rise of Negro preachers of merit in the Baptist and Methodist denominations during the eighteenth century, and the founding of the first churches by Negroes of these sects. Among these he mentions the first African Baptist Church by Andrew Bryan in 1788, the first African Methodist Episcopal Church by Richard Allen in 1794, and the first African Presbyterian Church by John Gloucester in 1807.

The factors which caused the cleavage of the white denominations into North and South, the causes of the separation of the Negro communicants from the whites and the threefold cleavage of the Negro Methodists are adequately discussed. Attention is given also to the increase in the number of churches and the State and national centralization of the churches within the respective denominations. The ante-bellum beginnings of the only Negro education which aimed to develop Negro preachers through instructors of both races, the importance of Negro churches in developing race leaders, educators, and statesmen who figured in the economic, social and political life of the Negro after the war, are ably treated. The book gives an account of the rise of the conservative and progressive elements within the church and closes with a chapter on the present-day Negro church statistics which indicate the enormous spread of Christianity through the ascendancy of the Methodists and Baptists.

One can hardly appreciate the sympathetic and scholarly character of this work from the bald outline given above. Just therein may it be characterized as a pioneer work, a genuine contribution. In a larger sense it is more than the history of the Negro church; it is the very life history of the Negro race in America, so intimately have the spiritual strivings of the Negro been bound up with his sentiments and interests, his habits and endeavors, his situation and circumstances, his monuments and edifices, his poetry and song.

F. C. SUMNER

Unsung Heroes. By Mrs. ELIZABETH ROSS HAYNES. N. Y. DuBois & Dill. 1921. 279 pp. Illustrated.

One of the gravest problems now facing the Negroes in the United States, and a problem none the less grave because unrecognized by the unthinking majority, is that of reading for their children. Can anything be more dangerous than the continual subjection of our children to the influence of books, magazines, and newspapers in which their race is being held up constantly to pity or contempt? The use of opprobrious and insulting epithets with reference to the Negro is so common in English and American publications as to need no more than a mere reference here, and this practice is to be noted even in authors who are conscious of no active race hostility. If the psychological influence of such endlessly reiterated and therefore inescapable slurs is bad for adults, how much worse must it be for children. In *The Brownies' Book*, published by DuBois and Dill, a most praiseworthy attempt has been made to meet this need in the form of a children's magazine free from all objectionable matter, and it is nothing short of a national calamity that this periodical has been forced to suspend publication because of a lack of sufficient patronage. It is fitting, then, that the same publishers should issue the book now under our hand, a fine specimen of the printer's art in paper, presswork, binding, and illustrations.

In it the author, the wife of Dr. George E. Haynes, the well-known sociologist, has set forth in a language and style suited to young readers the lives of seventeen of the most celebrated men and women of Negro descent. Eight of them—Douglass, Harriet Tubman, Banneker, Phillis Wheatley, Josiah Henson, Sojourner Truth,

Attucks, and Paul Cuffé—belong to the ante-bellum period in America; five—Dunbar, Booker Washington, B. K. Bruce, Crummell, and Langston—to the reconstruction and late nineteenth century periods; and four—Pushkin, the Russian; L'Ouverture, the Haytian; Coleridge-Taylor, the Englishman; and Alexandre Dumas, the Frenchman—belong across the ocean. It will be seen that the selection is a representative one, and that no living person is included. The material chosen from each life is carefully selected, too, to suit the minds and tastes of children. There are six illustrations by four of our well-known young artists. Altogether the book is the most satisfactory addition yet made to our children's literature in this country, and should be in every home where there are colored children, and in every library in which they are readers.

E. C. WILLIAMS

Les Daïmons du Culte Voudo. By DR. ARTHUR HOLLY, Port-au Prince, Haiti, 1919. Pp. lx-523.

The author of this unique volume declares himself "boldly, but without vanity, or false modesty" an esoterist, that is to say, one who is an adept at the interpretation of the occult and secret doctrines. This book, an exposition of the secret doctrine, is not, therefore, as its title might suggest, a scientific treatise upon the Voudo cult as it has existed and as it still exists in Haiti. It is rather an interpretation and defense of the primitive religion of Africa, particularly as it is represented in the religious customs and practices of the common people in Haiti today.

The sentiments which have inspired this undertaking are altogether admirable. "Haitiens," he says, "have reached a point in their efforts to conform to an alien culture where they are in danger of losing their personality as a people as well as their native culture." But now if ever is the moment, after the great cataclysm in Europe, to lift the ancestral cult from the dust and make it worthy of Haiti, of the African race.

"We are," he continues, "African-Latins. But our Latin culture is all on the surface. The old African heritage persists in us and controls us to such an extent that under certain circumstances we feel ourselves moved by mysterious forces when the silence of the night, throbs with the irregular rhythm, melancholly, passionate and magical, of the sacred dances of *Voudo*."

Dr. Arthur Holly is evidently learning, but he draws his knowledge from sources that are esoteric and therefore inaccessible to all except the adepts. What he has written is, therefore, neither science nor history. It has the character rather of revelation. It is impressive, but not intelligible to the uninitiated.

From his introduction, however, one gathers that he intends to show that Christianity and Voudoism are from a common source, that "the Bible," as he says, "belongs to us," *i.e.*, the black people, but that this earlier and more primitive form of religion which is revealed in it has been corrupted by the white race.

It is an interesting idea, but more interesting is the evidence that it offers of the rise, among the Negro people of Haiti, of a racial consciousness which embraces in one conscious unity the Negro peoples of Africa and America. It is another spontaneous manifestation of that unrest of the black man which has found expression in pan-Africanism and in the movement in this country headed by Marcus Garvey, whose program is Africa for the Africans.

ROBERT E. PARK

UNIVERSITY OF CHICAGO

The Wings of Oppression. By LESLIE PINCKNEY HILL. The Stratford Company, Publishers, Boston, Massachusetts. Price by mail, $2.15.

Bearing the certificate of the Lyric Muse, Mr. Leslie Pinckney Hill, schoolmaster of Cheney, Pennsylvania, and authentic singer, is the newest arrival on the slopes of Parnassus. A first glance tells that he is an agile climber, sinewy, easy of movement, light of step, with both grace and strength. Every indication in form and motion is for some point far up toward the summit. Youthful is he, ambitious plainly, and, in spite of a burden, buoyant. "Climber," I said. I will drop the figure. Poets were never pedestrians. Mr. Hill comes not afoot. If not on the wings of Pegasus, yet on wings he comes—*the wings of oppression*. Sad wings! Yet it must be remarked that it is commonly on such wings that poets of whatever race and time rise. And Mr. Hill's race knows no other wings. On the wings of oppression the Negro poet and the Negro people are rising toward the summits of Parnassus, Pisgah, and other peaks. This they know, too, and of it they are justly proud.

In his *Foreword* Mr. Hill thus states the case of his people, and, by implication, of himself:

"Nothing in the life of the nation has seemed to me more significant than that dark civilization which the colored man has built up in the midst of a white society organized against it. The Negro has been driven under all the burdens of oppression, both material and spiritual, to the brink of desperation, but he has always been saved by his philosophy of life. He has advanced against all opposition by a certain elevation of his spirit. He has been made strong in tribulation. He has constrained oppression to give him wings."

The significant thing about these wings, in a critical view, is that they fulfill the proper function of wings— bear aloft and sustain in flight through the azure depths. Mr. Hill's wings do bear aloft and sustain: if not always, nor even ever, into the very empyrean of poetry, yet invariably, seventy times, into the ampler air. Like all his race, he has suffered much; and, like all his race still, he has gathered wisdom from sorrow. As a true poet should have, he has philosophy, also vision and imagination—vision for himself and his people, imagination that sees facts in terms of beauty and presents truths with vital imagery. Add thereto crafts-manship acquired in the best traditions of English poetry and you have Hill the poet.

The merits of this book cannot be shown by the quoting of lines and stanzas. As ever with true art, the merit lies in the effect of complete poems. Still, we can here detach from this and that poem a stanza or two, despite the wrong to art. The first and fourth stanzas of the title-poem will indicate Mr. Hill's technique and philosophy:

> I have a song that few will sing
>
> In honor of all suffering,
>
> A song to which my heart can bring
>
> The homage of believing—
>
> A song the heavy-laden hears
>
> Above the clamor of his fears,
>
> While still he walks with blinding tears,
>
> And drains the cap of grieving.
>
> .   .   .   .   .   .
>
> So long as life is steeped in wrong,
>
> And nations cry: "How long, how long!"
>
> I look not to the wise and strong
>
> For peace and self-possession:
>
> But right will rise, and mercy shine,
>
> And justice lift her conquering sign
>
> Where lowly people starve and pine
>
> Beneath a world oppression.

Significant as interpreting the character and temper of the Negro with whom today the white world has to deal, are the following lines from the blank verse poem entitled *Armageddon*:

> Because ye schooled them in the arts of life,
>
> and gave to them your God, and poured your

blood

Into their veins to make them what they are,

They shall not fail you in your hour of need,

They hold in them enough of you to feel

All that has made you masters in your time—

The power of art and wealth, unending toil,

Proud types of beauty, an unbounded will

To triumph, wondrous science, and old law—

These have they learned to value and to share.

If these poems, taken collectively, do not declare "what is on the Negro's mind," they yet truly reveal, to the reflecting person, what has sunk deep into his heart. They are therefore a message to America, a protest, an appeal, and a warning. They will penetrate, I predict, through breast armor of *aes triplex* into the hearts of those whom sermons and editorials fail to touch in the springs of action. Such is the virtue of music wed to persuasive words.

A sonnet entitled *To a Caged Canary in a Negro Restaurant* will present the poet's people and his own manner of poetic musing:

Thou little golden bird of happy song!

A cage cannot restrain the rapturous joy

Which thou dost shed abroad. Thou dost employ

Thy bondage for high uses. Grievous wrong

Is thine; yet in thy heart glows full and strong

The tropic sun, though far beyond thy flight,

And though thou flutterest there by day and
night

Above the clamor of a dusky throng.

So let my will, albeit hedged about

By creed and caste, feed on the light within;

So let my song sing through the bars of doubt

With light and healing where despair has been;

So let my people bide their time and place,

A hindered but a sunny-hearted race.

It would be an injustice to this poet did I convey the idea
that his seventy-odd poems are exclusively occupied
with race wrongs and oppression. Not a few of them
bear no stamp of an oppressed or afflicted spirit,
though of sorrow they may have been nurtured.

A lyric of pure loveliness is the following, entitled:

To a Nobly-Gifted Singer

All the pleasance of her face

Telleth of an inward grace;

In her dark eyes I have seen

Sorrows of the Nazarene;

In the proud and perfect mould

Of her body I behold,

Rounded in a single view,

The good, the beautiful, the true;

And when her spirit goes up-winging
On sweet air of artless singing,
Surely the heavenly spheres rejoice
In union with a kindred voice.

The Wings of Oppression strikes a high level of artistic expression and makes a quite extraordinary appeal. It is intense poetry, lyrical and meditative.

Here is that solid body of thought which, in addition to artistic expression, is requisite to poetry that attains and holds a high place of esteem. Great variety of form is also here; excellent blank verse with a movement at once easy and restrained, an equable, strong flow, bearing lofty meditations; sonnets after the manner of the masters; octo-syllabics of sententious felicity; various apt lyrical stanzas. Culture alone, of which there is abundant evidence, could not have produced these poems. The poetic endowment, thoroughly disciplined, was necessary. Mr. Leslie Pinckney Hill is a poet. His powers are rich, varied, and developing. His second book will be better than this excellent first.

But more than the merit that has been intimated there is in these lyrics and measured musings a pathos, a restrained Laocoön cry, that must be to thousands an arresting revelation of the unimagined sufferings of the cultured colored people of our land. Mr. Hill's *Wings of Oppression* has a message in it for America.

ROBERT T. KERLIN

LEXINGTON, VA.

NOTES.

By aiding the education of Negroes in rural communities with the assistance of State governments and of Negroes themselves Mr. Julius Rosenwald has been making an important chapter in the history of this race during the last generation. The significance of this achievement is apparent when one merely glances at these statistics:

1223 buildings (2812 teachers).

Total Cost	$4,012,923
Negroes	$1,139,165
Whites	277,668
Public Funds	1,840,210
Rosenwald aid	755,880

These schoolbuildings have been built in the States as follows: Alabama 234, North Carolina 175, Mississippi 145, Louisiana 136, Tennessee 114, Virginia 105, South Carolina 73, Arkansas 54, Georgia 53, Kentucky 52, Texas 50, Maryland 16 and Oklahoma 15.

By types these buildings include:

357	one-teacher
464	two-teacher
191	three-teacher
106	four-teacher
39	five-teacher

32	six-teacher
5	seven-teacher
5	eight-teacher
1	nine-teacher
2	ten-teacher
1	eleven-teacher
1	twelve-teacher
1	sixteen-teacher
18	Teachers' Homes
1223	

The fact that over $4,000,000 has been invested in these buildings is worthy of comment as is the added fact that more than one-fourth of this large total has been raised by the Negroes themselves. While the figures are of buildings which have been actually completed, it is well to note that there are in progress now, some of them nearly finished and all of them to be finished before June 30, 1922, other buildings which will increase the total to 1500, will show a total outlay of $5,500,000, will bring the total of contributions by the Negroes up to $1,500,000, and make Mr. Rosenwald's contribution over $1,000,000. These school building projects and the financial outlays for them have been definitely approved, and all that is lacking is the actual completion of contracts let.

When the work was first undertaken, the thought was to build one-room rural schoolhouses. Under the developing interest, however, larger and better buildings have been erected. As the teacher capacity is an important thing, the total number of teachers has been given to serve as another index to the value of this achievement.

Still another significant thing should be noted. All of the construction now going on is being done through the States themselves. Every project is presented for approval by the State educational authorities, and is certified as completed by the same officers. The interest manifested is sincere and continuing, and in North Carolina, for example, there are no fewer than eight people connected with the office of the Superintendent of Public Instruction who are giving their time toward Negro education.

There is another point too which may be interesting. The buildings are constructed according to definite plans and specifications and no building receives Rosenwald aid unless it conforms to the details of such plans and specifications. As a result in the Rosenwald schools the windows are so placed as to give the right kind of light; the blackboards too are properly located; and the equipment in the way of desks is the best available for the funds on hand. No school building is paid for until inspection has shown it to be built according to the approved ideas.

The following extract from *Current History*, Vol. XV, pages 771-772, sets forth the participation of Alice Ball, a scholarly Negro chemist, in the treatment of leprosy through the use of chaulmoogra oil extracted by a difficult scientific process.

"Credit for initiating a revolutionary method of

treatment is generally ascribed to Dr. Victor Heiser of the United States Public Health Service in the Philippines. Instead of giving raw chaulmoogra oil in doses, as had been the custom for centuries, he gave it by injection to the muscles. Mixed with olive oil and drugs, it was efficacious and helped all patients treated. The old method of taking the oil through the mouth, even in capsules, produced such violent nausea that very few could retain it. If retained, it was healing; the best remedy then known. The success of the Heiser treatment led physicians generally to adopt injections as the best method of giving the oil, but it was thick and not easily absorbed. This led Dr. Harry T. Hollman, a member of the Government Medical Corps at Honolulu, to call for a more diluted form of the oil, one freed from extraneous matter, an ethyl ester, or the vital principle, if there was one. The decomposition of the oil, he said, should be accomplished outside the body.

"After securing the approval of his superiors, Drs. McCoy and Currie, he asked the Chemistry Department of the University of Hawaii to liberate this essence from the vegetable compound. President Dean, himself an expert chemist, became greatly interested. He assigned to the task Miss Alice Ball, a young negro woman and an expert chemist, who found the task exceedingly elusive. She gave it all her time and secured a light essence, which Dr. Hollman administered with improved results; but he still insisted it could be improved. Miss Ball's health failed, possibly from chemical poisoning, and she went to California to recuperate. On her return she again took up the task, aided by Dr. Dean, but was again forced to give up the work entirely and soon afterward died in California.

"President Dean then entered upon the task with redoubled enthusiasm. He was encouraged from results obtained to give every possible aid to the indomitable and optimistic Dr. Hollman. There were months of persistent effort, the devising of expensive and complicated apparatus, including a special furnace for intense heat. At last the precise ethyl ester desired—with a number of others—was secured. Injections were made as before into the hips of patients—the large muscles were selected to avoid any possible introduction of the medicine into the large veins or arteries. The improvement following in every case was so marked as to cause surprise and decided gratification."

On the 3rd and 4th of April, the Association for the Study of Negro Life and History will hold its spring conference in New York City. This meeting will come as a climax of a nation-wide membership drive now being conducted by the Association. The plans are to have present a large representation of persons from the various parts of the country that steps may be taken for a more thorough prosecution of the work.

THE JOURNAL OF
NEGRO HISTORY

VOL. VII—JULY, 1922—No. 3

THE ANDERSON FUGITIVE CASE

The recent decision of the Canadian government not to allow deportation to proceed in the case of Matthew Bullock, a Negro whose return was asked by the State of North Carolina, has served to recall to public attention in Canada certain cases occurring during the period of slavery in the United States when the Canadian courts were asked to order the return of fugitives. The most famous of these was the Anderson case tried before the Canadian courts at Toronto, in 1860, interest in which stirred the British provinces from end to end.

The Bullock case, recently decided, has some points of similarity to the Anderson case, though the circumstances vary greatly. Bullock was charged with participation in race riots in North Carolina in January 1921. He had made his way to Canada and succeeded in evading the immigration authorities in entering the country. It was admitted by the Canadian authorities that he was in the country illegally but in the final decision it was stated that, as he had conducted himself in an exemplary manner since entering, he would be allowed to remain. On behalf of the fugitive it was freely hinted that should he be returned to North Carolina he would risk being a victim of mob justice. While this plea doubtless influenced the Canadian immigration authorities, it could not, of course, be stated as their reason for allowing the man his freedom.

The Anderson case of 1860, to which so much newspaper reference was made during the progress of the Bullock case, came just on the eve of the American Civil War. In some respects it looked to be one of the last efforts of the slave-owners to secure complete enforcement of the Fugitive Slave Law of 1850. That measure, so detested by the North, became a dead letter in many sections by the force of public opinion but was also weakened by the fact that the fugitive in the North could soon cross into Canada, if threatened by any sudden enforcement of the law. An arrest under the Fugitive Slave Law in any northern city was usually followed by a swift trek into Canada of other Negroes who feared that they might be the next victims. But what if there could be found some means of using British law to secure the return of fugitives from Canada? This appears to have been in the minds of those who tried to get Anderson out of Canada in 1860. It is difficult to account, otherwise, for the strenuous efforts that were made to secure his extradition. That the Missouri slaveholders felt they were performing something in the nature of a public service by fighting this case in the Canadian courts, is evidenced by their request that the State should reimburse them for their outlay.[1]

John Anderson appears to have arrived in Canada in November 1853, crossing over the Detroit River to Windsor where he stayed with Mrs. Bibb, mother of Henry Bibb, who was attempting to organize a refugee settlement not far from that frontier point. Mrs. Laura

S. Haviland, a philanthropic Michigan woman who was doing missionary and educational work among the fugitives, met him soon after his arrival and learned his story. She says that he came to her asking that she write a letter for him. This letter revealed the tragedy in which he had recently figured and that had caused him to flee to Canada. She had noted the sadness in his face which indicated the stress through which he had passed. He told her that to satisfy a debt he had been sold by his master, Seneca Diggs, and was to be separated from his wife and four children. Husband and wife pleaded not to be separated but the reply was that the buyer desired only the man. Later, however, the master indicated that some other arrangement might be arrived at but the man was suspicious and armed himself with a dirk. His suspicions were further aroused when he was told to come to the woods where some trees were to be chopped and when he noticed that the master had a stout rope under his coat. The slave kept at a distance from the master until the latter finally frankly admitted his purpose. The slave declared that he would never be taken but at this point another man appeared and Anderson began to run. The slavers followed him for seven miles and finally had him cornered. Anderson flourished his knife and threatened to kill the first man who laid hands upon him. All stood back but Diggs who, with a knife in his hand, rushed at the slave. In the melee the master was stabbed and the slave escaped into the woods. That night he saw his wife and family for the last time. The woman informed him that he had killed his master and that if he were caught he could expect to be burned alive or chopped to pieces.

She urged him to flee to Canada, and if he arrived there safely, he was to write to her father who was free. This is the story as he told it to Mrs. Haviland and it was the letter to his father-in-law that he wished her to write.

Mrs. Haviland shrewdly suspected that a letter from Canada addressed to a Negro related to Anderson would not likely reach its destination and would also give a clue to the fugitive's whereabouts. Accordingly she dated the letter from Adrian, Michigan, and asked that the reply be sent there. The answer, which came shortly after, said that Anderson's wife and four children were being brought to him. Mrs. Haviland replied to this letter but warned Anderson not to cross the Detroit River as she suspected a plot. In her message she asked the party to come to Adrian, Michigan, and inquire for Mrs. Laura Haviland, a widow, from whom information could be had regarding Anderson. A few days later a white man called, very clearly a southerner, and informed her that Anderson's family was in Detroit staying in the home of a Negro minister named Williams. The visitor seemed exceedingly anxious to find out where Anderson was and Mrs. Haviland finally told him that the man was in Chatham and advised that his family should be sent there. At this the visitor's face reddened rather noticeably. Mrs. Haviland lost no time in sending a message to Anderson advising him to leave Chatham. He got out none too soon for within a few days white men were in Chatham inquiring for him. They were told that he had gone to Sault Ste. Marie and they followed the trail there but without success. Finally they disappeared after leaving with

Detroit people power of attorney to arrest Anderson, if he could ever be decoyed over the river or should be found there.

Mrs. Haviland, in her memoirs, says that after this effort to capture Anderson as a murderer she wrote a letter to Lord Elgin, the Governor of the Canadas, setting forth the facts, and that she received this reply from him: "In case of a demand for William Anderson, he should require the case to be tried in their British courts; and if twelve freeholders should testify that he had been a man of integrity since his arrival in their dominion it should clear him."[2]

There is a rather curious similarity between the latter part of this statement and the recent decision from Ottawa in the Bullock case, namely, that as the latter had conducted himself well since entering the country he should not be deported.

About three years after the events mentioned above, which would be about 1856, Mrs. Haviland records a meeting with D. L. Ward, a New Orleans attorney, who said to her: "We are going to have Anderson by hook or by crook; we will have him by fair means or foul; the South is determined to have that man."

The whereabouts of Anderson between 1853 and 1859 is not on record. Probably he lived most of that time in southwestern Ontario where his own people were most numerous. It is stated that he had worked in Hamilton and Caledonia. In the fall of 1860 he was working near Brantford when it came to the ears of a magistrate at Brantford, Matthews by name, that at some time in the past this Negro had committed a crime and was a fugitive from the justice of his own State. Matthews had the Negro arrested and locked him up. It would appear that he had no evidence of any kind other than rumor. S. B. Freeman, who defended Anderson later, says that he went to the Brantford magistrate and made inquiries about the prisoner, being told that the fugitive was held pending the receipt of necessary evidence. According to Freeman's charges, which were made publicly in *The Toronto Globe* of December 11, 1860, Matthews communicated with private detectives in Detroit who passed the word on to friends of the deceased Diggs in Missouri and they promptly applied at Washington for extradition papers. *The Hamilton Times* charged that Matthews had subjected his prisoner to most rigorous prison life for two months, keeping him ironed, permitting no Negro friends to see him, not even admitting Rev. Walter Hawkins, the Negro preacher who afterwards became a bishop.[3] It required very much persuasion on the part of Freeman, and apparently some threats as well, to induce the Brantford magistrate to release his prisoner. When let out of jail Anderson went to Simcoe and was working there when again arrested, this time, it would appear, on a warrant sworn out by a Detroit man named Gunning. There are indications in the press reports of the time that the Brantford magistrate was much aggrieved at his prisoner getting into other hands and sought to have the case transferred to Brantford, being aided in this by the county Crown attorney.

In a letter to the *Hamilton Spectator* Freeman made this

charge against the magistrate: "Mr. Matthews arrested him as having been guilty of murder without any legal evidence of a murder having been committed, or, in fact, of any one having been killed by him. And after he had him in custody he communicated with the authorities for the necessary evidence."[4]

On November 24 Anderson was brought before the Court of Queen's Bench consisting of Chief Justice Robinson and Justices Burns and McLean. S. B. Freeman appeared for the prisoner and Henry Eccles and R. A. Harrison for the attorney-general. Freeman read the warrant of committal by William Matthews and the two other Brantford magistrates who had been associated with him. The evidence was to the effect that on September 28, 1859 (sic), Anderson was on the estate of Seneca T. P. Diggs in Howard County, Missouri, and that Diggs, while attempting with Negro help to arrest Anderson, was stabbed twice and later died. The question was whether Canada was to administer the slave laws of Missouri. The counsel for the Crown admitted that Anderson's act, if committed in Canada, would not be murder.

The Anderson case was practically the last important case to come before Chief Justice Sir John Beverly Robinson, and around perhaps no decision of his whole legal career did more excitement center. While the justices were considering the evidence public meetings were being held, not only in Toronto but in other Canadian cities. Newspapers were furiously defending the fugitive and the judgment of the court was being awaited with tense interest.

It was understood on November 30 that the Chief Justice was ready to give decision but that he deferred for his associates. On that date there were special police on duty about the court in fear of an attempt at rescue by the Negroes and others. *The Globe* of that date contended that the question of surrendering the man, being a matter of a treaty, should have been dealt with by the executive and not by the courts at all.

"The universal heart and conscience of the people of Canada and of the British nation will say upon the facts of the case that Anderson is not a murderer in the sight of God, or under British law," was a part of its comment editorially upon the case. A day or two later the paper pointed out the significance of this particular case. If Anderson were given up, it maintained, "no fugitive slave in Canada is safe on our soil ... there is not a fugitive in Canada whose extradition may not be demanded upon evidence sufficient to put the accused upon his trial."[5]

The court finally gave its judgment on Saturday, December 15. The papers of the following Monday say, that as the decision was being given, police stood about the court with muskets and that a company of Royal Canadian Rifles were also under arms at the Government House.

In its decision the court was not unanimous. The Chief Justice and Justice Burns favored extradition while Justice McLean dissented. The biographer of the Chief Justice says of this judgment: "Their decision was neither in support of nor against slavery but was based entirely upon the consideration of the treaty existing between the United States and Canada." The biographer quotes also as follows from an English contemporary: "These judges, proof against unpopularity and unswayed by their own bitter hatred of slavery, as well as unsoftened by their own feelings for a fellow man, in agonizing peril, upheld the law made to their hands and which they are sworn faithfully to administer. Fiat justitia. Give them their due. Such men are the ballast of nations."[6]

Gerrit Smith, the famous abolitionist, was one of those who acted on behalf of the fugitive, and his plea made a strong impression. He argued that Anderson was not guilty of murder but at the worst of homicide, that the Ashburton case did not require the surrender of fugitives and that in any case Anderson's delivery was a matter for the English courts to decide.

On the evening of December 19, 1860, a huge mass meeting was held in St. Lawrence Hall. The mayor of the city presided and the chief speaker of the evening was John Scoble, the abolitionist.[7] He was able to throw considerable light upon the exact meaning of the extradition treaty, having interviewed both Lord Aberdeen and Lord Brougham on its terms in relation to fugitive slaves at the time that it was passing through the British Parliament. He was at that time the secretary of the Anti-Slavery Society of England which had become alarmed over the possibilities to fugitives in Canada of the extradition clauses.[8]

Ashburton told him, he said, "that the article in

question was no more designed to touch the fugitive slave than to affect the case of deserters or parties charged with high treason." Lord Aberdeen stated that instructions would be sent to the Governor of Canada that in the case of fugitive slaves great care was to be taken to see that the treaty did not work their ruin. Sir Charles Metcalfe, Governor of Canada, was quoted by the speaker as having said that he would never be a party to wronging fugitives.

In the course of his address Mr. Scoble gave some information about the arrest of Anderson. He said that he personally went to Brantford as soon as Anderson was taken up in April and tried to get a writ of habeas corpus but could get no help from counsel in Brantford. At the Brantford spring assizes Anderson was released by the judge, since there was no evidence against him, but was rearrested three days later. Other speakers at the St. Lawrence Hall gathering were Rev. Wm. King, M. C. Cameron, Rev. Dr. Willis, Rev. Dr. Burns, Peter Brown and Rev. Mr. Marling. At the close of the meeting there were cheers for Anderson and others and groans for Magistrate Matthews.

There was much comment in the Canadian press on the case as a whole and upon the judgment in particular. *The Montreal Herald* of December 19, 1860, said: "We hope that the day will never come when the wretches who traffic in the bodies and souls of their fellow creatures will be able to say to any British subject, 'And thou also art made like unto us.'" *The Quebec Mercury* said: "The judgment of the court in Anderson's case is one of those infamous prostitutions of judicial power to political expediency which in this degenerate age have too frequently polluted the judicial ermine." *The Montreal Witness* said: "Such a gigantic wrong cannot exist on the same continent with us without affecting the people of Canada in one way or another. Slaveholders long looked at Canada with evil eye. If the slavers get Anderson back they will execute him before the slaves. It would be worth hundreds of thousands of dollars to them annually."

Speaking on the evening of December 20 before the St. Patrick's Literary Society of Montreal, Hon. Thomas D'Arcy McGee condemned the decision in the Anderson case. "As a fugitive slave has never been yielded by this province," he said, "I cannot believe that we are going to take upon ourselves the yoke of that servitude just now. We have no bonds to break or keep with the 'peculiar institution' of the south; and the true voice and spirit of this province is that when the flying slave has once put the roar of Niagara between him and the bay of the bloodhounds of his master—from that hour, no man shall ever dream of recovering him as his chattel property."

As soon as the decision of the Court of Queen's Bench was given, abolitionists in Toronto decided to carry the case to English courts and did so, securing from the Court of Queen's Bench at Westminster an order to bring Anderson there. In the meantime the case was carried to the Court of Common Pleas in Toronto and there on February 16, 1861, Chief Justice Draper acquitted Anderson, for the following reasons, as quoted in *The Toronto Leader*: "In the first place, the magistrate's warrant was defective inasmuch as the words used in the warrant did not imply the charge of murder, though perhaps expressing more than manslaughter; secondly, the warrant of commitment was also defective in not adhering to the words of the treaty."

It would take long to list all the meetings, petitions, resolutions, and protests that were brought forth by the Anderson case. The Anti-Slavery Society of Canada, with headquarters in Toronto, was, of course, active throughout the whole case. Early in January it was reported that a petition signed by more than 2500 people had been forwarded from Montreal on behalf of Anderson and from elsewhere in Canada came similar protests.

With the decision of Chief Justice Draper the Anderson case was closed and the fugitive disappears. As a result, however, of the unseemly action of the Brantford magistrate the Canadian law was revised so as to take from the control of ordinary magistrates jurisdiction as regards foreign fugitives from justice, leaving such cases with county judges and police justices.

FRED LANDON.

The Public Library,
 London, Ontario.

FOOTNOTES:

[1] On March 27, 1861, certain Howard County citizens petitioned for money advanced by them to prosecute Anderson in the Canadian Courts (*Session Laws*, 1860, p. 534).

[2] For Mrs. Haviland's story see her book, "*A Woman's Life Work*," published at Grand Rapids, Mich., in 1881. Anderson's story as told to her is found on pages 197-8.

[3] See *The Toronto Globe*, Nov. 14, 1860.

[4] Quoted in *The Toronto Globe*, Nov. 29, 1860.

[5] The Toronto Globe, Dec. 3, 1860.

[6] Life of Sir John Beverly Robinson, London, 1904, pp. 326-7.

[7] The proceedings of this meeting are reported at length in *The Globe* of the following day.

[8] Article X of the Ashburton Treaty, dealing with extradition, reads as follows: "It is agreed that the United States and Her Britannic Majesty shall, upon mutual requisition by them, or their ministers, officers, or authorities, respectively made, deliver up to justice all persons who, being charged with the crime of murder, or assault with intent to commit murder, or piracy, or arson, or robbery, or forgery, or the utterance of forged paper, shall seek an asylum, or shall be found within the territories of the other; provided that this shall only be done upon such evidence of criminality as, according to the laws of the place where the fugitive

or person so charged shall be found, would justify his apprehension and commitment for trial, if the crime or offence had there been committed, etc."

A NEGRO SENATOR

Incredible as it may sound to the twentieth century reader, the Commonwealth of Mississippi was for six years ably represented in the United States Senate by a distinguished Negro Senator, the Honorable B. K. Bruce. So inspiring is the story of Senator Bruce's efforts in the defense of humanity that it ought not to be permitted to lie in obscurity for want of a sympathetic pen. The present venture, therefore, is an attempt, though belated, to recount some of the achievements of this statesman whose public career looms up as a monument to the American Negro's self-confidence, resolution, and persistency.

Senator Bruce's career in the upper chamber of Congress began on March 5, 1875, at the special session of the Forty-fourth Congress, called by President Grant. His name appears in the *Congressional Record* of that session as "Branch" K. Bruce, Floreyville, Mississippi. He was assigned to the *Committee on Manufactures* and to the *Committee on Education and Labor* and later to the *Committee on Pensions* and the *Committee on the Improvement of the Mississippi River and its Tributaries.*[1]

Antedating his election to the United States Senate, Senator Bruce had held positions of trust and honor in the State of Mississippi. He had been Sheriff, Tax-Collector, Commissioner of the Levees Board, and

County Superintendent of Education. Moreover, he had served as Sergeant-at-Arms of the first State Senate after the Reconstruction Period, and Commissioner of Elections in a county that was reputed as being the most lawless in the State. In all these positions, Senator Bruce had displayed such integrity of purpose, sagacious statesmanship, and tireless industry that his election to the United States Senate followed as a logical and merited promotion.[2]

Senator Bruce's "maiden speech" in the Senate was delivered shortly after he took his seat during the special session. The speech was a vigorous protest against the proposed removal of the troops from the South, Mississippi in particular, where the military authorities were still in control. The speech made a profound impression on the Senate and clearly indicated the manly stand which Senator Bruce was preparing to take against the injustices practised against Negro citizens both North and South.[3]

The regular session of the Forty-fourth Congress, which convened on Monday, December 6, 1875, gave Senator Bruce numerous opportunities for energetic efforts. Early in the session, he presented a petition of the Sons of Temperance of the District of Columbia, praying for legislation for the District of Columbia and the Territories; for the prohibition of the importation of alcoholic liquors from abroad and that total abstinence be made a condition of the civil, military, and naval service. Later he introduced a Bill "to provide for the payment of bounties, etc., to colored soldiers and sailors and their heirs."[4] His first important opportunity for valuable service came during the discussion of the resolution to admit former Governor Pinchback as a Senator from Louisiana. The resolution had been presented on March 5, 1875, at the special session of the Senate—"That P. B. S. Pinchback be admitted as a Senator from the State of Louisiana for the term of six years, beginning with the fourth of March 1873." Senator Bruce delivered the following address:

When I entered upon my duties here as Senator from Mississippi, the question ceased to be novel, and had already been elaborately and exhaustively discussed. So far as opportunity has permitted me to do so, I have dispassionately examined the question in the light of the discussion, and I venture my views now with the diffidence inspired by my limited experience in the consideration of such questions and by a just appreciation of the learning and ability of the gentlemen who have already attempted to elucidate and determine this case.

I believe, Mr. President, whatever seeming informalities may attach to the manner in which the will of the people was ascertained, Mr. Pinchback is the representative of a majority of the legal voters of Louisiana, and is entitled to a seat in the Senate. In the election of 1872, the white population of the State exceeded, by the census of 1872, the colored population by about two thousand, including in the white estimate 6,300 foreigners, only half of whom were naturalized. This estimate, at the same ratio in each race, would give a large majority of colored voters. The census and registration up to 1872 substantially agree, and both sustain this conclusion. The census of 1875, taken in pursuance of an article of the State constitution, gives, after including the foreign population (naturalized and unnaturalized) in the white aggregate, a majority of 45,695 colored population.

This view of the question is submitted not as determining the contest, but as an offset to the allegation that Mr. Pinchback does not fairly represent the popular will of the State, and as a presumption in favor of the legal title of the assembly that elected him.

The State government elected in 1872, and permanently inaugurated in January 1873, in the face of contest and opposition, obtained for its authority the recognition of the inferior and supreme courts of the State. When organized violence threatened its existence and the United States Government was appealed to for troops to sustain it, the national Executive, in pursuance of his constitutional authority and duty, responded to the demand made for help, prefacing said action by an authoritative declaration, made through the Attorney General, addressed to Lieutenant-Governor Pinchback, then Acting Governor, of date of December 12, 1872, that said Pinchback was "recognized as the lawful executive of Louisiana, and the body assembled at Mechanics' Institute as the lawful Legislature of the State"; and similar recognition of his successor was subsequently given. When in September 1874, an attempt was made to overthrow the government, the President again interposed with the Army and Navy for its protection and the maintenance of its authority.

This government has proceeded to enact and enforce

laws for three years, which not only affect life, liberty, and property, but which have received the general obedience of the citizens of the State. The present government also has frequently been brought in official contact with the United States Congress—through its legislatures of 1873 and 1875, by memorials and joint resolutions addressed to the respective Houses; and through its executive, by credentials, borne by Congressmen and by Senators—and in no case has the legitimate authority of the Legislature been excepted to save in the action of electing a United States Senator; and in no instance has the sufficiency of the executive's credentials been questioned, in either House, except in the matter of the senatorial claimant.

Now, sir, shall we admit by our action on this ease that for three years the State of Louisiana has not had a lawful Legislature; that its laws have been made by an unauthorized mob; that the President of the United States actively, and Congress, by non-action at least, have sustained and perpetuated this abnormal, illegal, wrongful condition of things, thereby justifying and provoking the indignant and violent protests of one portion of the people of that State, and inviting them to renewed and continued agitation and violence? Such action by us would be unjust to the claimant, a great wrong to the people who sent him here, and cruel even to that class who have awaited an opportunity to bring to their support the overwhelming moral power of the nation in the pursuit of their illusion—which has so nearly ruined the future of that fair State—a government based upon the prejudices of caste.

I respectfully ask attention of Senators to another view of this subject, which is not without weight in determining the obligations of this body to the State of Louisiana and in ascertaining the title of the claimant. If the assumption that the present government inaugurated in 1873 is without legal authority and usurpation is true, the remedy for the state of things was to be found in the exercise of Congress through the joint action of the two Houses of the powers conferred under the guaranteeing clause of the Constitution relative to republican forms of government in the several States.

Failing to exercise her power and perform her duty in this direction, and thus practically perpetuating the present government, I submit that, in my judgment, we cannot now ignore our obligation to give the State her full representation on the score of the alleged irregularity of the government through which she has expressed her will; and there does seem to me, in this connection, something incongruous in the proposition that we may impose upon the people a government without legal sanction and demand their obedience to and support thereof, said government meanwhile determining the character of its successors and thus perpetuating its talent, and yet are powerless to admit a Senator elected thereby.

In my judgment, this question shall at this juncture be considered and decided not on abstract but practical grounds. Whatever wrongs have been done and mistakes made in Louisiana by either party, the present order of things is accepted by the people of the State and by the nation, and will be maintained as a final settlement of the political issues that have divided the people there; and no changes in the administration of public affairs can or will be made except by the people, through the ballot, under the existing government and laws of the Commonwealth.

Under these circumstances, holding the question in abeyance is, in my judgment, an unconstitutional deprivation of the right of a State, and a provocation to popular disquietude; and in the interest of good-will and good government, the most judicious and consistent course is to admit the claimant to his seat.

I desire, Mr. President, to make a personal reference to the claimant. I would not attempt one or deem one proper were it not that his personal character has been assailed.

As a father, I know him to be affectionate; as a husband, the idol of a pleasant home and cheerful fireside; as a citizen, loyal, brave, and true. And in his character and success we behold an admirable illustration of the excellence of our republican institutions.[5]

This speech, printed in its entirety, is an honest, frank, and convincing enunciation of republican truths. It is an unselfish and sober appeal for justice to another member of the Negro race. Bereft of all rhetorical embellishments, as the speech is, it may well pass for a masterpiece of logical thought and dynamic expression. It is the forerunner of even mightier utterances.

Long before Senator Bruce donned his senatorial toga, rioting in Mississippi had become prevalent. In fact, his own county, Bolivar, was perhaps the only one in the State which had not furnished a stage for bitter race feuds; and even this county narrowly averted a calamity. Back in the early seventies, a report gained currency that in a few days there was to be a "shooting up" in Bolivar. Guns and ammunition were being stored, and the outlook became menacing. The riot, however, was averted because Senator Bruce went personally to the controlling citizens and succeeded in arousing a strong sentiment against the threatening disorder. Bolivar County was thus enabled to boast that it had never been stained with bloodshed, and even today the memory of Senator Bruce is held in highest respect in Bolivar County.

In other sections of the State, rioting became so prevalent, especially on election days, that the returns of the elections were open to serious doubt. The United States Senate was forced to take cognizance of this condition. On Friday, March 31, 1876, a Resolution was introduced appointing a Committee "to investigate the late election in Mississippi." Senator Bruce embraced this opportunity to give a clear exposition of the condition of affairs in his State. His speech on this occasion reveals him as a broad-minded and courageous statesman free from the curse of narrow dogma and paltry aim. He began by announcing the basic principles of a democracy that will survive:

The conduct of the late election in Mississippi affected not merely the fortunes of the partisans—as the same were necessarily involved in the defeat or success of the respective parties to the contest—but put in question and jeopardy the sacred rights of the citizens; and the investigation contemplated in the pending resolution has for its object not the determination of the question whether the offices shall be held and the public affairs of the State be administered by Democrats or Republicans, but the higher and more important end, the protection in all their purity and significance of the political rights of the people and the free institutions of the country.[6]

He continued by referring to the evidence which proved that the voters of Mississippi in the "late election" had not had an actual opportunity to cast their votes:

The evidence in hand and accessible will show beyond peradventure that in many parts of the State corrupt and violent influences were brought to bear upon the registrars of voters, thus materially affecting the character of the voting or poll lists; upon the inspectors of election, prejudicially and unfairly, thereby changing the number of votes cast; and finally threats and violence were practiced directly upon the masses of voters in such measure and strength as to produce grave apprehensions for personal safety and as to deter them from the exercise of their political franchises.

It was in this speech that Senator Bruce replied to the erstwhile criticism that the Negro was a coward because he endured every kind of indignity without retaliating. Taking the prevalent view of progressive thought of the nineteenth century, he spoke as follows:

It will not accord with the laws of nature or history to brand colored people a race of cowards. On more than one historic field, beginning in 1776 and coming down to the centennial year of the Republic, they have attested in blood their courage as well as a love of liberty. I ask Senators to believe that no consideration of fear or personal danger has kept us quiet and forbearing under the provocations and wrongs that have so sorely tried our souls. But feeling kindly towards our white fellow-citizens, appreciating the good purposes and offices of the better classes, and, above all, abhorring war of races, we determined to wait until such time as an appeal to the good sense and justice of the American people could be made.[7]

This pronouncement of Senator Bruce exalting the manly virtue of patience, even in the face of grave injustices, was preeminently representative of the most highly educated Negro thought of the century in which Senator Bruce lived, and must be interpreted in terms of the philosophy of his day. If it should be objected to by some of the most highly developed Negro thought of the present day, the increasing tendency towards retaliation should be attributed partly to the American Negro's metamorphosis since the colossal struggle for that Utopian dream—a World's Democracy.

Perhaps the part of Senator Bruce's speech which has given most impetus to similar modern expression is contained in the following excerpt:

The sober American judgment must obtain in the South as elsewhere in the Republic, that the only distinctions upon which parties can be safely organized and in harmony with our institutions are differences of opinion relative to principles and policies of government, and that differences of religion, nationality, or race can neither with safety nor propriety be permitted for a moment to enter into the party contests of the day. The unanimity with which the colored voters act with a party is not referable to any race prejudice on their part. On the contrary, they invite the political cooperation of their white brethren, and vote as a unit because proscribed as such. They deprecate the establishment of the color line by the opposition, not only because the act is unwise, but because it isolates them from the white men of the South and forces them, in sheer self-protection, and against their inclination, to act seemingly upon the basis of a race prejudice that they neither respect nor entertain. They not only recognize the equality of citizenship and the right of every man to hold without proscription any position of honor and trust to which the confidence of the people may elevate him; but owing nothing to race, birth, or surroundings, they above all other classes, in the community, are interested to see prejudices drop out of both politics and the business of the country, and success in life proceed upon the integrity and merit of the man who seeks it.... But withal, as they progress in intelligence and appreciation of the dignity of their prerogatives as citizens, they as an evidence of growth begin to realize the significance of the proverb, "When thou doest well for thyself, men shall praise thee"; and are disposed to exact the same protection and concession of rights that are conferred upon other citizens by the Constitution, and that too without humiliation involved in the enforced abandonment of their political convictions.

The speech closes with an enthusiastic expression of confidence in American institutions and in the American Negro:

I have confidence, not only in my country and her institutions, but in the endurance, capacity and destiny of my people. We will, as opportunity offers and ability serves, seek our places, sometimes in the field of letters, arts, science and the professions. More frequently mechanical pursuits will attract and elicit our efforts; more still of my people will find employment and livelihood as the cultivators of the soil. The bulk of this people—by surroundings, habits, adaptation, and choice will continue to find their homes in the South and constitute the masses of its yeomanry. We will there, probably of our own volition and more abundantly than in the past, produce the great staples that will contribute to the basis of foreign exchange, aid in giving the nation a balance of trade, and minister to the wants and comforts and build up the prosperity of the whole land. Whatever our ultimate position in the composite civilization of the republic and whatever varying fortunes attend our career, we will not forget our instincts for freedom nor our love for country.[8]

A careful study of the speech shows what a model it has been for speakers and writers of a much later period. It deals openly and frankly with the Southern question, and is prophetic of President Harding's recent utterances on the Negro's political status in the South.

During the second session of the Forty-fourth Congress, Mr. Bruce confined his efforts largely to the relief of the legal heirs of Negro soldiers who had fought to preserve the Union. Consequently, he introduced a number of bills praying that arrears of pensions be granted. In this way, he became the benefactor of many persons who otherwise might never have received their pensions. In addition to such relief legislation, he presented for the second time a petition praying for a general law prohibiting liquor traffic, and introduced a bill for certain improvements in the Mississippi River.[9]

The Forty-fifth Congress was not especially eventful. Senator Bruce, however, continued to introduce bills for the relief of legal heirs of soldiers. During the second session of this Congress, he took an active interest in the Chinese Exclusion Bill, registering his vote against the measure which seemed to him to be contrary to American principles. His denunciation of the selfish policy of the United States toward the Indian was more pronounced than that of his dissatisfaction with the restriction of the immigration of the Chinese. He believed that the attitude of the Americans toward the Indian bred hatred and discontent and made the Indian a fugitive and a vagabond. He believed that the United States Government should do something to civilize the Indian rather than to restrict him. The Indian could be made a desirable citizen if the best elements of his nature were developed to enable him to exercise the functions of citizenship. He early advocated, therefore, that the Indians should cease to be dealt with as tribes and should receive consideration as individuals, "subject to American law and beneficiaries of American institutions." The Indian then, when no longer branded as an outlaw, would in the very near future advance to the position when the cooperation and the protection of the white man would be welcomed as that of friends.[11]

It was during the Forty-sixth Congress that Senator Bruce was most active. Senator Bruce did most constructive work in advocating the improvement of the navigation of the Mississippi river. The importance of this question today is not so striking as it was at that time for the reason that little had been done to protect life and property from the inundations of that stream. Senator Bruce kept this important problem before Congress urging not only that the interest of the people in the valley itself be taken care of, but that this river should by adequate facilities be made the highway of interstate and foreign commerce. Toward this end Senator Bruce offered several bills meeting the exigencies of the time and providing for future needs. As the foresight of a majority of the members of Congress at that time was not sufficient to appreciate this statesmanlike effort of Senator Bruce, his program for this important internal improvement was not carried out, although some important efforts since then to supply this need in our economic development must be considered as due in some measure to the persistence and the courage of Senator Bruce in keeping this question before Congress.[12]

Senator Bruce, moreover, had been watching, with increasing misgivings, the affairs of that notorious banking bubble, more pretentiously known as the Freedman's Savings and Trust Company. To protect the rights of the depositors of the defunct institution, he offered the following resolution, on April 7, 1879:

That the President of the Senate appoint a committee of five on the Freedman's Savings and Trust Company to take into consideration all matters relating to said institution, and that said committee be authorized to employ a clerk, and that the necessary expenses be paid out of the "miscellaneous items" of the contingent fund of the Senate.[13]

The resolution was considered by unanimous consent and agreed to. The Vice President, the Honorable William A. Wheeler, subsequently appointed Senator Bruce as Chairman of this committee. The other members were Senators Cameron of Wisconsin, Gordon, Withers, and Garland. To head such a committee was, indeed, an enviable privilege, but the real opportunity lay in the kind of service which the entangled affairs of the bank made possible. At this time, the affairs of the bank were in the hands of three commissioners, each receiving $3000 a year, and no promise of winding up the business of the bank was foreshadowed. Thus the available assets were reduced annually by the total amount of these salaries. The assets, of course, were to be paid *pro rata* to the depositors.

In order that his committee might have more power to go into the management of the bank, Senator Bruce offered the following resolution on May 16, 1879:

That the Select Committee on the Freedman's Savings and Trust Company appointed by resolution of the Senate of April 7, 1879, is authorized and directed to investigate the affairs of said savings and trust company and its several branches, to ascertain and report to the Senate all matters relating to the management of the same and the cause or causes of failure, with such other facts relating thereto as may be important to a full understanding of the management and present condition of the institution and to a more economical administration and speedy adjustment of its affairs.

Following this resolution, Senator Bruce presented a petition of R. M. Hall, M.D., and others, citizens of Baltimore, Maryland, praying the passage of an act requiring the commissioners of the Freedman's Savings and Trust Company to close up the affairs of the institution and distribute the assets among the creditors thereof. This petition was presented on May 27, 1879.

The resolution and the petition had their desired effect. The services of the commissioners were dispensed with, thus saving $9000 a year for the depositors; and the final settlement of the claims was turned over to the Controller of the Treasury. To Senator Bruce's Committee, therefore, goes the credit of bringing a speedy close to the affairs of the defunct Freedman's Savings and Trust Company, with the minimum of further loss to the depositors. Later, Senator Bruce made a strong, but vain, appeal to reimburse the colored depositors of the Freedman's Savings and Trust Company for losses incurred by the failure of the bank.

His final dealings with the Freedman's Savings and Trust Company came in the third session of the Forty-sixth Congress, when he introduced the following bill:

That the Senate authorize and direct the purchase by the Secretary of the Treasury, for public use, the property known as the Freedman's Savings and Trust Company, and the real estate and parcels of ground adjacent thereto, belonging to the Freedman's Savings and Trust Company, and located on Pennsylvania Avenue between Fifteenth and Fifteenth-and-a-half Streets, Washington, District of Columbia.

The bill was considered, amended, and passed.[14]

Ever alert to the educational needs of the colored youth, Senator Bruce introduced, among many other bills, during the second session of the Forty-sixth Congress, a bill:

To provide for the investment of certain unclaimed pay and bounty moneys now in the Treasury of the United States and to facilitate and encourage the education of the colored race in the several States and Territories.

The bill was referred to the *Committee on Education and Labor*, amended by Mr. Pendleton of Ohio, and reported back adversely and postponed indefinitely.[15]

Senator Bruce was not returned to the Forty-seventh Congress. The record, however, which he made in the Forty-fourth, Forty-fifth, and Forty-sixth Congresses will ever maintain for him a prominent place among the progressive and constructive statesmen of this country. And here our account should end if it were not for the fact that some of our readers will want a glimpse of some of the significant events in Senator Brace's life, exclusive of his career in the Senate. A condensed account of such facts will suffice.

Senator Bruce was not a native Mississippian. He was born in the little town of Farmville, Virginia. At an early age, he made his way to Missouri, thence to Mississippi where he arrived in 1868. In 1878, he married Miss Josephine B. Wilson, of Cleveland, Ohio, a lady of most excellent parts and refined culture. A son, Roscoe Conklin, was born in 1879—a polished gentleman by birth, an educator by training, an orator and debater by choice, and a scholar by nature. Both wife and son survive the late Senator.[16]

Senator Bruce belonged to that rugged, self-made type of manhood that did right to prosper in this world and hope for felicity in the next. He studied under private tutors and spent two years at Oberlin College. Like many successful statesmen, he served his time in the classroom as a teacher. It was during his teaching career that he was persuaded by Henry Ward Beecher to enter the Christian ministry, but the inward voice did not respond to the ministerial call.

Though his tenure of office as United States Senator lasted but one full term of six years, he was given further opportunities for public service. From 1881 to 1885, he served as Register of the Treasury, having been appointed to this office by President Garfield. In 1889, during the administration of President Benjamin Harrison, he was appointed Recorder of Deeds when the office was operated under a system of fees which netted from twelve to fifteen thousand dollars a year.

President McKinley called him a second time to the office of Register of the Treasury, in which position he remained until his death in 1898.

G. DAVID HOUSTON

FOOTNOTES:

[1] *Congressional Record*, 44th Congress, First Session.

[2] Simmons, *Men of Mark*, 699-703.

[3] *Congressional Record*, 44th Congress, 1st Session, pp. 2100-2105.

[4] *Ibid.*, pp. 736, 1547, 5138.

[5] *Congressional Record*, 1st Session, pp. 1444, 1445.

[6] *Congressional Record*, 44th Congress, 1st Session, pp. 2100-2105.

[7] *Congressional Record*, 44th Congress, 1st Session, p. 2104.

[8] *Congressional Record*, Forty-sixth Congress, 1st Session, p. 2104.

[9] *Ibid.*, p. 2105.

[10] *Ibid.*, p. 2105.

[11] *Congressional Record*, Forty-sixth Congress, 2d Session, pp. 2195-2196.

[12] *Congressional Record*, Forty-fifth Congress, 1st Session, pp. 201, 245; 3d Session, pp. 1314, 1316, 2309.

[13] *Ibid.*, Forty-sixth Congress, 1st Session, pp. 45, 71, 435, 1679, 2415; 3d Session, pp. 632, 668.

[14] *Congressional Record*, Forty-sixth Congress, 2d Session, pp. 45, 273, 538.

[15] *Ibid.*, pp. 1619, 1953, 2053, 2384, 4563.

[16] See Simmons, *Men of Mark*, pp. 699-703.

LINCOLN'S EMANCIPATION PLAN

There was some slavery in the Northwest Territory to which Lincoln moved with his father from Kentucky, for although that section had been dedicated to freedom by the Ordinance of 1787, slavery in a modified form existed there for three reasons. The Ordinance was not considered emancipatory so far as it regarded the British slaves held in such service prior to 1795, those of French masters prior to 1763 and those already in that condition when the Ordinance was passed. Furthermore, after separating from the Indiana Territory, Illinois legalized slavery by indenture, provided for the hiring of slaves from Southern States to supply labor in its various industries, and at the same time passed a stringent law to prohibit the immigration of free Negroes into that State. Later there followed an attempt to open the State to slavery by the Legislature of 1822–1823, but the slave party was defeated by the election of Governor Coles, who would not permit the reactionary element to reduce that commonwealth to a mediaeval basis.[1] Such slavery as existed in Illinois, however, differed widely from that in the South where it had become economic rather than patriarchal as it then existed in certain parts of the North.

On a trip by way of the Sangamon and the Mississippi to New Orleans in May 1831, Abraham Lincoln got his first impression of economic slavery when he "saw Negroes chained, maltreated, whipped and scourged."[2] He made no mention of this spectacle until a decade later when journeying from Louisville to St. Louis he saw ten or twelve slaves shackled together on a boat. This was sufficient to convince him that this institution was not only an economic evil but a disgrace to a country pretending to be free. Lincoln, therefore, early decided within himself that if he ever attained a position of sufficient power to do something for the extermination of this institution, he would count it the opportunity of his life.

There soon followed an occasion when Lincoln had an opportunity to show his constituents his position on this important question. As a result of the murder of Lovejoy the question of slavery was brought up at the session of the legislature held in 1837 and was referred to a committee. The report of this committee expressed disapproval of abolition societies and carried a declaration to the effect that the Federal Constitution secured the right of property in slaves, and the Government of the United States could not abolish slavery in the District of Columbia without the consent of its citizens. After much heated debate and filibustering these resolutions were finally passed, although Lincoln and five other members voted in the negative. Then there followed from Lincoln and Daniel A. Stone a protest, questioning and attacking the moral support of slavery, yet recognizing all the constitutional guarantees that protected it.[3]

Lincoln, as an Illinois Representative in Congress,

resorted to a similar procedure in that national body. At this time there was almost a pitched battle between the slave States and the free commonwealths, each one endeavoring to develop more strength than the other in the effort to dictate the policy of the nation with reference to the States to be formed out of the remaining western territory. Lincoln did not take any active part in the discussion of slavery during the first session of his service in Congress, but he always voted against any measure providing for the extension of the institution. However, he still adhered to his position as set forth in the protest in the Illinois Legislature, that Congress had power under the Constitution to regulate or prohibit slavery in all territory subject to its jurisdiction, provided that such power be exercised with due regard to constitutional rights. He, therefore, decided to test the question whether it was possible to remove from the seat of the Federal Government the offensive traffic in human beings. In formulating his plans to carry out this policy, he consulted the leading citizens of the District of Columbia and certain prominent men in Congress.

Having secured the approval of Mayor Seaton of Washington, a representative of the intelligent slave-holding citizens of the District of Columbia, and also the support of Joshua Giddings, the leading abolition member of Congress, Lincoln proposed a bill to this effect. Thereupon Giddings made these remarks: "This evening (January 11th) our whole mess remained in the dining room after tea, and conversed upon the subject of Mr. Lincoln's bill to abolish slavery. It was approved by all; I believe it as good bill as we could get at this time, and am willing to pay for slaves to save them from the southern market, as I suppose every man in the District would sell his slaves if he saw that slavery was to be abolished."[4]

In the meantime a less radical bill providing also for the abolition of slavery in the District of Columbia had been introduced by Representative Gott of New York. Lincoln, therefore, moved as an amendment on January 16, 1849, that a committee report a bill for the emancipation of all slaves in the District of Columbia. This measure prohibited the bringing of slaves into and selling them out of the District except in the case of those temporarily serving persons representing slave-holding States. It made provision for a tentative system of apprenticeship and the eventual emancipation of children born of slave mothers after January 1, 1850. It further provided for the manumission of slaves by the Government of the United States with compensation to the owners who might make application therefor, for the return of fugitive slaves from Washington and Georgetown, and finally for the submission of the bill to popular vote in the District of Columbia. This measure, however, and its probability of success so excited the proslavery members of Congress and the slave owners in the District of Columbia that a violent opposition thereto followed. So many influential forces were arrayed against the measure that its friends did not further endeavor to pilot it through the House.[5] This unsuccessful effort marked the expiration of Lincoln's term in Congress.

Declining to become a candidate for renomination to Congress, Lincoln returned to Springfield, partially withdrew from politics, and devoted himself largely to the practice of law. He reappeared as an active participant in politics in Illinois in 1854, when there appeared a new aspect of the question as reflected by the debate incident to the Kansas-Nebraska controversy. At this time Lincoln was called for in all directions to deliver addresses to inform the people on the issue of the day. In this connection he demonstrated his inalterable opposition to the extension of slavery.[6] He objected to the iniquitous doctrine of the Nebraska Bill in that it assumed that there was moral right in the enslaving of one man by another, and, further, that it tended to be unmistakably subversive of the basic principles of the Declaration of Independence. Lincoln was of the opinion that the salvation of the Union was dependent upon the extension or the restriction of slavery. Realizing the futility and the hopelessness of voluntary emancipation, he asserted that the "Autocrat of all the Russias" would resign his crown, and proclaim freedom to all his subjects sooner than the "American masters" would voluntarily give up their slaves.[7] It is remarkable that Lincoln's speculative affirmation was followed by what he thought an impossibility, for on the day preceding Mr. Lincoln's inauguration the "Autocrat of all the Russias," Alexander II, by an imperial decree emancipated his serfs; "while six weeks after the inauguration, the proslavery element, headed by Jefferson Davis, began the Rebellion to perpetuate and to spread the institution of slavery."

In 1857 came the Dred Scott decision, in which Chief Justice Taney of the Supreme Court dragged that tribunal into politics, aiming to settle the question of slavery in the territories, but it stimulated rather than suppressed the discussion of slavery, as was evident by its outburst in the debates between Mr. Lincoln and Mr. Stephen A. Douglas.[8] The main question was whether, according to the Constitution, Congress could prohibit slavery in the territories. Lincoln contended that it could but Douglas was evasive, as he hoped to reconcile his popular sovereignty with the Dred Scott decision. Lincoln, on the other hand, showed that the public estimate of the Negro had become decidedly lower than it was prior to the industrial revolution, when masters could emancipate their bondmen of their own volition. Since then it had become common for the State Legislature, which in the exercise of the sovereignty of the State had the power to abolish slavery within its limits, to withhold that power and to make legal restraints tantamount to prohibition.

Lincoln opposed Mr. Douglas in 1858 when he contested the latter's reelection to the United States Senate. Toward this end he launched a more determined antislavery program than ever before, advancing the doctrine that "a house divided against itself cannot stand" and likewise that "the Union could not endure permanently, half slave and half free."[9] He further declared that either the advocates of slavery would push the institution forward until it became alike lawful in both North and South, or the opponents thereof would arrest its extension. Douglas had charged the Republicans with the intent to abolish slavery in the States and had asserted that their opposition to the Dred Scott decision marked their desire for Negro equality and amalgamation.[10] To this charge Lincoln replied that the Republicans were not directing their efforts toward abolition in the slave States, but toward the exclusion of slavery from the territories. He forcibly denied the accusation that the Republicans solicited social equality and amalgamation with the Negro, declaring that there was a physical difference between the two races, which probably would forever forbid their living together on equal footing; and that, inasmuch as it became a necessity that there must be a difference, he, like Douglas, favored his race for the superior position. Lincoln admitted that in some respects the Negro, according to the Declaration of Independence, was not the white man's equal; that in color, size, intellect, moral development, or social capacity the Negro was not on a par with the white man; but that that instrument did, with tolerable distinctness, consider "all men created equal" with certain inalienable rights, such as "life, liberty, and the pursuit of happiness."[11] Lincoln held that, notwithstanding all these facts, there was no reason why the Negro was not entitled to all the natural rights embraced by the Declaration of Independence, which are enjoyed by the white man.[12] He interpreted the standard maxim that "all men are created equal" as being of no practical use in effecting the separation of the thirteen Colonies from Great Britain, and, on the contrary, contended that it was placed in the Declaration of Independence for future use in the attainment of democracy.

Lincoln failed to defeat Douglas for the United States Senate but he continued to discuss the constitutionality of the restriction of slavery. On more than one instance he limited his remarks to this question, irrespective of the type of his audience or character of the occasion. He persistently reiterated the doctrine that there was no provision in the Constitution that precluded the right of the Federal Government to control slavery in the territories.[13]

The crisis between 1850 and 1860 brought Lincoln's ideas before larger groups. Until that year the Democrats had apparently remained united. At the Democratic National Convention in Charleston, South Carolina, in April, 1860, there was a division.[14] The Northern Democrats, unable to comply with the demands of the slave power that the convention should adopt a platform requiring Congress to protect slavery in the territories and the Northerners to acknowledge and advocate the moral right of slavery, forced the South to the radical position of withdrawing from the Convention. Since no candidate could then be nominated, the Convention adjourned to Baltimore, in the hope that time would bring about a reconciliation; but in the end the Northern Democrats nominated Douglas, and the Southerners nominated Breckenridge.[15]

The Republican Convention was held in Chicago in May 1860, and there was adopted a moderate platform, with a denial of the right of Congress to interfere with slavery in the States. The Republicans reaffirmed the Declaration of Independence and declared that Congress should prohibit slavery in the territories. They repudiated the Dred Scott decision and advocated a protective system. Their most difficult problem was the selection of a candidate for the presidency. Inasmuch as Seward and Chase had alienated certain elements by their bold advocacy of advanced principles and Lincoln was comparatively unknown, the managers of the party finally accepted him because of his availability. This choice was received with much indignation among the antislavery leaders, for even Wendell Phillips and William Lloyd Garrison railed against the nominee and portrayed him as an obscurity.[16]

Lincoln's election forced slavery into the foreground. Without waiting for his inauguration, several Southern States, acting in accordance with their previous threats that they would secede if a Republican President were elected, withdrew from the Union. Others soon followed their example. Congress hastened to offer various concessions to the seceding States,[17] but these efforts for compromise were in vain. The die was cast. When Lincoln asserted that his oath of office bound him to preserve the Union at any cost, civil war became inevitable. The proslavery element opened fire on the American flag at Fort Sumter and forced its surrender April 14.[18] On the next day Lincoln issued a proclamation calling for 75,000 volunteers. 500,000 others were later called to defend the honor of the nation.

The emancipation of Negroes during the Civil War could not be kept down. It appeared first in the acceptance of Negroes in the Union army camps as contraband, on the ground that they were being used by the Confederates to build fortifications and the like and, if returned to the seceding territory, would be of further use in opposing the Federal troops. General Butler set this precedent when he was in charge of the forces at Fortress Monroe. At first there was some hesitation as to whether the administration should adopt such a policy. Butler's course, however, was approved by Cameron, the Secretary of War, May 30, 1861, although Lincoln was not pleased with it; for he did not desire to alienate the border slave States by radical steps toward emancipation. He was hoping that the nation would trust him, "as having the more commanding view, gradually to fix the attitude of the Government toward the subject,"[19] as the conquest of the Confederacy proceeded. The Federal troops, however, did not at first make much headway in the East, but events west of the Alleghenies progressed favorably for the Union cause, especially in Missouri. Taking advantage of this state of affairs, General John C. Fremont, in charge of this district, proclaimed military emancipation in that State on August 30, 1861. All persons with arms were to be tried by court martial and shot. Their property would be confiscated, and their slaves would thereby be declared free. He appointed a military commission, whose business it was to hear evidence and to issue personal deeds of the manumission of slaves.

When Lincoln was apprised of this proclamation, he forthwith took action. He feared that the provisions of General Fremont's drastic order, providing for the confiscation of property and the emancipation of slaves of traitorous owners, would alarm the Southern friends of the Union, would drive them over to the seceding faction, and perhaps would be instrumental in the loss of the border slave States. Fremont's action was diametrically opposed to Lincoln's policy, in that such emancipation was purely administrative and political, one of civil administration that could not be justified by military necessity. Consequently Lincoln issued an order instructing Fremont to modify his proclamation by striking out the disturbing provisions of the proclamation and substituting therefor the act to confiscate property used for insurrectionary purposes, passed by Congress on August 6, 1861, which authorized the President to cause property used or employed in aid of insurrection to be seized, confiscated, or condemned, providing, however, that such condemnation be made by judicial procedure.[20]

Lincoln, nevertheless, hoped to increase the number of free States through compensated emancipation, which he expected to come through voluntary action on the part of the slave States at the suggestion of the Federal Government. In his next annual message to Congress, however, he made no direct reference to any specific plan of emancipation, but discussed its practical necessities in general terms so as to leave himself in a position to decide later on a definite policy.[21] He endeavored to keep before Congress new and possible contingencies and emphasized the fact that, by virtue of the Confiscation Act, many of the slaves thus liberated were already dependent upon the United States for maintenance, and that they must be provided for. He recommended, therefore, that Congress provide for accepting such persons from States so affected in lieu of direct taxes, and that such persons accepted by the General Government be declared free immediately.

With his plan for compensated emancipation in mind, it was quite natural that Lincoln should look for a field of experimentation in a small State, such as Delaware, especially since there was in Congress from that State, Representative George E. Fisher, who was a staunch Unionist and a friend of the President. Fisher gladly cooperated with Lincoln in carrying out this plan. The Congressman tried to have the Legislature of Delaware pass an act for the gradual compensated emancipation of the 1,798 slaves which that State claimed according to the census of 1861, on the condition that the United States would pay the Delaware slaveholders $400 for each slave. During November of 1861, Lincoln wrote drafts of two separate bills to effect such an agreement. [22] The first bill provided that, on the passage of the act, all Negroes over thirty-five years of age should become free; that all born after the passage of the measure should remain free; and that the rest, after suitable apprenticeship for children, should become free in 1893, while the State in the meanwhile should prohibit the selling of Delaware slaves elsewhere. By the provisions of the second bill the United States Government should pay the State of Delaware $23,200 a year for thirty-one years and all Negroes born after the passage of the act should be declared free, while all others should automatically become free at thirty-five years of age until January, 1893, when all remaining slaves of all ages should become free, subject to apprenticeship for minors born of slave mothers up to the respective ages of eighteen and twenty-one.

One of the drafts was rewritten by the friends of the measure that it might embrace the details and alterations to conform with local opinion and law. It was printed and circulated among the members of the Legislature of Delaware and a special session of that body was called to consider the proposal. The bill, however, was never introduced, because it was feared that it would be voted down by the hostile proslavery majority. The proslavery element, moreover, prepared resolutions to the effect that the bill would encourage the abolition element in Congress, that it bore evidence of an effort to abolish slavery in the States, that Congress had no right to appropriate money for the purchase of slaves, that it was not desirable to make Delaware guarantee the public faith of the United States, that the suggestion of saving expenses to the people by compensated emancipation was a bribe, and that Delaware would abolish slavery of its own volition at a time when its lawmakers would deem it advisable. But these resolutions did not fare much better than Lincoln's bill, for in spite of the fact that they passed the House they were lost in the Senate.[23]

Although disappointed over the failure of his plans for compensated emancipation in Delaware, Lincoln, encouraged by the victories of Thomas and Grant in the West took his next step through Congress to the States. [24] Accordingly, on March 6, 1862, he sent to that body a special message, recommending the adoption of the joint resolution that the United States would cooperate with any State which might adopt gradual emancipation, giving such State compensation for all inconveniences produced by the change of any system within its confines.[25] Lincoln had figured out that less than the cost of the war for a half day would pay for all the slaves in Delaware at $400 each, and that less than eighty-seven days' cost of the war would compensate the slaveowners of Delaware, Maryland, the District of Columbia, Kentucky, and Missouri for all the slaves at the same rate.

The next step took the form of Roscoe Conkling's joint resolution to this effect recommended by Lincoln in his special message of March 6. At the same time Lincoln assembled the Congressmen from the border slave States of Delaware, Maryland, West Virginia, Kentucky, and Missouri at the Executive Mansion, where a prolonged discussion of the subject ensued. [26] Lincoln tried to convince these Congressmen of the good faith of the administration, and suggested to them that they take this question of gradual abolition into serious consideration, for the Government of the United States had no right to coerce them. He asserted that emancipation was exclusively a State affair; and that his purpose was simply to present the proposition. Yet probably one reason for the failure of these Congressmen of the border slave States to make a favorable reply or to commit themselves in any way was that they were well aware of Lincoln's determination, according to his special message of March 6, to use all means to save the Union; and they, furthermore, understood the hint that necessity might force him to resort to extreme measures. While this proposition gained no headway with the border slave States, the joint resolution was approved by Congress and received the signature of the President on April 10.

Congress then passed an important measure, the expediency of which Lincoln urged in 1849. This was emancipation in the District of Columbia. Lincoln made no specific recommendations relative to this in his annual message, but later sent a special message to Congress March 6, 1862, taking up the subject in its more extensive aspects. This bill provided for the immediate emancipation of slaves in the District of Columbia, and empowered a commission to distribute to slave-holders for their manumitted slaves a compensation not to exceed an aggregate of three hundred dollars a head, with an additional appropriation for $100,000 for expenses of voluntary emigration of freedmen to Haiti and Liberia.[27] Lincoln did not heartily approve this measure, however, for he did not want this to interfere with his policy of compensated emancipation in the border slave States. Even after the bill had been amended, according to his suggestions, he still hesitated and some of his friends thought that he might never sign it, but he did.

The question of emancipation appeared in another form when, upon the capture of Port Royal the previous November, many slaves, abandoned by the fleeing slave-holders, sought protection in the Union army. These slaves, thus dislodged by the misfortunes of war, outnumbered the whites five to one and had to be organized in groups for government protection. Relief societies in Boston, New York, and Philadelphia sent funds and teachers for the slaves. This educational enterprise received the official sanction of Secretary Chase at President Lincoln's request. Wishing further to improve their condition, General David Hunter, commander of the Department of the South, issued on May 9, 1862, an order of military emancipation, proclaiming the Department of the South under martial law and declaring persons in Georgia, Florida, and South Carolina, heretofore held as slaves, forever free.[28] Hunter regarded this an act of military necessity, not an instrument of political import as General Fremont's proclamation in Missouri, for Hunter's forces were insufficient for offensive movements, and he was doing this as the first step toward training and arming Negroes within his lines. Assuming that the instructions of the War Department conferred the necessary authority he proclaimed the order without delay.

The news of this proclamation did not travel rapidly. It was published in the newspapers one week later, owing to the slow mail by sea from the South. By this means even Lincoln first learned of this decree, on account of which he was being assailed in many parts. When the news reached Lincoln he took decisive and prompt action. On May 19, he published a proclamation in which he revoked the order of emancipation and recited that the Government had no knowledge of such a decree nor had it authorized General Hunter to give such an order.[29]

Lincoln, however, used this occasion for an admonition to the border slave States, although he carefully distinguished between the limited powers of the commanders in the field and his full executive authority. He reminded the border States of the joint resolution passed by Congress, to authorize compensated emancipation, and he warned them not to neglect this opportunity to obtain financial indemnity, for the "signs of the times" were multiplying to a degree that should have convinced the border States that slavery was doomed.

In the very beginning of the Thirty-seventh Congress there came a series of antislavery measures which constituted a complete and decisive reversal of the policy of the Federal Government.[30] On March 13, 1862, Congress approved an act, which prohibited all military and naval officers and enlisted personnel from returning fugitive slaves. Section 10 of the Confiscation Act, virtually an amendment of the Fugitive Slave Law, which withheld from the claimant the right to use his authority until he had taken an oath of allegiance, and made it tantamount to a crime for any person in the army or navy to surrender a fugitive slave or attempt to validate the owner's claim, was rigidly enforced. Wishing to see Liberia and Haiti welcomed into the family of nations, moreover, Lincoln in his annual message in the previous December recommended the recognition of their independence and the establishment of diplomatic relations with the new nations. This resolution was passed by a Congress and approved June 5, 1862. Lincoln then effected the passage of a measure to carry into execution the treaty between

Great Britain and the United States for the suppression of the African slave trade. Soon thereafter followed an act to secure freedom to all persons within the territories of the United States. The Republican party had thus carried out its platform by its restoration of the Missouri Compromise, its extension and application to all Territories, and as a logical result the rejection and condemnation of the Dred Scott decision and the subversive property theory of the secessionists.[31]

Then followed the Confiscation Act, the discussion of which was closely followed by Lincoln, who had his views incorporated therein by pointing out its defects and suggesting amendments. Whereas the act of August 6, 1861, freed slaves actually employed in military service, the new Confiscation Act of 1862 proved to be a law to destroy slavery under the powers of war. In conjunction with provisions for punishing treason or rebellion it declared free all slaves of persons guilty and convicted of these crimes, and provided that slaves deserted by rebels escaping from them or coming under control of the United States and slaves of rebels found on Union soil should be deemed captives and set free. Then again, there were enacted other provisions, which by implication permitted the employment of slaves in the United States army that they might work their own enfranchisement. Under this law the President was empowered to enroll and employ contrabands in such service as they were fitted for. Their mothers, wives, and children, if owned by rebels, should be declared free by virtue of such service. The eleventh section of the Confiscation Act authorized the President to employ as many Negroes as he might deem necessary for the suppression of the rebellion. The organization of the earliest Negro regiments resulted from this legislation.

Lincoln had some hesitation about signing this bill, however, for it had to be changed to conform to his views. But he signed it and also an anticipatory resolution of Congress to remedy its defects, placing himself on record by transmitting with his approval a copy of his intended veto, had certain defects remained. Mr. Lincoln objected to the expression that Congress could free a slave within a State, whereupon he suggested that it be changed to read that the ownership of the slave would be transferred to the nation, and that Congress would then liberate him.[32] The Democrats opposed this act, but antislavery opinion gained momentum by increasing accessions to the ranks of freedom and by that unusual ability of the highly talented patriotic membership of Congress. Yet to the proslavery element and the conservative Unionists, Lincoln's proposal of gradual compensated emancipation was a daring innovation upon practical politics. "In point of fact," say Nicolay and Hay, "the President stood sagaciously midway between headlong reform and blind reaction. His steady, cautious direction and control of the average public sentiment of the country alike held back rash experiment and spurred lagging opinion."[33]

Four months after Lincoln's proposal of compensated emancipation to the border slave States and its sanction by Congress, the situation seeming more complicated by the vicissitudes of war, Lincoln saw the necessity for uniting the sentiment of the North for a practical solution of the slavery problem. Looking forward into the future, therefore, Lincoln readily realized that the North must present a united front contending for a plain, practical policy, relative to things both political and military.

Consequently he again met the border State delegations on July 12, and made a second appeal to them to accept compensation for the emancipation of the slaves in their respective States while the opportunity was yet at hand.[34] He pointed out to them that the war would have been ended, had they considered the acceptance of the provisions of his first appeal for gradual emancipation, and that this plan would not be a slow and weak means of ending the war. Dissuading them from secession, he failed not to apprise them of the fact that, if the rebellion continued, their institution would be destroyed without any sort of indemnity or reparation. Again he referred to his revoking General Hunter's proclamation of military abolition, with the hope that he might possibly win them over to his plan, but his effort was futile. Most of them replied with a qualified refusal; twenty of them later presented a written reply, pledging themselves to continue loyal, but at the same time giving the reasons why they could not accept the plan of compensated emancipation.

In the meantime the capture of strategic points like Vicksburg and New Orleans had given the control of the lower Mississippi to the Union,[35] General Grant had crippled and driven back the Confederates in the West,[36] and prospects for military success in the East seemed to require some such a measure as military emancipation. After the refusal of compensated emancipation by the border slave States the President decided to emancipate the slaves of rebellious commonwealths by military order.[37] While riding with Mr. Seward and Mr. Welles one day, Mr. Lincoln made mention of emancipating the slaves by proclamation, if the rebels did not lay down their arms. He believed that such action could be guaranteed only as a military necessity. He thought that the slaves must be liberated, or the Union would be exterminated. Lincoln reached a final conclusion and called the cabinet together on July 21, the day preceding the close of that session of Congress.[38] Since he was at the end of his tether, he determined to take a more definite and decisive step. Accordingly, he prepared several orders which, gave authority to commanders in the field to subsist their troops in hostile territory and to employ Negroes as paid laborers, and further provided for the colonization of Negroes in some tropical country.[39]

As this discussion led to no definite conclusion, the subject was resumed at a meeting on the following day; but Lincoln decided that the time was inopportune. While he thought that more evil than good would be derived from the wholesale arming of Negroes, yet he was not unwilling that the commanders arm, purely for defensive purposes, those slaves who came within the Union lines. But the President had reached a decision on the correlated policy of emancipation with which it appears that his cabinet was not in accord. They were surprised when he read to them the first draft of a proclamation warning the rebels of the penalties provided by the Confiscation Act, suggesting the renewal of his proposition of compensation to the loyal States, and adding a summary order that, as Commander-in-Chief of the Army and Navy, he would declare free the slaves of all States that might be in rebellion on January 1, 1863. The Cabinet was somewhat "bewildered by the magnitude and boldness of this proposal."[40]

Only two members of the cabinet concurred in the proposal. Secretary Chase favored this plan of military emancipation, but could not approve the method of execution. Blair, the Postmaster General, deprecated this policy on the ground that it would cost the administration the fall elections. Secretary Seward approved it and yet questioned the expediency of its issue at that stage of the war, owing to the depression of the public mind and the repeated reversals for the Union armies. He further deemed it to be a last measure of an exhausted government that was crying for help, stretching forth its arms to Ethiopia instead of awaiting a reverse appeal from Ethiopia. Consequently he urged a postponement of the issue of the proclamation until the country was supported by military success. Lincoln, struck by the wisdom of Seward's views, which he had entirely overlooked, laid it away and postponed the proclamation on July 22 until the Union forces reported a victory. Instead, after a three-day interval, he issued a short announcement that contained warnings as required by the provisions of the Confiscation Act.

Lincoln's postponement of the issue of the proclamation was wise. Military reversals made the situation more serious for the President's supporters. The radicals and the conservatives, resorted to incessant criticism, railing against him and his policy. Lincoln, however, kept up appearances of indecision, even though his own course had been clearly and inalterably mapped out; but circumstances did not admit a revelation. His main object was to restrain impatience and zeal, and yet maintain the loyalty of both factions.[41]

Horace Greeley attacked Lincoln unmercifully in *The New York Tribune* and accused him of being responsible for the deplorable results coming from his failure to enforce the Confiscation Act. Lincoln, on the contrary, lost no time in replying to Greeley, and declared that he intended to save the Union by the shortest possible way in accordance with the provisions of the Constitution; that his paramount object in the struggle was to preserve the Union and not either to preserve or destroy slavery; that he would save the Union, either without liberating any slaves, or by freeing all the slaves, or by freeing some and leaving others in servitude; that, at any rate, he would save the Union; and that his efforts at emancipation would be determined by its bearing on the more important question of saving the Union.

The expected easy victory did not follow; but, on the contrary, came sad and humiliating defeat of Pope in the second battle of Bull Run in August, 1862. At this juncture Lincoln was urged by both individuals and delegations to follow one or the other decision relative to emancipation, but his attitude remained the same. On September 13, he informed a Chicago delegation that he was unable to free slaves by the Constitution, especially when the Constitution could not be enforced in the rebel States, and declared that any emancipation proclamation would at that time be as effective and operative as "the Pope's bull against the comet."[42] What the antislavery group wanted was not granted; but wholesale emancipation was going on by virtue of the provisions of the Confiscation Act, slavery had been abolished in the District of Columbia, and the territories had been restored to freedom. Lincoln, moreover, left himself a margin for action according to his declaration, in his interview with the Chicago delegation, that, as Commander-in-Chief of the Army and Navy, he had the right to take any measure which might best subdue the enemy.[43]

Upon hearing of the Union victory at Antietam three days after, Lincoln immediately seized this opportunity to announce the policy upon which he had already decided. He had promised to withhold his Emancipation Proclamation until the rebels were out of Frederick. Now that they had been driven from Maryland and Pennsylvania, Lincoln was ready to carry out his plan. On September 22, 1862, therefore, he announced, read, and published his preliminary Emancipation Proclamation.[44] It embraced propositions that provided for the renewal of the plan of compensated emancipation, voluntary colonization, military emancipation of all slaves in rebellious States on January 1, 1863, and the ultimate recommendation of compensation to loyal owners.

Although this proclamation was endorsed by an assembly of Governors from the Northern States, who had already convened at Altoona, Pennsylvania, to consider emergency measures for the protection of their respective States,[45] the political test of this announcement of military emancipation came, as expected, in the autumn elections. Popular discontent had arisen as the result of military failure. The Democrats boldly declared that the war of the Union had been changed to a war for abolition of slavery. Party conflicts became bitter and resulted in a loss to the Republicans although they still retained a majority.

In his next annual message, however, President Lincoln did not discuss the Emancipation Proclamation, but he renewed his argument for compensated emancipation. On December 11, 1862, George H. Yeaman of Kentucky introduced in the House of Representatives a resolution dubbing the President's proclamation as unwarranted by the Constitution and a useless and dangerous war message. This resolution was tabled by a vote of ninety-four to forty-five. Four days later Representative S. C. Fessenden of Maine, on the contrary, offered a resolution putting into affirmative form the identical phraseology of Mr. Yeaman's proposition, and secured its passage by a test vote of seventy-eight to fifty-four. No other action of consequence then followed except a manifestation of interest in compensated emancipation in Missouri.

At a cabinet meeting on the last day of December, 1862, Lincoln read the final draft of the Emancipation Proclamation and invited criticism. He made some revision of a minor nature but rejected the proposal to eliminate from the order the provision that the freedmen be armed. In this form the Proclamation was issued the following day, January 1, 1863. The constitutionality of this document has been questioned. It is conceded, however, that it did actually abolish slavery within the rebellious area and as a moral stimulus to the struggle for freedom, it proved to be of great value.

HARRY S. BLACKISTON

FOOTNOTES:

[1] *Edwards, History of Illinois, 179.*

[2] Nicolay and Hay, *Abraham Lincoln*, I, 72; W. H. Lamon, *Life of Abraham Lincoln*, 83.

[3] Nicolay and Hay, *Abraham Lincoln*, I, 15, 140, 151, 642.

[4] Nicolay and Hay, *Abraham Lincoln*, I, 148, 285-288.

[5] Nicolay and Hay, *Abraham Lincoln*, I, 286.

[6] *Ibid.*, I, 373, 375, 380-390.

[7] *Ibid.*, I, pp. 391, 392.

[8] Nicolay and Hay, II, 85, 89.

[9] Nicolay and Hay, II, 136-138, 143.

[10] Nicolay and Hay, II, 137, 156, 157; *Lincoln-Douglass Debates*, p. 8.

[11] Nicolay and Hay, II, pp. 75, 147.

[12] *Ibid.*, II, p. 149.

[13] Nicolay and Hay, II, 156, 157, 216.

[14] Murat Halstead, *Conventions of 1860*, 6.

[15] *Ibid.*, 7.

[16] Nicolay and Hay, II, 255.

[17] Nicolay and Hay, II, 287, 382.

[18] Rhodes, *United States*, III, p. 357.

[19] Burgess, *Civil War*, II, p. 76.

[20] Nicolay and Hay, *Abraham Lincoln*, IV, 416-420; V, p. 211.

[21] Burgess, *Civil War*, II, 79-80.

[22] Nicolay and Hay, V, 206.

[23] Nicolay and Hay, V, 207.

[24] Dodge, *View*, chap. xi.

[25] Nicolay and Hay, V, p. 209.

[26] McPherson, History of the Rebellion, p. 210.

[27] Nicolay and Hay, V, 214.

[28] *Ibid.*, VI, p. 90.

[29] Nicolay and Hay, VI, 94-96.

[30] *Ibid.*, VI, 97.

[31] Nicolay and Hay, VI, 99-100.

[32] Nicolay and Hay, VI, 103.

[33] *Ibid.*, VI, 107.

[34] *Ibid.*, VI, pp. 109-111.

[35] King, *New Orleans*, ch. xiii.

[36] Dodge, *View*, ch. x.

[37] Nicolay and Hay, VI, p. 121.

[38] *Ibid.*, VI, pp. 123-124.

[39] *Warden, Life of S. P. Chase, p. 439.*

[40] F. B. Carpenter, *Six Months at the White House*, pp. 20-22.

[41] Dodge, *View*, ch. xiv. Rossiter Johnson, *History of War of Secession.*

[42] Nicolay and Hay, VI, 155.

[43] Dodge, *View*, pp. 102-115.

[44] Nicolay and Hay, VI, pp. 168-169.

[45] Nicolay and Hay, VI, p. 164.

THE JOURNAL OF ISAACO[1]

I

The time approaches when all the wildness of this little world will be overrun and tamed into the trimness of a civilized parterre; when the last trail will have been trodden, the mystery of the last forest bared, and the last of the savage peoples penned into a League of Nations to die of unnatural peace. What will our children do then, I wonder, for their books of high romance? How satisfy their thirst of daring with nothing further to dare? Who will appease them, when

> "The Rudyards cease from kipling
>
> And the Haggards ride no more,"

when Robinson Crusoe and the classics are once read, and in a hencoop world no saga-man arises in their stead? They say that by then we shall have enlarged our borders and gone in our chariots of petrol to visit the wheeling stars. But I misdoubt these Icarian flights. It seems to me more likely that the harassed parents and publishers of those days will be driven earthward to rummage into the lumber of the past and bring out as new the obscure things that a former more heroic age had buried. In those stricken times, I hope someone may have the fortune to light upon my manuscript

Journal of Isaaco, a slim, alluring folio that now glitters in red-and-gold upon my study shelves. It would be a pity if Time, the All-Merciless, were allowed to throw the dust of oblivion over these pretty pages, for they possess in good measure that trait of "pleasant atrocity" which wins the attention of youth.

But who was Isaaco, and what was his *Journal* that it calls for the popularity of print? Those who have followed the harrowing tale of Mungo Park's *Travels* along the River Niger, in the years 1795 to 1797, and again in the fatal expedition of 1805, will be well acquainted with Isaaco. They will have smiled at his childish tempers, applauded his snakelike cunning, and laughed outright at his heathen superstitions. But the others must be gravely informed that Isaaco was a West African of the Mandingo tribe who was wont for dignity's sake to describe himself as a Mohammedan priest. Certainly he had the Pentecostal gift of tongues, for there was hardly a dialect of Bambouk, Fool-adoo, Jallonkadoo, Timbuctoo, and all the other tribes of Senegal and beyond, but he could deceive the wiliest natives in it. Moreover, as a professional guide he found it paid to keep a wife in every petty state. At the worst she served to exercise the tongue; at the best she was provisioner, geographer, and spy. Never tired, never sick, never at a loss, Isaaco was simply indispensable to the European merchants trading in Senegal. So, indeed, was he to Mungo Park, that doughtiest of Scotsmen, who dared on through Bambarra and Haoussa where no white-face had ever been. Without Isaaco's genius and gigantic strength, it is unlikely that the second expedition (in 1805) would ever have reached the Niger. It was Isaaco who nursed the forty brave men who one by one sickened of dysentery; supported them on their mules, even in delirium, when they cried like children for their homes; and buried them at the last with saphies or charms from the *Koran* over their unmarked graves. It was he who watched, while the others slept the dead sleep of exhaustion; piled up the camp-fires to scare off the lions and wolves, and, worse than the wolves, those thieves and murderers (the scum of Senegal) who ever dogged their steps. None like Isaaco could placate each chieftain with the gift that his soul desired (be it cowries, beads, looking-glasses, muskets, or multi-colored waistcoats); nor when these failed, could any but Isaaco win passports with the mere honey of his tongue. Nothing could swerve him from honesty or the performance of his task. He was tied to a tree and flogged in the presence of his local wife, set upon by the very white men he was serving, stung all over by a swarm of bees, and mauled in both thighs by a crocodile; but each time he turned up smiling and ready to go on. Nothing could stop him, for did he not keep the solemn ritual of the guides, sacrificing a black ram at the threshold of every country they entered, drawing the magic triangles and hieroglyphs on the sand of every desert they had to cross, and keeping fast in his scrip that lock of a white man's hair, which added all the knowledge of a European to the African natives who possessed it?[2]

II

The agreement of Isaaco was to guide the expedition to the Niger, whence it was to proceed under the direction of Amady Fatouma, another guide. Accordingly, when Sansanding was reached, Isaaco's work was accomplished. Some days he lingered to load the great canoe (large enough to carry a hundred men). In the evenings he taught Mungo Park the names of the necessaries of life in the tongues of the countries ahead. Then he took a last farewell of his master and carried back to the coast that famous letter to Lord Camden, the concluding lines of which are engraved below the writer's statue in the city of Edinburgh: "My dear friends Mr. Anderson and likewise Mr. Scott are both dead; but, though all Europeans who were with me should die, and though I were myself half dead, I would still persevere; and if I could not succeed in the object of my journey I would at least die on the Niger."

One by one the months wore on and no news came from the Niger. But in the next year (1806) there began to be rumors of a great disaster. Still nothing definite was heard, and Mungo Park's wife and his many friends hoped on. They knew his marvellous hardihood and resource, and that of the stalwart Scotsmen who were with him. In 1810, however, the Government, who were responsible for the second expedition, thought it time to inquire what had befallen it; so they told the Governor of Senegal to find Isaaco and offer him £1,000 to explore after the explorer and put all doubts at rest. Now the manuscript which I possess, and of which a *précis* follows, is Isaaco's account of his travels in search of Mungo Park, by which he earned his thousand pounds and did the last sad offices to his master's memory. In my judgment it contains as much of the spirit of adventure as Mungo Park's own journals, and, being written by a native, gets nearer to the life and mind of the African Negro than any white man, writing from outside, could hope to do. For that reason I often wonder why the successive editors of Park's *Travels* have passed it over, printing only the last page or two, wherein Amady Fatouma relates the explorer's end. One thing I know has been against its adoption, to wit, an insufferably dull style. Seeing that it is difficult to be dull in the Arabic tongue, and that it was impossible for Isaaco to be so in any of the tongues he used, I suspect the English translator (no doubt a mere clerk in Governor Maxwell's Office) of pruning away the flowers of speech, and making all as prim and exact as an affidavit. Or possibly Isaaco simulated dullness. He meant to have that thousand pounds, and could afford to take no risks. A tropical, luxuriant style would certainly have put his credibility in question. As it was, many of the learned societies doubted his word, and one of them roundly asserted that he had sat outside Senegal and fabricated at ease the history of his travels. It was only after Bowditch, Denham, Clapperton, and Landor had explored after the explorer that Isaaco's credit was established and the learned societies put to shame.

In the abridgment that follows I have tried to preserve not only the spirit, but wherever possible the very words, of Isaaco's manuscript *Journal*. Whatever has been discarded is of little consequence and of less grammar.

III

Isaaco left Senegal by ship on the 22d day of the Moon Tabasky (January 7th) in the year 1810; but apparently the moon was not propitious, for he was nearly cast away in the lighter, trying to cross the bar, and in the ensuing confusion the larger part of his baggage was stolen. When he discovered this two days later at Goree and attempted to return, the winds rose and tossed the vessel about for nine days and drove him back to Goree. After some negotiation with Governor Maxwell by courier, the baggage was rescued and sent to Isaaco by road. The next few pages of his *Journal* are difficult and barren reading, bristling with nothing but the uncouth names of places where the good ship passed or anchored for the night, and with the hours duly entered as in a log book, according to the Mohammedan hours of prayer. Sailing by way of Yoummy, Jillifrey, Tancrowaly, and Jaunimmarou, they came on the eighth day to Mariancounda, where Isaaco landed. This was the home of Dr. Robert Ainsley, who had so often befriended Mungo Park, fitted him out with the necessaries of life, and started each expedition on its way. Under the same hospitable roof Isaaco lodged for the inside of a week, and then, enriched with the gift of a horse and an ass and twenty bars of beads, went into the wilds to search for the fate of his master. To open the road through Giammalocoto and Tandacounda, Isaaco wisely paid court to the King of Cataba, and showered upon him an old musket and a string of amber of the quality No. 4. The next halt was at Sandougoumanna under a tamarisk tree (Isaaco always notes the trees under which he sleeps). From the shade of this in the early morning he sent presents to the kings who barred the way; tobacco to him of Sallatigua, and scarlet cloth to him of Mansangcoije. Three villages on, Isaaco's company was suddenly increased by members of his own family, fleeing before the army of Bambarra—all but his mother, who had refused to leave her kraal. Three days later he was with her, in his native place of Montogou, and there stayed forty days, whether carousing, or fighting, or praying, he does not say. Then, prudently burying his heavy luggage, he departed, still carrying his people with him—through Moundoundou, where the chief killed a sheep in his honor and was rewarded with a flask of powder— on through Couchiar, a sleepy sort of place by name and situation, with a spreading bark tree, beneath which he drowsed the length of a day—on to Saabic, a village solely inhabited by Maraboos or priests. To gain the goodwill of Allah, he dwelt there a few days, and discovered a relation of one of his wives (no rare occurrence, seeing how many he kept) whose heart he rejoiced with some gunpowder and a gay piece of cloth. At the very next village, Tallimangoly, he fell across another, who cost him three grains of amber. Indeed, it seemed as though his store of presents would never hold out; for, no sooner had he digested the sheep his cousin killed for him, than the Bambarra army came up, and with fear and trembling Isaaco must needs dole out a whole heap of stuff—10 flasks of powder, 13 grains of amber (this time No. 1), 2 grains of coral (No. 1) and a handsome tin box. These to the King. And the King's chamberlain, goldsmith, and singing men had to be tipped as well.[3]

IV

So they paid their way through Sangnonagagy and Saamcolo (where there was a "grand palaver" to rescue Isaaco's dog, which had bitten a man and been condemned to die), on to Diggichoucoumee, a place as long as its name, which took them four days to get through. It took still longer to get clear of the next village of Dramana, for the family of one of his wives came up and bitterly opposed her going with him on a journey so hazardous. There was another "grand palaver." In the end Isaaco lost his temper and divorced his wife; and, as the law required her to return what she had received at marriage, he came rather well out of it—to be exact, with a bullock and four sheep. A little further on Isaaco met an Arab with an exceptionally fine mare, which he bought with his wife's dowry and so consoled himself. He found the mare more tractable than a wife with obstinate relations. After this episode the pace of the party mended. Numbers of villages with unpronounceable names were hurried through. The river Senegal was crossed, and a country entered, that of Bambarra, where only women could be found. Every man, even the children and the aged, had gone away with the army. At the ill-sounding place Ourigiague, just beyond, they were royally entertained. A whole bullock was roasted for them. So, too, at Medina, where they were forced to waste twelve days and devour five sheep, because one of Isaaco's servants made off with the aforesaid mare and Isaaco's precious musket. A trustier servant was despatched on his trail. In due time he returned with the mare and the musket, and preferred not to say what had happened to the thief. The petty kingdom of Casso, which they came to next, proved very trying. There were six rivers to cross, full (says Isaaco) of alligators and hippopotami. There was the forbidding rock of Tap-Pa in the desert of Maretoumane to get by. And there was the mountain of Lambatara, on the top of which they were attacked by a cloud of bees. Maddened with the stings, the Negroes ran everywhere; the mules broke loose and threw their packs down the hill. Poor Isaaco had to collect them all, physick the dying and distressed, and number the living and the lost. At nightfall he slept like a log "under a monkey-bread tree." The following day was darkened by an ominous message from the King of Bambarra. There was evidently trouble brewing ahead. To gain some friendship in the capital, Isaaco decided to bribe. To Sabila, the Chief of the King's slaves, he sent a pair of scissors, a snuff-box, and a looking-glass, and desired to be his friend. And to his old friend Allasana Bosiara, then ambassador at Bambarra from the King of Sego, he sent a piece of silver "as a mark of being near him," and begged him not to leave until he was in safety. As he drew nearer, other signs made Isaaco convinced that "something unpleasant was planning." He was refused lodgings and water by the chiefs. A friendly merchant who had travelled under his protection was secretly warned to take himself and his goods away before it was too late. Thereupon Isaaco retired to another monkey-bread tree, ringed his little company about with muskets, double-barrelled guns, and assegais and "waited for what should happen." The following morning the King tempted them away with the friendliest of welcomes and gave them lodging and water at Wassaba, near the Royal Palace. His suggestion, however, that Isaaco should sleep separately from his people, was courteously but firmly declined. Indeed, Isaaco left nothing to chance. He first fortified the lodgings assigned to him, and then set out to find Sabila. But the King's spies who dogged his steps gave him the wrong directions, and at last he abandoned the quest. It seemed clear that Sabila did not wish him well. The next day the King sent word that he would like to see Isaaco. It had to be. Taking his life in his hands, as he had done a thousand times before, the old guide mounted his horse and rode off to the royal quarters. On the way, a friend whispered to him that he was betrayed; and on no account must he tell the King that he was bound with presents to the King of Sego; for there was not a being he hated and feared so much as that monarch, who usurped his rightful throne. "But," replied Isaaco, "he knows already I am bound there. To Sego I was sent and to Sego I must go unless force or death prevents." Arrived at the King's door, Isaaco was told that he was sleeping (yet another ruse) and that he must remain in the guard-room. It was then about sunset. For hours Isaaco waited, but the King slept on and not a soul of Isaaco's friends in the capital came to relieve his suspense. They knew he was marked down to die. "The only person," he writes, "who came to comfort me was a Griot, that is, a dancing woman. On leaving me she went, as I afterwards learned, to the Ambassadors of Sego and said to them: 'Oh! me, oh! me, my back is broke (which is an expression of sorrow among the Cassoukes). They are going to kill Isaaco.'"

V

Meantime, as the guards were dancing, singing, and drinking, Isaaco stole out unperceived and made good use of his time. To the keeper of the inn, with whom he had formerly stayed, and who had some influence with the King, he gave one of his wives' necklaces and seven grains of coral. From him he went to Madiguijou, a Counsellor of State, explained his mission to Sego, and hinted what Governor Maxwell would do if he were put to death. He even crept into Sabila's hut, and told him the same thing; but the chief of the slaves smiled and promised nothing. Isaaco plied him with more amber No. 1, but he "smiled and smiled and still remained a villain." Then Isaaco thought it wiser to get back into the guard-room, before the drunken soldiers grew sober and looked for him. In the morning he played his last card by getting into touch with the Ambassadors from Sego. These distinguished gentlemen were by no means eager to take on the burden of his protection, but Isaaco bade them know that the present which Mungo Park had promised King Mansong, he (Isaaco) was commissioned to bring to their King Dacha, his son. If they were determined to go without him, they might do so; but whether he lived or died they should hear of it at Sego. That fetched them. They were by no means pleased with the picture Isaaco drew of their sufferings, and proceeded to save themselves by saving him. As the King their master could simply eat up the King of Bambarra and his army at one swallow, they commanded the release of Isaaco and twenty men to conduct him on his way. At this peremptory message, King Figuing Coroba found it politic to wake, and summoned Isaaco to his presence. The latter obeyed, went through the highest salutations, and proffered a tin box by way of asking: "Is it peace?" But there was no sign of peace. The King suddenly lost his temper, raged at the King of Sego, and, swearing he would seize everything Isaaco possessed, hurled the tin box at his head. Isaaco discreetly withdrew, while Sabila promised to pour oil on the troubled waters. The next day Isaaco, not the least daunted, presented himself with the aforesaid tin box and in addition a quantity of amber, and gunpowder, and the horse Robert Ainsley had given him. Sabila was bribed once more, and the King's singer was won over with a snuff-box. At the sight of his share, the King's anger melted like wax, and he not only gave Isaaco leave to depart that same day, but promised an escort too.... Isaaco coolly answered that he was in no hurry and would wait a day or two—an exhibition of nerve that quite astonished the King. "You see," he said to Sabila, "Isaaco appears to be a courageous man. If he had been of a weak-spirited mind, he would have run away and left his things in my hands." To confirm his friendship, the King called up the heir to the throne, and made him swear protection to Isaaco, an oath which the Prince hinted should be cemented by the gift of a *cousaba* or shirt. But Isaaco delicately replied that he had none quite clean enough to present. When he returned to his own country, he swore to bring him a new one. So Isaaco triumphed and returned to his own people, who were mourning him as dead. Nor did he come empty-handed, for he met a man on the way who wanted a priestly charm or amulet (*grisgris*). Isaaco scribbled an Arabic prayer on a leaf and received a bullock in exchange. This he slaughtered forthwith, feasted his large family, and made a sacrifice of thanksgiving to his god.

VI

Three days after this distressing delay, Isaaco set out for Sego, and was brought in safety to the end of the Bambarra dominions. For further guidance he then hired four promising natives; but, having landed the party in the midst of a gloomy forest, they grew superstitious and ran away. "I was much disappointed," says the mild Isaaco, "at their behavior." More likely he was speechless with rage.[4] But there was nothing to do but to press on, and that they did through forest and desert to the lakes of Chicare and Tirium. As they reached the mud-walled village of Giangounta, one of the fatting pigs, which were to be given to King Dacha, became too fat to carry. Isaaco begged the chief of the village to look after it until it could be fetched, but he objected, "being afraid to take charge of an unknown animal." However, Isaaco explained all about its ways, wrote a *grisgris* to ward off all evil, and dumped it on the still-astonished hamlet. Thence over more lakes by canoe, through Toucha, where they found the trees from which African gunpowder was made, and by a great pyramid with a large stone on its head, where the murderous Moors lie in wait. Going by night to avoid them, Isaaco did not till day discover that one of his servants had made off with his box of jewellery and his one and only *cousaba*. Then he swore as only a Mohammedan priest can, and rode after the thief. In three days he was back with the felon, whose death penalty he postponed for a time on condition that he carried the remaining pig into Sego. At Sannanba, Isaaco found again the sister and the wife he had left there five years before. He seems to have quite forgotten them; but they had faithfully waited his return, knowing that nothing would kill him. It was from them that he first learnt that Mungo Park was dead. They had seen Alhaji Beraim,[5] who had been shown the canoe in the country of Haoussa, where Park met his end. However, Isaaco was determined to go on and learn for himself on the spot. So he dismissed his sister with a piece of muslin, took on the wife, and released the prisoner, for (he says) "I was certain, once in the King's power, he would be put to death." At Counnow, a little further along the road, Isaaco came upon "an enormous large tree inhabited by a large number of bats. Another such tree lies on the west of the village, likewise full of bats; but what is most extraordinary, the bats of the east constantly go at night to the west, and return to the east at the approach of day; those of the west never go to the east. And the natives say their lawful King (Figuing Coroba who had been driven out to the petty kingdom of Bambarra) lies upon the west."

Impressing four men of every district to carry the pig to the next, Isaaco journeyed on through Dedougou, Issicord, and five other villages, all deserted. At Yamina, one of the women slaves whom Isaaco had redeemed, and who had followed his expedition, found her long-lost husband. There was much rejoicing and dancing and exchange of presents all round. Then after crossing the Niger at Jolliba, they struck Sego Coro, the ancient palace of the kings, where to that day (and possibly to this) the King resorted when war was declared, to have his amulets prepared, and don his forefathers' armor. There, too, the royal prisoners were wont to be brought for confinement until the fasting moon, and then cruelly murdered in the House of Death. For eight days after it was against the law for anyone to pass the house without putting off his hat and shoes. In the reign of the great warrior-king, Walloo, not a moon passed without the sacrifice of blood.

VII

The next day Isaaco was summoned to the presence of the King, who scented his presents from afar. Indeed the royal message was concerned only with the pigs: they were to be brought in the same ingenious manner by which Isaaco had tied them for transit. In this fashion then, with the swine, like peace-offerings, suspended in advance, Isaaco's motley company, begrimed with eight months' travel, came straggling into Sego.

Encircled with his companies of guards, "young, strong, and beardless," the great King Dacha squatted on the ground. Behind and beside him, standing upright in the earth, glittered the four broadswords which Mungo Park had given. As a sign that he had loosed his hounds of war, the King was dressed in his military coat, shining with countless amulets of gold. In the wild flaming sky burned the remnants of the storm which had just driven him back from Douabougou. So squatted King Dacha, and with royal impassive face, showing no mark of the boiling curiosity within, stared at those unknown animals, the swine. Hard on their heels shuffled Isaaco, himself also on all fours in a deep obeisance. Behind him the bearers of the inevitable bribes: a drum, two blunderbusses, a bed, a piece of scarlet cloth, and a solitary dog. (There should have been another, but it had bolted far back at Mariancounda.) Then said Isaaco: "Maxwell, Governor of Senegal, salutes you and sends his compliments to you. Here is the present your father asked of Mr. Park and which he promised to send him." "Is the Governor well?" asked Dacha. "Yes," replied Isaaco, "he is well and desired me to beg your assistance to discover what has become of Mr. Park. We would know if he is dead or alive." After these civilities they fell to business, and Isaaco bargained for a canoe to row as far as needful down the Niger. The King hesitated over the Governor's offer of two hundred bars, for was he not far enough away to break his word? But when the two pigs got loose and waddled about, he became as happy as a child, and was no more trouble to Isaaco. To confirm his goodwill, he killed a bullock for him, and begged him to remain as his guest throughout the remainder of that moon. After a fortnight's festivities, Isaaco was preparing to depart, when the King's mind was suddenly turned another way. A message was brought in that the Prince of Timbuctoo was at hand and desired an audience. King Dacha scowled. Then he leapt to his feet, summoned his 600 guards, and went out in full war-paint to meet him. The Prince rode up airily and said: "Being a friend of your father, I thought it my duty to let you know of my coming to take a wife, promised to me in your tribe." "And why," asked Dacha in his dreadful voice, "why have you permitted the people of your country to plunder one of my caravans, and why did *you* yourself plunder another?"

With no more said, the King returned to his kraal. It was from others the Prince learned that the merchants of the caravans had denounced him before the King, that his betrothed had been given to another, and that he was in danger of being plundered of his life. With almost indecent haste he despatched three horses to the King, gave pieces of colored stuff to all the captains of the guards, and slunk back ashamed to Timbuctoo. But King Dacha was so furiously enraged, he could neither stay in his kraal nor allow Isaaco to take leave. Away he rode to Impelbara and Banangcoro, with Isaaco trailing behind, very much out of temper and somewhat out of breath. It seemed, as the chief slave tried to explain, that when the King was angry, he pacified himself by visiting his children. Apparently he visited his wrath on them. Isaaco groaned and wondered how many there might be, and in what score of villages they dwelt apart. But he cheered up when they told him the legitimate children were six. There had been more, but by an ancient law of Sego, if a male child was born of one of the King's wives upon a Friday, its throat was cut immediately. This had accounted for three. After a decent interval, Isaaco made it known to the King that he also was very angry, and demanded to have his canoe and go after Mungo Park. The King then sent for him, apologized for forgetting all about him, and pointed in justification to the pigs, which, like a good father, he had brought along to please the children. He himself could hardly keep his eyes off such fat and unusually happy creatures. The next day Isaaco pressed the bargain, and, though it was Friday, steered away in the King's canoe for Sansanding, where he had parted from Mungo Park. And then, with the prospect of hundreds of miles in hostile country before him, he had a stroke of good fortune; for in the next village of Medina, whom should he run against but Amady Fatouma! As one might expect, Isaaco nailed him to the spot with a hundred questions. Poor Amady began to weep. "They are all dead," he sobbed. Isaaco demanded to know when and where and why. "They are all dead," the guide repeated. "They are lost for ever. It is no use asking. It is no good looking for what is irrecoverably lost." Like a sensible man, Isaaco checked the ardor of his curiosity. It certainly was hopeless to ply Amady with questions; his tears threatened to flood the Niger; it was not safe to stay there. So Isaaco gave him a day or two to subside, and arranged a meeting higher up the river.

VIII

Amady's tale has often been printed, and there is no need here to repeat anything but essentials; his padding is even more woolly than Isaaco's. In the great canoe,[6] which Isaaco had helped to load before departing, Mungo Park rowed away on November 17th, 1805, with the survivors of his company of forty, namely, four white men and five Negroes, including Amady, for crew. From the very outset the voyage proved unpropitious. Almost every village they passed on the river bank came out against them in canoes, armed with bows and arrows, pikes and assegais. Each member of the crew kept fifteen muskets in action; to kill and kill was the only chance of forcing a passage through. There was no Isaaco to try the magic of conciliation. Once indeed, when they had beaten off sixty canoes with appalling slaughter, Amady ventured to remonstrate. "Martin," he said, taking hold of his arm, "let us cease firing: we have killed too many already." "On which," he comments, "Martin wanted to kill me and would have done so had not Mr. Park intervened." The troubles thickened. The news of their coming had evidently been spread in advance. Just beyond Gotoigega they encountered a whole army, comprised of the Poule nation, such beasts themselves, that (says Amady) they possess no beasts of any other kind. They were suffered to go by in ominous silence—only to fall foul of a squadron of hippopotami, who nearly washed them over. At an island just beyond, Amady was landed to forage for milk; but there was no milk to be had, not even the milk of human kindness. The natives took him prisoner and decided he should be done to death. But Mungo Park was watching; and by a fortunate chance two canoes full of natives, bringing fresh provisions for sale, had come alongside at that moment. Mungo Park made it abundantly clear that he would kill every man-jack of them if a hair of Amady's head were touched. So the prisoners were exchanged. It was a narrow escape for Amady; and the uneasiness it caused was increased by the constant cries from the shore, "Amady Fatouma, how can you pass through our country without giving us anything?" "I seriously promised," he observed, "never to pass there again without making considerable charitable donations to the poor." As they came to the frontiers of Haoussa another large army of Moors watched them from a mountain. Fortunately they had no fire-arms, and could do no harm. On reaching Yaour, the first place of any size in Haoussa, Amady was landed, as his bargain was to bring the party only so far. In addition to his pay, he conveyed Mungo Park's presents to the King; but, instead of delivering these in person, gave them to the Chieftain of Yaour, who promised to forward them. A little slip, it seems, but fraught with deadly consequence. The Chieftain, finding out from Mungo Park that he did not intend to return that way, determined to keep the presents for himself. The next morning, as Amady was paying his court to the King and expecting the presents to come, two horsemen rode in from Yaour and said: "We are sent from the Chief to let you know that the white men went away without giving you or him anything. They have a great many things with them and have given nothing. This Amady Fatouma now before you is a bad man, and has made a fool of you." Poor Amady was forthwith put in irons and all his goods confiscated, with the exception of his Arabic charms, which they dared not touch. The next morning the King sent his army to Boussa and posted it on a rock which straddled the width of the river, leaving only a narrow opening for the current to race through. Mungo Park, seeing the danger, nevertheless resolved to force a passage. But the odds were terrific. It took half the men to keep the canoe moving against the current, while the rest fired at the enemy as they hurled stones and assegais upon their heads. At last the two steersmen were slain, and the canoe went adrift. In a desperate attempt to lighten it, they cast all the baggage into the river, but still could make no headway. Overpowered by numbers and fatigue, and with no chance of killing a whole army, they saw but one hope of escape—namely, to make for the shore and get away into the bush. Taking hold of one of the white men, Mungo Park leapt into the river, Martin, with another white man, following after; but, fine swimmers as they were, the current proved too strong for them and all four were drowned. The one Negro left in the canoe surrendered, and both he and the canoe were dragged to shore and carried to the King.

After being kept three months in irons, Amady was released and in part consoled with a concubine. But he made it his first business before departing to visit the slave taken in the canoe, and learn from him the sad details of Mungo Park's destruction. The only thing that was found in the canoe after its capture was a sword belt which the King used as a saddle-girth for his horse.

IX

Such was Amady Fatouma's tale, that Isaaco had journeyed for nine months to hear. And as he was a "good, honest, and upright man" and had sworn truth upon the *Koran*, there was nothing to do but believe and carry back the mournful tidings. To make "assurance double sure," Isaaco sent to Yaour a native who bribed a slave girl to steal the sword belt from the king's charger. Then, passing homeward through Sego, he told the news to Dacha, who was so furious that he despatched his army to wipe the country of Haoussa off the face of the earth. But Isaaco set his face for Senegal, to exchange his Arabic *Journal* for a thousand pounds.

Louis N. Feipel

FOOTNOTES:

[1] Extract from *The Cream of Curiosity*, by Reginald L. Hine, 1920, pp. 291-316.

[2] To this day no news has reached England of Isaaco's death, and indeed after all he survived it seems impossible that he should ever die.

[3] Isaaco was better able to appreciate their music than Mungo Park. In one item of his accounts, the latter writes: "To the native singers for singing their nonsense."

[4] It must be remembered that Isaaco was writing a government report and careful to suppress all signs of indecorum. What a heap of money one would give to possess his private, unexpurgated journal!

[5] A priest of Yaour to whom Amady Fatouma, the guide, had given a small present from Mungo Park.

[6] Mansong had sold it to Park for a quantity of firearms. It was half rotten and took eighteen days to make water-tight. Forty feet long by six broad and flat-bottomed. They christened it "His Majesty's Schooner Joliba."

CARTER G. WOODSON

COMMUNICATIONS

Mr. A. A. Taylor, who contributed the article on *Negro Congressmen a Generation After* in the April number, recently received from Mr. Henry A. Wallace, a participant in the Reconstruction in South Carolina, the following important letter:

326 FLOWER ST.,
CHESTER, PA.,
APRIL 19, 1922.

PROF. A. A. TAYLOR,
The West Virginia Collegiate Institute,
Institute, W. Va.

Dear Sir: I am still confined to the house, not having been outside since the last week of December. When we get some good sunshiny weather I will venture out. I am writing this to let you know how much I enjoyed reading your very interesting article "Negro Congressmen a Generation After," in the April number of The Journal of Negro History. This article and Dr. Woodson's "Fifty Years of Negro Citizenship as Qualified by the United States Supreme Court" are worth the subscription price to The Journal.

As your article is now in permanent form and no doubt will be quoted frequently, there are one or two little slips that I would like to invite your attention to, feeling that you, like myself, believe in accuracy.

On page 130, foot note relative to Mr. Rainey you have not included his service in the 41st Congress. He was seated in that Congress on December 12, 1870, to succeed Mr. Whittemore, who was unseated on account of a serious charge brought against him. Mr. Rainey was the first Negro Congressman. Mr. Long was seated in the same Congress, but later—January 16, 1871. This would give Mr. Rainey a record of five Congresses. On the same page (130) foot note relative to General Smalls, you have him as a member of five Congresses. My record does not show him a member of the 47th Congress. Mr. Rainey holds the record for length of service. In connection with Mr. Rainey's record I will state that he was the only one of the Negro congressmen who presided over the House of Representatives, that courtesy was extended to him by Speaker Blaine. Altho the House was democratic he was honored by the Republican caucus at one time for Clerkship of the House, showing the esteem in which he was held by his colleagues, after he retired from the House. Page 134—High Hollow Academy should be High Holborn Academy. On the same page, foot note, it is stated that Gen. Elliott resigned from Congress to accept the office of sheriff. While Gen. Elliott had his official residence in Aiken county, he and Mrs. Elliott had their home in Columbia, one of the show places of the city. I cannot conceive of him resigning the position of congressman to accept the insignificant office of sheriff of the small county of Aiken. He resigned in order to go to the House of Representatives at Columbia for the purpose of being elected Speaker of that body, and he succeeded. The other time he resigned was for the purpose of being a candidate for the U. S. Senatorship, but the Pennsylvania R. R. interests put John J. Patterson, who was a Cameron protege, over. Had he been elected sheriff of Aiken county it would have necessitated his living there.

On page 139—"From the year 1871—the period of service of the first Negro in Congress" should be *1870*—Rainey, Dec. 12, 1870.

The greatest compliment I think that was ever paid to a Negro by a prominent white man was that by Benjamin F. Butler, the distinguished Union General, afterwards Governor of Massachusetts, and who had charge of Sumner's civil rights bill in the House of Representatives. In the prefatory remarks to his speech on the day following the great speech made by Gen. Elliott on the same bill, he said:

"I should have considered more at length the constitutional argument, were it not for the exhaustive presentation by the gentleman from South Carolina (Mr. Elliott) of the law, and the only law quoted against us in this case that has been cited, to wit, the Slaughter-House cases. He, with the true instinct of freedom, with a grasp of mind that shows him to be the peer of any man on this floor, be he who he may, has given the full strength and full power of that decision of the Supreme Court."

Garfield, Cannon, Frye, Hale, Hawley, Hoar (Geo. F.),

Platt, Dawes, Phelps, Lamar, Beck, Stephens (A. H.), Randall, Mills, Cox, and Barnum, were among the prominent members of the House at that time, many of whom afterwards reached the Senate, and Garfield, the presidency. General Butler was considered one of the great constitutional lawyers of that period.

The following relative to Senator Bruce and Mr. Langston may interest you if you have not already heard of the incidents:

It is always customary when a new Senator appears with his credentials for his colleague to escort him to the Vice-President's desk to be sworn in. When Senator Bruce presented himself, his colleague, Senator Alcorn, was not present. Senator Roscoe Conkling taking in the situation, walked over to Senator Bruce and escorted him up the aisle and the oath was administered. For this gracious act Senator Bruce named his son, recently of Washington, after the distinguished senator from New York.

As Mr. Venable, the democrat, was given the certificate of election by the Virginia officials for the Congressional seat, Mr. Langston made the contest. The Committee on privileges and elections voted in favor of Mr. Langston. When the time set for action on the case arrived, the whole democratic membership withdrew from the House, thinking that they would catch the Republicans napping and without a quorom, the republican majority being small. The Republicans, however, got wind of what the Democrats were doing and had all of their members rounded up. They not only seated Mr. Langston but the chairman of the elections committee took advantage of the absence of the Democrats and called up the case of Miller versus Elliott from South Carolina and then seated Miller, though the case was not slated for that time. The feelings of the Democrats can be better imagined than described when they returned to the House and found two of their colleagues unseated and two Negro Congressmen seated in their places. The Democrats never again resorted to such tactics.

VERY RESPECTFULLY,
HENRY A. WALLACE.

DOCUMENTS

The following extracts from the *Daily Record*, Greensboro, North Carolina, February 2nd and 3rd, 1911, setting forth the reminiscences of Captain Ball, a participant in the Reconstruction of the Southern States, gives valuable information as to the troublous times of that period:

New York, Feb. 2.—I have now told nearly all of the authenticated facts concerning the Stephens murder; the rest is merely speculative. There have been stories coming from the negroes which are interesting, even if not strictly true. A negro has quite an imagination. I will relate some of these stories, without expressing an opinion, leaving others to decide as to their accuracy and naturalness.

Much of what follows comes from Governor Holden, at the time an aged man, retired (perhaps not voluntarily) from public life. The tendency of his political opinions in his later years was toward "Conservation." I called upon him in February, 1885 (twenty-six years ago) and took notes of what he said, because of its inherent interest. His memory was clear and comprehensive. While governor—he was elected by the Republicans in 1868—and before his impeachment and removal from office by the Democratic legislature of 1870, he sought to unravel the mysteries of the Kuklux brotherhoods;

and tried in every way to discover the perpetrators of the Stephens assassination.

It has already been stated that Stephens, on the fatal Saturday, was in attendance upon a Conservative meeting in Yanceyville, and that he went out of it with Wiley. It is reported that Wiley, on his way home, took supper at the house of a Mr. Poteat. Now the negroes are not only full of curiosity, but take risks to gratify it. Nothing was more common than for them to listen from behind doors, through keyholes and in the corners of the houses where they were employed as servants. Thus it happened that the conversation at the supper-table at Poteat's—so the story goes—was overheard by a negro woman (and other servants), who had been waiting upon the table, and a most pitiful recital it was! The servants had retired from the dining-room, and being in the passage way, outside, and hearing Stephens's name called, they listened.

Governor Holden said that Wiley was speaking of how Stephens had been killed that day; that he (Wiley) had done a good day's work and that he, and the others, had toled (that is enticed) Stephens down stairs to talk with Wiley about being a candidate for sheriff; that they got Stephens to the door and threw the noose over his neck and dragged him inside, and choked him down; that while this was going on, in the room below, old man Bedford Brown was making a speech up-stairs, and the applause was continuous, to drown any outcry; that after Stephens was choked the noose was loosened, as they wished if possible not to kill him; that he was told if he would denounce the Republican party and leave the State, they would spare his life; that he refused and said he would die first; that he then begged them, as their purpose was to kill him, to let him go and see his family; that he said to them, "Gentlemen, you know me, that I am a man of my word and will come back;" that they refused his request; that he then begged them to let him take a last look of his house; that they led him to the window, holding the rope behind him, and he saw his children playing upon the green; that they told him his time was up and pulled him back and again choked him down upon the table; that they loosened the rope when he said, "Gentlemen, I surrender—spare my life and I will do anything you say;" that a young man (whose name I will not give, as Governor Holden gave it to me) said, "No, damn you, you die," and struck him with his knife on his throat and vest, and then they finished him. The negro woman, horrified as she listened, upon hearing all this, exclaimed aloud, "There, by God!"

The supper party heard her words and the story ceased. Wiley left almost immediately; and then they asked the old woman why she said those words and she told them, "because the coffee burned her." They asked her if she had been listening and she declared she had not.

Next day, a younger brother of Poteat sent for her to work in his tobacco field, and asked her the second time the reason of her outcry the night before. He said, "You mind what you are doing—if you 'cheep,' (*i.e.*, tell) about this thing, I will put a ball through you."

Wiley went home (the story goes on) and walked up

and down his piazza, until late that night, attracting the attention of his family by his singular conduct. A negro man, on the watch, had followed him, and had hidden under the house, to hear what was said. The dwellings of the South are frequently without cellars and, in the country, are often sustained by brick and log supports; so it would be easy to crawl underneath. This negro claims to have heard some of Wiley's family ask him why he did not come to bed, and he replied that he was waiting for the wagon.

It was rumored among the negroes, that the purpose was to carry Stephens's corpse to a church near Wiley's, called "Republican Headquarters," and there leave it, to produce the impression that Stephens's political associates had killed him. There was a sprinkle of rain, after nightfall, and fresh wagon tracks were seen, which approached near to Yanceyville, and returned almost to Wiley's. Perhaps, if this was true, the scheme to steal away the body from the court house was baffled by the vigilance of the guards.

The effort was several times made to make it appear that Stephens had been slaughtered by his political friends, to get rid of him, or for effect. For instance, six years had elapsed when the Milton Chronicle, published in Caswell county, charged by innuendo, under the head of "Revelations," that "Hester, Holden, Settle, Smith, Albion (meaning Judge Tourgee), Albright, Boyd, Ball and Keogh" had accomplished this murder most foul. But Mr. Boyd, at the time of the Stephens homicide, was himself a member, in full standing, of the White Brotherhood. This silly charge was made during the

Tilden-Hayes campaign of 1876; Judge Settle then being the Republican candidate for governor and William A. Smith for lieutenant-governor. The others named were all Republicans of more or less prominence. Of course the editor of the Chronicle, and his patrons, knew that the story was a lie.

While I was at Yanceyville, at the inquest, William Henry Stephens—(usually called Henry) as I could not at once go home, thought it would be better for me to stay all night at his late brother's residence. My sojourn at the dwelling, that night, gave me my first opportunity to see how it was fortified. The lower story was protected by thick planks, bullet-proof. The stairway was fixed with a trap door, which could be let down, by its hinges, from above; and then no one could go upstairs without forcing his way against great odds. There was a plentiful supply of firearms with abundant ammunition. Twenty men could resist successfully a hundred, or more, if the attacking party had no artillery. But if a lodgment could be effected below, what could prevent the firing of the dwelling and the destruction of its inmates?

Here Stephens had lived and kept his enemies at bay; and he was as brave as any of them and much more desperate. The cowards who attacked negro cabins in the dead of night, with overwhelming numbers, never invaded Stephens's premises, for that sort took no risks. Yet he felt secure, for he had said that he suffered none to approach him, but those he knew to be his friends. I suppose he thought Wiley was his "friend."

Let us go back a few weeks. At spring term (April, 1870)

of the Caswell Superior Court, an alarm was given that the Kuklux were coming to kill Stephens, Judge Tourgee, and all Republicans and break up the court. This disquieting intelligence was conveyed to me by Judge Tourgee himself. At the time, I occupied a room in Mitchell's house, already mentioned. My apartment, although joined to the dwelling, had no door opening into the main building, so that one had to go into the yard to get to the entrances of that part of the structure. Hon. James T. Morehead, an aged lawyer, who had been famous in his day, and now attended the court from habit, occupied a room of the same size as mine, and opening into it, and detached, as mine was, from the main building.

On Monday afternoon, the first day of the term, Judge Tourgee told me that one Hemphill had informed him of the contemplated raid, and that it was to occur the next Wednesday night. He desired me to go with him to Stephens's house (where the judge boarded during the court), as one of the garrison, to help defend it. The proposition looked absurd to me and it seemed that, if I went, it might subject me to ridicule. No one likes to be ridiculed; at least, I do not.

It may be remarked, in passing, that Judge Tourgee had offended the lawyers, because he boarded with Stephens. They considered it beneath the dignity of so high an official to make his home with a man so low in the social scale, and they were all the more hostile toward the judge because he would do this. They insisted that they would have treated him with respect, if not with cordiality, had he not shown these degraded tastes. As it was, they had no more courtesy for him than for Stephens, believing the judge to have disgraced his office.

It was the effort of the lawyers of North Carolina, in those days, to avoid close contact with the populace and to preserve an esprit de corps. They believed that their only associates, on terms of equality, should be of their own order, as the clergy or medical profession, representing an educated aristocracy. The masses were illiterate, unpolished and, in the estimation of the lawyers, unfit for companionship with the cultivated classes, whose policy it was to inspire the plain people with profound respect for their superiors.

The statements here made of early ideas and feelings, largely result from conversations with Col. Thomas Ruffin, a man of aristocratic lineage and unusual powers of mind. He was a son of the late Chief Justice Ruffin, of the Supreme Court of North Carolina, and afterward himself was an associate justice of that eminent tribunal. He informed me of the sentiment among the lawyers against Tourgee, because of his intimacy with Stephens. And once, when as a matter of course, with my New York education, I had offered to make oath to an affidavit, in a Caswell county lawsuit, wherein I was associated with Col. Ruffin, he advised me against it, and said it had been the custom, in North Carolina, for lawyers never to be sworn, in the conduct of their cases, it being considered that their mere word was sufficient; and so, as I afterward understood, the judges generally so regarded it.

Any one can see, however, the mischiefs which might occur from such a custom; as, after the verbal statements of lawyers, disputes might arise as to what had been said, and no one would be able to decide, and no one would try to do so, for fear of a quarrel. Happily the people, in spite of the traditions of slavery, are rapidly emerging from their blind gropings, as an outcome of the freedom thrust upon them by the civil war, and the younger members of the legal profession now aid in the work of educating the illiterate, knowing that it is better for the commonwealth that all should be taught.

The social conditions existing in North Carolina in the early days mentioned, may help to explain the intense bitterness manifested on all occasions toward men like Stephens. He was of humble parentage, but had been put forward by Governor Holden as a trusted agent of the State government. Thus was invaded the prerogatives of the privileged classes. The prejudices of the leaders were communicated to their followers (who did the voting to keep their rulers in power).

Judge Tourgee, and all carpet-baggers (myself included, of course), were esteemed to be opposed to the dominion of the aristocrats; some of whom, nevertheless, were themselves quite ordinary persons, but puffed up with pride, God knows what for!

Judge Tourgee also invited J. R. Bulla, Esquire, the solicitor, to help defend Stephens's house. Mr. Bulla was a native Republican. Neither he, nor I, believed at the time, that the Kuklux were banded together for serious mischief; although, as I afterward learned, a plot was laid, in those days, by the Randolph county Kuklux, to take Mr. Bulla out and whip him. Had this been done it would have been a wanton outrage. Mr. Bulla never knew of the plan. The scheme was prevented by the interference of a mere youth, Tom Worth, from whom I had the facts.

Both Mr. Bulla and myself decided to remain in our rooms. Out of deference, however, to Judge Tourgee's intelligence, I agreed, in case of an alarm, to go over and help fight it out. There were sixteen resolute fellows there, under the leadership of Judge Tourgee, all well armed and with enough ammunition. Had an attack been made it would have been a lively conflict. Mr. Bulla, born a Quaker, would not agree to join in the battle, preferring, I suppose, in accordance with his tenets, to be murdered in cold blood.

The raid did not take place, however. The judge had caused all the roads leading to Yanceyville to be patrolled, and it was understood that if any considerable body of men approached from any direction light-wood fires would be kindled as warnings.

Tuesday night of the same week, I was invited, and so was Mr. Bulla, to a supper at Judge Kerr's. Nearly all of the members of the bar in attendance upon the court, were guests. Among them I remember Col. Ruffin, General Alfred M. Scales, Col. Junius I. Scales and Col. Dillard. Judge Tourgee was not invited.

Before I went to the supper Judge Kerr, whose residence was not far off, came to my room and smoked his pipe, with its long reed stem. Sometimes he walked the floor, and then sat down, then walked again, and so on. His manner was uneasy, a characteristic of the man. Several times he seemed ready to speak and then restrained himself. He had professed a liking for me, and as he was an impulsive man, I thought he might wish to say something about the threatenings in the air; but finally he kept whatever was on his mind to himself. He had fine traits, but was pompous in demeanor. Those who liked that style were fond of him.

At the April term of the court, the evidences of the presence of the Kuklux in Caswell county, accumulated. After partaking of supper with Judge Kerr and his guests, I retired to rest in my room, quite uneasy because of the rumors. I had fallen into a doze, when my ears were disturbed by voices and singing and a guitar tinkled. My venerable neighbor, Hon. James T. Morehead, was being serenaded. After the music (so-called) had ceased "Uncle Jimmy" made a little speech to the boys. From this, and the conversation ensuing, I learned that it was confessedly a Kuklux serenade. The venerable Nestor of the bar said to his visitors that there were many worse things than the Kuklux—among them the Union League and the Republican party. And so the young men were encouraged.

I was glad when the time came to go home; which I did on the 14th day of April, 1870. I started from Yanceyville in a buggy, with a Mr. Fowler, a resident of Greensboro. Had I previously doubted the existence of the Klans, I must have been convinced, after that ride, unimportant in itself, but memorable for the events which lately had taken place. The remarks and manners of my companion were peculiar. He had a furtive, scared expression as night enclosed us. He was a native Democrat—and I was amazed at his evident trepidation.

We were striving to reach Ruffin, a little station on the Richmond and Danville railroad (now called the Southern Railroad) a few miles south of Danville. Although spring was opening, there was no foliage on the trees, except tiny leaflets bursting into life. Night advanced and the moon shone effulgent, but her rays were obscured by the divergent limbs of the forest, when we sometimes plunged into its depths. The gloom was intensified by drifting clouds, hanging low; but these momentarily lifted, briefly restoring the cheery moonbeams and silver roadway. Many tree-trunks were white, contrasting with the darkness within the dense woods, glistening like spectres, as the tremulous light glimmered through the branches. There was no sound in the forest, except the solemn wail of the wind, and the steady tramp, tramp—tramp, tramp of the hurrying horse. My flesh crept and shuddered under the drastic influence of the chill night and the doleful croakings of my companion; who talked continually of the Kuklux, and peered through the bushes and under-growth, as if expecting to see rise from the ground a full cavalcade of shadowy night-riders.

We reached Ruffin, nevertheless, in good time, and went whirling home in a comfortable railway coach, filled not with hobgoblins, but with civilized human beings.

Afterward I learned that the companion of my

night-ride (who was a tailor) had sewn together the diabolical garbs of the White Brotherhood of his vicinity. Remembering this hideous livery of the devil, it was no wonder he was afraid, even of the peaceful moon, as she benignantly observed him through the arms of the forest.

New York, Feb. 2.—The result of the election (Nov. 8) was rather shocking, but not unexpected. I think the Republicans deserved the drubbing. A hundred and ninety thousand of them, in New York, did not vote; so to punish somebody for something, they let Tammany obtain control.

Governor Dix doesn't say anything; but Governor Wilson says enough for both. It remains to be seen whether or not the latter has not bitten off more than he can masticate.

In the course of my life I have been shocked more than once, mostly, while living in North Carolina. For instance, in 1876, when it was supposed that Tilden had been elected, the young men of Odell's store thought it a good joke and decorated my fence with black calico. Our colored cook, thinking it would hurt our feelings, stripped it all off early in the morning before we got a sight of it, much to our regret. But Madam was equal to the emergency and had the girl gather up the black stuff and take it to Odell's store to sell for paper-rags! The cook was received with shouts of applause, showing that Odell's young men fully appreciated the humor of the occasion.

Odell had a big store, but all the black calico in stock

must have been cleaned out on that occasion. As I understand at the time, the fences of Judge Dick, Postmaster White, Col. Keogh, Judge Settle and Judge Tourgee were all decorated. The last named, characteristically, sought to make capital out of the episode, which was only a joke.

When I went to bed very late the night before (or rather in the morning) I thought Tilden had really been elected and I did not enjoy the sensation. Nevertheless I did not feel as I did six years before, in the Ku Klux times. We lived then in the little cottage opposite the jail. The election was in August. Madam had gone North to visit her home-folks. I was alone in the house. Diagonally across the street was a disreputable bar-room, where all the "roughs" assembled every night; and for no less than three weeks after the "Conservative" victory these fellows kept up a shouting and howling, which was far from agreeable to me.

Those were the Kuklux days and the times were very uncomfortable, especially for a carpet-bagger, whose party had been overwhelmingly defeated. But I did not know anything about the Kuklux and was simple-minded enough not to fully credit their existence.

I had become a citizen of North Carolina in November, 1868; but being unaccustomed to the ways and prejudices of the people, I was not prepared to believe what was said about the Klans. Respectable Southern gentlemen denied their existence and I felt bound by their protestations. Yet a "den" met frequently in Greensboro; sometimes in Bogart's Hall; sometimes in the old Caldwell Institute (now torn down), again upstairs over the Lindsay corner (recently destroyed) opposite the court house and more often in the woods in the northern suburbs of the town, not a great ways from the residence of Judge Dick.

These meetings were occurring after the beginning of my residence in Greensboro, for nearly a year, but I did not know of them. Indeed, young men with whom I was well acquainted, actually were members of the fraternity—men whom I met every day, on social terms, in my boarding house at Mrs. Gilmer's. I had not reason to suspect their membership. Of course the assemblages were as secret as could be. When they were held in Bogart's Hall, for example—so I have since been told by participants—the only light was a candle, placed under a table, so that its rays could not shine through the curtained windows.

While I myself was incredulous, my political friends, Union men, natives of the South, familiar with the methods and peculiarities of the people, were firm believers in the entity of the Kuklux. They saw and understood the most trivial signs and signals. These men had been on the spot when the rebellion raged and had, in many instances, belonged to the "Red Strings," and other secret societies, banded together for mutual help and protection, and to aid the Union cause, in which they implicitly believed; and to assist escaping prisoners of war through the military lines. If therefore they observed a peculiar mark upon a tree, or figures upon the ground, they knew there was some meaning intended.

But the time soon came when I had to believe. In the latter days of 1869, Judge Tourgee, then of the Superior Court, issued a bench warrant for the arrest of several citizens of Caswell county. They were charged with having visited in disguise the cabins of a number of negroes, whom they took out and whipped. I was employed by Gov. Holden to conduct the examination of witnesses for the State; but the defendants easily proved alibis, as usual in such cases.

A few months afterward I was notified by the Governor to attend similar examinations before Mr. John W. Stephens (called "Chicken Stephens" by Jo. Turner). Mr. Stephens was a justice of the peace in Yanceyville. He was likewise a State Senator, but the legislature was not then in session.

I proceeded to Yanceyville via Danville, Va., leaving the railroad at the latter town, and driving sixteen miles across the country. Reaching Yanceyville in the forenoon, I noticed several groups of men, apparently laboring under suppressed excitement. Beginning to understand the popular temper I feared a riot if the cases should go on before the magistrate that day.

I stated my apprehensions to the Honorable John Kerr, the leading attorney for the defendants and suggested that, to avoid a possible riot, his clients should waive examination, and give bail for their appearance at the next term of the Superior Court, which they could do easily.

All of the Yanceyville lawyers appeared with Judge Kerr for the defendants, doubtless volunteering their services with patriotic fervor. After further consultation, my suggestion was adopted and thus, it may be, bloodshed was then avoided. At any rate, events soon to follow in Yanceyville, justify the belief that Stephens would have been put out of the way on the spot, had the trials proceeded.

When the cases had been disposed of, Stephens came to my room. He was a slender, sinewy man, with fair complexion, pale blue eyes and light brown hair, not prepossessing in manners or appearance; illiterate and unpolished, but very earnest; belonging to the plain classes of the South. His origin was respectable, although born into a poor family, in Guilford county. He had courage and tenacity. He was the leader of the Caswell county Republicans, being one of the few white men who dared to profess Republican principles in that locality. He was bitterly hated by the "Conservatives," and this boded him no good. Yet knowing it all, accused of petty crimes, which he had not committed, held up to ridicule by such a man as Jo. Turner, then a veritable potentate, Stephens had stood up boldly in the midst of a hostile population, with no backers but the timid negroes, which only intensified the hatred of his enemies. No romance of chivalry has ever invested its heroes with a nobler spirit than his, which was more than equal to that of the bravest of his traducers—for who of them all would have faced the dangers that he was facing?

He resided about a quarter of a mile from the Yanceyville court house, within plain view of it. His house was veritably his castle, where he had fortified himself. He was besieged at home and was under obsession every-where; yet he seemed to hold danger in contempt.

On this occasion he wore a sack-coat of medium length, with side-pockets. He said he had been warned by anonymous letters to leave the State. "But," he said simply, "I have a right to be here and can't be scared away from my home and family." Continuing, Stephens told me how well he was prepared for emergencies; and he displayed two single-barreled, breech-loading Derringers. He showed me how rapidly he could load them and seemed expert in handling the weapons. He carried a pistol in each side-pocket of his coat, within easy reach. He said he never permitted any one to approach unless he knew him to be a friend; that he always carried the Derringers, but that on "public days," he also had with him what I understood to be a seven shooter.

In his estimation this was a public day, because a crowd was in town, attracted by the cases before his magis-trate's court. Yanceyville was but a small village, with a court house and a few dwellings, stores and shops, and ordinarily not many persons were on the streets. There was no hotel. Throwing back his coat, Stephens, displayed to me his other weapon. With his temper and dangerous surroundings, he was a man to be dreaded by his foes, for he meant to kill any assailant. He could be overcome only by treachery, as will be seen hereafter.

To me, his words had peculiar significance, when considered in connection with the occurrences of the next few days; for it should be noticed that he declared he never suffered any one to approach, unless he knew him to be a friend. "But," he added, "I think the worst is now over and they," (meaning the Kuklux) "are becoming frightened at their own acts." Alas, how little he knew or understood the venom of his enemies! Our conversation was on Monday. The next Saturday, May 21, 1870, Stephens was murdered in a lower room of the Yanceyville court house.

A vivid account of the assassination is given in "A Fool's Errand," where John Walter Stephens is called "John Walters." Whether it is all true as therein narrated, I cannot say for certain; but the story, confessedly fiction, is no more monstrous than the reality. It was a ghastly murder. As those who know best about it (if still alive) have told nothing, and will not, any narrative of the circumstances must be imperfect.

On the day of the homicide Stephens had attended a Democratic meeting, upstairs in the court house, in the audience-room. According to his custom he had been taking note of the speeches.

Sometimes he used the room where his body afterward was found, for the trial of his magistrate's cases. This room was at the time occupied for no other purpose, and was devoid of furniture, except an old table and a chair or two. A pile of fire-place wood extended across it, on the north side, next to the wall, one end of the pile being near a window. There were three windows, two of them overlooking the court house yard, opposite a street. On the other side of the street were several negro houses. Stephens's dwelling could be seen plainly from the windows, being southeast from the court house. The only door entering the room was from the hallway, which passed entirely through the building from north to south. The door of the room was within a few feet of the rear hall entrance.

Stephens, after being in the meeting upstairs, until about 5 o'clock in the afternoon, was called out by a man named Wiley; with whom Stephens had been in frequent conversation during the day, trying to induce Wiley to become an independent candidate for sheriff. Wiley was a Democrat and Stephens had pledged him the Republican vote of Caswell county. After the two went out together Stephens was not seen alive by any one innocent of the murder.

No doubt Wiley enticed Stephens from the meeting and admitted it. But according to a letter from Hon. R. Z. Linney (recently deceased) published in the *News-Observer*, Dec. 29, 1891, credited to the *Statesville Landmark*, "a gentleman of intelligence who was at Yanceyville at the time of the tragedy," declared that he had information regarded by him as altogether reliable, that Wiley was not in the room when Stephens was killed, but had arranged to get him from the court-room, to extort from him a promise to leave the county; and the promise not being given Stephens was killed. According to the "gentleman of intelligence," Wiley was "very angry" with the men who had slain Stephens—a lame excuse, it must be admitted; although his "anger" was quite creditable.

Mr. Linney, it may be stated, in passing, said in his

letter, that Wiley died at his (Linney's) house near Taylorsville, and that the "measure of the corpse was about seven feet in length." This statement seems astounding, but as I recollect him, Wiley was a very tall man. Upon one occasion, during the Kuklux troubles, I saw him on horseback, going from Yanceyville, with a long rifle resting in the hollow of his arm—an incident characteristic of the times. He looked like a wind mill on horse back.

MATERIALS FROM THE SCRAPBOOK OF W. A. HAYNE COLLECTED IN 1874[1]

William A. Hayne was a native of Charleston, and a free man of free parents. His mother's father and his father's father were white. He was educated in the Charleston school of free Negroes. He attained the position of Representative in the Legislature and served the State efficiently. Hayne passed away in 1889.

The recent meeting at Barnwell Courthouse was by far the largest held there since the war. The meeting was called to order by Dr. J. W. Ogilvie as temporary chairman. A committee of five, consisting of Col. Counts, Captain F. M. Wanamaker, Dr. J. C. Miller, and Messrs. W. T. Blanton and J. M. Hudson were appointed to select permanent officers, and nominated the following gentlemen: General Johnson Hagood, President; Messrs. Counts, Sojourner, Blanton, Killingsworth and Ogilvie, vice-presidents; J. M. Ryan, secretary.

General Hagood, who was at the front end of the hall, some distance from the chair he was to occupy, upon the invitation of the temporary chairman, advanced to take his seat as presiding officer amidst deafening applause. On taking the chair, General Hagood said: "I understand the purpose of this meeting to be to consider the misgovernment in South Carolina, which running through ten long years, has culminated in the shameful and shameless proceedings of our present Legislature. It is not for me, here, to recall this disgraceful history in all its details. You have borne with it till patience has ceased to be a virtue, and from one end of this American Union to another, regardless of section or party the press—that mighty engine and exponent of popular sentiment—is now ringing with the denunciation of the last wrong inflicted upon you, and with commendation of the true and faithful man who, with a heroism surpassing that of the battlefield, which is wielding such weapons as the executive army can furnish in your temporary defence. This thing has gone far enough: This crowded hall—these earnest faces over which a light flickers that carries me back to a time since when my head and heart have alike grown gray, tell me so. Every instinct of self-preservation tells me that the time has come when all in South Carolina who are fit to live outside of her penitentiary, or expect to within her borders an inheritance for their children, must enlist in this struggle. It will be a contest in which no half-hearted recruit is wanted. It is a fight for life and property, in which you will have to do all that a citizen may do—and, if need be, all that may become a man." (Applause.)

Mr. Alfred Aldrich rose and said: A short time ago, in this house, I said among other things to the taxpayers, that I had "implicit confidence in the people of Barnwell County, but none in Governor Chamberlain." In the light of recent events, I desire to make the Amende honorable to Governor Chamberlain, and here, with equal unreserve as when I made the declaration alluded to, I wish to submit the charge in my opinion embodied in the following resolutions:

Resolved that Governor Chamberlain, from his first ... to his last veto, has carried ... knowledge to the platform on which ... if he does not receive the support of the leading men of his own party, is entitled to the confidence and will receive the cordial sympathy and merited aid of the honest and good men in South Carolina.

Resolved, that in rising above party to vindicate the civilization and ancient good name of the States over which he presides, by his rebuke to the Legislature for the election of corrupt and incompetent judges, as he has shown large statesmanship, integrity of purpose and courage of performance that command the respect and approval of all good men, irrespective of party.

Resolved: that the Governor, having taken care of the Charleston and Sumter circuits by refusing to commission Whipper and Moses and not being able to reach Wiggins in the same way, we of the Barnwell circuit must see that he does not defile the bench and debauch the county now adorned by the virtue and the learning of the incorruptible Maher.

Resolved: That we recognize and appreciate the difficulties that the Governor has had to contend against to maintain his position as a political reformer, that we acknowledge probity in redeeming the pledges contained in the platform on which he was elected to office, and admire his boldness in resisting the pressure of those who were not in earnest when they made them; that we are fully sensible of the opposition that he encountered and the difficulties that have environed him in acting his arduous role, and that we take this occasion to show him and the men of his party who endorse him, of our cordial support.

The resolutions were unanimously and enthusiastically adopted. The Honorable A. P. Aldrich by invitation, then addressed the meeting. We have already published his remarks.

It was resolved that the President appoint, at his leisure, an executive committee of five to carry out in Barnwell County such recommendations as might be made by the Central Democratic Executive Committee, at its meeting in Columbia on the instant.

Mr. Simms then offered the following resolutions, which were carried out unanimously: Resolved, that in view of our repeated failures to reform the State Government by the policy of co-operation with the Conservative element of the Republican Party, who professed the same object, and of recent events we recognize the absolute and immediate necessity of reorganizing the Democratic party to restore an honest and economical government.

Resolved: That the Democratic Party of South Carolina will in the future, as it has in the past, support principles, not men, and we hereby extend a cordial invitation to all men in the State, who desire honest government, to unite with us, at least until we have accomplished our purpose.

Resolved: That the co-operation now invited is not with the bad men who have heretofore deluded, deceived and betrayed our colored fellow-citizens, but with the great mass of that class who, we believe, are willing to rescue the State from the grasp of these unprincipled adventurers.

Resolved: That the President appoint a committee of five to carry out the recommendations of the State executive committee to meet in Columbia on the 6th instant.

The following resolutions offered by Col. Counts, were adopted without a dissenting voice.

Whereas, by an indiscreet action of the Legislature of this State an insult of the grossest nature—an insult to all common decency and to all civilization, has been thrust into our faces by way of an election for judges of the respective circuits of Judges Maher, Reed and Shaw; and whereas, it was not expected or desired by either political party of said circuits that either of the present incumbents should be defeated; and whereas, we regard this act as a public declaration against the peace, prosperity and happiness of all virtue and intelligence, now, therefore, be it

Resolved, That we, the people of this section of the second circuit, not wishing to make an issue with any individual or party, and not being willing to risk our lives and property in the hands of the newly elected judge, P. L. Wiggins, for reasons obvious, do earnestly request the said P. L. Wiggins to tender his resignation to the Governor at once, and that the Governor do declare said vacancy be filled by an election to take place before the close of the present session of the Legislature.

Resolved, That a memorial be prepared by such persons as the president of this meeting shall designate, asking for the re-election of Judge Maher, and that said memorial (by request of this convention) be presented to the Legislature by the Hon. Chancellor Johnson.

Resolved, That a memorial be prepared by such persons as the president of this meeting shall designate, asking for the re-election of Judge Maher, and that said memorial (by request of this convention) be presented to the Legislature by the Hon. Chancellor Johnson.

Resolved, That a committee of two be appointed by the president of this meeting to communicate with the action of this meeting to communicate with Solicitor Wiggins, and to notify him of the action of this convention; and that said committee be instructed to assure him that this convention is not prompted by any impure motives or personal animosity for him in taking this action, but alone for the interest of the country, and for the peace,....

VOTE OF MARION COUNTY IN 1870

	Reform	Republican
Marion	372	511

Friendship	79	65
Mars Bluff	84	192
Berry's X Roads	196	178
Mullins	196	124
Aliens	72	33
High Hill	176	37
Old Ark	23	17
Cains	121	120
McMilans	105	36
Little Rock	277	204
Aeriel	130	57
Stones	62	73
Jeffries Creek	67	224
Old Neck	80	67
Campbells Bridge	151	56
Totals	2191	1994

"It will be seen from the above statement that the reform movement in 1870 carried the county by a majority of 207 votes. In that election the fight was between the Conservatives and the Republicans—the whites against the blacks. In fact it was a question of color, for both races voted solidly. Now it is different. The Republicans have inaugurated the Reform movement, and the fight on the 3d of November will be between the two wings of this party. The problem then is easy to solve. The Reform movement will carry Marion County by an overwhelming majority."

\

THE SPEAKING TOMORROW 1870

The representatives of both wings of the Republican party will speak at the Courthouse tomorrow. We hope every Republican in the county will be present and hear what both sides have to say. The Republican voters of the county who have any doubt as to their duty at the coming election, for whom they should vote, we hope, will be sufficiently enlightened to cast their votes for honest men and an honest Government.

We hope, for the character of Marion, that, those who come to the Courthouse on this occasion, will come for the purpose of enlightening themselves on a subject which involves the salvation of the State, and that each and every one will constitute himself a keeper of the peace, and that good order will be preserved during the day.

ROLL OF MEMBERS OF THE UNION REPUBLICAN STATE CONVENTION, 1874

Aiken—R. B. Elliot, C. D. Hayne, Gloster Holland, W. M. Peel.

Abbeville—H. Wideman, J. R. Tolbert, R. Griffin, A. H. Wallace, A. J. Titus.

Anderson—John R. Cochran, C. A. Mathison, W. R. Parker.

Barnwell—W. J. Whipper, C. P. Leslie, E. M. Sumter,—Jackson.

Beaufort—Robert Smalls, N. B. Myers, R. H. Gleaves,

T. E. Miller, Thomas Hamilton, S. J. Bamfield, Hastings Gantt.

Charleston—W. R. Jervey, E. W. M. Mackey, Aaron Logan, S. E. Gaillard, W. J. McKinlay, T. H. Jones, E. B. Seabrook, J. L. Walker, W. T. Oliver, W. G. Pinckney, Stephen Brown, Edward Petty, J. A. Williams, J. W. Reid, J. A. Mushington, P. P. Hedges, R. B. Gathers, A. C. Richmond.

Chester—T. J. Mackey, D. J. Walker, Barney Humphries.

Chesterfield—T. L. Weston, Robert Brewer.

Clarendon—J. D. Warley, Syfax Milton.

Colleton—W. M. Thomas, A. C. Schaffer, A. P. Holmes, T. H. Grant, W. F. Myers.

Darlington—T. C. Cox, B. F. Whittemore, Jordan Lang, J. B. Middleton.

Edgefield—J. H. McDevitt, Lawrence Cain, Paris Simkins, David Graham, Ned Tenant.

Fairfield—Daniel Bird, Thomas Walker, William Boler.

Georgetown—J. H. Rainey, W. H. Jones, Jr., R. M. Herriott.

Greenville—J. M. Runion, Thos. Brier, A. Blythe, Zion Collins.

Horry—T. C. Dunn, H. W. Jones.

Kershaw—J. A. Chestnut, N. W. Blair, Frank Carter.

Lancaster—Jos. Clarke, Allen Hudson.

Laurens—Y. J. P. Owens, H. McDaniels, James Young, Jos. Crews.

Lexington—R. H. Kirk, S. L. Lorick.

Marion—C. Smith, W. A. Hayne, M. K. Holloway, Anthony Howard.

Marlboro—H. J. Maxwell, D. D. McColl.

Newberry—H. C. Corwin, C. David, Henry Gillem.

Oconee—M. D. Singleton, Elisha Jenkins.

Orangeburg—T. C. Andrews, R. R. Duncan, C. W. Caldwell, E. I. Cain, Samuel Lewis.

Pickens—O. C. Folger.

Richland—C. M. Wilder, J. J. Patterson, F. L. Cardoza, C. S. Minort.

Sumter—Samuel Lee, F. J. Moses, Jr., W. E. Johnson, J. M. Tindall.

Spartanburg—J. Winsmith, T. B. Hartwell, S. T. Poinier, Alex Jones.

Union—June Mobley, S. Hawkins, J. H. Goss.

Williamsburg—S. A. Swails, J. T. Peterson, Wm. Scott.

York—J. H. White, R. M. Crook, M. L. Owens, Nelson Davis.

MARION COUNTY

For Governor,
JOHN T. GREEN

For Lieutenant-Governor,
MARTIN R. DELANEY

For Congress,
SAMUEL LEE

State Board of Equalization,
B. D. TOWNSEND, OF DARLINGTON
W. B. SMITH, OF CHARLESTON
W. D. MARS, OF ABBEVILLE
G. W. MELTON, OF CHESTER
S. J. LEE, OF AIKEN

Representatives,

W. D. JOHNSON W. A. HAYNE
B. G. HOWARD A. H. HOWARD

Judge of Probate,
JOHN WILCOX, SR.

School Commissioners,
J. A. SMITH

County Commissioners,
T. W. AYRES A. J. FRYER
J. P. DAVIS

A GREEN POW WOW

CONFUSION TRIUMPHANT

To THE EDITOR OF THE CHARLESTON CHRONICLE:

A mass meeting of those of the Republicans of this County who are credulous enough to espouse the bolters movement, was held here on Tuesday the 29th inst, at the Court House under the call of one Dr. J. B. Thompson, temporary County Chairman, who was sent down here by Senator T. C. Dunn, with a handsome and carefully prepared set of Resolutions, for adoption, pledging the entire County for Green and Reform, and lauding Senator Jones, for his steadfast adherence to the cause; and with equal warmth denouncing the other of our delegation for daring to exercise their untrammelled opinion in their support and advocacy of Daniel H. Chamberlain. The resolutions, however, were never introduced as intended owing to the fact that the Chairman, the said Dr. Thompson, had not the temerity to call his own meeting to order, nor did he put in an appearance at any time during the proceedings. The recollections of the bombardment of Castle Jones, on the memorable night of the 13th of August was too vivid upon his memory. But about the meeting.

It was a Babel of confusion from beginning to ending. This arose principally from an evident disposition on the part of the most prominent Greenites, to thrust the notorious Bowley upon the people as a Delegate, against their will and wishes. The meeting was really a Pow Wow. A motion of any description could not be heard and the meeting adjourned without coming to any effectual conclusion.

The majority of the people are under such a feeling having been foiled, deceived, and deserted by the men whom they have elevated for honor, that they now have inscribed upon their banners:

"Judge Green may try with might and main, But he'll never beat Daniel H. Chamberlain."

REPUBLICAN.

MATTERS IN MARION

FREAKS OF A JACK-IN-OFFICE—THE PROCEEDINGS OF THE DISTRICT CONFERENCE

Correspondence of the News and Courier

MARION, S. C., JULY 20, 1874.

One W. A. Hayne, of nondescript complexion and Radical persuasion, whose frantic speeches and other wild performances during a political canvass several years ago procured him the sobriquet of "Notoriety," is just now lording over our unhappy people in the guise of a United States commissioner. In this potential capacity he has commenced active operations against those who he or his ebon emissaries choose to suspect of transgressing the internal revenue law. Farmers who may have been in the habit of purchasing small quantities of tobacco just as they purchase other supplies for the use of the laborers on their planta-tions, have all at once become victims of vindictive prosecutions—the officers who make the arrests, and the over-zealous witnesses for the government, all being negroes. It is said that a farmer must not buy tobacco for his hands without having obtained a regular license therefor. While this may or may not be true, it seems to be certain that the warlike commissioner is enforcing the decision not so much in the spirit of the law, which he pretends to vindicate, as with a malicious propensity to annoy his political opponents. He was not gracious enough to consider that our farmers were without perhaps a single exception, ignorant of the existence of so stringent a ruling, (if, indeed, it does exist,) and he did not see the propriety of advertising it for the benefit of those whose character would belie the suspicion of an intention to defraud the revenue. It may be that "Noteriety Hayne," by thus flaunting in our faces his puissant commission, means to enhance his consequence as a prospective candidate far the Legislature, or that he thereby seeks to ingratiate himself with the colored people who relish (as he may suppose) the persecution and humiliation to which the planters are subjected by such wanton abuses of misplaced authority.

The transaction from this topic to matters of religion may be somewhat violent; it is, nevertheless, a relief. The Marion District Conference of the Methodist Church convened here on Thursday last, and remained in session four days. An unusually large number of delegates were in attendance. The delibera-tions, which were presided over by Rev. W. C. Power, were conducted in a spirit of earnest devotion to the important interests which came up for consideration. The reports from the various charges in the district, which embraces the Counties of Marlboro', Marion, Horry and Georgetown, and portions of Darlington and Williamsburg, exhibited a most gratifying state of the church. The Sunday-Schools were shown to be in a very flourishing condition, and the cause of temperance was making headway against all opposition. The Rev. Drs. Shipp and Jones, presidents respectively of Wofford and Columbia Female Colleges, were present, and their fine pulpit ministrations added much to the interest of the occasion.

DIVIDING THE NEGRO VOTE

WHY THE SOUTH HAS FAILED TO ACCOMPLISH IT

A Northern Journalist's Impressions of the Palmetto State

The following extracts from a letter of Mr. John Russell Young, published in the New York Herald, are well worthy of attentive consideration; but we need hardly say that in our opinion Mr. Young is wholly mistaken in holding the white responsible, during the last five years at least, for the solidity and infrangibility of the negro in the South:

The Letter

Why is it that the Southerners, the whites who masters before the war, have not devided the negro vote, and uniting with those who were intelligent, gained control of the State so as to secure it an efficient government? It would seem to the ordinary political thinker that even three-sevenths whites could control the four-sevenths blacks. One thinks of the Saxon in India with the Hindoo, in Canada with the French, in Jamaica with the Negro, in Ireland, after a turbulent fashion, with the mailed hand, and yet his rule is now absolute. Why is it that in South Carolina it is otherwise? My gifted and honored colleague, Mr. Nordhoff, in his series of letters from the South, says it is because he has been corrupted by the carpet-bagger. With all deference to that distinguished authority, his answer is an imperfect solution. Surely the Negro who knows his old master, who has lived with him during his life, who in most cases looks with affection upon him and all who belong to him— surely in the new relation he will look to the master as a friend, and take his guidance in so solemn a duty as entering upon citizenship. This too because as we learn from all authorities, and from none more clearly than Mr. Nordhoff, that the master, "accepts the new relation" and has no purpose of renewing the war, and, so far as from wishing to return the negro to slavery, feels that the old system was an error, even from an economical point of view, and that in time its abolition will prove to be a blessing to the white, whatever it may be to the black. Why, then this being the case, has the carpet-bagger been able to strangle a commonwealth like South Carolina, and with the aid of the Negro, plunder his old master? The only answer that I can see is that the whites have not taken any pains to cultivate the blacks, who would naturally go with them, or the intelligent and honest Northern men who came here, meaning in good faith to make the South a home and to grow up with the Southern people. In nearly every case with scarcely an exception, the whites have drawn a line, just as Jefferson Davis drew when he embarked upon the Confederacy. They alone have a right here. Whoever opposes him is a "scalawag," a "carpet-bagger," or a "nigger." A "scalawag" if as a Southern born man he votes with the Republicans; a "carpet-bagger" if he comes from the North, no matter how he votes. This line is drawn with severity and with scarcely an exception. A worthy citizen of Charleston, who came from the North in the beginning of the war, from motives of philanthropy, to educate the blacks, who has lived in the state ever since, and holds a high reputation from all classes because of his integrity and ability, told me that he had never been asked to the home of a Southern man since he came into the State. "They do business with me, meet me in public places and show me all respect, but never open the latch key". A reverend and highly esteemed prelate of the Methodist Church in the North came here to attend a gathering of African churches. He was in an official position, for these churches were under the control of his denomination. He remained here several days presiding over the gathering. He was known to be an honored prelate, whose life was given solely to his religious duties. He told me that during his stay in South Carolina he had not received a single attention from his Southern fellow Methodists. The clergy had not noticed his presence nor asked him into their pulpit. He saw only fellow Christians who had come from the North or Negroes, I cannot imagine how the line can be more closely drawn, and now speak of what happened only a few days since.

The Negro and His Northern Ally

The negro, then has been thrown back upon his Northern ally. Every memory, every name, every anniversary of the war, is cherished as sacred. All the rest is an abomination. You may well ask: "Why should not this be so, for are not these memories dear to them by the blood slain brothers and children?" Truly so, and far be it from me to profane so holy a thought as that which would honor them. But I am answering the question propounded some time since as to how it is that the Southern whites have never succeeded in dividing the colored vote, so as to give the states a good government. They have driven the Negro away. In Georgia when they gained power they have practically disfranchised him. But for the interference of the Federal Congress they would have forbidden his appearance in their legislatures. I do not think that any frank Georgian will deny that this result was largely due to intimidation and force. In a State with 545,142 negroes in 1870, to 638,926 whites, they have virtually stamped out a Republican party. The negro is afraid to vote, is not in many places allowed on the jury, is punished severely for crimes, and Mr. Nordhoff has told you that at least 25,000 of them have left the State in the last five years; and yet in Georgia they pay taxes on a large property. The negro in South Carolina sees what has been done across the line, and he knows, or naturally fears, that should the white man rule here the same results will follow. As a consequence, therefore, the negro is in the hands of the adventurer. He fears that his master will make him a slave, or reduce him to a condition akin to slavery. The result is, therefore, that not one of them will vote the Democratic ticket. I have heard of Democratic negroes, but I have seen none. I have spoken on this subject with Southern men in Florida, Georgia, North and South Carolina, and there is only one story. "I have negroes here," said one eminent gentleman, "who were my slaves in the old time. They hang around my house. They will fight for me, work for me and bring me their money to keep. They take my advice in all things, and are trustworthy and devoted. They will not vote for me. My coachman there will vote against me and in favor of the meanest Republican in the county." The negro thus far sees nothing in politics but his own freedom. He votes for Grant all the time. His political education embraces a sentiment and a fact. The sentiment is Lincoln, the fact is Grant. I was talking to a woolly headed vagabond the other day, who had learned that I was a Northern man, and wanted to go home with me as an attendant. He was a worthless, ragged, shining darky, as black as night, and earned his living, he told me, by dancing the juba for gentlemen on the sidewalk when the police were not looking. During the war he was a slave lad. "Did you know you were free," I said, "before the war was over?" He told me that the news came very quickly; that they all kept "mighty shady," never pretending to know until "Massa Sherman came with the soldiers." But they knew it all the time, and there was never a night that his "old mammie didn't pray to Massa Lincoln." This is the thought that has burned deep into the negro mind. You cannot erase it. You cannot take it from him. He has heard the slaves' horn. He has worn the yoke and carried the scar into furrow and swamp. He has seen father and mother perhaps, taken to the block and sold into slavery. That memory ever lives as it would live with you and I, if such a career darkened our lives. So Moses may steal and Whipper may "administer justice," to him they mean freedom. Coming out of the night they find no hand to grasp but the hand of the adventurer. Is it any wonder then, that they follow him as blind men or those who see darkly?

Better Signs

I cannot resist the conclusion, and it grows upon me every day, in the South, that for much of the wrong, that has been done in these States the old Southerners are to blame. I say this in sorrow and with no harshness of feeling to them, and not without making allowance for a feeling which, after all, is one of human nature, a feeling of hatred of the men who defeated their hopes of empire and of contempt for the negro, who is today a senator, but who yesterday could have been sent to the whipping post. It is not easy for a planter who has not enough to eat to rejoice over the fact that the servant who once washed his beard is now his ruler of the State. But, whatever the motive of the feeling, the negro in South Carolina is at the feet of Moses and Whipper, because he was driven there. The old master has as yet made no sign of sympathy or friendship. I am profoundly convinced that if, instead of mourning over the lost cause, as in the past they were wont to bluster about the Yankees and slavery, these people had dealt wisely with the negro and generously with the Northern immigrant, these States, and South

Carolina especially, would be free and powerful. I hail the Chamberlain movement in one of its aspects as the opening of a new era. The support which that officer receives from the leading journal in the State, and one of the leading journals in the South—*The News and Courier*—shows the awakening of a new spirit. This paper thoroughly Democratic, its editors gentlemen who were in the Confederacy through the whole war and firm in their devotion to the lost cause, sees that the only hope for South Carolina is supporting the honest, intelligent New England Governor, who says he is Republican from conviction and never ... a Democrat; that he has no sympathy for Democracy or desire to be in its councils ... that as Governor he means to give ... honest government. The news ... takes the Governor at his word and ... him on, while newspapers over the border in Georgia mock and deride. If Chamberlain succeeds he will divide the colored vote, and for the first time array parties upon some other dividing line than that laid down by Jefferson Davis when he founded his Confederacy.

Hope for Carolina

But whether he succeeds or not the movement which he began a year ago, and which is now almost national in its extent, must go on. There is no way for South Carolina to win a good government except on this basis. Here the negroes are and in a large majority. They cannot be driven away, they cannot be slain, they cannot be disfranchised. They must be asked to take part in government, to unite with honest men in punishing crime. Education makes this more and more easy, and amid all this sorrow and strife and tumult the work of education goes on. The negro pants for the primer and the speller as the hart for the water of the brook. I have taken pains, in some bookstore loungings, to inquire about this. I learned in nearly every case that the negroes were constant purchasers, and almost invariably of school-books—elementary and advanced. I am told that the negro is as anxious to read and write as he used to be to own a yellow cravat. I do not suppose this education goes far, but it is something. It is there I see day—there, and nowhere else. This old feeling must die out. These memories of the Southern Confederacy must be put away with the family laces and grandmother' samplers. Leaders like Toombs and Hill must be superseded. These negroes must be taught that freedom means responsibility, and that honesty is safety and peace. These lands and ports, these watercourses, these widely stretching and vast acres, must respond to capital and energy, the money and the skill of the North. Here is room in South Carolina alone for all of New England, and in no State could the spirit of New England work such marvels. But so long as the fogs of slavery and misgovernment and ostracism and social hatred hang over them like the malaria of their own rice lowlands, so long South Carolina will be a prostrate State, crying for sympathy and help. Let us trust that the time has come for the people to help themselves, and in doing so, raise their Commonwealth to a pinacle of grandeur and prosperity such as even its proud history has never known.

"REPUBLICAN PRINCIPLE" AND THE INDEPENDENT REPUBLICAN MOVEMENT

The burden of the song of the Chamberlain Ring and their organs is that the integrity of "the party" is of more consequence than honest government, and that any Republican who votes for Green and Delaney is a traitor to the Republican party and false to Republican principles. In all humility we beg leave to suggest that the persons who are candidates for office in the interest of a corrupt Ring, and the few newspapers which live and move and have their being by and in that Ring, are hardly the disinterested and unselfish counsellors that they claim to be. It is safer to go outside of the charmed circle, and ascertain what is advised by Republicans whose honesty is as great as their integrity, who were Republicans when Democracy was in the ascendant, and who are as true now to Republicanism as they were while slavery existed and most of the South Carolina white Republicans were red-hot Democrats in the South or obscure demagogues in the North. Their opinions are entitled to weight, and for that reason they are carefully excluded from the columns of the organs of the Chamberlain Ring. It is in our power, however, to lay these opinions before the public, and we mean to do it.

1. *The New York Times* is known everywhere as a powerful Republican newspaper; it advocates Republican principles in season and out of season. This paper heartily approves of the Independent Republican movement, and says that, whatever may be the immediate result, "The final effect cannot be

good." It says, further, that, in the organization of the Independent Republican movement, the colored people have made "a long step forward."

2. *The New York Evening Post*, a Republican newspaper which circulates among the upper-ten, declares that "the political signs from South Carolina are favorable"; and that it has very gratifying assurances that "the colored voters are beginning to perceive that they have been used too long by unscrupulous politicians" (of the Chamberlain-Bowen school) "who have employed partisan prejudices to promote their own private fortunes." And *The New York Tribune*, an unfaltering friend of the colored Republicans, talks in the same strain, and gives the Independent Republican movement its warm approval.

3. One of the strongest Republican newspapers in New England is *The Springfield Republican* (Mass.) which sees in the new movement an evidence of good faith on the part of the Conservatives, and of sagacity and honesty on the part of the Independent Republicans.

The newspapers whose opinions we have quoted represent, in large part, the sentiments and opinions of the people who pushed the war against the South, and insisted on the abolition of slavery. They say, without a dissenting voice, that the Independent Republican movement is right and wise and just. On the other side, a marked man, stands C. C. Bowen, who, in printed handbills, speaks of Judge Green as "the Democratic candidate for Governor." Colored Republicans! whom will you believe, the men and newspapers who fought your battles when you were powerless to help yourselves, or the men and the newspapers whose love for you only began when you had office and public plunder to bestow upon them?

Sunday Morning, July 12, 1874

The Warning

If there be anything wanting to the argument we have persistently urged upon the Republicans of this State, it is contained in the following extract from an editorial in *The New York Times*, General Grant's especial organ. In speaking of what General Grant has said about South Carolina, the *Times* says: "He (General Grant) further added that unless a true reform was begun at once in South Carolina, the Republican party would this fall repudiate the so-called Republicans of the State. In fact, this is what the Republicans of the North have already done. The Triumph of Moses and his gang would be only the triumph of corruption, and that the people of this country will not stand.

If we do not heed this warning in time, there will not be enough left of our organization next year to make a respectable ward meeting. We cannot fight the Democrats here, General Grant and the whole country beside. We cannot afford to commit political suicide, and we are not going.

CHARLESTON, S. C., FRIDAY EVENING, OCTOBER 2, 1874

THE FAIR PLAY MEETING

*A Grand Gathering of Republicans and Conservatives —
Harmony Prevails and Nothing Asked but Fair Play*

The meeting last night was one of the most extraordinary gatherings ever held in Charleston. Upwards of four thousand of our citizens irrespective of party, assembled together and raised their voices in the interests of fair play for one and all.

Men of culture and wealth, stood side by side, with the honest and industrious workingmen. Republican and Conservative, white men and colored men, Chamberlain men and Green men stood shoulder to shoulder bearing in mind the great object of the meeting and for the time being casting aside all thoughts of party spirit. It seemed to be well understood by each and every man in the vast assemblage that this was not the time nor place to urge the claim of any particular candidates, and the harmony that prevailed reflected the most unbounded credit on the citizens of Charleston.

Let it here be distinctly understood that the objection to the commissioners of election does not imply an objection to either of them individually but it is claimed that one of them should at least give place to a representative of the other side. If Thompson and Smith are candidates for election to any office, and the three commissioners of election are all Thompson men, it is natural that the supporters of Smith should be dissatisfied, but by appointing one Smith man all suspicions of unfair play will be removed.

Col. E. W. M. Mackey called the meeting to order from the steps of the City Hall at 8 o'clock and upon his motion it was organized with the following officers:

President—The Hon. H. D. Lesesne.

Vice-Presidents—Mayor C. I. Cunningham, Ex-Gov. Wm. Aiken, Coroner Aaron Logan, Mr. E. B. Seabrook, Mr. S. Y. Tupper, Alderman W. J. McKinlay, Senator S. E. Gaillard, Hon. Henry Gourdin, Mr. John F. Taylor, Rev. E. J. Adams, Mr. Andrew Simonds, Mr. H. H. DeLeon, Mr. C. O. Witte, Alderman S. B. Garrett, Mr. Hugh Ferguson, Mr. J. W. Reed, Alderman John A. Godfrey, Mr. B. Bollman, Mr. B. O'Neill, Capt. J. C. Clausen, Mr. Stephen Brown, Mr. W. A. Courtenay.

Secretaries—Mr. J. A. Mushington, Mr. C. O. Trumbo, Capt. Alex Williams.

Mr. Lesesne opened the meeting with a most appropriate address, in which he stated ... meeting, at his leisure, who shall present by letter or otherwise, the foregoing preamble and resolutions to the Governor of the State, and require of him, as necessary for the preservation of public peace, that he do remove the said commissioners of election, or a majority of them, and appoint, in their stead, commissioners of known integrity, intelligence and impartiality, who will see that in every matter pertaining to the election, equal and exact justice shall be done to all citizens, irrespective of class, color or political party; and further, that the said committee shall, in the event of the refusal of the Executive to grant this request, call a mass meeting of the people to take such action as will then be necessary.

Resolved, That a committee of five be appointed by the chairman of this meeting, at his leisure, who shall immediately ascertain what protection can be secured to the voters of Charleston County under the United States laws relating to elections, which committee shall immediately report the result of their investigations, through the public prints, with such recommendations for the guidance of the citizens as they may deem advisable.

After the reading of the above preamble and resolutions, Mr. Joseph W. Barnwell addressed the meeting, and was followed by the Hon. G. A. Trenholm, who spoke with much eloquence and at considerable length.

Mr. Trenholm, holding the Chronicle in his hand, read therefrom the following extract from the third plank of the Republican platform: "We shall hold all men as enemies to equality of rights who interfere with the ballot or deny the free and lawful exercise of its use to any citizen, whatever may be his party creed."

He called attention to the fact that these sentiments were in the Republican platform and were published in the Charleston Chronicle, the only Republican paper in this city; but, strange to say, this portion of his speech does not seem to have made a great impression on either the News and Courier reporter or the Sun man. For the News and Courier fails to report it, and the Sun does not shine upon it.

The Hon. A. J. Ransier then took the platform, but his address was interrupted by an unlooked for incident.

A number of policemen having in charge some of the men who were wounded in the fracas with the strikers, of which an account is given elsewhere in this issue, were seen marching down Meeting street followed by a considerable crowd. The bigger crowd seeing the others, and not knowing what was up, became demoralized, and a panic ensued followed by a general stampede.

SPEECH OF W. A. HAYNE, OF MARION,

On Outrages In Edgefield County S. C.

The House, in Committee of the Whole, having under consideration the following message from His Excellency:

STATE OF SOUTH CAROLINA,
EXECUTIVE CHAMBER,
COLUMBIA, MARCH 1, 1876.

HON. ROBERT B. ELLIOTT, Speaker House of Representatives:

Sir:—I have the honor to acknowledge the receipt of a copy of a resolution adopted by the House of Representatives and concurred in by the Senate, by which I am requested to report to this General Assembly at the earliest practicable moment all the facts and information in my possession in relation to outrages alleged to have been committed recently in Edgefield County.

I have the honor, in reply, to say that the information received by me respecting the matter referred to is, in substance, that, on the night of the 11th of February, some twenty-five or thirty mounted men, in disguise, went to the house of James Perry, living near Ridge Spring, in the County of Edgefield; that they found in the house Freeman Gardner, his wife, Julia Brooks, a woman between seventy and eighty years of age, and Zilpha Hill, a young woman—all colored; that this disguised band took all four of the immates of the house to a point of about a mile and a quarter distant and then stripped and whipped them all; that after the whipping was over, the woman, Patsey Gardner, was severely and systematically burned by the application of liquid sealing wax or burning pitch to her back and limbs; that the young woman, Zilpha Hill, who was pregnant was also beaten and severely abused, to such an extent as to endanger her life; that the only pretext for this conduct was given in a remark of one of the disguised band about John Gaston's goods.

This is the account given by the victims of the outrage, and the condition of the woman, Patsey Gardner, seems to indicate the truth of her statements as to the injuries inflicted upon this woman.

This is the substance of the information in my hands at the present time.

VERY RESPECTFULLY,
(SIGNED) D. H. CHAMBERLAIN, GOVERNOR.

Mr. Hayne said:

Mr. Chairman—Perhaps no member regrets this outrage more than I do, for in the last campaign it was my earnest desire, yea, the height of my ambition, to bring about not only purity in my party, but harmony between the two races, and therefore my regret. I am disappointed, almost discouraged, for it seems as though 'tis love's labor lost. But, sir, just so long as the newspapers of the country continue to exert their influence in this direction will our State be disgraced by these foul outrages. They fire up the hatred of the hot headed, indiscreet youths of the State by their incendiary articles, and make them believe that to slay and scourge all who differ from them in opinion are doing God and their country a service. They never heap the ashes of charitable oblivion upon the coals of prejudice and hate, but continue to replenish it with the most exciting and fiery appeals. The Edgefield paper makes light of this dastardly violence done to aged and inoffensive women by ascribing it as the work of "rash boys." Manly pastime for these brave boys! a crime sir, that in any other State, and done to any other class, would have demanded and met with immediate punishment, perhaps in the Court of Judge Lynch, as was the case in Marlboro County a few weeks ago, when a white lady was abused, the perpetrators, two colored men, met with immediate punishment. They would not have brooked the law's delay. Yea, sir, an outraged community would have taught these "rash boys" a lesson that I fear they will learn in no other school, and the courteous Sheriff would not have been put to the trouble of "inviting them to be arrested."

But, Mr. Chairman, it happens to be the poor despised Africans who have tilled their fields for centuries, educated and amassed for them princely fortunes, and while they were engaged in riveting tighter the chains of bondage, were engaged in the care and protection of their defenceless families. Mr. Chairman, I ask, is this the mode to bring about harmony and prosperity? Will this tranquilize this already distracted country? No, sir. On the contrary, it will raise to its highest temperature the ill feelings of an outraged people, and cause them to adopt for their redress *lex talionis*, in opposition to the Edgefield *lex loci*, as Mr. McDuffe truthfully says, "God has planted in the breast of man a higher and holier principle than that by which he is prompted to resist oppression; the vilest reptile that crawls on the earth, without the gift of reason to comprehend the injustice of its injuries, would bite, or sting, or bruise the hand by which they were inflicted. Is it to be expected, then, that freemen will patiently bow down and kiss the rod of the oppressors?" I had hoped that the swift retribution that followed the K. K's reign, and the withering rebuke administered by their own counsel, (Hon. Reverdy Johnson,) would have put an end to these inhuman and disgusting outrages; but, sir, the newspapers must live and thrive, and this can only be done by a healthy subscription list, and, in order to swell that list, they must excite the worst passions of depraved men and pander to their prejudices.

Are the disgraceful scenes that darkened the history

of South Carolina and cast a foul blot upon her proud escutcheon to be re-enacted? It must not. If we expect to enjoy peace and prosperity in our State, we must be more mindful of the rights of each other, more tolerant in our political views, and finally, leave the punishment of violators of the law to Courts of Justice, and not constitute ourselves a Vigilance Committee for every imaginary wrong. The Courts are certainly doing their duty, as our increased appropriation for the penitentiary will evince. If this course of action is followed, then, and not until then, will South Carolina blossom as the rose, and peace and prosperity flow as a river within her borders.

Again, Mr. Chairman, if the people of that and any other County would only turn away from the siren voice of selfish office-seekers, and put in office men who would dare to do their duty at all times and in all places, without fear, favor or impartiality, then, sir, would their rights be secured, and they would sit down under their own vine and fig-tree, with none daring to molest or make afraid; then would these lawless men respect the rights of the occupants of the humblest cabin; for the law properly administered would indeed be a terror to these evil doers, and wherever that aegis of America's honor, and her citizen's protection floats, men would fear to disregard the rights of his fellows or take the law into their own hands; and, my fellow-citizens, let me entreat you, in the exercise of your rights as citizens hereafter, select only such men as are worthy of these high offices—men who will do their duty. When I have given such advice hitherto you have scorned it, but take heed in future, for your interests, the security of your rights, make it an imperative duty on you.

Mr. Chairman, if departed spirits are visitants of this earth, and familiar with the actions of men, the spirits of the patriotic Rutledge and of the sainted Gasden must have wept tears of anguish over the degeneracy of these men bearing their patronymics as they witnessed the outrages (the details of which are heart sickening) which were perpetrated upon those inoffensive women. Has the chivalry of South Carolina degenerated thus far? Is this the work of her brave sons? Could they find no more worthy foe than an aged, infirm woman, brutally maltreated and her person exposed, who, even if guilty, should have excited their sympathy? Another, in a condition that would have appealed not in vain to the protection of savages, much less civilized men, cruelly beaten, and her life and that of her unborn child endangered thereby. Shame on you, degenerate sons of a brave and chivalrous ancestry! The recording angel in heaven's chancery must have shed tears as, with his diamond pen, he noted this additional evidence of man's depravity. I am no advocate of the "bloody shirt" doctrine, neither do I endorse the rash sentiments expressed by the member from Charleston, (Mr. Davis); but inasmuch as His Excellency has furnished this House with official information of this outrage, I have felt it my duty as a representative to express in positive, forcible terms my utter abhorrence and condemnation of this brutal outrage. The Governor has faithfully performed his duty in furthering the arrest of the guilty parties, and I hope the Court of justice will administer a lesson that will not soon be forgotten by that community. The laws are adequate; we simply require efficient and faithful officers to execute them; and as a legislative body we have done our duty in condemning this outrage, the punishment of which we leave to another tribunal—the Nemesis of justice.

THE HIPPODROME

SECOND DAYS EXHIBITION!

They go for a Reporter And Catch a Tartar!

Large Attendance but Poor Performance.

The exhibition at this place of amusement yesterday was of only an indifferent character. Unless the managers improve the show in some way, it will hardly draw for many more performances. True, the tricks of the acrobats are worthy of mention; the riding passable, and the performance of the numerous ring-masters tolerably creditable; but the "dagger pitchers" and "revolver-swallowers," and inferior parts assigned to the clowns in the ring, were altogether too limited to please the amusement-loving public. There must be more robber declarations and full-blooded excited performances anxious for bloody fames, or the thing will be a failure. This pretense of fight won't do; there must be a regular shooting and dying for principle, or we shall pronounce your cheap show a humbug; and some of you at least know that no third rate "Punch and Judy" exhibition will be tolerated by the party in power in South Carolina. With this warning and introduction, we proceed to give an account of the performance.

The mob was called to order precisely at 1 o'clock, temporary President Swails in the chair. The proceedings of the previous day were read from *The Union-Herald* in his hand, and called the attention of the assemblage to an article in that paper touching upon the subject of the raising of a chair by some member for the purpose of annihilating the present Governor of South Carolina. Smalls succeeded in raising a turbulent discussion about nothing, and a general discussion of the subject by the windy members of the convention, for some two hours, in which many of the "end men" took part.

The more intelligent members of the hippodrome took no part in the discussion, with the exception of the Governor, who, in a very dignified manner, informed them that he had feared no bodily harm from any of them; that he had witnessed such scenes before, and was quietly engaged in preparation for any trap that might be sprung upon the decent members of the convention, after the riot should have spent itself.

At this point, Maxwell, the tragedian from Marlboro, obtained the floor. He is one of the most amusing characters connected with the big show. He hadn't "seen any chairs raised," and, folding his arms and throwing himself back in a tragic and majestic position, said: "I, gentlemen, was the coolest of the cool." This remark, brought the house down. The worst of them were compelled to laugh; especially those who know he never keeps cool. He wound up his harangue by saying that the day was fast approaching when men would seek their rights on the ... face to face with newspaper men ... got the floor....

After other speeches, of a like nature, Captain Canton, city editor of *The Union-Herald*, stepped in front of the reporters table, read the article, and explained to them how he obtained his information and what he saw with his own eyes, winding up, after being interrupted several times, by telling them that "newspaper men were abundantly able to take care of themselves."

The discussion continued until Elliott moved that the whole matter be laid upon the table, which was agreed to.

Mr. Keegan, the correspondent of *The Washington Chronicle*, had listened to their foul language of denunciation of himself and others of his profession, and seeing the question closed, the vilified correspondent, sought his hat, and turning round to the assembled mob, told them they had denounced him like a dog, and had denied him the right to defend himself. This remark of the correspondent cowed the more ignorant portion of the gang, and the resolution was withdrawn, which permitted him to explain to them as the representative of a Republican paper, a gentleman and a soldier; that he had fought to free them; fought against his own father, who owned 150 of their kind, and was a Major in the 5th Louisiana Regiment; that he fought for principle, while his father fought for property; that he had been sent to Columbia to report their doings and sayings, and to see if there was a possible hope of good government in South Carolina.

This stopped the war upon the newspaper men. We devoutly hope that when he goes back across the Potomac he may....

ROBERTSON'S EXPULSION

An Interesting Report of the Proceedings in the House

The School-Book Culprit's Speech in His Own Defense—His Attack Upon Mr. Cathcart and The News and Courier—A Pleasant Colloquy Between Hamilton and Leslie—The Close of the Discussion and Its Result

(From our special correspondent)

Columbia, S. C. February 25.—This has been a regular field day in the House, very nearly the entire session being devoted to a discussion of the report of the committee on privileges and elections concerning the guilt and expulsion of J. D. Robertson, of Beaufort.

Mr. Crittenden resumed, in a review of the evidence. He briefly reviewed his own remarks of yesterday, and then proceeded to quote from the letters of Robertson, while so endeavoring to benefit the children of South Carolina, had never informed the commission of his plans up to December 30th. One point Mr. Robertson had made was that Ivison, Blakeman & Co. were disappointed and for that reason they had made an attack upon him. This, Mr. Crittenden said, was too thin, as the publishers referred to were not that kind of men. He then concluded by saying that he hoped the time had come when the people of South Carolina would show to the world that the time had passed when the adventurers could come from other portions of the country, and with professions of love for the negroes and children of the State, take advantage of their own pockets. The colored people had learned better sense than to trust such people any longer.

Curtis, who was acting speaker, here asked what construction the House placed on Act 2, section 16 of the constitution, which relates to the number of votes required to expel a member, from the floor. Mr. Orr held that the Supreme Court had decided that two-thirds of the number present were competent to expel. Some one else claimed that it required two-thirds of all the members on roll. The speaker here cited a case in the House Journals in which it was decided that two-thirds of the members present was sufficient. Mr. Brayton stated that two-thirds of the House and two-thirds of the Senate were necessary to impeach a judge, and he thought that as much consideration should be shown to the members of the House. In justice to themselves they ought to insist upon the passage of the following resolution:

Resolved, that it is the sense of this House that in order to expel a member a two-thirds vote of all the members elected is required.

Freeman, of Charleston, spoke against the resolution, taking the same ground as that held by Mr. Orr.

Bampfield rose to a point of order that it was the duty of the chair to decide. If necessary an appeal could be had.

The chair stated that if he decided it would be in

favor of the view that it required two-thirds of the members present.

Freeman thought it very strange that no defense had been offered by the friends of the accused, and proposed to amend Brayton's resolution by striking out "elected" and inserting "present."

Mr. Orr said that no resolution of ruling of the chair was necessary as they had the decision of the Supreme Court on the matter, and that was their law. Richardson's Supreme Court Reports, volume 4, has already decided this question, and he didn't see the use of construing the law when it was already construed by such authority.

Chancellor Johnson stated that the matter was purely a constitutional question, and he quoted from the Constitution to show that the House had the right to decide all such questions, for itself.

On motion the resolution of Mr. Brayton was laid on the table.

Hirsch then called for a ruling from the chair, and the chair decided that it would require two-thirds of the members present. The Saint here became very much agitated, and requested that he be allowed to speak in his own behalf, as no one else saw fit to take up his cause. The request was granted, and he then spoke as follows:

Gentlemen of the House of Representatives: I will in the outset simply draw your attention to the fact that my accuser has never put his foot on the soil of South

Carolina. If the House will not defend me the courts will. No witnesses have been called here, and when I asked you for your protection I am taunted with the fact that I have offered no defence. If I had been accused in a trial justice's court I would have had the proofs, and would have the right to meet my accuser face to face. But here, when my reputation and the reputation of my innocent children are at stake, I am proved beyond doubt, and by respectable witnesses, to be a wilful falsifier and perverter of the truth. Take notice of this telegram from an honorable house, Messrs. Armstrong, Scribner & Co.: "We have heard threats that the books chosen shall not succeed, and that you shall be ruined." This is not the first time that Ivison, Blakeman & Co., have made a similar fight to this in the North. They have done so hundreds of times. I ask the patience of the House, which has my future weal or woe in their hands, to hear me yet further. Strike if you will but for Heaven's sake hear me. Another curious phase of this matter is that the house of Ivison, Blakeman & Co., when it suits their convenience, do not hesitate to publish confidential communications. And I would say here that a member of this House has done the same thing, viz, has divulged to the press what took place in the committee room, for his own ends.

Mr. Orr here rose and said that if Robertson referred to him he told a malicious falsehood, and that he would get his pay for it.

Robertson said he had no doubt he would get paid for it; that he had not mentioned Orr's name, but if he saw fit to appropriate the remark he could not help it.

The speaker here interrupted, and put an end to the controversy.

Robertson continued: That he had married into one of the best families of the State, and that his blood was mingled with theirs, &c.

Holland, a coal-black representative, for what purpose or actuated by what impulse must ever remain a mystery, here interrupted, and asked if Robertson referred to him. Mr. Robertson said no, he did not refer to him. This produced a roar of laughter all over the House which the speaker had great difficulty in suppressing.

Robertson continued: I have written some foolish things, it is true, but I am done with Cathcart and Ivison, Blakeman & Co. Remember the words of the Holy Writ: "Judge not that ye be not judged." I will now refer to the letter which the gentleman from Greenville rolled as a sweet morsel under his tongue yesterday. That letter was confidential, and you must remember that all this trouble is made up out of confidential letters. Which of you would be willing to have his confidential letters published? Concerning Guerad, I certainly did offer to help him get a situation, as he was worthy and needy. I was asked by him and endeavored to get it for him; and who would not do the same? Mr. Robertson then referred to his letter in *The News and Courier*, which, he said, the publishers of the paper had done him the justice to publish, and which contained a full account of the whole matter in plain terms, without any attempt to conceal or pervert the facts.

Mr. Robertson's time here expired, but on motion of Whipper he was allowed fifteen minutes longer. He continued: Recollect that two constructions can be placed upon this matter. One will ruin me and the other will not. Choose between them.

Hamilton interrupted. What particular portion of the letters do you deny?

Robertson. What I object to in this investigation is that copies of letters are given here purporting to be mine, when I cannot tell whether they are mine or not. Gentlemen, what can I say more? I built the first school-house that was ever built in my district, and supported the first teacher we had to teach the colored children in it. And now, gentlemen for this I am to be expelled; expelled because I have labored for the good of the children of the State; because in my anxiety I wrote letters which the secretary of the commission ought to have written himself. Gentlemen I am done. "Let him that is without sin among you cast the first stone."

Hamilton. Keep down then, it is where you belong, and if you had your deserts you ought to be down and out of the House. Hamilton then went on, saying that he proposed to divest himself of all personal feelings. He proposed to speak as he thought the people would have him speak—justly. The first ground that he took against Robertson was that he believed him guilty and thought that every man in South Carolina believed the same and I will say as he says, "Out of thy mouth thou shalt be convicted." No private confidential letters could benefit the children of the State; they benefit only the man who writes them. These letters undoubtedly were written to benefit himself, not the children. I express the sentiment of my people when I say that he is guilty of murder, not of manslaughter. This man and such as he have done an immense harm, and it is time we were getting rid of them. We can't hold that class of men and be successful in politics. It is with pain that I utter what I do. If this were some other occasion, and the gentleman was from some other county, I ... of ... Cathcart. Hayne then went into a review of the testimony, concluding with the remark that as to the expulsion of Mr. Robertson bringing disgrace upon his children he did not deny; it was mournful that the sins of the fathers should be visited upon their children.

Black ... Davis then got up, and, as usual, talked a great deal and said very little. The general tenor of the harangue, however, was that if they expelled Robertson they would establish a precedent that would work harm for the party. They would be opening a door that they might not be able to shut when they wanted to. That Republican material was scarce, and if they punished this man it would discourage other white carpet-baggers from coming down and help lead the party in this State.

Freeman of Charleston, then followed in a strong speech against Robertson. He said that the question was one of peculiar significance. It was whether the colored men of the State were able to lead themselves, and capable of upholding their self-respect. He had remained silent until he had heard the defence entirely exhausted, and he was forced to say that the accused had in his defence done nothing but make an admission that the charges were true. He then read a letter of Robertson's dated June 2d. This, he said, was a confidential letter, and no public servant had the right to write such confidential letters to put money in their own pockets. If he (Robertson) knew that it was the character of these Northern firms to defraud the people of the different States, as he says he did, then why did he go to them? If he knew that they were swindlers, why did he go to them to strike a bargain for the State. Robertson had cast an insult upon the colored men that would not be tolerated by any other race upon the face of the globe. He had flung out to the world the insinuation—nay, the assertion—that the colored members of the Legislature were for sale on every question. He hoped that the colored members would assert their self-respect and hurl back the charge with scorn, and show to the world that they had some sense of honor, and will not be duped by unprincipled carpet-baggers any longer.

Whipper then followed in a harangue in support of Robertson, taking the old ground that the letters were not certified to, and incompetent as testimony, &c., and wound up with a customary slash at *The News and Courier*.

Mr. Brayton, of Aiken, followed Whipper in a strong technical argument in support of Robertson, in which he claimed that the form of trial was illegal, and the testimony was insufficient and ex parte; not touching upon the guilt or innocence of Robertson at all.

The accusers and defenders had exhausted their

rhetoric and the patience of their audience and themselves, so a vote was taken on the question of expulsion, and resulted as follows—56 yeas and 25 nays. A few moments later and the hall was silent and in darkness.

Nesbit and Pinckney, however, it seems, hadn't had enough of the fight inside, but went to abusing each other about the course they had pursued. Pinckney voted for expulsion and Nesbit against it, and after some words they went to bruising each other in a way that must have shocked the effigy of the father of their country, around whose bronze form they shinned so mildly. The entertainment broke up, however, before the gladiators had entirely demolished each other.

The discussion of the Robertson matter in the House, if it has done nothing else, has very clearly demonstrated that the majority of the colored people of the State are tired of their carpet-bagger leaders, and do not propose to be led by them any longer.

FOOTNOTES:

[1] These articles were arranged by Monroe N. Work.

BOOK REVIEWS

Fifty Years in the Gospel Ministry. By Theophilus Gould Steward. The African Methodist Episcopal Book Concern, 631 Pine Street, Philadelphia, 1922. Pp. 520.

This is an autobiography covering the period from 1864 to 1914. It carries an introduction by Dr. Reverdy C. Ransom, the editor of the *African Methodist Episcopal Church Review*. Inasmuch as it is the record of a distinguished minister in one of the leading Negro denominations, it throws much light on this period, not only in ecclesiastical affairs but in matters touching the life and development of this race during that period. This is apparent to one observing that the book covers the author's twenty-seven years in the pastorate, sixteen years as a chaplain in the United States army, seven years as a professor in Wilberforce University, two of his trips to Europe and one to Mexico. The book is illustrated, but it has no index.

Taking up the work of the General Conference of 1864, the author says much to give the reader an insight into the characters and efforts of the leading churchmen of his denomination at that time. Among those passing in review are Bishops Quinn, Payne, and Nazrey, and others like H. M. Turner and Alexander W. Wayman who later became bishops of that denomination. Then follows his trip South, when the author had the opportunity to participate in the early efforts for the uplift of the freedmen, serving in Georgia and in South Carolina. He then tells how he arose to a position of usefulness and later served larger groups of communicants in Philadelphia and the District of Columbia. Referring to his record as a chaplain in the United States army, the author shows a larger acquaintance with the leading Negro statesmen through whom he obtained the position. The account of his services in this capacity, both in this country and abroad, and especially in the Philippine Islands, sets forth information, not only as to what that portion of the world was doing, but the reaction of this educated Negro to this panorama. Other interesting experiences appear in the account of his extensive travels.

The value of the book is incalculable when one takes into consideration the dearth of such literature bearing on Negroes. This work takes rank with the recent volume of Bishop Coppin entitled *Unwritten History*, for certainly there are to be found therein interesting romances taken from the life of the Negro and recorded by one of the race in the manner in which these things were impressed upon him and found expression in his mind. This is the sort of literature for which the public has patiently waited and it is devoutly to be desired that other churchmen may find time to leave a written record like these of Bishop Coppin and Chaplain Steward. For anyone desirous of studying the history of the Negro in its various ramifications, such works are indispensable.

The Negro in Literature and Art. By BENJAMIN BRAWLEY. Duffield and Company, New York, 1921. Pp. 197.

This is a revised edition of Professor Brawley's work

which appeared in 1918. It follows the general outline of the first edition and sets forth additional facts but not sufficient to justify this claim to revision. The work is biographical, largely devoted to the narrative of the careers of Phyllis Wheatley, Paul Laurence Dunbar, Charles W. Chesnutt, W. E. B. Dubois, William Stanley Braithwaite, Frederick Douglass, Booker Washington, Henry O. Tanner, Meta Warrick Fuller, and Charles S. Gilpin. The unsatisfactory short sketch of Gilpin constitutes the best claim of the work to that of a revised edition.

While this work does not show by historic or philosophical development the evolution of the Negro mind as expressed in the achievements of the race in literature and art, it has some value. To have a publisher place before the public the sketches of so many prominent Negroes who might otherwise remain unknown to the public is a service to be appreciated. The world has too long considered the Negro a human machine restricted to drudgery. Any successful effort, therefore, to bring before the public from time to time the achievements of worthy Negroes, although it may be a repetition of what may be well known to the better informed few, must be welcomed as an undertaking having a direct bearing on popularizing the record of a neglected seventh of the population of the world.

Let us hope, however, that in the near future some other author, grasping more correctly the needs of the time, may set forth in literary form the interesting story of how history has been influenced by the Negro during the various stages of the world's progress and especially how the Negro of today functions efficiently in the life of Europe and America. The public will welcome too a work treating the eloquent appeals of Negro orators, the beautiful poetry voicing the strivings of this oppressed group, and its peculiar philosophy of life constructed while enduring the ordeal of racial proscription.

The Free Negro in Maryland, 1634–1860. By JAMES M. WRIGHT. Longmans, Green and Company, New York; P. S. King and Son, Ltd., London, 1921. Pp. 362.

This is a study in a neglected field of American history. Hitherto very little has been done to inform the world as to the actual contribution of the free Negro prior to the Civil War. Few persons realize that there were half a million such Negroes in the United States at that time. It is a mistake, therefore, to consider this better selected group of the race so insignificant as not to influence the history of the communities in which they lived. A number of histories have been written since the Civil War, however, with a view to meeting this need for a treatment of this neglected group. There have appeared John H. Russell's *Free Negro in Virginia* and Brackett's *The Negro in Maryland.* But unfortunately such works have been too rigidly restricted to the discussion of the Negro's legal, social, and religious status as determined by the laws enacted for these purposes in the South rather than to the study of the free Negro himself. As it is well known that many of these laws were never enforced, we are still at sea as to what the free Negro actually was and what he was doing.

While Professor Wright has not altogether succeeded in meeting the requirements for this more scientific study of the free Negro, he has done his task much better than those who have hitherto invaded this field. In addition to covering the ground of other such studies he has undertaken to give the historic background and by statistical method he has presented valuable information as to the apprenticeship of Negro children, the occupations and wages of free Negroes, their acquisition of property, their education and their religious strivings.

In his long-drawn-out conclusion he does not seem to have an altogether favorable impression as to the rôle played by the free Negro in the State of Maryland. He shows that the Negro was led to despise himself in keeping with the policy of regarding the white man as the superior and the Negro as the inferior. Professor Wright says, however, that the perpetuation of such a handicap for the most needy part of the population was probably not sound social policy. Upon the whites the effects were first to cause at least a formal realization of race solidarity, and secondly, to intensify class lines within the ranks, although not to define the "poor whites" as rigidly as in certain of the sister slave States. On the whole, Professor Wright believes that the free Negro was an asset to the State, but one laden with many of the characteristics of a liability. "The managers of the corporate body to which he (the Negro) belonged," says the writer, "would have been relieved, could they have written him as an item off their accounts. Nevertheless the sympathetic personal attachment of many whites to individual negro servants, whether slave or free, was permanent." Thus ends an informing book with several misconceptions, but nevertheless fraught with valuable facts.

Batouala. By RENÉ MARAN. Albin Michel, Editor. Paris, 1921. Pp. 189.

This is a novel which was awarded the Goncourt prize in 1921. Inasmuch as it is socially historical, it contains many facts throwing light on the conditions of Africa. Born on the Island of Martinique where the conditions of colonial rule were different from those obtaining in Africa, the scenes of which inspired this indictment of the white man's civilization, René Maran doubtless found the situation there so revolting that it evoked from him this work. Without concealing the faults of the natives, Maran discusses the robber concession companies in Africa, forced labor, high taxes and exorbitant prices for goods sold to the natives. Inasmuch as there were no railroads or "pack animals," the Negroes themselves were impressed into a "pack-man system" which together with the Tsetse fly has worked havoc in Africa. The author maintains that this "pack carrying" has caused the death of more than one million Negroes and cites as evidence that in one town the blacks rebelled against this portage service because it was considered better to die than to undergo such a hardship. The book is intended to emphasize the importance of remedying these abuses and suggests as the proper reform that the concessions granted these private companies should be withdrawn and that nature should be given the opportunity to repair the damage done by white men.

This is a stirring note from a man of African blood speaking for Africa from the point of view of the native himself. It is a distinct contribution in that we have a different view from that appearing in the works of white men who have travelled through that continent, seeing it from the outside and then only "through a glass darkly." The cause of truth in that quarter is now fortunate in having there a number of intelligent Africans who, after having been trained in the mission schools and in the best universities of Europe and America, are now beginning to give the other phase of the social, economic, and political questions in Africa. Many of the conditions which have long obtained in that continent have continued for the reason that persons on the outside who might have been struck with holy horror, had such been known, have never learned and, therefore, can hardly realize that such appalling conditions exist. For this valuable contribution, not only from the literary point of view, but from that of the investigator of social and economic problems, the public must feel indebted to René Maran.

NOTES

The first Spring Conference of the Association for the Study of Negro Life and History was held in the city of New York on April 3d and 4th. There was a preliminary mass meeting on Sunday, the 2d, at the Mother A. M. E. Zion Church, where Mr. James F. Morton, Prof. John R. Hawkins, and Dr. C. G. Woodson delivered addresses which were enthusiastically received.

On Monday and Tuesday, the 3d and 4th, when the actual meeting began, a larger number of persons from afar were present. The day sessions were held at the 135th Street Branch Library where, on Tuesday morning, Dr. George E. Haynes, Secretary of the Race Commission of the Federal Council of the Churches of Christ, opened the discussion of the question "Why one race should know the other one." Other persons participating in the discussion and giving additional information as to the bright prospects for the cooperation of the races in the country were Bishop R. A. Carter, and Cleveland Allen who availed himself of the opportunity to emphasize the importance of placing the bust of Frederick Douglass in the New York Hall of Fame.

At the first evening session held at the Concord Baptist Church in Brooklyn the following evening there was a large attendance. The meeting was opened by preliminary remarks by the Director. He was followed by Prof. Albert Bushnell Hart of Harvard University who delivered an informing address on "Involuntary Servitude." Remarks as to the importance of this organization and how the work may be more success-fully prosecuted were made by Bishop R. A. Carter of the C. M. E. Church, Bishop Lee of the A. M. E. Z. Church and by Dr. George Frazier Miller, Dr. H. H. Proctor, Dr. W. H. Brown, and Rev. J. B. Adams.

On the following day, the morning session opened with a discussion on "How to promote the Study of Negro History in the Schools," led by Mr. Thomas C. Williams of the Bordentown Industrial School. He brought forward valuable statistics out of his own experience as a teacher in this field and presented several sugges-tions and plans for the promotion of this work. There followed some discussion of an informing nature by Dr. I. Garland Penn, Secretary of the Methodist Episcopal Church Board of Education for Negroes, and by Dr. W. Y. Bell, who spoke of his researches in the sources bearing on the history of the Negro in Africa.

The Conference closed with an evening session at the Mother A. M. E. Zion Church where addresses were delivered by Dr. I. Garland Penn and Dr. C. G. Woodson. The address of Dr. Penn dealt primarily with the Negro as a factor in church history. Beginning with the early struggles of the denominations and their relations to the Negroes, Dr. Penn enlightened the audience on facts which are not generally known to the public. He closed his informing address with the expression of faith in the importance of the church as a factor in the progress of the Negro. The address by the Director had to do primarily with the history of the Negro by cycles, showing the varying attitude of the white man toward the Negro and the successful efforts of the Negroes to rise in the midst of trying difficulties and to convince the world of their worth. On the whole, this first Spring Conference was a success and justified itself as an innovation.

The Quadrennial Address of the Bishops of the Colored Methodist Episcopal Church to the Fourteenth Session of the General Conference, held in St. Louis on the 3d of May, contains not only the information bearing on the church but a valuable retrospect as to the conditions among the Negroes after the World War. Among other topics are mentioned racial retrospect, race prejudice and race superiority, the aftermath of the war, the church and world conditions, and the reaction of white Christianity to lawlessness.

THE JOURNAL OF NEGRO HISTORY

VOL. VII—OCTOBER, 1922—No. 4

BRAZILIAN AND UNITED STATES SLAVERY COMPARED

A General View

Whether the Teutonic races are superior to the Latin races is a mooted question, subject to prejudiced points of view. However, there is no doubt that there actually exists a great difference in the institutions of religion, law, language, customs, fashions, and moral precepts between, let us say, the Anglo-Saxon and the Portuguese. In other words, the English nation has evolved an English way of living, just as the Portuguese have adapted themselves to governing society, attacking nature in their own way.

Now assume that these two nationalities with their unlike national habits and traditions are planted in the new world. Assume the one as living in a warm temperate clime, and the other under equatorial conditions. Assume that the first nationality is self-sufficient to establish a colony, and opposed to intermarriage with other races; and then imagine the second case, where there exist a few colonists in womanless settlements with consequent marriages between the native and European common, and a large half-breed population as the result. With such diversities in national character, in the make-up of the individuals, in natural and social environment, could we expect the two peoples to react similarly to a given social institution? No wonder then, that slavery in the English colonies of North America was very much unlike the institution as it existed in Brazil.

Brazil was being tilled by slave labor long before the settlement of Jamestown, and still boasted of hordes of slaves on its plantations as late as a quarter century after the Emancipation Proclamation in the United States had been issued. As early as 1585, Pernambuco could claim 10,000 African slaves and Bahia something like three or four thousand,[1] whereas the first shipment of slaves to the English colonies in America was introduced into Jamestown harbor by a Dutch ship as late as August, 1619.[2]

In Brazil the slave trade received an impetus as a result of royal restrictions and Jesuits' opposition to the enslavement of Indians, thereby compelling the more law-abiding and docile settlers to turn from exploiting the native labor and to seek its labor supply from Africa. [3] The labor demands of the great sugar plantations, cotton fields, tobacco lands, and later the mines, kept the slave poachers on the Guinea and Angola Coast busy, so that by the middle of the eighteenth century slaves were entering Brazil on a vast scale. From 1759 to 1803, according to Keller, the colonial registers give as consigned from Angola to Brazil 642,000 Negroes. Thus, by 1800 fully one half of the total Brazilian population of 3,200,000 was slave, and by 1818 there were 1,930,000 slaves besides some 526,000 free

Negroes and mulattoes, in all about sixty-three per cent of the total.[4] By the middle of the nineteenth century there was something like three millions of slaves out of a population of seven and a half millions. Lord Palmerston estimated the total number of slaves in the sixties as being 3,000,000;[5] whereas a writer in the "Revue des deux Mondes" puts the number between 2,500,000 and 4,000,000.[6] Dawson quotes the number of slaves in 1856 as being approximately 2,500,000 or forty per cent of the total population.[7] Apparently there is no actual census available on the number of slaves for this period. Needless to say, the slaves easily comprised from forty to fifty per cent of the population, and if we add all those of mixed blood we have a majority of the inhabitants of Brazil.

Now let us turn to the Old South. Slavery we know progressed somewhat in the southern colonies, and to a negligible extent in the New England colonies. The "Asiento" in 1713, by which Great Britain at the close of the War of Spanish Succession secured the right to supply the colonies of Spain with 4,800 slaves annually,[8] augmented the slave trade throughout the new world. Negroes were in demand in the rice areas, cotton fields, and tobacco plantations. In 1710 there were only 50,000 slaves in the United States, the number increased to 220,000 in 1750, to 464,000 in 1770,[9] until by the year 1790 they numbered 697,624.[10] This number constituted one-fifth of our total population.

Slavery, however, was not a venerated institution in the Southland in the eighteenth century. In fact, it was rather supported through the force of habit and the fear of the results of emancipation. Then came Eli Whitney's invention of the cotton gin. The South went cotton mad. The United States now became the world's producer of raw cotton. Henceforth, slavery was held "the indispensable economic instrument of southern society."[11]

In the first half of the nineteenth century, then, American slavery was at its height. By 1850 the slaves numbered 3,204,313, about a few thousand less than Brazil, which at the opening of the century had so far led it in the number of slaves held.[12] Blake, writing in 1857, shows that by the last census, however, unlike Brazil, the proportion of black to white was not great, being in the neighborhood of fourteen per cent. However, taking the nation in sections, the ratio of black to white in the South was one to two, whereas in the North it was but one to sixty-eight.[13]

As to the extent of slavery in the two nations, in the United States slavery was largely confined to the semi-tropical country south of the Pennsylvania-Maryland line and the Ohio River. A slight form of domestic slavery had existed in New England, and to a greater degree in the Middle Atlantic Colonies, but was virtually unknown in the mines and cattle ranges of the West. In Brazil slavery existed practically everywhere the Europeans settled. There was no geographical section, whose sentiment and economic interests were antagonistic to slave holding. However, it was true that about the plantations of Pernambuco and Bahia slavery existed on a far more extensive scale than in the southern province of Rio Grande De Sul, where slavery was practised at a minimum.

In both the United States and Brazil there were diversified products of slave labor. In Brazil sugar was the great slave labor staple; in America, cotton. Besides cotton, the American slave was the cultivator of tobacco, rice, sugar, hemp, and molasses. In Brazil the other products were tobacco, cotton, and cattle, in addition to some cacao and rubber.

In the United States there were two types of slavery, one the storied domestic slavery of the towns, and the southern country seat, where the Negro was usually benevolently treated and loved as though one of the family. This type of slavery was most common along the Mason–Dixon line. The other type was determined by the large scale enterprises in the cotton and rice fields in the "southern" South, where absentee ownership was often the rule. Here frequently masters knew little about their slaves, and the driving of the mobs of laborers gave Harriet Beecher Stowe, no doubt, her concept of a Simon Legree.[14] In Brazil slaves did every type of work. First of all, they furnished the labor for the great sugar plantations of Pernambuco and also the cotton districts of the north. In the provinces of the south of Brazil, contrary to conditions in the United States, they were employed on cattle ranches. In Minas Geraes they were utilized in the mines. In the cities they carried on all the manual and menial work.

Henderson tells us of his observations of the African in urban occupations during the first decade of the last century in Rio. He relates that owners would send out slaves to do work for other employers, and to turn over their wages to their idle masters. He relates that masters sent slaves in pairs and threes, bearing baskets on their heads, soliciting work. This type was called "Negroes de ganho." Others bore great tubs on their heads with which they drew water from fountains to supply the inhabitants. At dusk the street was crowded with slaves carrying the refuse of the city to the dumps. Slave labor removed the imported goods from the docks. Few had the help of wagons. The English had tried to introduce carts to help the toiling slaves at the wharves, but the custom house clerks would have none of them, as they were making a "haul" on the city by hiring out their slaves, and wagons would lessen the amount of work to be done.[15]

In the United States slaves were owned by planters and private individuals exclusively. In Brazil besides the planter class, large plantations were owned by such religious orders as the Benedictine and Carmelite friars, who treated their slaves with the greatest regard for comfort and ease.[16] Furthermore, there were slaves belonging to the government. As late as the outbreak of the American Civil War, the annual report of the Brazilian minister of finance shows more than 1,500 government slaves.[17] One thing in favor of Brazil, however, was that the horrible shortcomings of absentee ownership on large plantations did not exist to any extent, since most of the proprietors resided on their own respective estates.[18]

Summing up the general condition of the Negro slave in

both lands, we notice that (1) Brazilian slavery antedated and postulated American slavery; (2) that there were a larger number of slaves and a greater proportion to the total population in Brazil than in America; (3) that Brazilian slavery received its impetus through the cutting off of the native labor supply and the growth of sugar cultivation; whereas American slavery was stimulated by the invention of the cotton gin; (4) that in both countries slaves were engaged in diversified occupations, except that in Brazil besides agriculture and domestic pursuits, slaves were employed in almost every variety of unskilled and semi-skilled labor; (5) that in Brazil slavery was homogeneously distributed rather than in sectional patches; and (6), finally, that both the state and religious bodies owned slaves in Brazil.

THE SOCIAL SIDE OF SLAVERY

The living conditions of the Negroes in both the United States and Brazil varied in relation to the type of work. Domestic slaves in the former were generally treated well in the households of their masters. In Brazil the domestic slave was usually a Creole.[19] But our interest centers largely on the manner by which the *agricultural* slave lived, for after all, in him lies the crux to the whole problem. In both Brazil and America slaves were quartered on the great plantations in rude huts. Their diet was simple. Corn meal, bacon, and sweet potatoes were chief items in the diet of the American slave. In Brazil the slave was fed farina (the flour of the mandioca root), salt fish or salt meat, sometimes bacon, and in the mining districts corn flour. In both countries the slave was rudely clad. In Brazil his outfit consisted of a shirt and pants of cotton and a straw hat.[20]

In the United States slaves on the large plantations began work at sunrise, and toiled to the crack of the whip on the great plantations until sundown. Women and children, only half grown, were compelled to do their share in the fields. In Brazil conditions generally were easier for the slave. The Portuguese planter was perhaps less anxious to "drive" the work out of his bondsmen than the more enterprising Anglo-Saxon. Accordingly, we are told that at three in the afternoon, at least at Pernambuco, the heart of the sugar belt, work ceased, and the slave had the remainder of the day to himself, time which many slaves employed in cultivating a private plot of their own, hoping some day to earn enough thereby to purchase their freedom. They, like their northern brothers, were supervised in the field by a "feitor" or taskmaster, usually white, though frequently a Creole, mulatto, freedman, or even in cases, another slave.[22]

Slaves in America welcomed Sundays and the days around Christmas as periods of rest and recreation. [23] In Brazil not only did the slaves have Sundays and Christmas, but something like over thirty holidays on the Catholic calendar. Incidentally, showing there was still a breath of humanity in a stifling age of oppression, it is declared in the "Correio Braziliense" for December, 1815, on page 738, that although the Portuguese had ceased to stop work on many of these holidays, the thirty-five holidays were still enforced as days of cessation of labor in Brazil in order that the slaves might still enjoy the days of rest.[24]

The Negro slave in Africa, according to DuBois, lived generally a polygamous family life. When he came to the Southern Colonies his whole family life was made irregular and unhappy, due to the evil conditions of slavery there. The slave might marry on the plantation, but the very next day he might be sold, and separated from his wife and parents. The auction block is the foulest stain on the whole parasitic institution of slavery in the United States. In Brazil the sale of slaves from one master to another apparently was never as extensive as in our own country.[25] Moreover, the sanctity of marriage was far more highly regarded in Brazil than in the United States. A slave, who wished to be married had first to learn the requisite number of prayers; he must understand the confession, and receive the sacraments. Then, having received the consent of the master, he was married by the vicar. A slave might marry a freeman. If the husband were free and the wife slave, the child of the union was a slave; vice versa, a slave father and free mother produced a free child.[26]

In language, we find in both the Old South and Brazil, that the Africans soon forgot their native dialects, and adopted the tongue of their new home, and their language did not materially influence that of their masters in America.

Religion was a vital factor in slave life. In the Old

South, religion was at first discouraged among the slaves. There was a reason for this, for masters knew that nowhere in Christian teachings were there provisions for enslaving Christians.[27] Never was religion encouraged to a great degree. In fact, as late as 1831, Virginia passed a measure, declaring that neither free nor slave Negro might "preach, exhort, or teach in any Negro assemblage." Nevertheless, religious sentiment waxed ever stronger. Beginning with the taboos of the deported tribal priest, and gradually becoming influenced by Christianity, the great Negro Church[28] grew. Sometimes the Negroes were allowed to worship under the same roof as their white superiors,[29] but they usually had to steal away to some secret place for this purpose. In Brazil, however, Christianization of the slaves was an essential. Before the Negroes in Angola (Portuguese West Africa) embarked on the slave vessel for Brazil, they were baptized "en masse." Arriving in the new world, they were branded with the crown, which proved that they had been baptized and that the king's duty on them had been paid. Next, they had to learn the doctrines of the Church and the duties of the religion they were about to embrace. Slaves from the other parts of Africa were Christianized after a year following arrival, during which time they had to learn certain prayers.[30] Most interesting is the existence among the Brazilian slaves of their own religious brotherhoods, to join which was the ambition of every Negro slave. These brotherhoods had their own versions of the Virgin Mary and Our Lady of the Rosary had her hands and face painted black.[31]

SLAVE RIGHTS

Properly speaking, a true slave has no legal rights. Perhaps the words privileges and permits are happier. At any rate, the obligations and restrictions in the Old South were far more stringent than those on the plantations and urban districts of Brazil. Privileges and restrictions for slaves in the South varied according to the laws of the States; whereas in Brazil the centralized colonial government tended to unify what slavery legislation there was.

In both countries, theoretically, a master was liable for indiscriminately killing his slaves or for practising cruelty. To be sure, the penalty was slight for so great an offense, but public opinion in Brazil, especially, more than once pointed its finger at the brutal master. In practice, even the slightest defense of a maltreated slave was rarely heard before the magistrates, for no slave in the case of the South could bear witness against a white. In Brazil the ouvidor of the province was the one to punish the cruel master, but then, who would dare report?[32] In Brazil, if a slave was unruly he was to be turned over to state authorities, and duly given a public punishment.[33]

In the Old South it was possible under certain circum-stances for the slave to buy his own freedom, that is, if the master was kindly disposed. In Brazil, it is commonly affirmed that the master was obliged to free his slave if the latter could furnish a sum equivalent to his market price.[34] As a matter of practice, it was easy for the master to deny freedom to his slave under such conditions, and the slave for lack of strength would have to accept the outcome meekly. Furthermore, Christie, British envoy extraordinary and minister plenipotentiary in Brazil during the period of the American Civil War, in a letter to Earl Russell in June, 1861, declares that no such law actually exists on the statute books of Brazil, as that the slave has the right to appear before a magistrate, have his price fixed and to purchase his freedom.[35]

Moreover, the Brazilian slave exercised some right to change masters. The master set a price upon his slave. Then the slave with a note, declaring the master's intentions, might seek out some neighboring planter with a good reputation, and if the desired new master decided to pay the price set, the old master, according to Luccock,[36] was obliged to sell the slave. In practice the plan did not work out so well, because one planter did not care to interfere in the other's affairs, and often the evaluation of the slave could not be agreed upon.[37]

A slave could be and was manumitted in both the United States and Brazil. In Brazil manumission could be accomplished in the following ways: (1) the slave could purchase himself; (2) his master could liberate him during his life; (3) or he could manumit him at his death; (4) a Negro woman who had brought ten children into the world by virtue of her tenth became free; (5) also, the price of a new-born babe was so slight, that often the infant was purchased its freedom by friends.[38] In fact, manumission had been so extensive, that by 1818 mulattoes and free Negroes had become a considerable part of the population.[39] In the United States there were 488,070 freedmen in 1860.[40]

As for holding common ordinary citizen's rights, the Negro slave in both countries was out of consideration. In the Old South, for instance, a slave could be arrested, tried, and condemned with but one witness against him, and without a jury.[41] In Brazil he was equally as defenceless. Professional slave runaway catchers might pounce upon a slave who was about his duty, imprison him, subject him to indignities, on the ground that he was a fugitive, and return him to his master, claiming money for their trouble. In such a sad case, no one would take the slave's part, none would believe his story.[42]

The privileges of the slave as to being secure against violent treatment, of securing his own freedom, of selecting another master, or of claiming any plain citizen's immunities whatsoever, then, were very slight in both Brazil and the United States, but even more so in our own Southland.

SLAVE RESISTANCE

Docile as the African slave was, he was bound at times to attempt to free himself from the drudgery and sufferings of his lot. Naturally the most direct, impulsive, and simple method was escape. Hence, we are brought to compare the fugitive slave problem in Brazil to the same problem in the United States.

In our own country the South had to combat an effective force which did not exist in Brazil, namely, the antagonism of an Anti-slavery North, which aided the Negroes by "underground railroads" to escape to free territory, or to cross the Canadian line, where slavery was prohibited. The Dismal Swamp in Virginia, and the Everglades of Florida were favorite hiding places for fugitives.[43] In Brazil the universal prevalence of slavery and the lack of opposition to the practice by any considerable group up to the last days of its existence gave the fleeing slave few friends. However, there was a trackless wilderness to which he might flee. Especially qualified runaway slave catchers were employed to trail such fugitives.

The other method of resisting the institution of slavery was by organized risings. Riots and local revolts occurred occasionally in the Old South, but were never serious and were easily quelled. The most noteworthy revolts of blacks in America were actually mere spouts. In the first half of the eighteenth century, for example, New York was thrown into hysteria at the rumors of a threatened Negro plot,[44] out of which nothing materialized. Gabriel's riot planned in Richmond, Virginia, in 1800, ended very much like that in New York. Another incident was the attempt in 1822 of a certain Negro, Denmark Vesey, to start an insurrection at Charleston, which utterly failed. Nat Turner, a religious fanatic, was the cause of the most serious uprising of all. In 1831 he organized a revolt in Virginia which cost the lives of several score of whites before it was quelled.[45] The other spontaneous turn of the worm was the *Amistad* incident,[46] in which Negroes of the slave ship *Amistad* rose and took possession of the ship, and ordered the crew to guide her back to Africa. Instead, the crew steered the vessel into a hospitable harbor, thus baffling its captors. The rising of the slaves of the *Creole* in somewhat the same manner was more romantic.

All these pin pricks in the South are now to be contrasted to a series of serious organized risings of slaves in Brazil, eruptions which at times threatened the political control or integrity of a whole district or province. In the United States the slave placidly submitted. In Brazil he was at periods actually class conscious.

In Pernambuco, the Brazilian government was actually challenged by slave rebels. It was during the chaotic days of 1630-1654, when the Dutch were in occupation of Pernambuco, and the Brazilians were at war with them, that hundreds of slaves fled to the interior, where they established an independent state, consisting of a cluster of fortified villages. Establishing a rude form of administration and a primitive adaptation of Christianity, they actually governed themselves. After the Dutch had been fairly well beaten, the whites turned to make war upon the villages. For fifty years the villages held out, until in 1697, Palmares, the last and most important of the fortresses, capitulated.[47]

Bahia lived in a perpetual fear of Negro uprising, and well were her fears grounded, for here the Negro was most assertive against his mistreatment. The population of Bahia in the first decade of the nineteenth century is estimated by Henderson as being in the neighborhood of 110,000, two thirds of which was slave. Once let the slave get a start and with such odds in his favor the masters had best beware. For this reason, slaves were prevented as much as possible from organizing. No bondman might go on the streets of Bahia after evening vespers, save with a pass from his master.[48] Yet the slaves did at times organize. In 1808, when John VI, the Portuguese king, arrived in Bahia, the slaves boldly communicated with him, asking that the punishment of one hundred and fifty lashes be abolished.[49]

A short time after this episode, matters came to a culmination. As was usual at holiday time, slaves congregated in plazas, chose a chief for the day, to whom they did homage. This was a customary feat, tolerated by the authorities of the city. On this particular occasion, a friend of Henderson noticed that a white man was being hanged in effigy. He sniffed trouble. Only a few months later the Bahian authorities were lucky, by timely arrests, to save the whole population from being massacred by the enraged slaves in an impending insurrection, whose purpose was nothing less than the wholesale slaughter of the entire white population of the city, with the exception of the governor, D'Arcos, whom the insurrectos were to raise as their prince. Already they had murdered many whites in the outskirts of the city.[50]

Thus, in the Old South, flight was the leading form of resistance to the institution of slavery; whereas in Brazil the more effective form of resistance by organized uprising was more frequently attempted.

THE RACE PROBLEM

Before concluding the theme, it is imperative that we hurriedly skim over the saddest and most serious by-product of United States slavery, race prejudice. We are familiar enough with the limitations of the man of color in the South today. In the days of slavery, discriminations were just as severe, if not more so, against any man of black skin, whether slave, mulatto, freedman, quadroon, or octoroon. The slightest strain of black in a man's pedigree made him a "nigger." A freedman was better than a slave only in an economic way. Otherwise he had virtually no rights. He could not vote, marry a white, hold office, give testimony in case of a white man on trial, and for militia services was limited to fatigue duty. In many parts, however, the freedman could keep his own money, possess land, have slaves, a wife, and even own one gun to protect his home.[51]

In Portuguese America it is often said that the race problem has been allowed to solve itself, which is largely true. The slave in Brazil was looked down upon as a menial laborer, rather than as an offshoot of a lower race. Marriages between the lower classes of either race were not scorned by society. Inter-racial marriages were legal, Brazilian society favoring the marriage of the higher type of the white to the lighter type of Negroid. Of course, among the highest class of the land, the wealthy planters and officials, unions with persons of non-genuine white ancestry were not relished. Here and there existed race prejudice in mild form.[52]

Mulattoes who were free were ranked above freedmen of pure ancestry. The former were generally considered as white, for as a rule in Brazil a man passed as white if he contained a fair degree of white blood in his veins. These free mulattoes had a regiment of their own with their own officers, as was the case with the blacks. Many wealthy planters at Pernambuco were men of color. Many of the Creole blacks in this region were mechanics, who sent out their slaves to do odd mechanical jobs for the owner's profit. The best church and image painter at Pernambuco was black. One of three commanders of the Brazilian forces against the Dutch in the seventeenth century was Henrique Diaz, a Negro.

All told, race prejudice, as a vast problem, was a peculiar complement of the Anglo-Saxon new world colonies' slave problem, for in virtually no other country has slavery ever so viciously contributed to race discord. Brazil, then, may pride herself upon emerging from a slave sustained society, free from the sores of a hideous race conflict.

AN AFTERTHOUGHT

In brief, it seems that the Brazilian institution of slavery was softer, far less brutal than the United States system. On the other hand, the United States slave system was probably more efficient, for the inefficiency of the management of the plantations of sugar in Brazil allowed the West Indies in the eighteenth century to take the lead in the sugar, rum, and molasses exports. The United States, under the slave system, secured pre-eminence in the production of the world's greatest textile staple, cotton.

It is to be regretted, of course, that slavery has persisted so long, and still thrives in certain Mohammedan lands. It stands today outlawed in the new world, but it will always be a source of regret to progressive citizens of the United States that their country clung to the institution up to within the memory of many yet living, and that she did not relax her tight grasp upon the slave until forced to immediate action in the stress of a fratricidal war. To humane thinkers of Brazil, it will ever be a source of sorrow that their nation has only been slave ridden within the present generation, and even then, egged on to emancipation by the reproaches of an at last awakened world.

Slavery must have differed in details in one country from that in another, but after all, it was shameful in Brazil, shameful in the United States, just as it is shameful at any other spot underneath the blue sky.

HERBERT B. ALEXANDER

FOOTNOTES:

[1] Keller, Albert Galloway, Ph.D., *Colonization*, Boston, Copyright, 1908, p. 145.

[2] DuBois, William Edward Burghardt, *The Negro*, New York, 1915, p. 164.

[3] Keller, pp. 156–157.

[4] *Ibid.*

[5] Christie, W. D., *Notes on Brazil*, London, 1821, pp. 69–76.

[6] Christie, pp. 69–76.

[7] Dawson, Thomas C., *South American Republics*, two volumes, first edition, vol. I, New York, Copyright, 1903, p. 481.

[8] DuBois, *The Negro*, p. 152.

[9] *Ibid.* p. 184.

[10] *Negro Population in the United States, 1790–1915, p. 33.*

[11] Ingram, J. K., *A History of Slavery and Serfdom*, London, 1895, p. 285.

[12] Bureau of Census (Dept. of Commerce and Labor), *A Century of Population Growth*, Washington, 1909, p. 80.

[13] Blake, William O., *A History of Slavery and the Slave Trade*, Columbus, 1857, p. 808.

[14] DuBois, *The Negro*, p. 190.

[15] Henderson, James, *A History of Brazil*, London, 1821, pp. 73–74.

[16] Koster, Henry, *Travels in Brazil*, second edition, in two volumes, vol. II, London, 1817, pp. 247–259.

[17] Christie, pp. 69-76.

[18] Koster, p. 123.

[19] *Ibid.*, pp. 247-259.

[20] Koster, pp. 247-259.

[21] *Encyclopedia Americana*, 30 volumes, vol. 27, New York and Chicago, 1919, pp. 395-396.

[22] *Americana*, pp. 395-396.

[23] Koster, pp. 229-231.

[24] Koster, pp. 246-247.

[25] Southey, vol. III, pp. 781-783, states that in Pernambuco masters were opposed to selling their slaves.

[26] Koster, pp. 246-247.

[27] Brawley, Benjamin Griffith, *A Short History of the American Negro*, N. Y., 1917, pp. 20-21.

[28] DuBois, p. 197.

[29] *Americana*, pp. 395-396.

[30] Koster, pp. 238-239.

[31] *Ibid.*

[32] Koster, pp. 236-238.

[33] *Luccock, John, Notes on Rio de Janeiro and the Southern Part of Brazil, London, 1820, p. 591.*

[34] Koster, pp. 229-231.

[35] Christie, p. 578.

[36] Luccock, p. 591.

[37] Koster, pp. 233-235.

[38] *Ibid.*

[39] Keller, pp. 156-157.

[40] Blake, p. 808.

[41] Brawley, pp. 20-21.

[42] Henderson, pp. 72-78.

[43] Brawley, p. 90.

[44] DuBois, p. 196

[45] *Ibid.*

[46] Brawley, p. 90.

[47] Dawson, p. 375.

[48] Henderson, pp. 339-340.

[49] Henderson, p. 340.

[50] *Ibid.*, p. 340.

[51] Brawley, p. 22.

[52] Koster, ch. XVIII

THE ORIGINS OF ABOLITION IN SANTO DOMINGO

Columbus discovered this island December 6, 1492. It is of the Great Antilles of the Caribbean Sea, and lies between Cuba and Puerto Rico. He called the island Hispaniola, but Hayti, or Haiti, was its original name. It seems beyond the power of language to exaggerate its beauties, its productiveness, the loveliness of its climate, and its suitability as an abode for man.

At the time of its discovery the island was divided into five states or cacicats. Thus divided it was easily conquered by the Spaniards who subjected the native Indians to slavery. Soon after the discovery, Spain began establishing a plantation colony as opposed to a farm colony. The work fell upon the subjected Indians, who vanished from the island, in about 50 years, leaving the problem of labor to the overseers and the colonists. To meet this need, the Spaniards repaired this loss by bringing in Africans, supplied by the Portuguese, who at that time occupied themselves with the slave trade. Hierrera, who claimed to be an authority, said that one Negro would do more work than four Indians. [1] In 1630, a number of French adventurers were expelled by the Spanish from St. Christophe, which they had taken possession of five years before under the leadership of Neil d'Enambroe of Dieppe. Shortly afterward they established themselves at La Fortue.

In 1650 the Spaniards still held the inner and greater islands, Cuba, Hispaniola, Puerto Rico, and Jamaica; though in Hispaniola French buccaneers were laying the foundations of the prosperous French Colony of St. Domingo. Smouldering resentment on the part of the Spaniards soon burst forth in open hostility, exhibiting more seriousness than before. Then followed savage contention between Spain and France, the Spaniards disputing the rights of the French, the French creeping steadily inward until 1697 by virtue of the treaty of Ryswick an end was put to this struggle. Louis XIV obtained, under this treaty, from Charles II of Spain, the cession of all the western part of the island, which for forty years belonged to the French by virtue of conquest. Spain kept the eastern portion of the island, calling it Santo Domingo. This cession was of great economic value to France, she increased her number of slaves and soon supplied all Europe with cotton and sugar. Santo Domingo, Spain's portion of the island, as compared with Haiti, was a sluggish community. Here also Negroes increased as slaves and soon the population of these two colonies was mostly Negro.

The distinct line between master and slave, white and black, was to become smeared. Soon there grew up four distinct classes. Miscegenation, the result of the contact of European masters with slave women, gave rise to a new class called mulattoes. These were usually given their freedom, and it was the practice to liberate the mother as well. This gave rise to another class, the free-blacks. The mulattoes and free-blacks obtained with emancipation no political rights whatever. At first this caused no worry or serious difficulty. Some of the mulattoes received vast wealth from their fathers and often they were educated abroad, usually in France. Some of the free-blacks accumulated a little property but in a far lesser degree, however. With the increase of mulattoes and free-blacks, and the return of those mulattoes from studies abroad, dissatisfaction grew into thought and subsequently into expression and agitation for political rights. Behind and beneath the growing dissatisfaction of these two classes, the mulattoes and free-blacks, was a resentful and restless slave population.

At the outbreak of the French Revolution, even before it, France had in her possession eight slave holding colonies, San Domingo, Martinique, Guadeloupe, Cayenne, Tabago, St. Lucie, the Isle of France, and the Isle of Bourbon. The most important of these being Martinique and Guadeloupe, with a white population of about 25,000, contained about 150,000 slaves and a small number of free Negroes; and then there was her flourishing colony of San Domingo. Martinique and Guadeloupe were represented in the National Assemblies which brought France into early contact with the issue rising out of racial color.[2] San Domingo with its large population and economic importance offered a more perplexing problem. The population there was large. Moreau de St. Méry quoted the official figures of 1790 as 30,826 whites, 24,262 free Negroes and mulattoes, and 452,000 slaves.[3]

The legal status of slaves here was substantially the same as that of slaves in the tropical colonies of other nations; in fact, the Western European slave code remains practically the same. This slave colony seems singular in being unfavorable to the health and life of the natives. The annual excess of deaths over births amounted to about two and one half per cent. Added to this death rate was the rapid spread of the feverish desire for wealth at any cost among the peoples of European countries. The slave trade was profitable. The demand for slaves was continual, amounting at this period to anywhere between 30,000 to 35,000 a year in the French West Indies. Human life and rights were subordinate to gold, despite the position assumed by these nations as champions of Christianity.

The question of mulattoes and freedmen and their descendants was peculiar to San Domingo. The free Negroes and mulattoes were four fifths the whites in number. When the offspring of illicit unions between slave women and their masters attained their majority they were emancipated, and in many cases their mothers were set free also. As follows a system of servitude,

> "The Sons of gods take the Daughters of men, but
>
> The Sons of men dare not touch the daughters of the gods."

And thus it came about the number of these classes increased rapidly. The poor laboring class of the community, corresponding somewhat to the class of "poor whites" within the slave section of our country, was made up of free Negroes.

"According to the *Code Noir* of Louis XIV, freemen and their descendants were entitled to all the rights and privileges of citizens of France. However, in defiance of the law, race prejudice had built up during the eighteenth century a special body of customary rules for their control, and this custom was recognized by numerous administrative edicts and royal ordinances." Great effort was put forth to keep the possibilities of uprisings at a distance. Any use of fire arms was prohibited even the mulattoes, and the commissioned officers of military service were kept white without exception. A trace of Negro blood was a bar to individual attainment, even marriage to a mulatto received its share of condemnation. A strong feeling of social repugnance was being brought into play which outlawed all social intercourse between the races. This sort of thing, going on in so many different places—practically wherever the Western European colonized—became imbedded in custom and in places was expressed in law.

While the *Code Noir* of Louis XIV went even so far as to lay down certain practices as the fundamental law of slavery, it was apparently only a "law." There was a lack of the moral support necessary to insure for it even a respectable amount of operation. There were at work, however, forces which sought to create a widespread social antipathy to slavery. This resulted somewhat from the situation in England where there was a strong sentiment against slavery. The Quakers in England, whose founder had been a fearless critic of the institution, were foremost in the attack on slavery. In 1727 the Society of Friends passed a resolution of censure against the slave trade, and in 1758 its influence was strongly exerted to keep its members from even an indirect connection with it. In 1765, Granville Sharp began to look after the interests of Negroes who were claimed in British ports as slaves, and in 1772 was instrumental in securing the famous Somerset decision that, as soon as any slave set foot on British soil he became free. In 1783 the Society of Friends submitted to Parliament the first petition for the abolition of the slave trade. In that same year Thomas Clarkson won the prize in a competition in Latin composition at Cambridge upon the assigned subject, "Whether it is right to enslave others against their will." His essay immediately became a standard authority among opponents of the trade and the institution. A greater consequence was that Clarkson himself was so inspired he devoted his life to the cause of the blacks. In 1787 a "Committee for Effecting the Abolition of the Slave Trade" was organized. It was composed chiefly of Quakers, having Granville Sharp as President and Thomas Clarkson as its most prominent member. Their work was organized to embrace appeals to the public and petitions to the government. Wilberforce, a member of Parliament and an intimate friend of Pitt, was to head the campaign in Parliament, while the Committee was to solicit funds, collect information and arouse public sentiment. This campaign lasted until the abolition of British slave trade in 1806.

This work in behalf of freedom soon extended to France. A little over three months after the London Committee was formed it received a letter from Jean Pierre Brissot, requesting that he and Etienne Clavière might become associates of the committee for the purpose of publishing French translations of its literature and collecting subscriptions to be remitted to London for the good of the common cause. The committee declined the offer of financial aid but elected Brissot an honorary member and recommended that a society be formed in France. Now both Brissot and Clavière were active figures in the Revolution. Clavière was at one time minister of finances and Brissot, most ardent of revolutionists, was a Parish Deputy during the Reign of Terror, and a leader of the Girondins from 1789 to 1792. Accordingly, a society was formed in Paris in February, 1788, under the name of the Society of Friends of the Blacks, with Clavière as President. It adopted the same seals as the Committee in England but was an entirely independent organization. Directly its influence began to draw within its folds powerful figures. The famous Comte de Mirabeau was a charter member, Marquis de Lafayette, an officer who had served in the American Revolution, and Condorcet, a member of the Convention, whose report as a member of the Committee of Public Instruction of the Legislative Assembly formed the actual basis of subsequent plans for education, were among the first additions to its membership. Other prominent members who came in later were Sièyés, Petion, Grégoire, Robespierre, and the Duke de la Rochefoucauld. Mirabeau issued the early publications of the society as supplements to his journal; at a later time Brissot's journal, the "Patriote francaise," became the organ of the society.

With Brissot's return from a visit to America in 1788, the society went seriously to work. In America he seems to have met some things which clinched his convictions and determinations. Coincidental, the National Assembly was about to meet, deputies were being elected, cahiers were being written, and the country was stirred up over the watchword liberty. This offered an exceptional advantage to the society. What better opportunity could one anticipate to secure the abolition of slavery and the slave trade, the most flagrant violations of the principles of equality and liberty ever known? On February 3, 1789, Condorcet, at that time the President, addressed a circular letter to all the bailiwicks of France, urging that there be inserted in the cahiers a demand that the Estates-General destroy the slave trade and make preparations for the ultimate abolition of slavery. The results of this campaign were disappointing. As a whole the cahiers made it perfectly clear to the Society and all concerned, that an attack on slavery was not a matter vital to the mass of the nation, and that success, if it came at all, must be due to the loyalty of the Estates-General to the principles of equality and liberty, and to the ability and energy of the little group of intellectual leaders who made up the Society of Friends of the Blacks. This was the status of the controversy. Anti-slavery agitation was confined to an intellectual élite, promoted by an appeal to the mind.

In the National Assembly the contest between Friends of the Blacks and defenders of slavery began in connection with the application of a delegation for admission to the

Estates-General as representatives of San Domingo. Early in 1788 there was formed in Paris an organization, the "colonial committee" by name, composed of certain colonial proprietors residing in France, a few merchants interested in colonial trade, and a small number of actual residents of San Domingo, which began an agitation for representation of the colony in the Estates-General, which had been promised for 1792. The committee circulated pamphlets and the like. It made a formal request of the king for representation of San Domingo. The request was refused by the Council of State. The agitators boldly drew up and sent to the colony a plan for electoral assemblies. These assemblies were held without any legal sanction, and thirty-one deputies were elected.

The committee continued its work in France, and succeeded in securing a demand for the admission of colonial deputies in at least fourteen cahiers of primary assemblies. Repeated applications were made to Necker and to the Minister of Marine, but without result, and when the Estates-General opened the representatives of San Domingo had no legal standing. Nevertheless part of the deputies presented themselves on June 8, making application separately to each of the three orders.

The third estate alone proved receptive. On June 20, eight San Domingo deputies were allowed to take the Tennis Court Oath. On June 27 the Committee on Credentials made a report unanimously recommending the admission of the colonial deputation but declared itself unable to agree on the number of deputies to which the colony was properly entitled. The Assembly accepted the report, apparently without a dissenting voice, and postponed discussion of the question of numbers to June 3. This brought squarely before the Assembly the delicate problem of slavery and the status of free-blacks under the new régime, and brought upon the colonial delegation the wrath of the powerful Society of the Friends of the Blacks.

The Friends of the Blacks recognized in this San Domingo delegation a foe. Mirabeau's newspaper challenged their right to count the slaves as a basis of representation, and taunted them with bitter words. "Either count your Negroes as men or as beasts; if they are men, free them, let them vote, let them be elected to office. If they are cattle, let the number of deputies be proportional to your human population; we have counted neither our horses nor our mules."[4]

Between the vote of admission on June 27 and the final debate on July 3 and 4 the Friends of the Blacks awoke to the importance of the issue. Condorcet published a vigorous pamphlet denouncing the slave holder and all his works. "We are tempted," said he, "to advocate a law which shall exclude from the National Assembly every man, who, as a slave holder, is interested in the maintenance of principles contrary to the natural rights of man, which are the only purpose of every political organization.... The natural rights of man to be governed only by laws to which he has given his consent cannot be invoked in favor of a man who is himself at the very moment violating the law of nature." The pamphlet closes with the remark that the planters can doubtless speak concerning their own interests, "but that on their lips the sacred word 'rights' would be blasphemy against reason."[5]

When the question was reopened on July 3, Mirabeau took the lead in the discussion, raising again the question of counting the slaves, and arguing further that the so-called deputies really represented only about one half the free population, since the whole body of free blacks and mulattoes had been excluded from suffrage. The spokesman of the colonial deputation was the Marquis de Gouy d'Arsy, a colonial proprietor residing in Paris, from the beginning a leader in the movement for colonial representation. Gouy made no attempt to defend the principle of slave representation. He based his claim for the admission of eighteen or twenty delegates on the wealth and commercial importance of the colony. His weak point was the exclusion of free tax-paying mulattoes from the electoral assemblies. He said that since the mulattoes were natural enemies of the whites it would be dangerous to give them any influence, an argument which made a bad impression on the Assembly. The debate was finished the next day, and the number of deputies was fixed by a compromise at six. The chief importance of this discussion was the prominence which it gave to two questions that the colonial deputies were anxious to keep smothered—slavery and the civil status of the free Negroes. During the debate on June 27 the Duke de la Rochefoucauld found opportunity to present the aims of the Society of Friends of the Blacks, and requested the future consideration of the problem of emancipation. Remarks by other deputies to the effect that something be done to improve the condition of slaves received hearty applause.

The French Revolution plunged the island into a state of chaos. The vast majority of the population of the western colony were slaves, and the number of free blacks and mulattoes were nearly equal to the number of whites. "The news of the Revolution had encouraged each class of the colonial population to expect the realization of its peculiar hopes. The planters desired freer access to the markets of the world, the poor whites hoped for the advantages that their richer neighbors alone enjoyed, the free blacks and mulattoes for civil equality; even the slaves cherished hopes of liberty."[6] The clash of interests brought on civil war in Santo Domingo. The situation here, the richest of the sugar colonies, was serious; it soon received special attention from the home government. A colonial assembly was chosen, and did in miniature what the National Assembly undertook for all France. It controlled royal officers and troops, attempted to reorganize the administrative system and the courts, and even opened the ports to products specifically excluded by a royal ordinance. The question of the status of the free blacks had reached an acute stage. As property holders their interests were identical with those of the whites, provided the whites did not exclude them from a share in the civil conquests of the French Revolution. The National Assembly finally gave to the colonies an organization similar to the local admin-istrative system of France except that it delegated executive powers to a governor. The constitution of the colony, once approved by the national legislature, could not be changed without the demand or consent of the local assemblies. To this local legislature was given the responsibility for the making of laws on all matters except trade and defense. If the governor did not withhold his consent in order that the authorities at Paris should first be consulted, laws could be put into force provisionally before they received the final sanction of the National Assembly and the Crown.

The free people of color petitioned the National Assembly for political rights and privileges in 1789. On May 15, 1791, on the question of the free blacks, the Assembly passed a decree declaring that people of color, born of free parents, were entitled to all the privileges of French citizens. When the news reached the island the mulattoes and free Negroes rejoiced. The whites were opposed to any such measure. Thereupon the governor of the island delayed promulgating the decree while he communicated with the home government. The free people of color were angered and civil strife followed. The mulattoes took up arms against the whites. To complicate matters, the slaves rose in insurrection in August, 1791. The whites, finding themselves in a perilous situation, decided to accede to the demands of the free people of color, who in turn promised to combine with the whites to suppress the revolt. Meanwhile, in the last days of the Assembly the friends of the planters succeeded in having the whole matter referred to the colonial assemblies. The people of color, mulattoes and free blacks, fled to arms again and joined the slaves, leading bands of them against the whites or remained indifferent in actual warfare. Then followed actual civil war. The French land owners or "colons" called in the English to help them combat the blacks.[7] The English came to their aid. By the end of 1793 the latter took possession of a part of the island which seemed lost to France, being occupied partly by Spaniards and partly by English, when Toussaint L'Ouverture, the bondman leading the revolting slaves, espoused the cause of France. Following months of bloody war, France, apprehensive of a British invasion in full force, and not being able to put down the insurgents, weary and tired of the struggle, conciliated. August, 1793, Universal Freedom was proclaimed—this measure was ratified by the National convention early the following year. This was the first time in the history of the world a legislative assembly ever decreed the abolition of human slavery.

The British, having taken Port-au-Prince and besieged the French Governor at Port-de-la-Paix when the blacks under Toussaint L'Ouverture defeated them and released the French Governor, abandoned the island in 1797. L'Ouverture, who up to forty years of age had been a slave, thus succeeded in ridding the island of the Spaniards and the English. The French government rewarded him by appointing him major-general and governor of the island.

This left L'Ouverture Commander-in-Chief and virtually dictator of the island. He set up a Republic, drew up a Constitution, which he sent to Napoleon. For answer Napoleon appointed Leclerc governor of the colony, and sent a formidable army to reduce the authority of L'Ouverture. War broke out again. After several engagements L'Ouverture surrendered and retired on his properties. He was subsequently decoyed on board a French vessel, kidnapped and deported to Paris. He was then placed by Bonaparte in a damp prison of the fortress of Joux on the chilly heights of Jura where he died. In September, 1802, the peoples of color took up arms against French domination under the leadership of General Dessalines and swore to die rather than remain subservient any longer.[8] By the end of 1793 Rochambeau, who on the death of General Leclerc was put in command by Bonaparte, was hard pressed in the city of Cape Haitien by black troops and was compelled to capitulate and "the power of France was lost on the island forever." On January 1, 1804, Haiti, as it was better known, proclaimed its independence with General Dessalines as ruler. Slavery was abolished forever. In 1822 Haiti, the western colony, controlled the whole of the island; but in 1844 the eastern part seceded and established an independent government known today as the Dominican Republic.

GEORGE W. BROWN

FOOTNOTES:

[1] *Mossell, Toussaint L'Ouverture, p. xiii.*

[2] *Hardy, Negro Question in French Revolution, p. 1.*

[3] Moreau de St. Méry, *Response, etc.,* 72.

[4]   Hardy,   The   Negro   Question   in   the   French Revolution, p. 10.

[5] Condorcet's *Works.*

[6] Bourne, Revolutionary Period in Europe, p. 110.

[7] American Encyclopedia—Haiti.

[8] Mossell, Toussaint L'Ouverture.

CANADIAN NEGROES AND THE REBELLION OF 1837

There are a number of interesting references in the literature of the times to the part played by Negro refugees in defending the frontier of Canada during the troubles of 1838. The outbreaks in both Upper and Lower Canada in 1837 were followed by a series of petty attacks along the border in which American sympathizers participated. Sandwich, on the Detroit River, was one of the objectives of the attacking parties and there were also threats on the Niagara River frontier. One of the parties of "rebels" had taken possession of Navy Island, in the Niagara River, and a small ship, the *Caroline*, was used for conveying supplies. A Canadian party under command of Colonel MacNab crossed the river, seized the ship and after setting it afire allowed it to drift over the falls. This gave rise to an international issue and was the occasion of much bluster on both sides of the line that happily ended as bluster. All along the border on the American side there were "Hunter's Lodges"[1] organized during 1838 and this movement, joined with the widespread political disaffection, made the times unhappy for the Canadian provinces.

Sir Francis Bond Head, who was Governor of Upper Canada when the troubles of 1837 began and whose conduct did not tend materially to quelling the unrest, wrote his "apologia" a couple of years later and in it he speaks of the loyalty of the colored people, almost all of whom were refugees from slavery. He says:

"When our colored population were informed that American citizens, sympathizing with their sufferings, had taken violent possession of Navy Island, for the double object of liberating them from the domination of British rule, and of imparting to them the blessings of republican institutions, based upon the principle that all men are born equal, did our colored brethren hail their approach? No, on the contrary, they hastened as volunteers in wagon-loads to the Niagara frontier to beg from me permission that, in the intended attack upon Navy Island, they might be permitted to form the forlorn hope—in short they supplicated that they might be allowed to be foremost to defend the glorious institutions of Great Britain."[2]

Rev. J. W. Loguen, in the narrative of his life, says that he was urgently solicited by the Canadian government to accept the captaincy of a company of black troops who had been enrolled during the troubles. As the affair was then about all over by the joint effort of the Canadian and United States governments, he did not accept the offer but he makes this interesting comment:

"The colored population of Canada at that time was small compared to what it now is; nevertheless, it was sufficiently large to attract the attention of the government. They were almost to a man fugitives from the States. They could not, therefore, be passive when the success of the invaders would break the only arm interposed for their security, and destroy the only asylum for African freedom in North America. The promptness with which several companies of blacks were organized and equipped, and the desperate valor they displayed in this brief conflict, are an earnest of what may be expected from the swelling thousands of colored fugitives collecting there, in the event of a war between the two countries."[3]

Josiah Henson, founder of the Dawn colony in Upper Canada and famous as the reputed "original" of Mrs. Stowe's Uncle Tom, says in his narrative that he was captain of the second company of Essex colored volunteers and that he and his men assisted in the defence of Fort Malden (Amherstburg) from Christmas 1837 to May of 1838. He says further that he assisted in the capture of the schooner *Anne*, an affair which took place on January 9, 1838.[4]

John MacMullen, in his *History of Canada*, says that among the troops on the border during 1838 "were two hundred Indians from Delaware, and a body of colored men, settlers in the western part of the province, the poor hunted fugitives from American slavery, who had at length found liberty and security under the British flag."[5]

A rather interesting aftermath of the rebellion is contained in an item appearing in the *Amherstburg Courier* of March 10, 1849, reporting a meeting of Negroes in Sandwich township to protest against the Rebellion Losses Bill.[6] Colonel Prince was thanked for his opposition to the measure.[7]

Eighty years after the rebellion the Negro men of Canada

were again called upon to fight, this time in another land and in a conflict that was destined to affect every race and every land. The service that was rendered in the Canadian army by the colored companies of pioneers will some day receive due recognition at the hands of an historian. In the meantime, it is not forgotten by the people of Canada.

FRED LANDON

THE PUBLIC LIBRARY,
  LONDON, ONTARIO

FOOTNOTES:

[1] A convention of Hunter's Lodges of Ohio and Michigan, held at Cleveland, September 16–22, 1838, was attended by seventy delegates.

[2] Head, Sir, F. B., *A Narrative* (London, 1839), page 392.

[3] *Loguen, J. W., The Rev. J. W. Loguen as a Slave and as a Freeman (Syracuse, 1859), pp. 343–345.*

[4] *An autobiography of the Rev. Josiah Henson, "Uncle Tom," from 1789 to 1881* (London, Ont., 1881), page 177. A sketch of Josiah Henson appeared in THE JOURNAL OF NEGRO HISTORY for January, 1918 (Vol. III, no. 1, pp. 1–21). This is condensed from his autobiography which appeared in several editions.

[5] MacMullen, John, *History of Canada from its first Discovery to the Present Times* (Brockville, Ont., 1868),

pp. 459-460. He gives as his authority Radclift's despatch, "10th January, 1838."

[6] The Rebellion Losses Bill proposed compensation for those who had sustained losses in Lower Canada (Quebec) during the troubles of 1837. It was fiercely opposed in Upper Canada (Ontario) by the element that regarded the French as "aliens" and "rebels." When Lord Elgin, the Governor, gave his assent to the bill in 1849 there were riots in Montreal in which the Parliament Buildings were burned.

[7] Col. Prince was one of the leaders in the defense of the Canadian frontier along the Detroit River during 1838, afterwards a member of the Canadian Parliament. During the troubles of 1838 he ordered the shooting of four prisoners without the form of a trial. The act was condemned by Lord Brougham and others with great severity and is one dark spot on the records of the Canadian forces during the trying period.

LOTT CARY,[1] THE COLONIZING MISSIONARY

With Lott Cary and Colin Teague[2] sailing for Africa in 1821, a new era of missionary expansion was begun by Negro Baptists. The distinctive feature of this epoch, which may be termed modern, is the fact that behind these men was the Richmond African Baptist Missionary Society, which gave them support, such as it was, and to which periodic reports were made. True enough, Lott Cary was under appointment of the General Missionary Convention of the Baptist Denomination in the United States of America but only that fact and the sum of $200 in cash and $100 in books appropriated for his use up to 1826[3] could not be sufficient evidence to claim him wholly as a missionary of the General Missionary Convention although he did receive some advisory instructions from its board. [4] Indeed, Lott Cary was the first American Baptist missionary in Africa, the first representative of a purely Negro missionary organization to labor beyond the limits of the United States.

PREPARATION FOR AFRICA

Lott Cary was born on the estate of William A. Christian,[5] in Charles City County, Virginia,[6] thirty miles from Richmond,[7] about four years after the signing of the Declaration of Independence. There was no exact record kept of the time of his birth, although it appears to have been about the year 1780.[8]

His mother and father lived together on the great plantation of their master, centering their attention on Lott, their only child. His mother gave no public profession of religion although she died giving evidence that she accepted the Christian faith. His father, however, was a pious man, a respected member of a Baptist church.[9] As a result, Lott received some early religious training which may have influenced his later life.

But there were temptings in his life; there were battles in his soul. Why should a slave boy hope? Could he ever become free? Why not drink life to the dregs? The chief among his playmates, he became the mischief-maker of the place. Profligate, profane, polluter was his title. Lott Cary tried to reform but he was only able to control himself a few days. Before long, in 1804,[10] he was hired out by the year as a common laborer[11] in the Shochoe tobacco warehouse at Richmond.[12] There he grew more intemperate and profane and showed little signs of reformation.

It was not reformation that he needed but regeneration as was evidenced one Lord's day in 1807[13] as he sat in the gallery of the First Baptist Church[14] and heard the minister preach. He was hopefully converted and was baptized by Pastor John Courtney[15] into the fellowship of the church. There he heard a sermon on the third chapter of the gospel of John which so inspired him that he obtained a Testament in order that he might read for himself the Lord's interview with Nicodemus. In a short time he knew the alphabet, and with very little assistance from the men at the warehouse,[16] he learned to read this chapter and also to write.[17]

Cary was a changed man—industrious, thrifty, Christian. Whereas he had been idle now he devoted his leisure time to reading and it is said that one of the books that he read was Adam Smith's *Wealth of Nations*.[18] By his application to reading and writing he was able in a little time to make dray tickets and to act as shipping clerk.[19] His work in the warehouse was "such as no person, white or black, has equalled in the same situation.... He could produce any one of the hundreds of hogsheads of tobacco the instant it was called for."[20] For these services he was often given a five dollar note and the privilege to sell small quantities of waste tobacco for his own benefit.[21] He saved the money obtained in this way, and with the aid of a subscription among his employers accumulated by 1813 $850 with which he purchased freedom for himself and his two children.[22]

The following extract of a letter from William Crane to the Rev. Obadiah Brown of Washington City, which he forwarded to the corresponding secretary of the Baptist Board of Foreign Missions, corroborates, in the main, the foregoing statements as well as gives some interesting sidelights on the lives of Cary and Teague:

RICHMOND, MARCH 28, 1819.

You will probably recollect, that I introduced you to two of our colored brethren in this place, who are accustomed to speak in public; one named Collin Teague, the other Lot Carey. Ever since the missionary subject has been so much agitated in this country, these two brethren, associated with many others, have been wishing they could, in some way, aid their unhappy kindred in Africa; and I suppose you have heard of their having formed a missionary society for this sole purpose. Some letters published in No. VI of the *Luminary* (written by Kizell, the Baptist leader in Sherbro Island and by some others) have served to awaken them effectually. They are now determined to go themselves to Africa; and the only questions with them are, in what way will it be best for them to proceed? and what previous steps are requisite to be taken? They think it necessary to spend some time in study first. They both possess industry and abilities, such as, with the blessing of Providence, would soon make them rich. It is but two or three years since either of them enjoyed freedom; and both have paid large sums for their families. They now possess but little, except a zealous wish to go and do what they can. Brother Lot has a wife, and several little children. He has a place a little below Richmond, that cost him $1500, but will probably not sell for more than $1000 at this time. Brother Collin has a wife, a son 14 years of age, and a daughter of 11, for whom he has paid $1300, and has scarcely any thing left. Both their wives are Baptists; their children, amiable and docile, have been to school considerably; and I hope, if they go, will likewise be of service. Collin is a saddler and harness maker. He had no early education. The little that he has gained, has been by chance and peacemeal. He has judgment, and as much keenness of penetration as almost any man. He can read, though he is not a good reader, and can write so as to make out a letter. The little knowledge he has of figures, has been gained by common calculations in business. Lot was brought up on a farm; and for a number of years has been chief manager among the labourers in the largest tobacco ware house in this city. He has charge of receiving, marking and shipping tobacco; and the circumstance that he receives $700 a-year wages may help you to form an estimate of the man. He reads better than Collin, and is in every respect a better scholar. They have been trying to preach about ten or eleven years, and are both about forty years of age.[23]

Cary had been licensed to preach by the First Baptist

Church, Richmond, and he exercised his talent every Lord's day among the colored people on plantations a few miles from Richmond.[24] It was not many months before he was the highly esteemed pastor of the African Baptist Church in Richmond. As a preacher, Cary was not polished, but "his ideas would sometimes burst upon you in their native solemnity, and awaken deeper feelings than the most polished, but less original" and artificial discourses.[25]

Lott Cary early exhibited the power of an organizer. In 1815, William Crane, who was a member of the First Baptist Church, felt that his ought to use his talent among the twelve hundred Negro members of that congregation. Consequently, he and David Roper[26] gratuitously opened a tri-weekly night school in the gallery of the old church with Lott Cary, Colin Teague and fifteen or twenty leading members of the church as pupils.[27] Now Crane was able to inspire such a group to practical missionary service, for he himself had been repeatedly urged to become a missionary and had had close contact with Luther Rice as one of the managers of the General Missionary Convention. But it was left to Lott Cary to excite among the Negroes a strong interest in behalf of Africa. The result was the formation of the Richmond African Baptist Missionary Society in 1815. Crane was the president or corresponding secretary. [28] This was necessary, for since the various uprisings of Negroes[29] were making Virginia a hotbed of discontent, the city of Richmond was wary of having Negro meetings unless they were sponsored by white persons. Crane represented the Society in the General

Missionary Convention,[30] formed in 1814, and remained its delegate for about twenty years.

At the first triennial session of the Convention at Philadelphia, in May, 1817, a letter was read from the corresponding secretary of the Richmond African Baptist Missionary Society and it was unanimously

Resolved, that the said letter be noticed on the minutes of the Convention, and that the Board, if they find it practicable, be advised to institute an African Mission, conformably to the wishes of the said African Mission Society; and that the Corresponding Secretary of the Board be requested to communicate this resolution together with an encouraging affectionate letter to that society.[31]

Feeling of sympathy for the African was high. Many slave-holding Baptists felt that they owed the Negro a debt which they should pay.[32] Moreover, the board of the Convention felt that the interest in Foreign missions manifested by the Negro Baptists of Richmond was a providential plan whereby the slaves brought from Africa might be converted and returned to evangelize that continent.[33] Since, therefore, mission work could be propagated in Africa in the English language and for one quarter the expense required for other lands,[34] the Convention felt no hesitancy in acknowledging the claims of Africa.

Luther Rice, while in Richmond during the winter of 1817, visited the African Missionary Society. "It afforded me much pleasure, indeed," he reported,[35]

"to observe the zeal, and intelligence and capacity, and success, discovered in the African Mission Society."

As a matter of fact, the formation of the Richmond African Baptist Society was an epochal event. The example was followed by the African Baptist Church of Philadelphia[36] and by the Baptists of Petersburg, Virginia.[37] The African mission spirit even permeated North Carolina and Georgia, for during the years 1816 and 1817 the Negro Baptists of those parts contributed $32.64 to the cause.[38] This contribution far outstripped the donation of the white Baptists to the same cause. During the same time they contributed only $14.27, $12.27 of which was given by the newly formed African Mite Society of Providence, Rhode Island.[39]

Lott Cary resolved that it was his duty to go and preach the gospel in benighted Africa. It was at Crane's night school that this intention was made known. After Crane had reviewed the report of Burgess and Mills, telling of their exploring tour on the coast of Africa, Lott Cary said: "I have been determined for a long time to go to Africa and at least to see the country for myself."[40] There is no doubt that to some extent Gary was awakened to a deep sense of responsibility for his brethren in Africa by that part of this report which dealt with John Kizell, the Baptist leader in Sherbro Island, the president of the Friendly Society established by Paul Cuffee, the escort and guide of Burgess and Mills on their exploring tour, the man directly responsible for the beginning of the impractical scheme of deportation on the continent of Africa by the American Colonization Society.[41]

But how was he to accomplish his object? Crane said,[42] "I had thought of addressing the Corresponding Secretary on their (Cary and Teague) behalf, for the patronage of the American Baptist Mission Society, but again thought, that the Colonization Society might be pleased with taking them under their care, and that their mission might bear a more imposing aspect under the auspices of this society than it would with the Baptists alone." Lott Cary was received by the Baptist Board of Foreign Missions, May 1, 1819, and was accepted by the American Colonization Society to work for them "without pay as other engagements would permit."[43]

The treasurer of the General Missionary Convention reported $2 for Africa received September 21, 1819, from a friend in Nashville Tennessee. The next year the society appropriated $200 in cash and $100 in books. Contrasted with this was the $483.25 paid April 17, 1820, by the Richmond African Baptist Missionary Society to the General Missionary Convention to be appropriated for Africa.[44] Thus the Convention served only as a clearing house for the funds contributed from Richmond. With this in mind we can more clearly understand the following order voted by the Baptist Board of Foreign Missions in 1820:

With African Mission Society, Richmond,
 To various exp. for Collin Teague and Lot Carey ... 500 25.[45]

Furthermore, the historian of the Convention up to the year 1840[46] relates that the Richmond African

Baptist Missionary Society, of which Lott Cary was the recording secretary, appropriated to the cause of African redemption $700, all of its funds collected during the first five years of its existence. For many years thereafter the Society collected and contributed annually from $100 to $150 to the mission in Africa.[47]

Lott Cary was giving up much to be an apostle to his people—a pastorate of nearly eight hundred members, a farm and house costing $1,500 and a salary increase of $200 a year if he would stay.[48] But he must go. There were promptings big and great. Cary and Colin Teague are said to have wished to be where their color would be no disparagement to their usefulness.[49] "I am an African," he is reported to have answered an intelligent minister who asked him why he was leaving,[50] "and, in this country, however meritorious my conduct, and respectable my character, I cannot receive the credit due to either. I wish to go to a country where I shall be estimated by my merits, not by my complexion; and I feel bound to labor for my suffering race."

It is highly probable that Cary possessed no such race consciousness as is portrayed in the foregoing reports of Crane and Gurley. True enough, the occasion for such sentiment was there in the institution of slavery but had Cary imbibed the spirit? On the one hand, the free Negro was not wanted in Virginia as is evidenced by an act which made unlawful the permanent residence in the State of any slave set free after May 1, 1806. But, on the other hand, this act was not generally enforced because of the economic value of many of the freedmen. [51] Thus it is doubtful whether Cary, whose salary would be increased if he remained in Virginia, and Teague, both effectual workmen whose industry was needed, would have to go away to gain a higher status.

Let us examine the facts further. Crane was certainly enthusiastic for African colonization and Gurley was the secretary of the American Colonization Society. Thus these statements, as well as similar ones which follow, seem like attempts on the part of the friends of colonization to make Cary say to the other free Negroes that colonization was a desirable thing. Certainly such an attitude would be a timely rebuttal of the anti-colonization sentiment of the Negro ministry in general.

Furthermore, this reason for going to Africa was not in accord with the one given at Crane's night school. Then he wanted to see Africa for himself; now he finds America no place for the Negro. He could have changed his point of view, but did he? If he did change his view, he had changed again in less than two years (March 13, 1821) when he wrote as follows to the corresponding secretary of the Board of Foreign Missions:

If you intend doing anything for Africa you must not wait for the Colonization Society, nor for government, for neither of these are in search of missionary grounds, but of colonizing grounds; if it should not suit missionary needs, you cannot expect to gather in a missionary crop. And, moreover, all of us who are connected with the agents, who are under public instructions, must be conformed to their laws, whether they militate against missionary operation or not.[52]

Thus if Cary made statements which favor colonization

he was very inconsistent, for it was he who was chiefly responsible for the colonists openly defying the Colonization Society in 1824. Nor could Cary write so well. It is most likely, therefore, that Lott Cary wanted to go to Africa simply to see the country and to do missionary work.

Prior to his public farewell, Lott Cary and Colin Teague were ordained and they, with their wives, Joseph Langford and wife and Hilary Teague, were organized in January, 1821, into a church. Lott Cary was elected pastor. The constitution of this body which they were to plant in Africa was modelled after the Samson Street Church of Philadelphia.[53]

Cary's farewell sermon, preached in the meeting house of the First Baptist Church, Richmond, was well ordered, without the rant common to some preachers of that day, dignified and pathetic, and left a lasting impression on the audience.[54] Teague had often remarked to William Crane, "Sir, I don't hear any of your white ministers that can preach like Lott Cary." Crane was anxious to hear him and after listening to his farewell message from Romans 8:32—"He that spared not his own Son, but delivered Him up for us all, how shall He not with Him also freely give us all things?"— he did not hesitate to declare: "I have a most vivid recollection of the manner in which, towards the close, he dwelt upon the word 'freely.' With thrilling emphasis he exclaimed over and over, 'He gave them freely!' He rang a succession of perhaps a dozen changes upon the word, in a manner that would not have dishonored Whitfield."[55]

Lott Gary closed his sermon with this thought:

I am about to leave you and expect to see your faces no more. I long to preach to the poor Africans the way of life and salvation. I don't know what may befall me, whether I may find a grave in the ocean, or among the savage men, or more savage wild beasts on the Coast of Africa; nor am I anxious what may become of me. I feel it my duty to go; and I very much fear that many of those who preach the Gospel in this country, will blush when the Saviour calls them to give an account of their labors in His cause and tell them, "I commanded you to go into all the world, and preach the Gospel to every creature;" (very emphatically he exclaimed) the Saviour may ask where have you been? What have you been doing? Have you endeavored to the utmost of your ability to fulfill the commands I gave you, or have you sought your own gratification, and your own ease, regardless of My commands?[56]

A distinguished Presbyterian minister said to Gurley, "A sermon which I heard from Lott Gary, shortly before he sailed for Africa, was the best extemporaneous sermon I ever heard. It contained more original and impressive thoughts, some of which are distinct in my memory, and never can be forgotten."[57] Elder John Bryce, assistant pastor of the First Baptist Church, afterwards confessed that he had never been so deeply interested in a sermon.[58]

READJUSTMENT ON AFRICAN SOIL

By the twenty-third of January, 1821, Gary and his church were ready to sail.[59] At half past six in the morning[60] the *Nautilus*, carrying 28 colonists and a number of children, left Norfolk, Virginia, en route to Sierra Leone.[61]

As the agents of the American Colonization Society, who made the journey, had not completed their negotiations for the purchase of a site for the settlers, the party remained at Freetown, Sierra Leone, for some months. [62] From there Cary wrote the Corresponding Secretary of the Baptist Board of Foreign Missions, March 13th:

Rev. and Dear Sir

I am happy that an opportunity is now afforded me, to inform the Board through you, the only proper medium of communication with them, that we all arrived safe in Africa. We had a long passage of forty four days, yet we were wonderfully preserved by the great Ruler of the winds and the seas....

I am truly sorry, that the hopes and expectations of the Board cannot be realized, as to our missionary labours; for, as it pleased you to have us connected with the Colonization Society, and the agents of the Society upon their arrival here, finding their prospects of getting lands very gloomy, so much so that they disowned us as colonists; and the government's agent had captured Africans for whom he was bound, by the laws of the United States, to procure a place, in order to settle them, or until there can be a more permanent settlement obtained, the agent received us as labourers and mechanics, to be settled with them in order to make preparations for the reception of others; we are therefore bound to the government's agent. He has rented a farm, and put us on it, and we must cultivate it for our support, and for the support of these Africans; and pay as much of the rent as we can. And as this obligation will last until lands are purchased by the agents of the Colonization Society, I am greatly afraid it will not end soon; and until it does end, our mission labours will be very few. Jesus Christ, our Saviour, when he came on his mission into this world, was found often with a broad axe in his hand: and I believe that a good many corn field missionaries would be a great blessing to this country, that is if they were not confined to the field by law and by necessity. We are bound by both. I converse very freely with you on this subject, because with me it is a very important one, and because of the interest which the Board has taken in this mission.[63]

Mrs. Cary, "a sensible woman and an exemplary Christian,"[64] was sick at this time and soon died, leaving her husband the care of their two children. [65] Despite this and the appalling circumstances of the first settlers, they wrote to the Board rejoicing that they were in the country of their forefathers and hoping that His gracious approbation would crown their labors.[66] Lott Cary kept constantly in mind the great object of his mission. He not only preached as often as opportunity would permit but he established a mission among the Mandingoes.[67]

Nevertheless, there was danger for some time that the whole enterprise would be abandoned. Whereupon, Captain Robert F. Stockton was sent to Africa in the armed schooner *Alligator* with full powers from President Monroe and the American Colonization Society to make arrangements for a new and permanent settlement.[68] On December 11, he and Doctor Eli Ayres, the Society's agent, who had left America in July, anchored off Cape Mesurado or Montserado and, with John Mills, an English mulatto and slave dealer, as interpreter, made negotiations with King Peter, the principal chief around the Cape, for the purchase of a settlement. After much parleying and delay on the part of the king and treachery on the part of Mills,[69] they finally exchanged gunpowder, tobacco, rum, iron pots, beads, looking glasses, "four Hats, three Coats, three pair Shoes"[70] and other minor articles not worth more than $300 for that valuable tract of land[71] which was the nucleus of what is now the Republic of Liberia.[72]

Arrangements were made for the colonists to take possession of their new home the 7th of February, 1822.[73] The territory, finally including ninety miles of coast lying between the Junk and Sesters Rivers and extending nearly seventy miles into the interior, presented, on the one hand, an excellent opportunity to work among the Bassa, Vey, Dey and Kroo tribes,[74] who numbered about 125,000, and exhibited, on the other hand, many obstacles, for the natives were hostile, and the rainy season was approaching, at the time when provisions were scarce.

The condition of the colonists was so appalling that many proposed to return to Sierra Leone. Just a few more hours and the Cape would have been abandoned, but when the Agent went ashore to prepare for departure he was informed by Lott Gary that he was determined not to go. Nearly all the colonists were induced to follow his example.

In the event they suffered severely; nearly 1,000 natives attacked them in November, 1822, but were repulsed. During this and similar encounters with the natives, which lasted through the months of November and December, Lott Cary cooperated wisely with the Agent, Jehudi Ashmun,[75] and, although several of the colonists were killed and wounded, with only 37 men and boys he, on one occasion, drove back with considerable loss 1,500 wild and exasperated natives who were bent on extirpating the settlement. Lott Cary compared the little company of disturbed settlers to the Jews, who "grasped a weapon in one hand, while they labored with the other" to rebuild the city. But he is said to have asserted: "There never has been an hour or a minute, no, not even when the balls were flying around my head, when I could wish myself again in America."[76]

These colonists planted their church at Monrovia and soon had under way the nucleus of a flourishing Sunday-school.[77] Cary extended his labors to communities far and near, and by 1823 had 6 converts. [78] The following resolution adopted by the General Missionary Convention speaks for itself the sentiment of that body respecting the work of Cary and Teague up to May 7, 1823:[79]

The committee states that the present condition and prospects of the mission are encouraging. Brethren Cary and Teague are at present much occupied in aiding in the establishment of the colony at Cape Mesurado. Their conduct has been good and that of the former, in particular, has been specially commended by the Agent of the Colonization Society. The committee recommends that an able white missionary be stationed, as soon as practicable, at Cape Mesurado. The mission has a double effect. While it tends to introduce the gospel into Africa, a mission establishment on the coast will essentially aid in the suppression of the slave trade.

In spite of the fact that his associate, Colin Teague, had returned to Freetown, Sierra Leone,[80] Lott Cary was adding some few of the natives to the church. In 1824, he baptized 9. One by the name of John from Grand Cape Mount, a town about eighty miles distant, proved a valuable helper by the good influence which he exerted. Some word from Hector Peters[81] had touched him and he came to the American settlement for instruction and baptism. Without being asked, he related his experience to the church.

"When me bin Sa' lone," he began, "me see all man go to church house—me go too—me be very bad man too—suppose a man can cus (curse) me—me can cus im too—suppose a man can fight me—me can fight im too.—Well, me go to church house—the man speak, and one word catch my heart (and at the same time laying his hand on his breast)—I go to my home—my heart be very heavy—and trouble me too—night time come—me fear me can't go to my bed for sleep—my heart trouble me so—something tell me go pray to God—me fall down to pray—no—my heart be too bad—I can't pray—I think so—I go die now—suppose I die—I go to hell—me be very bad man—pass all turrer (other) man—God be angry with me—soon I die—suppose man cus me this time—me can't cus him no more—suppose man fight me—me can't fight him no more—all the time my heart trouble me—all day— all night me can't sleep—by and by my heart grow too big—me fall down this time—now me can pray—me say Lord—have massey. Then light come in my heart— make me glad—make me light—make me love the Son of God—make me love everybody."

John was baptized the 20th of March, 1825. The church neatly dressed him, gave him an extra suit, about $10.50, 3 Bibles and 2 hymn books and sent him on his way rejoicing.[82]

The impetus received by the church was amazing. The membership by 1825 had increased to 60 or 70 and two or three pious emigrants were assisting in the work. This same year, Lott Cary directed the building of a substantial meeting house which would have been completed immediately if nails and boards could have been procured.[83] In a letter from Monrovia,[84] dated April 24, 1826, he wrote a brother in Norfolk: "We dedicated our meeting house last October; it was four weeks from the time we raised it to the time it was dedicated. It is quite a comfortable house, 30 × 20 feet, and ceiled inside nearly up to the plates, with a decent pulpit and seats. I feel very grateful to you for your services, and to the brethren and friends for their liberal contribution."[85]

This progress of the church might, at first blush, seem to say that everything was in a state of tranquility and peace. This is far from being the case. In the face of the record of Lott Cary as a Christian, a pastor, a representative of the Richmond African Baptist Missionary Society and a church builder in Africa, it is interesting to note the invective hurled against him by Governor Ashmun in 1823. The Governor's phraseology is unique. "Wretched," "morose," "obstinate," "soured," "narrow," "disobliging," "moral desert," "a corroding temper," and "destitute of natural affection," were some of the epithets used as over against "more obliging," "affectionate husband," "display of tenderness," "sweet and profound humility," "promoter of every commendable and pious design," "every laudable habit," "moral renovation," "habit of holiness," and "redeemed" when an understanding was perfected in 1824.[86]

The cause of the misunderstanding was of long standing. Agents of the American Colonization Society prior to Ashmun's time were accused of transmitting false reports to the board and of appropriating to their own use the provisions and supplies of the colonists. [87] It is also known that a commercial company of Baltimore, whose business it was to prosecute the African slave trade, was jealous of the Society and tried to undermine it. In addition, the trials and hardships incidental to founding the colony had reduced many of the settlers to want.[88] The most ignorant could thus fathom their condition: "We suffer: if the Society have means and does not apply them to our relief, it is without benevolence; if it have not means, it wants power and in either case is unworthy of our confidence."[89]

This lack of power showed itself in the helplessness of the government to restrain the first vestiges of insubordination and to enforce the law. Thereupon, the discontentment of Cary and one or two others became widespread.[90] Probably the manhood consciousness of Cary would not have asserted itself so soon had not the occasion arisen between August 31 and September 25, 1823, when the principal Agent attempted to redistribute the town lots of the earliest colonists who alleged that they held them under a former sanction of the Agent and so refused to have them redistributed. They resolved to appeal to the board of the American Colonization Society.[91] Moreover, they openly avowed that they would neither survey nor cultivate any of the lots (thickly covered with undergrowth) assigned to them nor aid in any public improvements[92] until they should hear from the board. On the 13th of December, Ashmun published the announcement that there were in the Colony more than a dozen healthy persons who would not receive any more provisions out of the public store till they earned them. Six days later the Agent ordered the rations of the offending persons to be stopped. Next morning a few[93] of the colonists assembled at the Agency House and vociferously demanded the Agent to rescind his order.

Ashmun was immovable. The colonists straightway hastened to the storehouse where rations for the week were then being issued and each seized a store of provisions and went home.[94] Lott Cary had no small influence and share in this seditious proceeding.[95] Toward evening, the Agent addressed a circular "to all the colonists" declaring that the impropriety of the morning's act would be communicated to the board. He further exhorted all to go to work and not to commit such an offence again for their sakes in this world or in the one to come. Lott Cary was not to perform any of his ministerial functions "till time and circumstances shall have evidenced the deepness and sincerity of his repentance."[96] Gurley states that the leaders of the sedition, led by Lott Cary, almost "immediately confessed and deplored" their error.[97]

It seemed in 1824 that the affair of the previous year would be repeated when, on March 17, the rations were reduced one half. The act was viewed by the colonists as oppression and they openly reproached Ashmun. Through all of this period, the spirit of disorganization was working so that the colonists furnished little support towards developing the government.[98]

In communicating the account of the disturbances to the board, Ashmun wrote, March 15, that "the services rendered by Lott Cary in the Colony, who has with very few (and those recent exceptions), done honor to the selection of the Baptist Missionary Society, under whose auspices he was sent out to Africa, entitle his agency in this affair, to the most indulgent construction which it will bear. The hand which records the lawless transaction, would long since have been cold in the grave, had it not been for the unwearied and painful attentions of this individual rendered at all hours—of every description—and continued several months."[99]

The General Missionary Convention was influenced very little, if any, by the report, if, indeed, they had received it officially. At the annual meeting of the Board of Managers, April, 1824, the committee on the African mission had "no hesitation in recommending a careful regard to this mission, which though it may seem to slumber for a moment, in their opinion promises great and extensive usefulness." The board recommended

That a constant correspondence be kept up with the brethren there by which their minds will be encouraged, and their hands strengthened and through which information may be received of the state of the Colony, the progress of the cause, and of the earliest opportunities which may offer for introducing the Gospel more extensively into the heart of Africa.[100]

There is no further account of this misunderstanding other than that from the pen of Ashmun. Mr. Taylor,[101] the biographer of Lott Cary, remarks: "He (Cary) was compelled, to some extent, to act the part of a mediator between the rebellious colonists, who considered themselves injured, and Mr. Ashmun, the Governor. While for a moment he might seem to act injudiciously, he possessed too much noble and generous feeling to be guilty of a dishonorable act." The Rev. G. Winfred Hervey[102] thinks that "in any controversy between mules and muledrivers, the latter have several advantages among which one of the most important is that they have the exclusive use of vocal attack and defence. Cary was too prudent a man to publish an apology for constructive sedition; and as he has not left us his own explanation of any of the facts in the case, we have not all the materials on which to base an impartial judgment."

The agitation at length had its effect. It was directly responsible for the establishment, in 1824, of a new form of government which was approved by Cary and his fellow-citizens and in which the colonists had a full expression.[103] Gurley[104] and Ashmun both testified that Cary readily entered into the spirit of the new government.[105] Only eight days, from August 14 to 22, were needed to organize a government that should be energetic and feasible.[106] "Beneath the thatched roof of the first rude house for divine worship ever erected in the Colony stood the little company of one hundred colored emigrants, who had ventured all things to gain for themselves and children a home and inheritance of liberty and before God pledged themselves to maintain the Constitution of their choice, and prove faithful to the great trust committed to their hands."[107] Despite the seeming repetition of the chagrin of past irregularities in September, 1824, however, the board of the American Colonization Society passed a motion, April 2, 1825, to organize, on the 18th of the next month, a permanent government for the colony.[108]

USEFULNESS OF THE MAN

During these times Lott Cary continued to increase his popularity by performing the pastoral duties of the Providence Baptist Church as vigorously as he could. [109] He preached several times each week, and, in addition, gave religious instruction to many of the native children. A day school of twenty-one pupils was begun April 18, 1825.[110] By June, the number had increased to thirty-two, nineteen of whom came from Grand Cape Mount, some miles distant.[111] Cary was handicapped in this work by the lack of funds, by the demoralizing gin traffic of the Europeans, by Mohammedanism, by the deadly climate and by degraded fetichism,[112] yet, in the course of seven weeks, he taught several children to read the Bible intelligently, although he could not devote more than three hours a day to this work.[113]

In the meantime, in keeping with the report of the Board of Managers of the General Missionary Convention in 1823, Governor Ashmun wrote to the American Colonization Society, March 20, 1825, that "the natives have universally a most affecting persuasion of the superiority of white men.... I cannot hesitate to say that the missionary, or principal of the proposed establishment (*i.e.*, a religious mission for Africa), ought by preference to be a white man."[114] The little colony of near 400 souls was suffering for an adequate educational program. Excepting Governor Ashmun, there was not an individual there who had ever received a plain English education.[115] Allowing that and granting that there were few intelligent Negroes in the United States,[116] Ashmun would have appeared more hopeful of Negro leadership had he made his request to the board more general.

Whether because of this appeal or not, it is singular to note that the Rev. Calvin Holton, a graduate of Waterville College (now Colby College), offered his service to the board the same year and, with 34 emigrants,[117] sailed from Boston in the brig *Vine*, January 4, 1826. He was employed to establish and direct a Lancastrian system of education for (1) the children of the colonists, (2) for the native children living in the settlement, (3) for the recaptured Africans who numbered about 120, and (4) for the young men and women who were teaching or preparing themselves for this profession.[118] His work was not of long duration for on the 2d of July, 1826, he died[119] and was succeeded early in 1827 by the Rev. G. M'Gill, "an intelligent and experienced coloured Teacher from Baltimore."[120]

About this time the number of native boys who received instruction was only 50. These were trained either to be interpreters to American and European missionaries or religious teachers. Lott Cary had 45 scholars enrolled in his school at Monrovia.[121] He was assisted by a lad of fourteen years and by the Rev. John N. Lewis, another missionary sent out by the Richmond African Baptist Missionary Society, but who, from lack of adequate support, turned to other business.[122]

Lott Cary had a large task to perform with this school. As a matter of fact, "the hopes of the African tribes," said Ashmun,[123] "from Gallinas to Trade Town, are at present suspended upon it. Most of the boys who attend it are sons of the principal individuals of the country, and more than half can read the New Testament intelligently, and understand the English language nearly as well as the settlers of the same age." The expense of a native boy was estimated at $25 and of a girl at $20.[124]

Gurley believed that the schools were numerous enough and amply able to afford instruction to every child in the colony. Although this instruction was compulsory, it is not altogether evident, however, that at any place save Monrovia a real educational program was begun. Ashmun related that about six out of every ten emigrants were illiterate and that just one pious individual assisted by two or three utterly illiterate exhorters was the only instructor around the settlement. "Not one in five of these people habitually attend, even on Sundays, such religious instruction as they possess." Consequently, he adds that the moral power exerted was not sufficient to offset "the demoralizing influence of corrupt examples."[125]

The Richmond African Baptist Missionary Society and Lott Cary, however, were expending their funds liberally on the schools. The surplus funds in the colonial treasury plus the subscription of $1,400 from the colonists (including $300 subscribed by Ashmun) were spent for education.[126] Yet from all sources enough money could not be raised to continue all the schools begun. Cary, in 1827, removed the day school from Monrovia to Grand Cape Mount. He made appeal after appeal to send the light to Africa. To prove that the natives would sooner steal the light than miss it he gives the following incident that occurred in removing the school establishment to Grand Cape Mount:

"I had upwards of forty natives," he said,[127] "to carry our baggage, and they carried something like 250 bars ($187.50); a part of them went on four days beforehand, and had every opportunity to commit depredations, but of all the goods that were sent and carried there, nothing was lost except fifteen spelling books; five of them were recovered again."

Mr. Cary's letter to Mr. Crane will explain somewhat the circumstances of the school at Grand Cape Mount.

JUNE 11, 1827.

On yesterday week, being our monthly meeting, I baptized one young man, and after preaching in the afternoon, we had the happiness to break bread together in the house of the Lord. I don't like to be too sanguine, but I think he will be a blessing to the church; his name is John Reavy (Revey)—came out in the first expedition, and has been engaged in teaching a native school on the Sherbro, with Nathaniel Brander, until the last two years, which he has spent at Sierra Leone.

For I fear I may not have another opportunity to write you again soon, I must again call your attention to the immediate establishment of a school at Cape Mount. Since writing the fore part of this letter, I have received an order for books from Cape Mount, which I have sent. I requested, at the same time, the native Brother,

John,[128] to come down immediately, and I would try and arrange business so as to send up a teacher with him; and on proposing the subject to Brother John Reavy, he is quite willing to go up to commence the school as soon as the Brother comes down. I expect to allow him $10.00 per month and find him. My means at present will not justify these engagements, but I know you will do what you can when there is an opportunity; if you cannot send out tobacco or other articles, send out the money. United States bank notes pass as well here as they do with you. I shall try to keep the wheels going until you can send out supplies. I want some writing paper and ink powder or ink, and wish the Society (Richmond) would send me a bbl. of single nails. You will please make my respects to all the brethren and friends, and accept the same for yourself and the Board.

Lott   Cary.[129]

After many months of delay[130] the school was established November 10, 1827, at Big Town, Grand Cape Mount. John Revey was in charge. "The school room," says Cary,[131] "is nearly fifteen feet by thirty. We made arrangements to have worship in it on the ensuing Lord's day, and I had the honour to address a very attentive audience twice, through brother John. After service I informed the congregation that I should need their assistance the following day in preparing seats, &c., and they turned out like men, and performed more labour by eight o'clock, than I expected to have accomplished in the whole day. We got seats prepared for about 60 children by 4 o'clock, and gave notice that as the school would be organized on the day following, at 9 o'clock, A.M., all persons wishing to have their children instructed were requested to come at that time and have them entered, and the number received was 37. I read and explained a short set of regulations which I had drawn up; and as I had the king and his head men present, I got them to sign the articles of agreement in the presence of the whole congregation. For twelve months I think the school will, of course, be expensive. The present arrangement is—I agree to allow brother Revey $20 per month, and find him provisions, washing, &c."

Mr. Cary thought that by this arrangement the station at Grand Cape Mount would net better results than the one at Monrovia. Neither he nor the Richmond African Baptist Missionary Society were able to maintain both. Some funds were received[132] but it developed in about a year that the school had to be given up for lack of funds and assistants.[133]

Other duties, moreover, required some time. Lott Cary realized from the beginning of the colony that a missionary in Africa ought to be more than a corrector of moral ills and a "doctor" of divinity; he would be fortunate indeed if he could mend human bodies. As a result, Cary was constrained to forego much of the joy which he had anticipated from efforts to show men the living Christ by accepting the position of Health Officer of the colony, August 31, 1822.[134] He had no medical schooling but with the use of home remedies, patent medicines,[135] and common sense, he was able to cure some. Until the 31st of August, 1823, he was practically the only physician in the settlement (excepting Dr. Ayres who was present a part of the year 1822). After that Dr. Ayres returned on the *Oswego* in the late spring of 1825.[136] He and sixty emigrants who came with him were soon suffering from the disease of the country and had to rely on the medical experience of Cary. Eight emigrants died[137] and by December, Dr. Ayres was compelled to leave the colony. The climate was so unhealthy that hardly any one escaped its pestilence.[138] When, in addition, the poor housing conditions, the inadequate sanitation and the scanty hospital supplies[139] are considered, it is remarkable that so many escaped death.

Every ship[140] that brought emigrants meant more work for Cary. On February 13, 1824,[141] one hundred and five emigrants arrived in the ship *Cyrus* and in less than a month every one was prostrate with the fever.[142] "Astonishing," said Ashmun,[143] "that in this atmosphere should exist causes so universal in their operation, as amongst all the varieties of age, sex and habit, not to leave one in the whole number without disease, and that in less than four weeks; and stranger still, that the blast should be so tempered to the strength of the constitution of every individual, as only to have swept off three small children. Men may call these phenomena in human life, the effects of the laws of nature; I choose to call them singular proofs of the Providence of God over all his creatures."

When the brig *Hunter* arrived, March 13, 1825, with 66 settlers, nearly all of whom were farmers,[144] all were stricken during the first month. Although Cary himself was confined to his house nursing a severe injury, only a few children were fatally affected.[145]

Cary gratuitously spent about half of his time in caring for the sick of the colony. This fact was a matter of course as no funds were specially designated for this purpose. Cary was financially able to do such a thing. He had defrayed no small share of his own expense[146] in equipment for Africa, and when the colonists were in need of medical aid, he spent much of his means in this direction.[147] In 1825 he still owned a house and lot near Richmond which he was desirous of selling.[148]

Lott Cary was so occupied with caring for the sick that his prospective trip to America in the spring of 1826 had to be postponed.[149] He was also physician to Governor Ashmun. The governor was very ill in May after an exposure of four hours in attempting to save the schooner *Catherine* from destruction. "The prescriptions of our excellent and experienced assistant physician, the Rev. L. Cary," the Governor said,[150] "under the blessing of Divine Providence, so far succeeded as to afford complete relief, only leaving me in a very emaciated and enfeebled state, about the end of the first week in July."

All of this was just part of the work that Lott Cary had set himself to accomplish. By his unselfish labors and untiring efforts he had won the hearts of the natives. He had been indefatigable in his efforts to uplift the colony. The morale of the settlement was greatly lifted. Drunkenness, profanity and quarreling were unknown;

the Sabbath was observed with strictness.[151] Nearly the whole adult population had come under the influence of Christianity. On the site of a once desolate forest consecrated to demon worship was erected the commodious chapel which stood as a monument of the overthrow of heathenism and as a tribute to the Son of God.[152]

But in the sight of this landmark of Christianity, the slave trade was carried on extensively.[153] In 1825 from eight to ten, even fifteen traders were engaged at the same time off the coast. In July "contracts were existing for eight hundred slaves to be furnished in the short space of four months within eight miles of the Cape. Four hundred of these were to be purchased for two American traders. During the same season, a boat belonging to a Frenchman, having on board twenty-six slaves, all in irons, was upset in the mouth of the St. Paul River and twenty of their number perished."[154] Between October, 1825, and April, 1826, no less than one hundred and eighty Negroes were reclaimed from slave traders and taught the Scripture.[155]

When Gurley visited the colony in August, 1824, he found the state of religion and morality hopeful, defenses adequate, quiet Sabbaths and physical improvements which indicated that a considerable amount of labor had been done. For twenty-two months following, the jails were in disuse.[156] By 1826 the people had developed from inexperienced immigrants to efficient citizens. No family was without ample food and wearing apparel. Wages were high and employment could be found everywhere. The common laborers were receiving from $.75 to $1.75 a day, while the mechanics got $2 a day. Houses were built and a telegraph system was soon to be installed. There were also two corps of militia, an artillery battery of fifty men and forty infantrymen. These had charge of the fifteen large carriages and three small pivot guns.[157]

A printing press costing more than $1,000, in addition to the salary of a printer, had been sent out. The citizens of Liberia expressed their thanks by subscribing nearly $200 "toward the immediate issue and support of a publick newspaper."[158] One thousand volumes of books, a complete set of the North American Review, a gift of Editor Sparks, and many other useful things were on hand.[159]

Economic effort, however, did not at first play as conspicuous a part in the missionary adventure of Lott Cary as it did in the lives of the pioneers, George Liele and David George, who left this country primarily to be able to make a living.[160] Nevertheless, the economic feature developed after a time. The agricultural progress of the country was rapidly promoted. The sultry and moist climate greatly accelerated[161] the growth of coffee,[162] rice and cassada. The Rev. Colston M. Waring was the first to attempt farming on anything like a large scale. His crop of rice and cassada on a ten acre farm failed and checked so bold an example from all except Lott Cary. He, too, lost a promising crop in 1825 on the same kind of land because of the birds and the monkeys.[163] This failure, however, showed him that either farming as the natives adopted (scratching the surface of the ground with a sharp stick) or more improved methods of thoroughly preparing the soil had to be tried.[164] In the following year, Cary enlarged his farm, had it cleared, dug it up with picks and hoes, and, in June, sowed about three bushels of rice to the acre. At the first cutting, on the 20th of October, it averaged 50 kroos (a measure varying from 3 to 5 winchester gallons) per acre.[165]

In one letter, he says:[166] "I have a promising little crop of rice and cassada, and have planted about 180 coffee trees this week, a part of which I expect, will produce next season, as they are now in bloom. I think, sir, that in a very few years we shall send you coffee of a better quality than you have ever seen brought into your market. We find that trees of two species abound in great quantities on the Cape."

On the 7th of July, 1825, Cary reported a discovery of gold in the sand near little Cape Mount.[167] The appearance of gold was certain to develop the country commercially; some trade was already being carried on. Endeavoring to participate therein, nine of the natives built a ten ton schooner which carried from four to eight thousand dollars' worth of goods each trip.[168] Doctor Alexander[169] relates that between the first of January and the fifteenth of July, 1826, fifteen vessels stopped at Monrovia.

Nevertheless, there were some anti-slavery leaders in America who seriously questioned the permanent utility and moral influence of the colony of Liberia. One of these anti-slavery groups, composed of free Negroes of Philadelphia, was led by Richard Allen, the founder of the African Methodist Episcopal Church.[170] In a letter to a gentleman in Richmond, Lott Cary makes mention, September 24, 1827, of the agitation carried on by these Negroes of Philadelphia. "Before I left America," he said,[171] "and ever since then, the coloured people in about Philadelphia, have been making efforts in opposition to the scheme of colonizing the free people in Africa; and as some of their very recent publications have reached this place, I felt that in justice to the cause, and my own feelings, I ought to undertake to point out to them their situation."

Unfortunately the letter closes shortly after this but singularly enough our sources supply an "Address, *By the Citizens of Monrovia*, to the free coloured people of the United States,"[172] which no doubt is referred to in the letter. The name of Lott Cary is not attached to this address, which boosts "the doings of the Colonization Society" and which points out the political, social, economic, educational and religious advantages enjoyed by the colonists. Nevertheless, the document could not fully express the sentiments of the colonists unless the feelings of the leaders were given. It is not too much to presume that the address was gotten up by Lott Cary, the outstanding leader of the colonists, but it is very doubtful whether he wrote it in its present form. The correspondence of Cary reveals that he did not express himself so clearly nor did he use so good English.[173] The antithetical style reminds one of the writing of Ashmun.[174]

Through all of the many affairs which Cary performed, he continued pastor of the church at Monrovia. A missionary society was formed in connection with the church in the spring of 1826. Cary was elected president.[175] At the first anniversary[176] on Easter Monday, in consequence of the failure of the Rev. Colin Teague to come from Sierra Leone, Lott Cary preached the introductory sermon.[177] This society contributed $50 for mission work during the year 1827.[178] By the following year, the church contained one hundred members and two ordained preachers, John Lewis and Colston M. Waring, besides exhorters.[179]

FINAL WORK AND WORTH

Lott Cary was none the less interested and active in the welfare of the government. From the first settlement in Cape Montserado, he was appointed Government Inspector at the same time he was selected Health Officer[180] and consequently he knew something of the working of the government. In September, 1826, he was unanimously elected vice-agent of the colony. The colonial agent had great confidence in his judgments, decisions and loyalty[181] and left the affairs of the colony in Cary's charge when he was advised in 1828 to return to America for his health.[182]

"I was able," Mr. Ashmun wrote to the board,[183] "to arrange the concerns of the Colony with Mr. Cary, even to the minutest particulars, and I have the greatest confidence that his administration will prove satisfactory, in a high degree, to the Board and advantageous to the Colony."

During the first six months, Cary's task was to see to it that every man and working family were self-supporting. "To effect this object, they must be furnished with a few simple tools—to pay for them if they can—if not, to receive them gratuitously. Their allowance must be withheld if they neglect or negligently follow the improvement of their lands, and the building of their houses. Much may be done by visiting the people separately, getting at their intentions and circumstances and spurring, advising or reproving as they may require. I am persuaded it will be useful, and in most instances possible to get at least all the men out of the public receptacles and on their lands before the rains set in." Respecting the buildings of the United States, those of the colony, the arms, forts, printing establishment, farms, Millsburg settlement, finances, etc., other particular regulations were suggested.[184] Lott Cary kept Ashmun and the American Colonization Society informed about the condition of the colony. [185] On his death bed, Ashmun again expressed his confidence in Cary and urged that he should be permanently appointed to conduct the affairs of the colony[186] which now contained upwards of 1,200 settlers.[187]

The only trouble that Cary had while he was vice-agent was with the natives.[188] The factory belonging to the colony at Digby, a settlement just north of Monrovia, was robbed by them and general hostilities threatened when satisfaction was demanded and refused. A letter of protest to a slave dealer who had stored his goods in the house where stores of the colony had been deposited was intercepted and destroyed by the natives. Immediately, Cary prepared to defend the rights and property of the colony. He called out the militia and began with others, in the evening of November 8, to make cartridges in the old agency house. In some manner, a candle was accidentally upset and almost instantly the entire ammunition exploded, entirely destroying the house. Eight people died; six of the number survived until the next day; Lott Cary and one other until November 10, 1828.[189]

The unbelievable news of the death of Lott Cary spread like a mighty conflagration to the organizations which he represented. The following is the resolution read and adopted at the annual meeting of the Richmond African Baptist Missionary Society in 1829:[190]

The loss which has been sustained, cannot in our estimation, be easily repaired. This excellent man seems to have been raised up by divine providence, for the special purpose of taking an active part in the management of the infant settlement. His discriminating judgment, his honesty of heart, and decision of character, qualified him eminently, for this service. But, especially, in relation to your society is his death to be sincerely lamented. It will be recollected, that he was a principal instrument in the origin of this society, and for several years acted as its recording secretary. A little more than eight years ago, he received his appointment, and sailed, as missionary, in company with brother Teage, for the land of their forefathers. His exertions as a minister in that land have been of the most devoted and untiring kind. In the communications which have been received by the Board, he seemed to possess the most anxious concern for the salvation of the perishing multitudes around him. Through his instrumentality a considerable church has been collected together which seems to be in a prosperous and growing condition. Sabbath and week day schools have been instituted for the instruction of native children and the children of the colony, which have proved eminently useful. We were looking forward with confidence to the more perfect consummation of our wishes, when that moral desert should rejoice and blossom as the rose; but God has seen fit to cross our expectations, in calling from his station this laborious missionary. It becomes us to bow with submission to the stroke, and to realize the saying of the apostle, "how unsearchable are his judgments, and his ways past finding out." Although we were not permitted to receive his dying testimony to the trust, we have the fullest assurance that our loss is his unspeakable and eternal gain.

At the sixth triennial meeting of the General Missionary Convention, 1829, the committee on the African Mission made this report[191] which in some particulars was paradoxical:

This excellent man (it began) went to Africa, under the patronage of the American Colonization Society, as well as of this convention.... Could he have devoted his whole time to our service much good might have been expected to have resulted from his labors. But he was under necessity to assist in its government and defense, as well as to act as its physician.

It is a source of consolation to the friends of Mr. Cary that though his life was terminated in an unexpected moment and in a most distressing manner, the unwearied diligence and fidelity with which he discharged the important trust confided to his care—his zeal for the honor of religion, and the purity and piety of his general conduct have gained him a reputation which must live in grateful remembrance, as long as the interesting colony exists, in whose service he lived and died.

Your committee cannot help expressing their regret that so small a portion of benevolent feeling has been exercised towards this mission, and that so little has been accomplished during the eight years of its existence.

The next item of this report is an appeal for "some brethren of competent talents" to go and labor there.

There surely was ground for regret that so small a portion of benevolent feeling was exercised towards this mission. Some individuals did contribute now and then; "A Georgia Planter" sent a part of $10;[192] a "poor woman" of the Rev. H. Malcom's congregation sent $3 for the African mission;[193] "a friend to Africa avails of jewelry for mission to Liberia, per Mr. E. Lincoln, $6";[194] the Negroes connected with the First Baptist Church, Washington, sent $15[195] and, no doubt, some others contributed.

It is not quite clear, however, why William Crane, still representing the Richmond African Baptist Missionary Society in the Convention and the Rev. James B. Taylor, a delegate from Virginia and later the biographer of Lott Cary, did not challenge the statement that so little had been accomplished during the eight years of the existence of the African mission.

The Convention then adopted the following recommendation of the Committee:

Resolved, That this convention cherish a grateful recollection of the self-denying labors of our late lamented missionary to Africa, Rev. Lott Cary, and that we sympathize with his family, the American Colonization Society, and the church at Monrovia, in the loss they have sustained in his death.

Resolved, That it be recommended to the Board to take measures for supplying the vacancy occasioned by the death of Bro. Cary as soon as possible by an able white missionary, and that they endeavor to the utmost of their power to promote the success of this mission, as one in which the convention feel a special interest.

S. CORNELIUS, CHAIRMAN.

It was not until 1832 that the Convention saw the error of its conclusion and declared that it must depend "principally on *colored persons*, as missionaries and school teachers, in Africa."[196] Despite this color-phobia of the Baptists, nothing can explain away the fact that Lott Cary had lived helpfully and died honorably. Gurley[197] and Hervey[198] would make him a man of genius who, had he possessed educational advantages, would have won a worldwide reputation as preacher, as general or as chief magistrate. This square-faced, keen-eyed, reserved, cautious black held nothing back. From Charles City County to Richmond, from slave to freedman, from profligate to prophet, from sinner to saint, is a record that might have gone unnoticed; but from America to Africa, from governed to governor, from missionary to martyr is Lott Cary.

For over a score of years the little village of Carytown was the only memento of the man. But in 1850, the Rev. Eli Ball, an agent of the Southern Baptist Convention, while visiting all the Liberian Baptist Mission stations, found with difficulty the final resting place of Lott Cary. The next year a marble monument was sent out and placed over his grave.[199]

MILES MARK FISHER

FOOTNOTES:

[1] This spelling seems more correct than either the short form, *Lot Cary*, used by the Rev. D. Stratton, D.D. of St. Albans, West Virginia, in his "Life and Work of Lot Cary, Missionary in Africa," or the longer form, *Lott Carey*, used by the Rev. James B. Taylor in "The Biography of Elder Lott Carey" and by many other writers for the following consideration: There is no trace of Cary spelling his name Lot Cary. In the American Baptist Magazine and Gammell's "A History of American Baptist Missions" there are letters from or references to Cary marked Lott Carey, which are no doubt presumptions on the part of the printer or writer that the name is spelled like that of the Rev. William Carey. If, on the other hand, Lott Cary spelled

his name either *Carey* or *Cary*, that would only argue that his name would be better spelled Lott Cary as a means of distinction from the Rev. William Carey. "The Biography of Elder Lott Carey" written in 1837 is the source of much that is known of the man but seems to draw heavily from the "Life of Jehudi Ashmun, late Colonial Agent in Liberia, with an Appendix Containing Extracts from His Journal and Other Writings, with a Brief Sketch of the Life of the Rev. Lott Cary," written in 1835 by Ralph Randolph Gurley, Secretary of the American Colonization Society. Many incidents of the life of Lott Cary are taken from the life and writings of Mr. Ashmun. It would therefore seem consistent to follow his spelling of the name. In this work, the name, Lott Cary, is used frequently—even signed to a letter to Mr. Gurley—and many references are made to it by Mr. Ashmun who probably knew Cary better than anyone else. Only once in the entire work, on page 126, never in the "Brief Sketch of the Life of the Rev. Lott Cary," is the name spelled *Carey*. This could be a typographical error. Furthermore, Mr. Randall who went to Africa as Governor of Liberia about a month and a half after Cary's death said, respecting a native settlement, "I propose to have it called after him, Carytown." (*The African Repository*, Vol. V, p. 1.) Appletons' *Cyclopaedia of American Biography*, Vol. I, p. 548, follows this spelling.

[2] This name is also variously spelled—Collin or Colin and Teague or Teage. The above spelling is from the American Baptist Missionary Union in their Missionary Jubilee volume, pp. 215, 267.

[3] *Proceedings of the Fifth Triennial Meeting of the Baptist*

General Convention, 1826, p. 22; Earnest, The Religious Development of the Negro in Virginia, p. 95; $150 was appropriated for the mission May 23, 1823. Proceedings, 1826, pp. 22, 32.

[4] *Report of the Board of Managers of the General Convention in The Latter Day Luminary, Vol. II, pp. 396 ff.*

[5] *The American Missionary Register, Vol. VI, p. 340.*

[6] *Hervey, The Story of Baptist Missions in Foreign Lands, p. 199.*

[7] *Gurley, Life of Jehudi Ashmun, appendix, p. 147; Peck, History of the Missions of the Baptist General Convention in the History of American Missions to the Heathen, p. 443.*

[8] Hervey, *op. cit.*, p. 199.

[9] *The African Repository*, March, 1829, p. 11; Gurley, *op. cit.*, appendix, p. 147.

[10] Hervey, *op. cit.*, p. 200.

[11] *The American Missionary Register, Vol. VI, p. 340.*

[12] Peck, *op. cit.*, p. 443.

[13] *The African Repository*, March, 1829, p. 11; Gurley, *op. cit.*, appendix, p. 147.

[14] The gallery was reserved for the slaves connected with the church and congregation. Hervey, *op. cit.*, p. 202.

[15] *The American Missionary Register, Vol. VI, p. 340.*

[16] Ibid.

[17] *The African Repository*, March, 1829, p. 11; Gurley, *op. cit.*, appendix, p. 147; Peck, *op. cit.*, p. 443.

[18] Gurley, *op. cit.*, appendix, p. 148; Peck, *op. cit.*, p. 443.

[19] The American Missionary Register, Vol. VI, p. 340.

[20] Gurley, *op. cit.*, appendix, p. 148.

[21] Peck, *op. cit.*, p. 443.

[22] *The American Missionary Register*, Vol. VI, p. 340. His wife died shortly before this time, *The African Repository*, March, 1829, p. 11; Gurley, *op. cit.*, appendix, p. 147.

[23] Fifth Annual Report of the Baptist Board of Foreign Missions in The Latter Day Luminary, Vol. I, pp. 400f.

[24] *The African Repository*, March, 1829, p. 12.

[25] *Ibid.*, Gurley, *op. cit.*, appendix, p. 148.

[26] Cathcart, *The Baptist Encyclopaedia*, Vol. I, p. 288.

[27] The Missionary Jubilee, pp. 17, 18, 19; Tupper, A Decade of Foreign Missions, p. 875.

[28] Peck, *op. cit.*, p. 444; The Missionary Jubilee, p. 214; Tupper, *op. cit.*, p. 875.

[29] The outbreaks of Toussaint L'Ouverture in Hayti in 1789 and especially Gabriel in Richmond had not died away. Gabriel in 1800 organized 1000 Negroes in Henrico County. The plot, however, was betrayed by a slave Pharaoh and amounted to no lives lost except

those of Gabriel and Jack Bowles who were executed. A public guard of 68 policed the city for some months afterwards. Cf. Ballagh, *Slavery in Virginia*, p. 92.

[30] From Article I of the Constitution of this body it is presumed that the Richmond Society contributed "a sum amounting to at least one hundred dollars" for their membership fee.

[31] *Proceedings of the General Convention, 1817, p. 134.*

[32] *Gammell, A History of American Baptist Missions, p. 256.*

[33] *The Third Annual Report of the Baptist Board of Foreign Missions, p. 180.*

[34] *Proceedings of the Baptist General Convention, 1829, p. 34; Gurley, op. cit., appendix, pp. 30, 32.*

[35] Letter to Doctor Staughton, dated Philadelphia, April 30, 1818, in the *Fourth Annual Report of the Baptist Board of Foreign Missions.*

[36] *Third Annual Report of the Baptist Board of Foreign Missions, p. 180.*

[37] *Cf. Letters and Addresses of Lott Cary.*

[38] August 5, 1816, the Negro Baptists of Warren County, North Carolina, contributed $5.15; August 18, of the County Line Association, Caswell County, North Carolina, $.69; September 1, of the Shiloh Association, Culpepper, Virginia, $1.90; October 21, of the Pee Dee Association, Montgomery County, North Carolina, $2.19; May 7, 1817, "a col. Wom." of Georgia, $1; June

2, "Coloured Brethren" of the Sunbury Association, Georgia, $21; June 16, "a man of colour 15 cts.—a woman of col. 6 cts." and August 1, "a man of col. 25 cts."—*The Third Annual Report of the Baptist Board*, pp. 146-149; *The Fourth Annual Report of the Baptist Board*, pp. 206, 208.

[39] *The Fourth Annual Report of the Baptist Board of Foreign Missions, pp. 206, 208, 210.*

[40] Peck, *op. cit.*, p. 444; Hervey, *op. cit.*, p. 201.

[41] *Cf. Journal of Mills in Spring, Memoirs of the Rev. Samuel J. Mills.*

[42] Letter dated Richmond, March 28, 1819, to the Rev. Obadiah B. Brown, Washington City.

[43] *The Missionary Jubilee, p. 215.*

[44] *Sixth Annual Report of the Baptist Board of Foreign Missions in The Latter Day Luminary, Vol. II, p. 141.*

[45] *The Latter Day Luminary, Vol. II, p. 141.*

[46] Peck, *op. cit.*, p. 439; cf. also The Missionary Jubilee, p. 215. The constitution of the Richmond African Baptist Missionary Society restricted its funds to Africa.

[47] *The African Repository*, March, 1829; Gurley, *op. cit.*, appendix.

[48] This would have increased his salary to $1000 annually.

[49] Letter of William Crane to the Rev. Obadiah Brown.

[50] Gurley, *op. cit.*, appendix, p. 148.

[51] *Russell, The Free Negro in Virginia, pp. 145-156.*

[52] *Seventh Annual Report of the Baptist Board of Foreign Missions in The Latter Day Luminary, Vol. II, pp. 317f.*

[53] *Ibid.*, p. 399; *The American Missionary Register*, Vol. VI, p. 341; Gurley, *op. cit.*, appendix, p. 159; Peck, *op. cit.*, p. 439; *The Missionary Jubilee*, p. 215.

[54] Peck, *op. cit.*, p. 444; Hervey, *op. cit.*, p. 202.

[55] Hervey, *op. cit.*, pp. 201f.

[56] Gurley, *op. cit.*, appendix, p. 149.

[57] *Ibid.*, p. 148; *The African Repository*, March, 1829, p. 12.

[58] Hervey, *op. cit.*, p. 202.

[59] Earnest, *op. cit.*, p. 95.

[60] Journal of Cary in *The Latter Day Luminary*, Vol. II, p. 399.

[61] *The American Baptist Magazine, Vol. III, p. 181.*

[62] Hervey, *op. cit.*, p. 202.

[63] *The Latter Day Luminary, Vol. II, pp. 397f.*

[64] Peck, *op. cit.*, p. 439.

[65] Gammell, *op. cit.*, pp. 247, 249.

[66] *The American Baptist Magazine, Vol. II, p. 181.*

[67] *Alexander, A History of Colonization on the Western Coast of Africa, p. 245.*

[68] *Latrobe, Maryland in Liberia, p. 9.*

[69] *The American Missionary Register, Vol. VI, pp. 149f.*

[70] *Cf. Letters and Addresses of Lott Cary.*

[71] *The Fifth Annual Report of the American Society for Colonizing the Free People of Colour of the United States, pp. 55–64.*

[72] Liberia was named at the annual meeting of the Colonization Society, February, 1825. Fox, *The American Colonization Society*, p. 71.

[73] Gurley, *op. cit.*, appendix, p. 149; Hervey, *op. cit.*, p. 202.

[74] *Warneck, Outline of a History of Protestant Missions, p. 193.*

[75] Gurley, *op. cit.*, appendix, p. 149; Hervey, *op. cit.*, p. 203.

[76] Gurley, *op. cit.*, appendix, p. 149; Hervey, *op. cit.*, p. 203; *The African Repository*, March, 1829, p. 13; *The American Missionary Register*, Vol. VI, p. 341.

[77] Gammell, *op. cit.*, p. 244; Peck, *op. cit.*, p. 441.

[78] Peck, *op. cit.*, p. 439; Gammell, *op. cit.*, p. 244.

[79] *The American Baptist Magazine, Vol. IV, p. 142.*

[80] *The American Missionary Register, Vol. VI, p. 341;*

Gammell, op. cit., p. 244; Tupper, The Foreign Missions of the Southern Baptist Convention, p. 277.

[81] A Negro Baptist preacher who accompanied David George to Sierra Leone from Nova Scotia in 1792. For a detailed account cf. Rippon, *The Baptist Annual Register,* Vol. I, pp. 478-481.

[82] *The American Baptist Magazine, Vol. V, pp. 241f.; The American Missionary Register, Vol. VI, pp. 222f.*

[83] *The American Missionary Register, Vol. VI, pp. 222f.*

[84] At the annual meeting of the American Colonization Society, February, 1825, on motion of General Robert G. Harper, the settlement was named Monrovia, in honor of the President of the United States. Fox, *op. cit.,* p. 71.

[85] *The American Baptist Magazine*, Vol. VI, pp. 244f. In the Report of the Board of Managers of the General Missionary Convention, May, 1825, "Lott Cary ... states that hostilities ... of the natives had ceased.... He asks for assistance to complete the work (on the church); and the Board feel pleasure in recommending the case to the hearts of all who are interested in the melioration of the condition of the African Race." Ibid., Vol. V, p. 216.

[86] *Cf. Letters and Addresses of Lott Cary.*

[87] Gurley, *op. cit.,* p. 196.

[88] Gurley, *op. cit.,* p. 213.

[89] *Ibid.,* p. 214.

[90] *Ibid.*, p. 213.

[91] *Ibid., op. cit., p. 182.*

[92] The laws of the Society required every adult male to work two days a week for the public good while receiving rations from the public store. This rule was dispensed with providing each colonist would cultivate his own land. *Ibid.*, p. 186.

[93] *Ibid.*, appendix, p. 150.

[94] Gurley, *op. cit.*, p. 187.

[95] *Ibid.*, appendix, p. 150.

[96] Fox, *op. cit.*, p. 72.

[97] Gurley, *op. cit.*, appendix, p. 150.

[98] *Ibid.*, pp. 190ff.

[99] Gurley, *op. cit.*, appendix, p. 150.

[100] *The American Baptist Magazine, Vol. IV, p. 423.*

[101] Hervey, *op. cit.*, p. 204.

[102] Gurley, *op. cit.*, p. 203.

[103] Gurley, *op. cit.*, p. 214; Hervey, *op. cit.*, p. 204.

[104] *Ibid., op. cit.*, p. 215; *ibid.*, appendix, p. 150.

[105] *The American Missionary Register, Vol. VI, p. 143.*

[106] Ibid.

[107] Gurley, *op. cit.*, appendix, p. 49.

[108] *Ibid.* p. 246.

[109] Gammell, *op. cit.,* p. 247.

[110] *The Missionary Jubilee, p. 215.*

[111] The Veys inhabit this healthy country and are very intelligent. They have a written language although no books. Peck, *op. cit.,* p. 441.

[112] Warneck, *op. cit.,* p. 189.

[113] Peck, *op. cit.,* p. 441.

[114] Gurley, *op. cit.,* appendix, p. 30.

[115] *The American Missionary Register, Vol. VI, p. 341.*

[116] *Cf. Jones, The Religious Instruction of the Negro in the United States.*

[117] These emigrants with one exception were from Newport, Rhode Island. Eighteen of them were, just before their departure and at their own request, organized into a church. Gurley, *op. cit.,* pp. 308, 310.

[118] Gurley, *op. cit.,* p. 309.

[119] *The American Baptist Magazine, Vol. VI, p. 368; Gammell, op. cit., p. 247; Peck, op. cit., p. 442; The Missionary Jubilee, p. 215.*

[120] Gurley, *op. cit.,* p. 356.

[121] The schools and scholars in Liberia in 1827 were as follows:

Rev. Mr. Gary's school for native children	45
Rev. Mr. M'Gill's classes	16
Mr. Stewart's school	44
Miss Jackson's school	40
Mrs. Williams' school	30
Mr. Prout's school	52

Gurley, *op. cit.*, p. 350.

[122] *The American Baptist Magazine*, Vol. VI, pp. 272f.; *ibid.*, Vol. VII, p. 166.

[123] Gurley, *op. cit.*, p. 357.

[124] *The American Baptist Magazine, Vol. XXI, p. 183.*

[125] Gurley, *op. cit.*, appendix, pp. 32, 35, 36, 37.

[126] *Ibid., op. cit., p. 356.*

[127] *The American Baptist Magazine*, Vol. VIII, p. 144; cf. also Alexander, *op. cit.*, pp. 248f.

[128] Baptized eighteen months before by Cary. He was a native evangelist at Big Town, Grand Cape Mount and styled himself John Baptist. Letter of Cary dated Monrovia, June, 1827, to Crane.

[129] *The American Baptist Magazine, Vol. VII, pp. 305f.*

[130] *The American Baptist Magazine, Vol. VIII, pp. 143f.*

[131] *Ibid.*, pp. 53f.

[132] The General Missionary Convention made a

remittance of $90 on February 15, 1828. *The American Baptist Magazine*, Vol. VII, pp. 170, 176.

[133] Peck, *op. cit.*, p. 442.

[134] Alexander, *op. cit.*, p. 181.

[135] *Cf. Letters and Addresses of Lott Cary.*

[136] *The American Missionary Register, May, 1825, p. 142.*

[137] Gurley, *op. cit.*, p. 182.

[138] *Ibid.*, p. 190.

[139] *Ibid.*, p. 182.

[140] *Cf. Letters and Addresses of Lott Cary.*

[141] *The American Missionary Register, Vol. VI, p. 142.*

[142] Peck, *op. cit.*, p. 439; Stratton, *Life and Work of Lot Cary, p. 3.*

[143] Gurley, *op. cit.*, p. 190.

[144] Gurley, *op. cit.*, p. 232.

[145] *The American Baptist Magazine, Vol. V, p. 242.*

[146] *The American Missionary Register, Vol. VI, p. 340.*

[147] *Cf. Letters and Addresses of Lott Cary.*

[148] *The American Missionary Register, Vol. VI, p. 340.*

[149] This trip was to influence the free people of color in the United States to emigrate to Liberia. Gurley, *op. cit.*, appendix, p. 151.

[150] Gurley, *op. cit.*, pp. 340f.

[151] Peck, *op. cit.*, p. 554.

[152] *The American Baptist Magazine, Vol. VI, p. 216.*

[153] *Gurley, Life of Jehudi Ashmun, p. 157.*

[154] *Ibid., op. cit., p. 261.*

[155] *The American Baptist Magazine*, Vol. IX, pp. 212f.; Peck, *op. cit.*, p. 442.

[156] *The American Missionary Register, Vol. VI, p. 142.*

[157] *The American Baptist Magazine, Vol. VI, p. 216.*

[158] *The Liberia Herald* ran for three issues. Then the printer, Mr. Charles L. Force, died. *Ibid.*, pp. 214ff.

[159] Ibid.

[160] Rippon, *op. cit.*, Vol. I, pp. 334, 482; Alexander, *op. cit.*, p. 41; Crooks, *A History of the Colony of Sierra Leone*, p. 36.

[161] Gurley, *op. cit.*, appendix, p. 66.

[162] *Ibid.*, p. 56.

[163] *Ibid.*, p. 131.

[164] Gurley, *op. cit.*, appendix, p. 132.

[165] Ibid.

[166] Alexander, *op. cit.*, p. 247.

[167] Gurley, *op. cit.*, appendix, p. 126.

[168] *The American Baptist Magazine, Vol. VI, p. 216.*

[169] *History of African Colonization, p. 225.*

[170] *Cf. Adams, The Neglected Period of Anti-Slavery in America, p. 92; Cromwell, The Early Negro Convention Movement, pp. 3-5.*

[171] *The American Baptist Magazine, Vol. VIII, pp. 53f.*

[172] *Cf. Letters and Addresses of Lott Cary.*

[173] Cf. especially Gurley, *Life of Jehudi Ashmun,* appendix, pp. 153, 157. In speaking of going to Grand Cape Mount, Mr. Cary says, "I should have went up last year ... we may anticipate a middling severe struggle from the Mandingo priests who have been for years propagating their system of religion among that nation. They are a kind of Mahometan Jews—they are very skilful in the Old Testament...." *The American Baptist Magazine*, Vol. VII, p. 305. Moreover, there is no known evidence that any other of the colonists could have written so well.

[174] Compare the Address of the Citizens of Monrovia to the free colored people of the United States with the account given in Gurley, *Life of Jehudi Ashmun,* pp. 136-138.

[175] *The American Baptist Magazine, Vol. VIII, p. 203.*

[176] $1 was the annual membership fee; 45 names were enrolled and the money paid. $7.25 was collected at the door. Ashmun contributed $5 extra. *The American Baptist Magazine*, Vol. VII, p. 305n.

[177] *Ibid.*, p. 305.

[178] *Ibid.*, Vol. VIII, p. 170.

[179] *Ibid.*, Vol. IX, p. 195; Peek, *op. cit.*, p. 443.

[180] On August 31, 1822, Alexander, *op. cit.*, p. 181.

[181] *The African Repository, Vol. V, p. 14.*

[182] Gurley, *op. cit.*, appendix, p. 153.

[183] *Ibid., op. cit., p. 385.*

[184] Gurley, *op. cit.*, p. 385; cf. Journal of Lott Cary in Gurley, *Life of Jehu Ashmun*, appendix, pp. 153-156.

[185] Cf. Appendix L.

[186] Gurley, *op. cit.*, appendix, p. 159.

[187] *The American Baptist Magazine*, Vol. IX, p. 212; Alexander, *op. cit.*, p. 279.

[188] Alexander, *op. cit.*, p. 261.

[189] *The African Repository*, Vol. V, p. 10; Gurley, *op. cit.*, appendix, p. 160.

[190] Alexander, *op. cit.*, pp. 254f.

[191] *The American Baptist Magazine*, Vol. IX, pp. 212, 215, cf. also p. 195.

[192] Cf. a letter to the treasurer of the Massachusetts Baptist Education Society in *The American Baptist Magazine*, Vol. VI, p. 181.

[193] *The American Baptist Magazine, Vol. IX, p. 255.*

[194] *Ibid.,* p. 214.

[195] *The American Baptist Magazine, p. 215.*

[196] *Proceedings,* 1832, pp. 10, 33.

[197] *Op. cit.,* appendix, p. 160.

[198] *Op. cit.,* p. 207.

[199] Hervey,*op. cit.,* p. 206.

COMMUNICATIONS

The correspondence of the editor often has an historical value as the following communications will show:

FEBRUARY 13, 1922.

Dear Dr. Woodson:

Your JOURNAL OF NEGRO HISTORY has been so full of good material that I hesitate to call attention to two things in the last (January) number that seem unsuitable.

The first is the leading article on Slave Society on the Southern Society. For more than thirty years I have been combating with all my might the theory of slave-holding sovereignty set forth in that article. It is the essentially Southern view—a magnified view and an unreal view. The article is practically a mild form of the panegyric of the slave plantation which has been the stock in trade of defenders of slavery for a hundred years.

The reasons for slavery given on pages 1 and 2 do not accord with the facts, and if they were true would have minimized the protests against slavery, past and present. It is ridiculous to say that white men endanger their lives by working in the South when you consider how large a part of the cotton crop is raised entirely by white men.

The description of what was said to be the "usual" type of plantation house does not in my opinion apply to more than two hundred or three hundred plantations in the South at the outside. I have traveled very extensively in the South and have never seen more than three or four such mansions. The testimony of Olmsted and other writers is that ordinarily the slaveholder's house was poor and that he lived in a very poor fashion. As for the twelve sons and daughters in the planters' families, and the fifteen to twenty-five children in the negro families, it is perfect gammon. Not one family in a thousand had such numbers. None but a very few of the richest planters lived in the profusion described on page four. As for the enrolment in colleges between 1859 and 1860, and the incomes of the higher institutions, that is all bosh. Francis Lieber was a German by birth, found his service in South Carolina very uncongenial, and stood by the union. To compare slavery to apprenticeship is an affront. The day's work set down by Murat (whose history of the United States is a very obscure work) is contrary to evidence North or South. Regular nurseries were built only on a few large plantations. The arguments in favor of slavery on pages nine and ten are stated without qualification or contradiction. I deeply regret that a Journal of Negro History should admit an article so full of statements both untrue and dangerous to the Negro race.

The experience of a Georgia peon "seems to me very doubtful. I am personally acquainted with the story of Dade's stockade, and have passed within a few miles of it, and I do not believe in the least that there is now, or has been in the past thirty years, any plantation in the South where families are brought up in servitude. The only Ponce-de-Leon spring that I know is in Florida, which is not on the road between Georgia and Mississippi. The man seems to think that Chattanooga is on the west side of the river. It is a dangerous thing to accept any such statement without thorough investigation and calling upon the relater to state exactly where these things happened, and what was his course of travel.

I should not venture to write so decidedly but that you have done so much for the cause of the Negro race, and I don't like to see you give ammunition to the enemies of your race.

SINCERELY YOURS,
ALBERT BUSHNELL HART.

326 FLOWER ST.,
CHESTER, PA.,
JUNE 26, 1922.

CARTER G. WOODSON, Ph.D.,
The Journal of Negro History,
Washington, D. C.

My dear Doctor Woodson:

The following list of Negro delegates to the Republican National Conventions from 1868 to 1920, inclusive, from South Carolina, may be of sufficient interest for publication. As the proceedings of the conventions do not differentiate as to the racial identity of the delegates it is necessary that this data should be collected before it is too late, especially as it pertains to the Reconstruction period. While a reduction in the numbers of delegates from South Carolina, as well as from most of the Southern States, was made by the Republican National Committee in December, 1913, the State still sends a majority of Negro delegates:

1868—Chicago, Ill., May 20-21.
 Robert Brown Elliott, Henry B. Hayne,
Stephen A. Swails,
 Joseph H. Rainey, Wm. J. McKinlay, Robert Smalls,
 Henry L. Shrewsbury.

1872—Philadelphia, Pa., June 5-6.
 At-Large—Alonzo J. Ransier.
1st District—Stephen A. Swails, F. H. Frost, Henry J.
Maxwell.
 2nd District—Robert Smalls.
 3rd District—Robert Brown Elliott, Wm.
Beverly Nash.
 A. J. Ransier on Committee to notify nominees.
 At the Convention of 1872, General Elliott was called
 upon from the floor to address the convention. His
 speech will be found in the proceedings of the
convention.

1876—Cincinnati, Ohio, June 14-16.
 At-Large—Robert Brown Elliott, Richard H. Gleaves.
 1st District—Stephen A. Swails, Joseph H. Rainey.
 2nd District—Wm. J. McKinlay.
 3rd District—Wm. Beverly Nash.

5th District—Lawrence Cain, Robert Smalls.
Joseph H. Rainey on Committee to notify nominees.

1880—Chicago, Illinois, June 2-8.
 At-Large—Robert Brown Elliott, Samuel Lee.
 1st District—Wm. A. Hayne.
 3rd District—Charles M. Wilder.
 4th District—Wilson Cooke.
 5th District—Wm. F. Myers, Wm. J. Whipper.
 Messrs. Hayne, Myers and Whipper went
down to defeat
 with General U. S. Grant. All received medals for
 their loyalty.

1884—Chicago, Illinois, June 3-6.
 At-Large—Samuel Lee, Robert Smalls.
 1st District—John M. Freeman.
 2nd District—Paris Simpkins, Seymour E. Smith.
 4th District—Charles M. Wilder, Wilson Cooke.
 5th District—Eugene H. Dibble.
 6th District—Edmund H. Deas.
 7th District—Wm. H. Thompson.
 Samuel Lee on Committee to notify nominees. Major
 John R. Lynch, delegate from Mississippi, was elected
 temporary chairman, the first and only time
that a colored
 man ever presided over a Republican National
Convention.

1888—Chicago, Illinois, June 19-25.
 At-Large—Wm. F. Myers, Robert Smalls.
 1st District—John M. Freeman.
 2nd District—Fred Nix, Jr., Paris Simpkins.

3rd District—F. L. Hicks.
4th District—Peter F. Oliver, F. A. Saxton.
5th District—Charles C. Levy, Zachariah E. Walker.
6th District—Edmund H. Deas.
7th District—George E. Herriott.
Paris Simpkins on Committee to notify nominees.
Peter Oliver seconded the nomination of
General Alger
for president.

1892—Minneapolis, Minn., June 7-10.
At-Large—Edmund H. Deas, Dr. Wm. D. Crum.
1st District—John H. Fordham.
2nd District—Paris Simpkins, Seymour E. Smith.
3rd District—A. S. Jamison.
4th District—Irwin I. Miller.
5th District—Wm. E. Boykin.
6th District—Rev. Joshua E. Wilson.
7th District—R. H. Richardson.
E. H. Deas on Committee to notify presidential nominee.
J. H. Fordham on Committee to nominate
vice-presidential
nominee.

1896—St. Louis, Mo., June 16-18.
At-Large—Dr. Wm. D. Crum, Robert Smalls.
1st District—Robert C. Brown.
2nd District—Wm. S. Dixon.
4th District—Charles M. Wilder.
5th District—Wm. E. Boykin.
6th District—Edmund H. Deas, Rev. Joshua E. Wilson.
7th District—Zachariah E. Walker, John H. Fordham.

E. H. Deas on Committee to notify presidential nominee.

1900—Philadelphia, Pa., June 19-21.
 At-Large—Edmund H. Deas, Robert Smalls.
 1st District—Dr. Wm. D. Crum.
 2nd District—Wm. S. Dixon, B. J. Dickerson.
 5th District—Wm. E. Boykin.
 6th District—Rev. Joshua E. Wilson, Wm. H. Collier.
 7th District—John H. Fordham.
 E. H. Deas on Committee to notify presidential nominee.

1904—Chicago, Illinois, June 21-23.
 At-Large—Edmund H. Deas, Dr. Wm. D. Crum.
 1st District—Wm. F. Myers, A. P. Prioleau.
 2nd District—Wm. S. Dixon, E. J. Dickerson.
 4th District—Pratt S. Suber.
 5th District—Wm. E. Boykin.
 6th District—J. R. Levy, J. A. Baxter.
 Dr. Crum on Committee to notify vice-presidential
 nominee.

1908—Chicago, Illinois, June 16-19.
 At-Large—Edmund H. Deas, Thomas L. Grant.
 1st District—C. M. English, P. T. Richardson.
 2nd District—Wm. S. Dixon.
 3rd District—G. C. Williams.
 4th District—Dr. Wm. Tecumseh Smith.
 5th District—Wm. E. Boykin.
 6th District—J. A. Baxter, J. R. Levy.
 7th District—Wm. T. Andrews.

Thomas L. Grant on Committee to notify presidential nominee.

1912—Chicago, Illinois, June 18-22.
At-Large—Wm. T. Andrews, J. R. Levy.
1st District—Thomas L. Grant, A. P. Prioleau.
2nd District—Wm. S. Dixon.
4th District—Thomas Brier.
6th District—Rev. Joshua E. Wilson, J. A. Baxter.
7th District—Dr. J. H. Godwyn.
Rev. J. E. Wilson on Committee to notify presidential nominee.

1916—Chicago, Illinois, June 7-10.
At-Large—Dr. J. H. Goodwyn, John H. Fordham.
1st District—Gibbs Mitchell.
2nd District—Wm. S. Dixon.
4th District—J. A. Brier.
6th District—J. R. Levy.
7th District—L. A. Hawkins.
J. R. Levy on Committee to notify presidential nominee.
W. S. Dixon on Committee to notify vice-presidential nominee.

1920—Chicago, Illinois, June 5-9.
At-Large—W. S. Dixon, Dr. J. H. Goodwyn.
1st District—Gibbs Mitchell.
2nd District—J. M. Jones.
5th District—G. A. Watts.
6th District—I. J. McCottrie.
7th District—L. A. Hawkins.
W. S. Dixon on Committee to notify

presidential nominee.
I. J. McCottrie on Committee to notify
vice-presidential
 nominee.

HENRY A. WALLACE.

140 COTTAGE STREET, NEW HAVEN, CONN.,
June 26, 1922.

DR. CARTER G. WOODSON,
 1216 You Street, N. W.,
Washington, D. C.

My dear Dr. Woodson:

Your studies in the history of the Negro people have greatly impressed me with their value and I trust that they will be continued in the many fields which call for new and careful investigation. I think there is especial need for exact and detailed information about the period of "reconstruction" in the South. Reviewing in my memory the whole period since the civil war I find a great change in prevalent opinion in the North concerning the events of the reconstruction. It seems to me that the champions of secession, of slavery and the southern oligarchy, have been heard in justification of everything they did and in arraignment of every-thing that defeated their designs with an unsuspicious confidence that has enabled them to mislead sentiment in the North, especially among the younger people. For example: a Yale professor of history had an article in the New York Times, a while ago, declaring that the constitutional amendments conferring citizenship on the Negroes were wrong and that the reaction against them in depriving the Negroes of the vote was justifiable; to which I wrote a reply, mostly in the language of Mr. Flemming, a native Southerner who had represented Georgia in Congress, arguing that the amendments were not only justifiable but indispensable, and the Times would not publish it, so that I had to give it to the Post. There is a prevalent opinion that the "carpet baggers" were a sort of monsters. I have known some of them as estimable men and practical public spirited citizens of a very high type: Judge Henderson of Wilcox County, Ala. for example.

Now if you can go to the roots of history in this period and investigate the facts, with biographical sketches of leading men as they actually were and authentic records of things that were actually done, it might help to clarify history.

The incessant whining and propaganda of Southern bigots devoted to the old regime naturally have an undue influence on sympathetic listeners. I am afraid that this influence will not be counteracted as it ought to be till Negro investigators, historians and journalists learn to tell their side of the story with greater thoroughness.

Very truly yours,
G. S. DICKERMAN.

NEW BEDFORD, MASS., MAY 15TH, 1916
ROOM 6, ROBESON BLDG.

DR. CARTER G. WOODSON,
WASHINGTON, D. C.

My Dear Sir:

In reply to yours of the 8th, please find herewith a contribution in the line of my suggestion to Mr. Baker. I did not mean to imply I had much material of that nature, and what is sent is that I could readily find, and would need to take time to go through my papers to really know what I have. If you can use it all right; if not, consign it to the waste basket, and no complaint will be coming.

What I had more in mind was this: In many communities can be found some one person who has contributed services of value to race, none the less appreciable from the fact that their interest and value seem circumscribed locally. That they are so limited I do not believe, but think of each as the centre of an ever widening, circling influence for good. To illustrate:

Paul Cuffee was born at Cuttyhunk, Mass., in 1758; was an early defender of the rights of colored men; when the selectmen of the Town of Dartmouth, refused to admit colored children to the public schools, and to make separate provision for their education, he refused to pay his school taxes, was imprisoned, and when liberated, built a school house at his own expense, on his own land, employed a teacher at his own expense, and then opened his school *without* race discrimination, a privilege which his white neighbors availed themselves of as his school was more convenient and equally as good as those of the town. The result was colored children ceased to be proscribed along educational lines. He was a ship owner, builder and export trader. His story has been published at length, in one of our dailies, with all the documents in the case. It seemed to me that such stories would be of general as well as local interest. If you agree with me in this, Mr. Jourdain would without doubt forward the clipping to you.

The first colored school-teacher in Boston, was Prince Sanders, Secretary African Lodge F. & A. M., the first Lodge of colored Masons in America. He taught a colored school in the basement of the old Joy Street Church from 1809 to 1812. The first colored school, private, was opened in 1798, at the residence of Primus Hall, corner of West Cedar and Revere Streets, Boston, and was taught by a white man, by name, Sylvester. Its curriculum was limited to the three "R's."

I am sending you in mail with this a pamphlet copy of "Proceedings" etc., on pp. 12, 16, 17, you will find statements of services given by Prince Hall, of general as well as of local interest and value.

Yours sincerely,

Frederic S. Monroe.

DOCUMENTS

LETTERS, ADDRESSES, AND THE LIKE THROWING LIGHT ON THE CAREER OF LOTT CARY[1]

PHILADELPHIA, JANUARY 6, 1621 (1821).

The Board of Managers of the General Convention of the Baptist Denomination in the United States, to their coloured brethren, Collin Teage and Lott Carey, present the assurance of their sincere affectionate esteem. They have heard with pleasure, that, by a vessel about to sail from Norfolk to the coast of Africa, an opportunity is presented for accomplishing those benevolent desires which, for many months past, you have been led to entertain. At the present time, they possess a deep anxiety for your preservation in a country where so many colonists have frequently found a grave. They most fervently commend you to the gracious protection of that God in whose hand your breath is, and whose are all your ways. May you make the Lord your refuge, even the Most High your habitation. It is a source of much encouragement that you will be able to collect useful information from the experience of your predecessors; and it is hoped that by the advice of your brethren who have already reached the shores of your forefathers, you will be enabled to adopt the most prudent measures for the health and safety of yourselves and families.

The Board earnestly recommend, what they cheerfully anticipate, that your conduct before your fellow passengers on the ocean, be pious and exemplary. Endeavour to secure their good will by every office of kindness; and, above all, cherish and discover a solemn concern for their everlasting salvation. Arrived in Africa, you will find much that will require patience, and prudence, and mutual counsel. You will have to bear with prejudices that have descended on the minds of the inhabitants, after having been cherished for ages, and to instil the sacred truths of the gospel with meekness and wisdom. While your conversation shall be without blame, the Board advise you in your ministry to dwell much on the doctrine of the cross, a doctrine which has been found in every age of the church of Christ, the power of God.

Have as little to do as possible with what may be called the politics of the country. Be content with the silence so divinely exemplified in the Lord Jesus and his apostles to render unto Caesar the things which are Caesar's. Cultivate a tender regard for each other. If difference of opinion on any measures occur, never suffer it to produce alienation of affection. You have already had opportunities of improving your minds by reading, and the Board are gratified by the reflection that you bear with your books that are calculated to add to your general and spiritual knowledge.

Give yourselves to reading still; and, above all, let the word of God dwell in you richly. Be much engaged in prayer. If troubles rise around you, the delightful thought that you have a Father, a Saviour, in heaven, with whom you are so happy as to hold communion, will not only soften their severity, but in a good degree elevate you above their influence.

Let nothing discourage you. Ethiopia shall stretch forth her hands unto God. You are engaged in the service of Him who can make the *crooked straight*, and the *rough places* plain.

The Board wish you, as you shall find opportunity, to write. They will rejoice to hear that a church, on the principles of the gospel, is founded as the fruit of your labours. They trust that at no distant period, many such churches will rise, and the solitary place be glad for them. They will be happy to facilitate your prosperity to the utmost of their power.

They pray that the grace of our Lord Jesus Christ may be with you, with your families, and with all who sail or settle with you; and that the American Colonization Society, and all its sister institutions, may be rendered instrumental in diffusing literary, economical, and evangelic light, from the Mediterranean to the Cape of Good Hope, and from the Atlantic to the Red Sea and Indian Ocean.

BY ORDER OF THE BOARD,
WM. STAUGHTON, COR. SEC'RY.

Seventh Report of the Board of Managers of the General Convention, in *The Latter Day Luminary*, Vol. II, pp. 396f.

A RESOLUTION

A communication having been received from the

Petersburg African Mission Society, and also from brother Colston W. Waring, a preacher of colour at Petersburg, desiring the patronage of this Board in favour of the said Waring, as a missionary to Africa.

Resolved, That the said communications impart pleasure to this body, and that the Board will cheerfully countenance and encourage the said Waring as their missionary to Africa, provided the expenses of his outfit, &c. can be met by his own resources and those of his brethren in that quarter.

Sixth Annual Report of the Board, in *The Latter Day Luminary*, Vol. II, p. 134.

A CONTRACT

KNOW ALL MEN, That this Contract, made on the fifteenth day of December, in the year of our Lord one thousand eight hundred twenty-one, between King Peter, King George, King Zoda, and King L. Peter, their Princes and Head-men, of the one part; and Captain Robert F. Stockton and Eli Ayres, of the other part; WITNESSETH, That whereas certain persons Citizens of the United States of America, are desirous to establish themselves on the Western Coast of Africa, and have invested Captain Robert F. Stockton and Eli Ayres with full powers to treat with and purchase from us the said Kings, Princes, and Head-men, certain Lands, viz: Dozoa Island, and also all that portion of Land bounded north and west by the Atlantic Ocean, and on the south and east by a line drawn in a south-east direction from the north of Mesurado river, We, the said Kings, Princes, and Head-men, being fully convinced of the

Pacific and just views of the said Citizens of America, and being desirous to reciprocate the friendship and affection expressed for us and our people, DO HEREBY, in consideration of so much paid in hand, viz: Six muskets, one box Beads, two hogsheads Tobacco, one cask Gunpowder, six bars Iron, ten iron Pots, one dozen Knives and Forks, one dozen Spoons, six pieces blue Baft, four Hats, three Coats, three pair Shoes, one box Pipes, one keg Nails, twenty Looking-glasses, three pieces Handkerchiefs, three pieces Calico, three Canes, four Umbrellas, one box Soap, one barrel Rum; And *to be paid*, the following: three casks Tobacco, one box Pipes, three barrels Rum, twelve pieces cloth, six bars Iron, one box Beads, fifty Knives, twenty Looking-glasses, ten iron Pots different sizes, twelve Guns, three barrels Gunpowder, one dozen Plates, one dozen Knives and Forks, twenty Hats, five casks Beef, five barrels Pork, ten barrels Biscuit, twelve Decanters, twelve glass Tumblers, and fifty Shoes, FOR EVER CEDE AND RELINQUISH the above described Lands, with all thereto appertaining or belonging, or reputed so to belong, to Captain Robert F. Stockton and Eli Ayres, TO HAVE AND TO HOLD the said Premises, for the use of these said Citizens of America. And we, the said Kings, and Princes, and Head-men, do further pledge ourselves that we are the lawful owners of the above described Land, without manner of condition, limitation, or other matter.

The contracting Parties pledge themselves to live in peace and friendship for ever; and do further contract, not to make war, or otherwise molest or disturb each other.

We, the Kings, Princes, and Head-men, for a proper consideration by us received, do further agree to build for the use of the said Citizens of America, six large houses, on any place selected by them within the above described tract of ceded land.

In WITNESS whereof, the said Kings, Princes, and Head-men, of the one part; and Captain Robert Stockton and Eli Ayres, of the other part; do set their hands to this Covenant, on the day and year above written.

(SIGNED)
KING PETER, X HIS MARK.
KING GEORGE, X HIS MARK.
KING ZODA, X HIS MARK.
KING LONG PETER, X HIS MARK.
KING GOVERNOR, X HIS MARK.
KING JIMMY, X HIS MARK.

(Signed)
CAPTAIN ROBERT F. STOCKTON.
ELI AYRES, M.D.

WITNESS, (SIGNED)
JOHN S. MILL.
JOHN CRAIG.

AGREEMENT WITH J. S. MILL

I HEREBY CONTRACT, for the consideration of one barrel of Rum, one tierce of Tobacco, one barrel of Bread, one barrel of Beef, one barrel of Pork, and one piece of trade Cloth, to give to Captain R. F. Stockton and Eli Ayres all my right and title to the Houses situated on the Land bought by them on Cape Mesurado.

In Witness whereof, I have here unto signed my name, on this sixteenth day of December, one thousand eight hundred twenty-one.

(SIGNED) JOHN S. MILL.

Witness, (Signed)
CHARLES CAREY, X his mark.
WILLIAM RODGERS, X his mark.

We promise to present to Charles Carey, one Coat.

(SIGNED) R. F. STOCKTON.
ELI AYRES.

The Fifth Annual Report of the American Colonization Society, pp. 64-66.

L— — C— —.

A black man, has been a member of this Colony since the beginning of the year 1820. He made a profession of religion in America: but never never since I knew him, either discharged its duties, or evinced much of its spirit, till within the last ten months. He was a man of good natural sense, but wretched in the extreme; and the cause of equal wretchedness to his young family. His wife, naturally of a mild and placid temper, failed in almost every thing to please him, or prevent the constant outbreakings of his morose and peevish humor. He was her tyrant—and so instinct with malevolence, the vain conceit of superiority, jealousy, and obstinate pride, as to resemble more an Arab of the desert, or a person destitute of natural affection, than a person by education and in name, a Christian. As a neighbor, his feelings were so soured and narrow, as to render him disobliging, suspicious, and equally an object of general dislike and neglect. His heart was a moral desert—no kind affection seemed to stir within it; and the bitter streams which it discharged had spread a moral desolation around him, and left him the solitary victim of his own corroding temper.

Such an ascendant had these evil qualities over the other faculties of his mind as in a great measure to dim the light of reason, and render him as a subject of the colonial government, no less perverse and untractable, than he was debased and wretched, as a man.

Several times have the laws, which guard the peace of our little community, been called in, to check the excesses of his turbulent passions, by supplying the weakness of more ingenuous motives. Still this person discovered, in the midst of this wreck of moral excellence, a few remaining qualities, on which charity might fix the hope of his recovery to virtue, usefulness and happiness. But these were few, and mostly of a negative kind. He was not addicted to profane discourse. He allowed himself in no intemperate indulgences. He observed towards sacred institutions a cold, but still an habitual respect. And, strange as the fact may seem, he was laborious in his avocations, even to severe drudgery, and equally a stranger to avarice, and a passion for a vain ostentation. Whether these relieving traits of his character were the effects of habit, produced by the influence of former piety; or whether they were the result of constitutional temperament, or of education, is not for me to decide. But such was L. C., until the autumn of 1824; when not only a reform but an absolute reversal, of every perverse disposition and habit in the revolting catalogue of his character took place. A more obliging and affectionate husband I am convinced is not to be found on the Cape, few in the world! And there is no appearance of constraint, or affection in this display of tenderness. It is uniform, untiring, cordial, and increasing, as far as it is permitted to any one, except the Searcher of hearts, to judge. In all his intercourse with his family, and neighbors, he carries with him, an inimitable air of sweet and profound humility. You would pronounce it to be the meekness of the heart springing from some deep-felt sentiment of the interior of the mind. But so far from abasing the possessor, in the estimation of others, this very trait commands their respect, and their love. It gives to him a value, which he never appeared to possess before. Ten months have I now had daily opportunities to observe this altered man in a great variety of circumstances, and some of them, it must be confessed, sufficiently trying. In one instance, I have had to regret, and censure the appearance of that perversity which made an important part of his character. But happily this fit of turbulence was of short duration; and some months have passed since, without witnessing a repetition of the infirmity. Were I this evening asked to name a man in the Colony, who would most carefully guard against offending, or causing even a momentary pain to any of his fellow-men, I should not hesitate to say that in my judgment, the man is L. C. On this point I insist, because it was precisely in his revolting and unfeeling churlishness, that his greatest and most incurable infirmity seemed to consist. I hardly need add, were silence not liable to misconstruction, that the duties and ordinances of religion are matters of his most devout and diligent observance. How often have I been awaked at dawn of Sabbath, by his devout strains of prayer and praise, sent up from the midst of a little company of praying people, who at that hour assemble for religious exercises in a vacant building near my residence. How sure am I to find him reverently seated in his place, among the earliest who assemble in the house of God. What an active promoter of every commendable and pious design, is sure to be found in him.

Every laudable habit, which had survived the general extinction of all practical virtue, seems to have acquired additional confirmation: and from the operation of higher principles, seems to follow of course, and derive the best guaranty of its continuance. I might go on to particularize; but it would only be to fill up the outline already sketched, and which, whether relating to his former or his present character, however, imperfect, is strictly true. Ask of him the cause of so obvious and surprising a change, and he humbly, but unhesitatingly ascribes it wholly to the power of the Divine Spirit, operating, he cannot tell how, but evidently by means of the word and ordinances of God, upon his whole mind. Such was the origin of this great moral renovation, and such are the agency and means by which its effects are sustained, and under the operation of which they are beginning to combine into a habit of holiness. He rejoices in the hope of its duration to the end of life, solely he would say from the confidence he has in the immutable love and faithfulness of the Holy Being, who has wrought so great a work in him. And let philosophers cavil and doubt, if they must; but this man's example is a refutation in fact of a thousand of their sceptical theories. He is a new man, and the change was effected chiefly before discipline, or example, had time to work it. He is an honest man, and soberly asserts that to his certain knowledge he did not perform the work himself. But where is the example to be found of *such* and *so great* a change, wrought by mortal means? The history of the human race is challenged to produce it. To God then who created man, to Christ who redeemed him, and to the Holy Ghost who sanctifies him, be ascribed without abatement, or reserve, the power and the grace displayed in this and every similar instance of the conversion of a blind, and hardened and wretched sinner.

Gurley, *Life of Jehudi Ashmun*, appendix, pp. 136–138.

"June 16th, 1827.

"To the Rev. R. R. Gurley.

"Rev. and Dear Sir, I transmit to you a few lines, which I trust may find you well. The last emigrants that you sent out, has fared remarkably well, as it respects the disease; we have only lost two children. We have several cases of bad ulcers; and from seeing advertised in the Compiler of Richmond, a medicine called Swaim's Panacea, said to be a sure cure for ulcers; please try if possible to procure some, and send out, for we should have very healthy inhabitants at present, but for the prevalence of that uncontrolable disease. We are also in want of Salts, Castor-oil, Cream of Tartar, mignesea, and Mustard, as much as you can send well put up. I am greatly in hopes to be over the next spring, and try to wake up my colored friends in Virginia. We have a plan in contemplation which if accomplished will, I think insure my making one visit to America, that is, to purchase, or aid in the purchase of a vessel to run constantly from this, to America, to bring out our own supplies, emigrants, &c. I hope sir, when such an attempt is made you will facilitate it all that you can.

"I think that you would be pleased with the improvements that we have made since you left if you were to make another visit to this country—both our civil and religious state I think has improved very much. No more but wishing that the blessing of the Lord may attend you,dministrations.

"Yours, &c.
"Lott Cary."

Gurley, *Life of Jehudi Ashmun*, appendix, p. 153.

Appendix F

"Monrovia, April 24th, 1826.

"Rev. and Dear Sir: I received your letter sent to me by the order of the Board of Managers of the American Colonization Society; and I expected until a few days ago that the return of the Indian Chief, would have enabled me in all respects to have realized their wishes. But on a more minute examination of the subject, Mr. Ashmun and myself both were apprehensive that my leaving the Colony at present, would endanger the lives of a number of the inhabitants; Mr. Ashmun, however, has made a full statement to the Board, which I have no doubt will be satisfactory to them. I think that through the blessing of the Almighty, I shall be able to get the last expedition through the fever with very little loss; we have lost only three, the Rev. Mr. Trueman, from Baltimore, and two children belonging to the Paxton family. But the emigrants who came out in the Vine, have suffered very much; we lost twelve of them. The action of the disease was more powerful with them than is common—they unfortunately arrived here in the most sickly month in the year, February. I am strongly of the opinion, sir, that if the people of New England leave there in the winter, that the transition is so great, that you may count upon a loss of half at least. They may, in my estimation, with safety, leave in the months from April to November, and arrive here in good time; I think it to be a matter of great importance; therefore I hope, that you will regard it as such.

"I am respectfully yours,

"Lott Cary."

Gurley, *Life of Jehudi Ashmun*, appendix, p. 152.

In April, 1826, Lott Cary made arrangements to embark for the United States. The following is extracted from a letter addressed by Mr. Ashmun to the Managers of the Colonization Society:

"The Rev. Lott Cary, returning by the 'Indian Chief,' has, in my opinion, some claims on the justice of the Society or Government of the United States, or both, which merit consideration. These claims arise out of a long and faithful course of medical services rendered to this Colony, (the only such services deserving much consideration, if we except those of Dr. Ayres and Dr. Peaco, since the commencement of the settlement, in 1820).

"It is perhaps known to the Board, that Mr. Cary has declined serving any civil office, incompatible with a faithful discharge of his sacred functions: and it may be added, that although one of the most diligent and active of men, he has never had the command of leisure or strength to engage in any Missionary duties, besides the weekly and occasional services of the congregation. More than one-half of his time has been given up to the care of our sick, from the day I landed in Africa, to the very moment of stating the fact. He has personally aided in every way, that fidelity and benevolence could dictate, in all the attentions which all our sick have in so long a period received. His want of science acquired by the regular study of Medicine, he has gone a long way towards supplying by an unwearied diligence which few regular physicians think it necessary—fewer super-ficial practitioners, have the motives for exercising.

"Several times have these disinterested labors reduced him to the verge of the grave. The presence of the other physicians has, instead of affording relief, only redoubled the intensity of his labors, by changing the ordinary routine of his attentions to the sick with the exhibition of their own prescriptions.

"Mr. Cary has hitherto received no compensation, either from the Society or the Government, for these services. I need not add, that it has not been in his power to support himself and family by any use he could make of the remnants of his time left him, after discharging the amount of duty already described. The Missionary Board of Richmond have fed, clothed and supplied the other wants of himself and family, while devoting his strength and time to your sick colonists, and Agents in this country. Justice seems to demand that he should be placed in a situation as an honest man, to refund the whole or part of the fund thus engrossed, not to say *misapplied*, to the Missionary Board.

"I beg leave also to state, that on the 15th of February, 1826, I came into an agreement with Mr. Cary, to allow him a reasonable compensation for his medical services, devoted to the then sickening company of Boston emigrants. His time has from the date of that agreement, to the present hour, been incessantly occupied in attending upon the sick."

Gurley, *Life of Jehudi Ashmun*, appendix, pp. 151f.

On the 25th of June Gary wrote to Ashmun:

"About three o'clock to-day, there appeared three

vessels—two brigs and a schooner. The schooner stood into the Roads, and one of the brigs near in, but showed no colours until a shot was fired by Captain Thompson; when she hoisted Spanish colours, and the schooner the same. All their movements appeared so suspicious, that we turned out all our forces to-night.—About eight this evening it was reported that they were standing out of our Roads; and at sunset, that the schooner had come to anchor very near the 'All Chance,' from Boston; and that the brig which had passed the Cape, had put about and was standing up, trying to double the Cape; and that the third vessel (a brig) was standing down for the Roads. The first mentioned brig showed nine ports a side. From all these circumstances I thought best to have Fort Norris Battery manned, which was immediately done by Captain Johnson. I also ordered out the two volunteer companies to make discoveries around the town, and the Artillery to support the guns, and protect the beach; which orders were promptly executed, and we stood in readiness during the night. At daylight the schooner lay at anchor and appeared to be making no preparations to communicate with us; I then ordered a shot to be fired at a little distance from her, when she sent a boat ashore with her Captain, Supercargo, and Interpreter. She reported herself the Joseph, from Havana, had been three months on the coast trading, but *not for slaves*, had one gun, and twenty-three men. Also, that the brig was a patriotic brig in chase of her, and that through fear she had taken shelter under our guns. The Captain wished a supply of wood and water; but I told him I knew him to be engaged in the slave trade, and that, though we did not pretend to attempt suppressing this trade, we would not aid it, and that I allowed him one hour, and one only, to get out of the reach of our guns. He was very punctual, and I believe before his hour."

Gurley, *Life of Jehudi Ashmun*, appendix, p. 157.

A letter to the American Colonization Society through her Secretary, July 17th (1828):

Until we can raise crops sufficient to supply a considerable number of new comers every year, such an arrangement (a vessel large enough to run down to Cape Palmas and occasionally to Sierra Leone) as will enable us to proceed farther to the leeward than we have ever done, in order to procure supplies, will be indispensably necessary; as there we can procure Indian Corn, Palm Oil, and live stock. For these, neither the slave traders nor others, give themselves much. Corn can be bought there for from fifteen to twenty cents per bushel. Fifteen or twenty bushels which I bought of Captain Woodbury, I have been using instead of rice for the last two months. Besides, it can be ground into meal, and would be better than any that can be sent. Upon the supposed inquiry, will not the lands of the Colony produce Corn? they will produce it in abundance; but with the quantity of lands appropriated at present, and the means to cultivate them, each landholder will, I think, be able to raise but little more than may be required by his own family, and consequently will have little to dispose of to new comers. (It has been resolved by the Board of Managers to increase the quantity of land alloted to each settler.)

Permit me to inform the Board, that proposals have been made by a number of very respectable citizens in Monrovia, to commence a settlement near the head of the Montserado River, which would be a kind of farming establishment; which, should it be the pleasure of the Board to approve, would be followed up with great spirit, and found to contribute largely towards increasing our crops, for the soil is very promising.

Gurley, *Life of Jehudi Ashmun*, appendix, p. 158.

ADDRESS

By the Citizens of Monrovia, to the free coloured people of the United States

As much speculation and uncertainty continue to prevail among the free people of colour in the United States, respecting our situation and prospects in Africa; and many misrepresentations have been put in circulation there, of a nature slanderous to *us*, and in their effects injurious to *them*; we feel it our duty by a true statement of our circumstances to endeavor to correct them.

The first consideration which caused our voluntary removal to this country, and the object which we still regard with the deepest concern, is liberty—liberty, in the sober, simple, but complete sense of the word:—not a licentious liberty—nor a liberty without government—or which should place us without the restraint of salutary laws. But that liberty of speech, action, and conscience, which distinguished the free, enfranchised citizens of a free state. We did not enjoy that freedom in our native country, and from causes which, as respects ourselves, we shall soon forget forever, we were certain it was not there attainable for ourselves, or our children. This then being the first object of our pursuit in coming to Africa, is probably the first subject on which you will ask for information. And we must truly declare to you, that our expectations and hopes in this respect have been realized. Our Constitution secures to us, so far as our condition allows, "all the rights and privileges enjoyed by the citizens of the United States," and these rights and these privileges are ours. We are proprietors of the soil we live on; and possess the rights of freeholders; our suffrages, and what is of more importance our *sentiments*, and our *opinions*, have their due weight in the government we live under. Our laws are altogether our own; they grow out of our circumstances; are framed for our exclusive benefit; and administered either by officers of our own appointment, or such as possess our confidence. We have a judiciary chosen from among ourselves; we serve as jurors in the trial of others; and are liable to be tried only by juries of our fellow-citizens, ourselves. We have all that is meant by *liberty of conscience*. The time and mode of worshipping God as prescribed in his word, and dictated by our conscience, we are not only free to follow, but are protected in following.

Forming a community of our own, in the land of our forefathers, having the commerce and soil and resources of the country at our disposal; we know nothing of that debasing inferiority, with which our very colour stamped us in America. There is nothing here to create the feeling on our part—nothing to cherish the feeling of superiority in the minds of foreigners who visit us. It is this moral emancipation—this liberation of the mind from worse than iron fetters, that repays us ten thousand times over, for all that it has cost us, and makes us grateful to God, and our American patrons, for the happy change which has taken place in our situation. We are not so self-complacent as to rest satisfied with our improvement either as regards our minds or our circumstances. We do not expect to remain stationary,—far from it; but we certainly feel ourselves, for the first time, in a state to improve either to any purpose. The burden is gone from our shoulders; we now breathe and move freely, and know not (in our present state) for which to pity you most, the empty name of liberty, which you endeavour to content yourselves with, in a country that is not yours; or the delusion which makes you hope for ampler privileges in that country hereafter. Tell us; which is the white man, who, with a prudent regard to his own character, can associate one of you on terms of equality? Ask *us* which is the white man who would decline such association with one of our number, whose intellectual and moral qualities are not an objection? To both of these questions we unhesitatingly make the same answer: there is no such white man.

We solicit none of you to emigrate to this country; for we know not who among you prefers rational independence and the honest respect of his fellow men, to the mental sloth and careless poverty, which you already possess, and your children will inherit after you, in

America. But if your views and aspirations rise a degree higher—if your minds are not as servile as your present condition, we can decide the question at once; and with confidence say that you will bless the day, and your children after you, when you determined to become citizens of Liberia.

But we do not hold this language on the blessing of liberty, for the purpose of consoling ourselves for the sacrifice of health, or the suffering of want, in consequence of our removal to Africa. We enjoy health after a few months' residence in the country as uniformly, and in as perfect a degree, as we possessed that blessing in our native country. And a distressing scarcity of provisions, or any of the comforts of life, has for the last two years been entirely unknown, even to the poorest persons in this community. We never hoped, by leaving America, to escape the common lot of mortals—the necessity of death to which the just appointment of Heaven consigns us. But we do expect to live as long, and pass this life with as little sickness as yourselves.

The true character of the African climate is not well understood in other countries. Its inhabitants are as robust, as healthy, as long lived, to say the least, as those of any other country. Nothing like an epidemic has ever appeared in this colony; nor can we learn from the natives, that the calamity of a sweeping sickness ever yet visited this part of the continent. But the change from a temperate to a tropical country is a great one; too great, not to affect the health more or less,—and in the cases of old people and very young children, it often causes death. In the early years of the colony, want of good houses, the great fatigues and dangers of the settlers, their irregular mode of living, and the hardships and discouragements they met with, greatly helped the other causes of sickness, which prevailed to an alarming extent, and was attended with great mortality. But we look back to those times as to a season of trial long past, and nearly forgotten:—our houses and circumstances are now comfortable, and for the last 2 or 3 years, not one person in forty, from the Middle and Southern States has died, from the change of climate.

People, now arriving, have comfortable houses to receive them, will enjoy the regular attendance of a Physician in the slight sickness that may await them; will be surrounded and attended by healthy and happy people who have borne the effects of the climate, who will encourage and fortify them against that despondency, which alone has carried off several in the first years of the colony. But, you may say, that even health and freedom, good as they are, are still dearly paid for, when they cost you the common comforts of life, and expose your wives and children to famine and all the evils of poverty. We do not dispute the soundness of this conclusion neither—but we utterly deny that it has any application to the people of Liberia. Away with all the false notions that are circulating about the barrenness of this country. They are the observations of such ignorant or designing men, as would injure both it and you. A more fertile soil and a more productive country, so far as it is cultivated, there is not, we believe, on the face of the earth. Its hills and its plains are covered with a verdure which never fades—the productions of nature keep on in their growth through all the seasons of the year. Even the natives of the country, almost without farming tools, without skill, and with very little labour, make more grain and vegetables than they can consume, and often more than they can sell.

Cattle, swine, fowls, ducks, goats and sheep, thrive without feeding—and require not other care than to keep them from straying. Cotton, coffee, Indigo, and sugar cane are all the spontaneous growth of our forests; and may be cultivated at pleasure to any extent, by such as are disposed. The same may be said of rice, indian corn, guinea corn, millet, and too many species of fruits and vegetables to be enumerated. Add to all this, we have no dreary winter here, for one half of the year, to consume the productions of the other half; nature is constantly renewing herself, and constantly pouring her treasures, all the year round, into the lap of the industrious. We could say on this subject more; but we are afraid of exciting too highly the hopes of the *imprudent.* It is only the industrious and virtuous that we can point to independence and plenty and happiness in this country. Such people are nearly sure, to attain in a very few years, to a style of comfortable living, which they may in vain hope for in the United States. And however short we come of the character ourselves, it is only a due acknowledgment of the bounty of Divine Providence, to say that we generally enjoy the good things of this life to our entire satisfaction.

Our trade and commerce are chiefly confined to the coast, to the interior parts of the continent, and to foreign vessels. It is already valuable, and fast increasing. It is carried on in the productions of the country, consisting of rice, palm oil, ivory, tortoise-shell, dye-woods, gold, hides, wax, and a small amount of coffee; and it brings us in return the products and manufactures of the four quarters of the world. Seldom indeed is our harbour clear of European and American shipping; and the bustle and thronging of our streets show something of the activity of the smaller seaports of the United States.

Mechanics of nearly every trade are carrying on their various occupations. Their wages are high, and a large number would be sure of constant and profitable employment. Not a child or youth in the colony, but is provided with an appropriate school. We have a numerous publick library, and a Courthouse, Meeting-houses, School-houses, and fortifications sufficient, or nearly so, for the colony in its present state.

Our houses are constructed of the same materials, and finished in the same style as in the towns in America. We have abundance of good building stone, shells for lime and clay of an excellent quality for bricks. Timber is plentiful and of various kinds, and fit for all the different purposes of building and fencing.

Truly we have a goodly heritage, and if there is any thing lacking in the character or condition of the people of this colony, it never can be charged to the account of the country. It must be the fruit of our own misman-agement or slothfulness or vices. But from these evils, we confide in Him to whom we are indebted for all our blessings, to preserve us. It is the topic of our weekly and daily thanksgiving to Almighty God, both in publick and private; and he knows with what sincerity, that we were ever conducted to this shore. Such great favours in so short a time, and mixed with so few trials, are to be ascribed to nothing but his special blessing. This we acknowledge. Judge then of the feelings with which we hear the motives and the doings of the Colonization Society traduced—and that too, by men too ignorant to know what that society has accomplished; too weak to look through its plans and intentions; or too dishonest to acknowledge either. But without pretending to any prophetic sagacity, we can certainly predict to that society the ultimate triumph of their hopes and labours; and disappointment and defeat to all who oppose them. Men may theorize and speculate about their plans in America. But there can be no speculation here. The cheerful abodes of civilization and happiness, which are scattered over this verdant mountain; the flourishing settlements which are spreading around it—the sound of Christian instruction, and scene of Christian worship, which are heard and seen in this land of brooding pagan darkness; a thousand contented freemen, united in founding a new Christian Empire, happy themselves, and the instruments of happiness to others—every object, every individual, is an argument, is demonstration of the wisdom and the goodness of the plan of Colonization.

Where is the argument that shall refute facts like these? and where is the man hardy enough to deny them?

The American Baptist Magazine, Vol. VIII, pp. 50-53.

JOURNAL OF LOTT CARY

The Colonial Agent, J. Ashmun, esq., went on board the brig Doris, March 26th, 1828, escorted by three companies of military, and when taking leave he delivered a short address, which was truly affecting; never, I suppose, were greater tokens of respect shown by any community on taking leave of their head. Nearly the whole (at least two-thirds) of the inhabitants of Monrovia, men, women, and children, were out on this occasion, and nearly all parted from him with tears, and in my opinion, the hope of his return in a few months, alone enabled them to give him up. He is indeed dear to this people, and it will be a joyful day when we are again permitted to see him. He has left a written address, which contains valuable admonitions to Officers, Civil, Military, and Religious. The brig sailed on the 27th. May she have a prosperous voyage.

THURSDAY, MARCH 27.

Feeling very sensibly my incompetency to enter upon the duties of my office without first making all the Officers of the Colony well acquainted with the principal objects which should engage our attention, I invited them to meet at the Agency House on the 27th, at 9 o'clock, which was punctually attended to; and I then read all the instructions left by Mr. Ashmun without reserve, and requested their co-operation. I stated that it would be our first object to put the Jail in complete order, secondly to have our guns and armaments in a proper state, and thirdly to get the new settlers located on their lands; as this was a very important item in my instructions. This explanation will, I think, have a good effect; as by it the effective part of the Colony is put in possession of the most important objects of our present pursuit; and I trust through the blessing of the great Ruler of events, we shall be able to realize all the expectations of Mr. Ashmun, and render entire satisfaction to the Board of Managers if they can reconcile themselves to the necessary expenses.

MARCH 29.

From a note received from Mr. James, dated Millsburg, I learn that he visited King Boatswain, and that the new road from Boatswain's to Millsburg will shortly be commenced.—The Headmen expect, however, to be paid for opening the road. Messrs. James and Cook, who came down this evening, state, that the Millsburg Factory will be ready in a few days for the reception of goods, and wished consignments might be made early. But as I had been on the 27th paying off the kings towards the Millsburg lands, and found that one hundred and twenty bars came so far short of satisfying them, I thought best to see them together before I should attempt to make any consignments to that place.

Know all men by these presents: That we, Old King Peter, and King Governor, King James, and King Long Peter, do on this fourth day of April, in the year of our Lord one thousand eight hundred and twenty-eight, grant unto Lott Cary, acting Agent of the Colony of Liberia, in behalf of the American Colonization Society, to wit:

All that tract of Land on the north side of St. Paul's

river, beginning at King James' line below the establishment called Millsburg Settlement, and we the
Kings as aforesaid do bargain, sell, and grant, unto
the said Lott Cary, acting in behalf of the American
Colonization Society, all the aforesaid tract of land,
situated and bounded as follows: by the St. Paul's river
on the South, and thence running an East Northeast
direction up the St. Paul's river, as far as he, the said
Lott Cary, or his successor in the Agency, or Civil
Authority of the Colony of Liberia, shall think proper to
take up and occupy: and bounded on the West by King
Jimmey's, and running thence a North direction as far
as our power and influence extend. We do this day and
date, grant as aforesaid for the consideration (here
follow the articles to be given in payment); and will
forever defend the same against all claims whatsoever.

In witness whereof we set our hands and names:

OLD X KING PETER,
LONG X KING PETER,
KING X GOVERNOR,
KING X JAMES>.

Signed in the presence of,

ELIJAH JOHNSON,
FREDERICK JAMES,
DANIEL GEORGE.

JUNE 18, 1828.

I found it necessary, in order to preserve the frame of the second floors of the Government House, to have the frame and ceiling painted, which is now doing. I have also been obliged to employ another workman to make the blinds, or else leave the house exposed the present season, as —— refused to do it under the former contract. On the 13th I visited Millsburg (named after Mills and Burgess) to ascertain the prospects of that settlement; and can say with propriety, that according to the quantity of land which the settlers have put under cultivation, they will reap a good and plentiful crop. The Company's crop of rice and cassada is especially promising. The new settlers at that place have done well; having all, with two or three exceptions, built houses, so as to render their families comfortable during the season. They have also each of them a small farm, which I think after a few months will be sufficient to subsist them. But I find from a particular examination, that we shall be obliged to allow them to draw rations longer than I expected, owing to the great scarcity of country produce, the cassada being so nearly exhausted, that it is, and will be, impossible to obtain, until new crops come in, much to aid our provisions, unless by going some distance into the country. Therefore I think it indispensably necessary, in order to keep the settlers to their farming improvements, to continue their rations longer than I at first intended; as I consider the present too important a crisis to leave them to neglect their improvements, although it may add something to our present expenses.

The people at Caldwell are getting on better with their

farms than with their houses. I think some of them are very slow, notwithstanding I have assisted them in building. The Gun House at Caldwell is done, and at present preparations are making for the fourth of July. I think that settlement generally, is rapidly advancing in farming, building, and I hope, in industry. Our gun carriages are done; the completion of the iron work alone prevents us from mounting them all immediately. We have four mounted, and I think we shall put them all in complete order by the end of the present week.

Captain Russel will be able to give something like a fair account of the state of our improvements, as he went with me to visit the settlements on the 13th and 14th, and seemed pleased with the project at Millsburg, Caldwell and the Half-way Farms.

Mr. Warner, who has been engaged nearly the whole of the last twelve months on business of negotiation with the native tribes to the leeward, is at present down at Tippicanoe, the place which I mentioned in my former communications, as being a very important section of country, since it would connect our Sesters and Bassa districts together. He is not, however, now engaged in business of negotiation, but only in business of trade.

Gurley, *Life of Jehudi Ashmun*, appendix, pp. 153–156.

In a letter to Mr. Ashmun, Mr. Cary wrote:

Things are nearly as you left them; most of the work that you directed to be done, is nearly accomplished. The plasterers are now at work on the Government House, and with what lime I am having brought down the river, and what shells I am getting, I think we shall succeed.

The Gun House in Monrovia and the Jail have been done for some weeks; the mounting of the guns will be done this week, if the weather permits.

The Houses at Half-way Farms are done; the Gun House at Caldwell would have been done at this time, had not the rain prevented, but I think it will be finished in three or four days. The public farm is doing pretty well. The Millsburg farms are doing very well. I think it would do you good to see that place at this time.

The Missionaries, although they have been sick are now, I am happy to inform you, recovered; and at present are able to attend to their business, and I regard them as entirely out of danger.

I hope we shall be able to remove all the furniture into the new house in two or three weeks.

Speaking of the celebration of the 4th of July under date of July 15th, Mr. Cary remarked to Mr. Ashmun:

The companies observed strictly the orders of the day, which I think were so arranged as to entitle the officers who drew them up to credit. Upon the whole, I am obliged to say, that I have never seen the American Independence celebrated with so much spirit and propriety since the existence of the Colony; the guns being all mounted and painted, and previously arranged for the purpose, added very much to the grand salute.

Two dinners were given, one by the Independent Volunteer Company, and one by Captain Devany.

Mr. Cary wrote to the Secretary of the Colonization Society, July 19th, 1828:

I have the honour to acknowledge the receipt of your letter, forwarded by Captain Chase of Providence, also your Report and Repository, directed to Mr. Ashmun, but owing to his absence, they have fallen into my hands; and permit me to say, that these communications are read with pleasure, and that nothing affords more joy to the Colony, than to hear of the prosperity of the Colonization Society, and that you have some hopes of aid from the General Government, which makes us more desirous to enlarge our habitation and extend the borders of the Colony.

I must say, from the flattering prospects of your Society, I feel myself very much at a loss how to proceed, in the absence of Mr. Ashmun, with regard to making provisions for the reception of a large number of emigrants, which appears to be indispensably necessary. Therefore, after receiving your communication, we conceived the following to be the most safe and prudent course. *First*, to make arrangements to have erected at Millsburg, houses to answer as receptacles sufficient to shelter from one hundred and fifty to two hundred persons, I have therefore extended the duties of Mr. Benson so as to embrace that object. I was led to this course from the following considerations. *First*, from the productiveness of the Millsburg lands and the fewness of their inhabitants. I know if Mr. Ashmun were present, it would be a principal object with him to push that settlement forward with all possible speed, and that for this purpose, he would send the emigrants by the first two or three expeditions to that place. I think that those from the fresh water rivers, if carried directly after their arrival here, up to Millsburg, would suffer very little from change of climate. *Second*, the fertility of the land is such a temptation to the farmer, that unless he possesses laziness in its extreme degree, he cannot resist it; he must and will go to work. *Thirdly*, it is important to strengthen that settlement against any possible attack; and though we apprehend no hostilities from the natives, yet we would have each settlement strong enough to repel them.

I am happy to say, that the health, peace and prosperity of the Colony, I think, is still advancing, and I hope that the Board of Managers may have their wishes and expectations realized to their fullest extent, with regard to the present and future prosperity of the Colony.

Gurley, *Life of Jehudi Ashmun*, appendix, pp. 156-158.

Letter to the treasurer of the Massachusetts Baptist Education Society:

Sir,

Here is a mite enclosed for your society. It is part of the proceeds of a cotton field, for benevolent purposes. I helped to plough the ground, plant, hoe, pick, gin and pack the cotton with my own hands. A part of the proceeds is for the Colonization Society. My servants would shew their large white teeth, when, to encourage them to do their work well, I informed them that this cotton was designed to be a means of enlightening their brethren in Africa. Don't you think that Christians by and by, will act more like stewards with the property God has given them? I think it better to give now and then a mite, which the Lord may have bestowed upon me, to advance his cause, than to lavish it on profligate and dissipated sons. Will not God at a future day require the property he has loaned us?

We see you Northern folks seem conscious of this, by the exertions you are using to advance the Redeemer's cause. This has become a fortunate legatee, in comparison with what it was fifty years ago.

We, down here, so near the equator, think we can discover the upper limb of the millennium sun already. Will he not get clear above the horizon by 1866.

A Georgia Planter.

The American Baptist Magazine, Vol. IV, p. 181.

FOOTNOTES:

[1] These extracts were collected by Miles Mark Fisher.

BOOK REVIEWS

The Master's Slave—Elijah John Fisher. By MILES MARK FISHER. The Judson Press, Philadelphia, Pa. Pp. 194.

This work is a biographical sketch of one of the most prominent Negro Baptist preachers of his time. The author, the son of the subject of the sketch, believes that too little has been said concerning the Negro Church, which is largely responsible for whatever advancement the race has made. To stimulate interest in this institution and to give it the proper place in the history of the race, this biography is given to the public.

The book contains an introduction by Dr. L. K. Williams, the popular successor of Dr. Fisher at the Olivet Baptist Church in Chicago, where the latter faithfully served many years. It contains also an appreciation by Martin B. Madden, Congressman from Illinois, who personally knew Dr. Fisher and speaks most commendably of his character and achievements in that State.

The actual sketch begins with the chapter entitled "Bound and Branded," presenting the life of Dr. Fisher during the slavery of the last decade prior to emancipation. Herein are set forth interesting facts showing the connection of the Negro with Africa and his status in the slave-holding South. The effects of the Civil War in this section appear also from page to page.

Then follows that part of his career when he as a youth undertook to secure an education by which he might be qualified for the serious duties of life. How he began as a teacher during the beginning of Negro education of the Reconstruction period, and how he finally became an exhorter and developed into a minister acceptable to the communicants of his denomination, make the story increasingly interesting. The sketch reaches its climax through a detailed account of Dr. Fisher's work at Atlanta, Nashville, and Chicago, emphasizing the last mentioned as the place of his most successful labor.

The historian will find this work valuable in that it illuminates one of the most interesting periods of Negro church history. It is not only a sketch of one distinguished churchman but a narrative presenting an important chapter of the story of the Baptists by relating the many incidents connected with the leading churchmen and ecclesiastical organizations inter-ested in the uplift of the Negro since the Civil War. This narrative, moreover, shows how the Negro minister, in keeping with the exigencies of the time, often had to be drawn into politics in self defense and that in the case of unselfish service like that of Dr. Fisher, he may come out of the controversy untarnished.

History of the United States. Vol. V. By EDWARD CHANNING. The Macmillan Company, New York City. Pp. 615.

This is the most recent volume of Professor Channing's eight volume History of the United States from the very beginning of our history to the present time. This particular volume covers the years from 1815 to 1848 and is entitled "The Period of Transition." It is written in keeping with the standard of thoroughness charac-teristic of the author and is made further informing by the use of ten valuable maps illustrating important facts in American History.

In this volume the author engages the attention of the reader with an account of the wonderful century in which he writes. He then discusses the westward movement of the population, urban migration, the rise of labor unions, giving more attention to economic matters than his predecessors have been accustomed to do in the treatment of this period. A study of the documentary history of the United States has convinced the author that these important factors in the making of this country have been neglected. His treatment, therefore, is a change in the point of view in American historical writing.

This volume does not show the usual interest in slavery and abolition. Only one chapter of this large work is devoted primarily to the plantation life and abolitionism. The author discusses the lot of the slave, accounting for his tendency to escape from bondage, the traffic in human flesh, the free people of color, the colonization movement in the South, and abolition in the North. This chapter culminates in a discussion of the efforts of William Lloyd Garrison, the agitating editor of the *Liberator*, of Wendell Phillips, the abolition orator, of Prudence Crandall, the sacrificing worker, and of Elijah Lovejoy, the martyr in the cause. Prof. Channing does not go into details as to the achievements of the abolitionists. His account is merely sufficient to connect this movement with other forces at work in the country at that time.

Most of this volume is devoted to changes in religion, education, literature, and politics, effected by such outstanding figures as James Monroe, John Quincy Adams, Andrew Jackson, Henry Clay, John C. Calhoun and Daniel Webster. The book shows an extensive treatment of the territorial expansion of that time, especially the efforts to secure Texas, California and Oregon, and the war with Mexico. On the whole, this book has a decided economic and social trend. It is an effort to account for the significant upheavals in our history through connection with important industrial and economic events which have materially influenced the history of the United States during the last century. The book emphasizes the fact that current history can not be easily written, that one must be far removed from situations in the past in order to weigh the influences having a bearing thereon to determine exactly how the country has become what it is today.

Recent History of the United States. By Frederick L. Paxson. Houghton Mifflin Company, Boston. Pp. 588.

This book beginning with the inauguration of Hayes shows how he reestablished home rule in the South, thus clearing the way for a realization of education and economic reconstruction of both South and North. The author then treats the civil and border strife as expressed in the Mexican Revolution of 1876, Indian wars, social unrest, national labor unions, and the War with Spain. Then follows the treatment of post-bellum ideals as expressed by literary periodicals and new writers showing a revolution in literature, and especially in historical writing.

In his treatment of silver, greenbacks, railroad and mine booms, and the like, he shows that the country had reached a new stage in its development when a transition both economic and political was apparent. This is made evident by his discussion of election frauds, Republican factions, office holders in politics, the abuse of patronage and the necessity for civil service reform. Next the author takes up the era of prosperity, the disappearance of the frontier, the land grants to railroads, the development of the telephone, telegraph, typewriter, electrical appliances, and the like, in their bearing on the industrial reconstruction of the whole country.

The author then discusses events more in detail, directing his attention to the tariff revision of the eighties, the "Mugwump Campaign" of 1884, the Wild West, labor ideals, protection, populism, the revival of the Democratic party through the leadership of Cleveland, industrial unrest, political schism, the Spanish-American War, business in politics, the career of Theodore Roosevelt, government control, insurgency, the rise of Woodrow Wilson, watchful waiting, neutrality and preparedness, the United States in the World War, and the League of Nations. Some attention is also given to the reconstruction and the election of 1920.

While the work is a valuable treatise from the point of view of a man who is trying to write the history of a particular race, it does not come up to the standard of history of the United States in all of its national and racial ramifications. So far as the Negro is concerned, it merely refers to his undoing as a political factor in the Reconstruction, the efforts for his education by northern sympathizers, the rise of Booker T. Washington, the elimination of the Negro as a factor in the South, the efforts to pass a force bill protecting the Negro in the exercise of the right of suffrage, and the continued control of the South of the Democratic party. A foreigner who reads this work might wonder whether the Negroes by this political upheaval have been exterminated or have emigrated from the country. Any student of the history of the whole Southland knows that it is centered largely around the Negro and any historian failing to take this into account cannot be recognized as an authority.

The Backbone of Africa. A Record of Travel during the Great War, with some Suggestions for Administrative Reform. By Sir Alfred Sharps, K. C. M. G., C. B., formerly Governor of Nyasaland. London, H. F. & G. Witherby, 1921. Pp. 232.

This is the reaction of a public functionary to the scenes of colonial life as they appeared to him from a different angle in a survey of the whole continent and under the circumstances of a political upheaval. He had in mind here the regions of Rhodesia, Nyasaland, Tanganyika, Ruanda, the Congo, and the Upper Nile. The book is illustrated, well written and suggestive throughout. It contains four valuable maps and has an index largely of names.

Writing from the point of view of the exploiter of Africa, the author considers such questions as the disposition of the German Colonies coming into the possession of England at the close of the Great War, the question of restitution, the partition of Africa, the suggested union of the Protectorates in Eastern Africa under a Governor General, the partition of German East Africa, the redelimitation of boundaries, problems of railway construction and a united East African Colony. He discusses also the Home Government, native taxation, local representation, land along with land laws, native rights, their education, the labor problem, migration, industrial questions, and missions.

Treating the colonial policy in dealing with the natives, the author shows some sympathy. He does not believe that the tax on natives has been wisely imposed and, therefore, asks for a uniform and more equitable system. To effect such a reform, however, he believes that the local government with increased authority in its own affairs should exercise such power rather than have such a policy determined by the Home Government through its appointive executive and legislators who act for the colonies though not of them. The question of native ownership of spare land, he believes, should be carefully considered, inasmuch as there has never been any real title to the possession of definite blocks of freehold lands in Native Africa. Native education also should be taken in hand and there should be adopted a suitable scheme, applicable to all the Protectorates.

"In the first place in one shape or another," says the author, "we introduce a direct but immoderate impost such as a hut-tax or a more general poll-tax, the money for which has to be earned. Next, we endeavor to create new wants: clothes, ornaments, manufactured goods and luxuries of all kinds. All this represents a gradual process of regeneration, as the native is by nature very conservative and, therefore, slow to adopt new tastes or acquire ambitions. But we endeavor to raise his ideals and to inculcate the view we ourselves hold: that man should not be satisfied with mere existence, like beasts in the field, but should adopt civilisation and everything that, in the main, we consider to be essential to civilised life. We ask him, therefore, to produce something—other than for his own immediate wants—whether it be by labour done for an employer, or on his own account."

NOTES

The next annual meeting of the Association will be held in Louisville, Kentucky, on Thursday and Friday, the 23d and 24th of November. The day sessions will be held at the Branch Library on West Chestnut Street and the evening sessions at the Quinn Chapel African Methodist Episcopal Church on the same street. The management is endeavoring to make this a national meeting effective in arousing universal interest in the study of Negro life and history.

During the academic year 1922-1923 Mr. A. A. Taylor, formerly Instructor in Economics at the West Virginia Collegiate Institute, will devote a part of his time to research in the field of Negro Reconstruction History as an investigator of the Association. The remaining portion of his time will be devoted to the completion of some graduate studies at Harvard University.

Mr. Taylor is a product of the Washington Public Schools and of the University of Michigan. He is the author of two articles recently published in THE JOURNAL OF NEGRO HISTORY, namely, "Making West Virginia a Free State" and "Negro Congressmen a Generation After." It is expected that Mr. Taylor may find it possible to devote his future to investigation under the auspices of the Association.

Mr. Hosea B. Campbell, who during his four years at Grinnell College held a Julius Rosenwald scholarship, has been awarded a fellowship of $500 by the

Association to prosecute at Harvard graduate studies in Negro American and African History.

An authorized translation into English of René Maran's *Batouala* has been published and is being sold throughout the United States. It is expected that in this form the work will more thoroughly inform the American public as to the African situation and as to the ability of this man of Negro blood to treat it.

Les Noirs de l'Afrique, an historical essay on the people of Africa, their customs and art, by Mr. Delafosse, appeared in Paris in 1921.

TRANSCRIBER'S NOTES:

Every effort has been made to replicate this text as faithfully as possible, including obsolete and variant spellings and other inconsistencies. The transcriber made the following changes to the text to correct obvious errors:

1. p. 5, professsors --> professors
2. p. 6, posssible --> possible
3. p. 34, Haper's Ferry --> Harper's Ferry
4. p. 51, tself --> itself
5. p. 54, Douglas --> Douglass
6. p. 61, banquent --> banquet
7. p. 70, Geogre --> George
8. p. 79, Ninteenth --> Nineteenth
9. p. 81, Footnote #19, Grimke's --> Grimké's

10. p. 81, No footnote marker for footnote #19.

11. p. 110, ecnouragement --> encouragement

12. p. 119, disfranchisment --> disfranchisement

13. p. 122, subscripion --> subscription

14. p. 133, Virgina --> Virginia

15. p. 137, successivly --> successively

16. p. 151, establisment --> establishment

17. p. 154, Eliott --> Elliott

18. p. 161, distinquished --> distinguished

19. p. 208, Piqua, --> Piqua.

20. p. 251, No footnote marker for footnote #10.

21. p. 334, villified --> vilified

22. p. 338, childern --> children

23. p. 355, No footnote marker for footnote #21.

24. p. 357, wheras --> whereas

25. p. 376, Footnote #8, Mossel --> Mossell

26. p. 381, missonary --> missionary

27. p. 385, Footnote #29, Toussiant --> Toussaint

28. p. 433, and and --> and

Also, many occurrences of mismatched single and double quotes remain as published.

www.ingramcontent.com/pod-product-compliance
Lightning Source LLC
Chambersburg PA
CBHW071526030726
47598CB00001B/7